THIRD SERIES

£5 Drama
Week 28.

General Editors: Richard Proudfoot, Ann Thompson,
David Scott Kastan and H.R. Woudhuysen

THE COMEDY OF ERRORS

D1323687

THE ARDEN SHAKESPEARE

* Second series

THE COMEDY OF ERRORS

Edited by

KENT CARTWRIGHT

Bloomsbury Arden Shakespeare
An Imprint of Bloomsbury Publishing Plc

B L O O M S B U R Y
LONDON · OXFORD · NEW YORK · NEW DELHI · SYDNEY

Bloomsbury Arden Shakespeare

An imprint of Bloomsbury Publishing Plc

50 Bedford Square	1385 Broadway
London	New York
WC1B 3DP	NY 10018
UK	USA

Imprint previously known as Arden Shakespeare

www.bloomsbury.com

**BLOOMSBURY, THE ARDEN SHAKESPEARE and the Diana logo
are trademarks of Bloomsbury Publishing Plc**

This edition of THE COMEDY OF ERRORS, edited by Kent Cartwright

First published 2017

The general editors of the Arden Shakespeare have been
W.J. Craig and R.H. Case (first series 1899–1944)
Una Ellis-Fermor, Harold F. Brooks, Harold Jenkins and
Brian Morris (second series 1946–82)

Present general editors (third series)
Richard Proudfoot, Ann Thompson, David Scott Kastan and H.R. Woudhuysen

British Library Cataloguing-in-Publication Data
A catalogue record for this book is available from the British Library.

ISBN: HB: 978-1-9042-7123-9
PB: 978-1-9042-7124-6
ePDF: 978-1-4081-5189-1
ePub: 978-1-4081-5190-7

Library of Congress Cataloging-in-Publication Data
A catalog record for this book is available from the Library of Congress.

Series: The Arden Shakespeare

Cover image © Den Reader/Arcangel

Typeset by Graphicraft Limited, Hong Kong

Printed and bound in India

To

Theresa M. Coletti
Theodore B. Leinwand
Maynard Mack, Jr

inspiring colleagues

CONTENTS

Contents

Contents

LIST OF
ILLUSTRATIONS

GENERAL EDITORS' PREFACE

The earliest volume in the first Arden series, Edward Dowden's *Hamlet*, was published in 1899. Since then the Arden Shakespeare has been widely acknowledged as the pre-eminent Shakespeare edition, valued by scholars, students, actors and 'the great variety of readers' alike for its clearly presented and reliable texts, its full annotation and its richly informative introductions.

In the third Arden series we seek to maintain these well-established qualities and general characteristics, preserving our predecessors' commitment to presenting the play as it has been shaped in history. Each volume necessarily has its own particular emphasis which reflects the unique possibilities and problems posed by the work in question, and the series as a whole seeks to maintain the highest standards of scholarship, combined with attractive and accessible presentation.

Newly edited from the original documents, texts are presented in fully modernized form, with a textual apparatus that records all substantial divergences from those early printings. The notes and introductions focus on the conditions and possibilities of meaning that editors, critics and performers (on stage and screen) have discovered in the play. While building upon the rich history of scholarly activity that has long shaped our understanding of Shakespeare's works, this third series of the Arden Shakespeare is enlivened by a new generation's encounter with Shakespeare.

THE TEXT

On each page of the play itself, readers will find a passage of text supported by commentary and textual notes. Act and scene divisions (seldom present in the early editions and often the product of eighteenth-century or later scholarship) have been retained for ease of reference, but have been given less prominence than in previous series. Editorial indications of location of the action have been removed to the textual notes or commentary.

In the text itself, elided forms in the early texts are spelt out in full in verse lines wherever they indicate a usual late twentieth-century pronunciation that requires no special indication and wherever they occur in prose (except where they indicate non-standard pronunciation). In verse speeches, marks of elision are retained where they are necessary guides to the scansion and pronunciation of the line. Final -ed in past tense and participial forms of verbs is always printed as -ed, without accent, never as -'d, but wherever the required pronunciation diverges from modern usage a note in the commentary draws attention to the fact. Where the final -ed should be given syllabic value contrary to modern usage, e.g.

Doth Silvia know that I am banished?

(TGV 3.1.214)

the note will take the form

214 **banished** banishèd

Conventional lineation of divided verse lines shared by two or more speakers has been reconsidered and sometimes rearranged. Except for the familiar *Exit* and *Exeunt*, Latin forms in stage directions and speech prefixes have been translated into English and the original Latin forms recorded in the textual notes.

COMMENTARY AND TEXTUAL NOTES

Notes in the commentary, for which a major source will be the *Oxford English Dictionary*, offer glossarial and other explication of verbal difficulties; they may also include discussion of points of interpretation and, in relevant cases, substantial extracts from Shakespeare's source material. Editors will not usually offer glossarial notes for words adequately defined in the latest edition of *The Concise Oxford Dictionary* or *Merriam-Webster's Collegiate Dictionary*, but in cases of doubt they will include notes. Attention, however, will be drawn to places where more than one likely interpretation can be proposed and to significant verbal and syntactic complexity. Notes preceded by *discuss editorial emendations or variant readings.

Headnotes to acts or scenes discuss, where appropriate, questions of scene location, the play's treatment of source materials, and major difficulties of staging. The list of roles (so headed to emphasize the play's status as a text for performance) is also considered in the commentary notes. These may include comment on plausible patterns of casting with the resources of an Elizabethan or Jacobean acting company and also on any variation in the description of roles in their speech prefixes in the early editions.

The textual notes are designed to let readers know when the edited text diverges from the early edition(s) or manuscript sources on which it is based. Wherever this happens the note will record the rejected reading of the early edition(s) or manuscript, in original spelling, and the source of the reading adopted in this edition. Other forms from the early edition(s) or manuscript recorded in these notes will include some spellings of particular interest or significance and original forms of translated stage directions. Where two or more early editions are involved, for instance with *Othello*, the notes also record all important differences between them. The textual notes take a form that has been in use since the nineteenth century. This comprises, first: line reference, reading adopted in the text and closing square bracket; then: abbreviated reference, in italic, to the earliest edition to adopt the accepted reading, italic semicolon and noteworthy alternative reading(s), each with abbreviated italic reference to its source.

Conventions used in these textual notes include the following. The solidus / is used, in notes quoting verse or discussing verse lining, to indicate line endings. Distinctive spellings of the base text follow the square bracket without indication of source and are enclosed in italic brackets. Names enclosed in italic brackets indicate originators of conjectural emendations when these did not originate in an edition of the text, or when the named edition records a conjecture not accepted into its text. Stage directions (SDs) are referred to by the number of the line within or immediately after which they are placed. Line numbers with a decimal point relate to centred entry SDs not falling within a verse line and to SDs more than one line long, with the number after the point indicating the line within the SD: e.g. 78.4 refers to the fourth line of the SD following line 78. Lines of SDs at the start of a scene are numbered 0.1, 0.2, etc. Where only a line number precedes a square bracket, e.g. 128], the note relates to the whole line; where SD is added to the number, it relates to the whole of a SD within or immediately following the line. Speech prefixes (SPs) follow similar conventions, 203 SP] referring to the speaker's name for line 203. Where a SP reference takes the form, e.g. 38+ SP, it relates to all subsequent speeches assigned to that speaker in the scene in question.

Where, as with *King Henry V*, one of the early editions is a so-called 'bad quarto' (that is, a text either heavily adapted, or reconstructed from memory, or both), the divergences from the present edition are too great to be recorded in full in the notes. In these cases, with the exception of *Hamlet*, which prints an edited text of the Quarto of 1603, the editions will include a reduced photographic facsimile of the 'bad quarto' in an appendix.

INTRODUCTION

Both the introduction and the commentary are designed to present the plays as texts for performance, and make appropriate reference to stage, film and television versions, as well as introducing the reader to the range of critical approaches to the plays. They discuss the history of the reception of the texts within the theatre and scholarship and beyond, investigating the interdependency of the literary text and the surrounding 'cultural text' both at the time of the original production of Shakespeare's works and during their long and rich afterlife.

PREFACE AND
ACKNOWLEDGEMENTS

This edition fell to me upon the untimely death of its initial editor, the distinguished scholar Gareth Roberts. Although it made sense to me to restart the project from scratch, I have consulted Professor Roberts's work with profit, especially his draft of commentary notes for the first three acts, and I have shared his interest in magic in the play. I am also indebted to the remarkable editorial work on *The Comedy of Errors* by ancients such as Pope, Theobald and Capell and by contemporaries such as Charles Whitworth, Standish Henning (who made his pre-publication work on the Variorum available to me) and the late R.A. Foakes. Foakes's edition for the Second Series of The Arden Shakespeare remains a classic. In addition, I owe much to the scholarship of Robert Miola on *Errors* and related subjects, and to him personally for his interest and help.

At Arden, the indefatigable publisher, Margaret Bartley, has overseen this project with a helpful sense of both urgency and camaraderie. Copy-editor Jane Armstrong's sense of exactitude improved the edition invaluably. To Henry Woudhuysen, the series general editor with whom I have worked most closely, I owe my greatest debt. He responded to my arguments and conjectures with a rigorous sense of evidence and logic, and offered sound advice on a host of matters, from the typographical to the conceptual. Any muddles that remain are of my own doing. I am thankful to David Scott Kastan for approaching me about undertaking this project. Richard Proudfoot provided important editorial feedback and insight in the edition's early stages, as did George Walton Williams, in conversation and with notes and postcards. Ann Thompson made helpful comments as the edition reached the stage of a completed draft.

Emily Hockley assisted efficiently with illustrations and permissions.

I am especially indebted to William Carroll for ongoing discussions of Shakespeare and all aspects of early comedy and for his counsel, encouragement and friendship. I have turned to his scholarly work and his model editing again and again. Bill kindly commented on an early, long version of the Introduction, as did my colleague Karen Nelson on a later one. Paul Werstine graciously reviewed Appendix 2: The text and editorial procedures. Paul's remarkable bibliographical work, buoyed by that of the helpful William Long, has significantly influenced my understanding of the text of *The Comedy of Errors*.

I have discussed *Errors* with numerous colleagues; regrettably, only a few can be mentioned here. During a year of residency at the Folger Shakespeare Library, Patricia Parker generously shared with me ideas about the play and about editing. In that period, Mariko Ichikawa likewise shared her vast knowledge of staging issues. Valerie Wayne has been a regular source of editorial fellowship and encouragement. Robert Hornback, in numerous conversations over many years, has inspired me with his fertile ideas about *Errors* and comedy in general. Stuart Sillars and his Bergen Shakespeare and Drama Network have provided multiple occasions for me to present work. Stuart himself has repeatedly shared his insight about paintings and illustrations of Shakespeare's works, along with his invaluable friendship and good humour. Fernando Cioni has listened to my travails, worked with me on various aspects of Shakespearean comedy, provided scholarly assistance and extended his warm friendship.

When I began this project, I had the benefit of a year-long National Endowment for the Humanities fellowship at the Folger Shakespeare Library. I am indebted to the Endowment, and even more deeply and lastingly to the Folger and its superb Reading Room staff, led by Betsy Walsh, as well as to Caroline

Duroselle-Melish, who helped me with illustrations. Most of my research and writing for this edition have been conducted at the Folger, and my thanks to that institution and to the extraordinary people who run it are beyond my capacity to express fully. At an early stage in this project, I also benefited from a semester-long Graduate Research Fellowship from my institution, the University of Maryland. For their support during this project, I am deeply indebted to my medieval, Renaissance and classics colleagues, past and present, as well as to others at the University of Maryland. They include: Sharon Achinstein, Amanda Bailey, Ralph Bauer, Kimberly Coles, Theresa Coletti, Jane Donawerth, Jeanne Fahnestock, the late Marshall Grossman, Judith Hallett, Donna Hamilton, Gary Hamilton, Theodore Leinwand, Maynard Mack, Jr, Thomas Moser, Jr, David Norbrook, Michael Olmert, Gerard Passannante, Kellie Robertson, Adele Seeff, William Sherman, Scott Trudell and Vessela Valiavitcharska.

Early in this project, I had the opportunity to be a Visiting Professor and to present work in the English Department at the University of Szeged, Hungary. I am grateful to György Szönyi for inviting me to teach and lecture at Szeged, to Attila Kiss for offering suggestions and support, and especially to Ágnes Matuska for engaging in a continuing conversation about comedy, which has been a source of illumination and inspiration. Late in the project, I had the privilege of being a Visiting Researcher for a year in the Department of Language Studies and Comparative Cultures at Ca' Foscari University of Venice. One of my best memories is of working in the department's library in Palazzo Cosulich, scenically sited on the Giudecca Canal. For their hospitality and interest, and for opportunities to present my work, I am thankful to Jeanne Clegg, Valerio de Scarpis di Vianino, Flavio Gregori, Loretta Innocenti, Laura Tosi and especially Shaul Bassi, who invited me to lecture on *Errors* and who provided myriad forms of help, encouragement and collegiality. Similar thanks are due to Rocco Coronato of the University of Padua and Fernando Cioni of the University of Florence.

Short on space but long on thanks, I would identify a group of individuals who have provided various forms of assistance and support: Charlotte Artese, Kathleen Bossert, Dennis Britton, Katherine Brokaw, James Bulman, Ralph Alan Cohen, John Cox, Alan Dessen, Elizabeth Driver, Charles Edelman, Andrew Fleck, John Ford, Jonathan Gil Harris, Donald Hedrick, Sean Keilen, Erin E. Kelly, Karen Kettnich, M.J. Kidnie, the late Bernice Kliman, Barbara Kreps, Jasmine Lellock, Jeanne McCarthy, Lawrence Manley, Robert Matz, Jean-Christophe Mayer, Kirk Melnikoff, Barbara Mowat, Leanne Palmer, Kaara Peterson, Lois Potter, Maggie Ray, Edward Rocklin, Heidi Scott, James Siemon, Alden and Virginia Vaughan, Melissa Walter, Lawrence Weiss, Sarah Werner, Deanne Williams, Jessica Winston, George T. Wright and Georgianna Ziegler.

Of all debts, my deepest personal one is to my wife, Pam.

Kent Cartwright
University of Maryland, College Park

INTRODUCTION

Audiences and readers have perennially delighted in the knock-about, laughter-inducing antics of *The Comedy of Errors*. Composed probably close in time to two other comedies rife with foolery, *The Two Gentlemen of Verona* and *The Taming of the Shrew*,[1] *Errors* has often been taken as the quintessential farce. It stitches together a crazy patchwork of lost family members, identical twins, mixed-up love relationships and seeming enchantments. A director need only add clownish bowler hats or Groucho spectacles with rubber noses and stand back for laughter. Yet for all its zaniness, *Errors* has structure and depth. Characters and events echo each other with an eerie, mathematical sense of patterning and an equal feeling of spontaneity: the play is a triumph of comic repetition-with-difference. The device of doubleness – two sets of identical twins, a city simultaneously humdrum and magical, incidents that seem recurrent, words layered with multiple meanings – fills *Errors*'s world with resonance.[2] Perhaps in no other comedy did Shakespeare combine compression and expansiveness to so much effect.

Errors brims with surprises. As farce, it resembles what aficionados call a 'door play', full of near-miss exits and entrances, with the greatest near-miss involving an actual door in 3.1. The audience, generally one step ahead of the protagonists, gets the pleasure of watching other people's befuddlements. But not always, because at times it will probably

---

1 The relative dating of these plays remains conjectural. Wells and Taylor place *Errors* (1594) chronologically after both *Two Gentlemen* and *Shrew* (see Oxf). Hodgdon speculates, however, that *Shrew*, the most problematic to date, may be post-1594 (35).

2 On mirroring scenes and episodes, see pp. 80–1.

be as confused as the characters about who is who; indeed, in the last act the spectators, like their stage counterparts, enjoy a shocking, rabbit-in-the-hat revelation. The proverbial rug keeps slipping from under our feet. The play delights in change: shifts in tone, in genre convention, in poetic or prose form. The effect can even become disconcerting, for poking through the surface of the buffoonery are intimations of sorrow, embarrassment, anxiety and suffered abuse – cries of the heart from the other side of farce. Audiences might find themselves experiencing a character's tribulations with unexpected empathy. A once-prosperous merchant, now destitute, falls into the clutches of the police in an enemy country and, because of his nationality, faces death. (The story already feels close to today's headlines.) Suddenly he sees his son in a crowd and calls out in desperate hope of rescue – but the son spurns him as a stranger. *Errors* exposes the audience to just such a moment of helplessness, the *doppelgänger* of delight. The play revels in contraries; it offers the grace of sadness turned to reconciliation and rings with laughter at the things that frighten us the most.

Although Renaissance thinkers understood the complexity of comedy, they also embraced its mirthful tone, with large-scale societal problems not so much solved in the ending as deferred by means of local accommodation. Comedy's gleeful business is to expose incongruities, yet also to release and exhaust inhibitions and to dissolve our misperceptions and fears into the elixir of hilarity. As Charles Armitage Brown observed, *Errors*'s 'action is serious', even though, oxymoronically, its 'mistakes . . . are ludicrous'.[1] Laughter at the ludicrous requires an act of sudden mental apprehension and thus expresses the 'instinct of reason' (Heller, 20). Not emotional in essence, laughter generates a shift in outlook and rational perspective that brings pleasure, such that getting the joke revitalizes.

---

1 Brown argued that *Errors* creates laughter more through action and 'situations' than through linguistic play (272).

Thus, we make temporary peace with ourselves and others and find our way through the maze of the world by laughing. Even more, comedy looks hopefully towards the future. Marriage in comedy stands for the possibility, if not always the fact, of happy outcomes; it constitutes the social symbol for joy in the gift of life.

As *Errors*'s performance history indicates, the play delivers such comedy at high-octane levels. It scrutinizes broken families and identity-troubled characters, while generating the kind of hilarious predicaments and slapstick that Abbott and Costello or Monty Python would appreciate. In 1838, for example, Brown remarked of a recent London production that 'the audience in their laughter rolled about like waves', as playgoers revelled in *Errors*'s 'unabated' 'drollery' (272–3). At the Folger Theater in staid Washington, DC, 166 years later, spectators, including sombre government officials and hard-nosed television journalists, doubled over in laughter and rose in standing ovation at the witty ribaldry of an *Errors* production (directed by Joe Banno). Laughter, anxiety, romance, perspicacity and sex folded into a madcap *tour de force*: you may never have more fun in the theatre.

Errors proceeds from an arresting premise: the shock of incomprehensibly losing one's identity to an unknown double – as if the play gathered up our primal intuitions about a charmed world of alter egos; as if we and our loved ones were not quite real or were suddenly under the influence of forces beyond our control. *Errors*'s uncanny underside can be glimpsed in the figure of Doctor Pinch.[1] This tawdry conjuror stands for the apprehensions of magic that trouble Syracusan Antipholus, and he likewise invades the memory of the twin brother, Ephesian Antipholus. The latter will torment Pinch vilely and then pillory him with equal passion (see 5.1.238–46),

---

1 On the uncanny, see Freud's famous essay 'The "Uncanny"' (1919), in Freud, 19–60.

to such a degree that the exorcist comes to suggest some unspeakable fear buried in the psyche. A scapegoat, yet one so disgusting and abused as to be slightly pathetic, Doctor Pinch represents a quality of experience both laughable and a bit unnerving.

Antipholus of Ephesus's denunciation of Pinch was memorable enough that Thomas Heywood apparently imitated it in a 1602 play: 'When didst thou see the starueling Schoolemaister? / That Rat, that shrimp, that spindleshanck, that Wren, that sheep-biter, that leane chittiface, that famine, that leane Enuy, that all bones, that bare Anatomy, that Iack a Lent, that ghost, that shadow, that Moone in the waine' (sig. E1$^\mathrm{v}$).[1] Other audiences remembered Pinch, too. When *Errors* was performed on 28 December 1594 during the Gray's Inn Christmas revels, it was probably intended as late-night relaxation for the brilliant ladies and lawyers who by then would have tired themselves in masquing and dancing. If an afterthought that night, *Errors* became the main topic the next day, when the previous evening's unexpected confusions were attributed to a conjuror (Doctor Pinch?) and the débâcle renamed 'The Night of Errors' (see pp. 108–9). The play made an impression – perhaps so much so that one of the Gray's Inn attendees may have recommended *Errors* for performance before King James twenty years to the day later (see p. 111). Since that time, the phrase, 'comedy of errors', promising both laughter and a touch of hysteria, has come down to us as the byword and matrix of all comedies.[2]

Yet *The Comedy of Errors* had a progenitor, for it adapts a famous comedy of ancient Rome, Plautus' *Menaechmi*, also about a twin in search of his lost, identical brother. *Menaechmi*

---

1 Heywood, *Wife* (sometimes attributed to Joshua Cooke). See Foakes, lii. Heywood's passage turns from verse to prose, as if the speaker were carried away by the force of the description.

2 Sidney calls comedy 'an imitation of the common errors of our life' (*Apology*, 98). Heller argues that 'every comedy is a comedy of errors' (44).

was perhaps the most read, performed and imitated Roman comedy in Italy and England in the fifteenth and sixteenth centuries. In England, the influence of Plautus and his successor, the more decorous and less madcap Terence, generated sparkling, often biting comic successors such as *Gammer Gurton's Needle*, *Ralph Roister Doister* and *Jack Juggler*, all created as English school plays in the mid-sixteenth century; some of Shakespeare's spectators would have known them. Roman farce continued to influence English comedy through the late 1580s (and beyond), as exemplified by John Lyly's *Mother Bombie* (Scragg, 10–11). *Errors*, then, builds upon a living classical tradition – and manages in its inventiveness to outdo its ancestor (see pp. 79–83).

In *Errors*, numerous of Shakespeare's formal strategies and pervasive thematic concerns intersect. In its prosody, the play shares its high percentage of verse with *Richard II* and *Love's Labour's Lost* and its verse experimentalism with *A Midsummer Night's Dream* (see pp. 64–73). Structurally, *Errors*'s framing device (the Syracusan family tragedy enclosing the Ephesian farce) has counterparts in the Induction of *The Taming of the Shrew*, in the contrasting locales of *A Midsummer Night's Dream* and *As You Like It* and even in the low humour set within high of *The Merry Wives of Windsor*. Other Shakespearean comedies employ farcical elements, such as Petruchio's wooing of Kate in *Shrew* or Falstaff's gulling by the merry wives; conversely, Portia and Belmont in *The Merchant of Venice* hail, like the Egeon family, from the generic world of romance. Shakespeare, that is, persists in exploring comic contrasts, especially those between farce and romance.

Errors's issues and geographic milieu anticipate much in Shakespeare's canon. Although *Errors* lacks the Italian setting of some of Shakespeare's comedies, its Ephesus resides in the same Mediterranean world (see Fig. 1). *Errors* also glances at the exotic east (see pp. 54–5), as does *A Midsummer Night's Dream*. The sea figures in *Errors* and in many other plays,

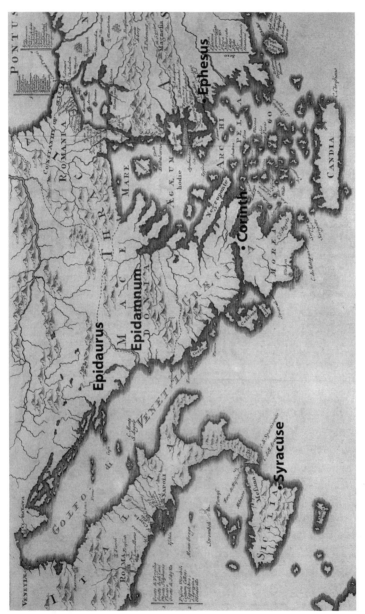

1 The north-eastern Mediterranean. Map from Cornelis de Bruyn, *A Voyage to the Levant* (London, 1702), with names of cities mentioned in the play added

including *Merchant*, *Twelfth Night* and *Pericles*, while separation of twins by shipwreck drives *Errors* as it later will *Twelfth Night*. The abstract problem of law versus mercy, introduced in the Duke's behaviour towards Egeon, becomes a feature of *Dream* and especially *Merchant*. The theme of magic will recur variously – in, for example, *1 Henry VI*, *2 Henry VI*, *Dream* and *The Tempest* – just as madness does in *Shrew* and *Twelfth Night*. *Errors*'s twin fascinations with the possibility of metamorphosis and the motif of oneself-as-another find expression in *Two Gentlemen*, *Dream* and *Twelfth Night* and return throughout the comic canon. Together with magic and madness, they show Shakespeare's interest in the potential instability of reality and the fluidity of personhood.

Shakespeare wrote *Errors* at a time when his thoughts were crystallizing around the problem of human identity – how do we know the self and others? – explored repeatedly from *Richard III* to *Hamlet* to *Antony and Cleopatra*. Identity issues are a common property of comedy, although here *Errors* assumes a special affinity with *Shrew*, where characters are so often not who we think they are. *Errors* ignores, however, the clash between love and friendship that features in *Two Gentlemen of Verona*, *Dream* and *Merchant*, and it attends less to premarital love relationships than do *Two Gentlemen*, *Dream*, *Love's Labour's Lost*, *Much Ado About Nothing* and most other comedies, while instead it scrutinizes marriage (as do *Shrew*, *Hamlet* and *Macbeth*). Finally, *Errors*'s climactic recognition of 'sympathy' (see 5.1.397 and n., on *symapthized*) – of occurrences so reciprocal and co-ordinated as to suggest a mysterious order – echoes throughout Shakespeare's comic and romantic oeuvre. In *Errors*, Shakespeare is formulating matters that will occupy him for the rest of his career.

Until *Errors* won redemption in the mid-twentieth century, however, critics shunned it as an aberration.[1] In 1709,

---

1 On *Errors*'s critical history, see Miola, 'Play'.

Shakespeare's first great editor, Nicholas Rowe, called *Errors* 'pure [i.e. simple] Comedy', faulted its 'Dogrel Rhymes' and dismissed the playwright's Latin competency – taking his cue from Ben Jonson's famous claim that Shakespeare had '*small* Latine, *and lesse* Greeke'[1] – as if he lacked sufficient learning to read *Menaechmi* in the original. Later editors disputed over Shakespeare's Latin skills while concurring that *Errors* amounts to little more than high-spirited farce. So unimpressed was Alexander Pope that he judged (in his 1728 edition) that 'only some characters, single scenes, or perhaps a few particular passages, were of his hand' (a description that Pope also applied to several other of Shakespeare's plays).[2] Thirty-five years later, George Steevens found in *Errors* 'more intricacy of plot than distinction of character', along with a banal predictability (Steevens, 221). In the early 1800s, Samuel Taylor Coleridge condemned *Errors* with quaint praise as 'the only specimen of *poetical* farce in our language' (1.213), while William Hazlitt equivocated that the 'curiosity excited' by the play 'is certainly very considerable, though not of the most pleasing kind' (331).

When in the 1940s T.W. Baldwin put paid to the allegation that Shakespeare possessed little Latin,[3] he opened the door for criticism to explore various new directions, as are discussed in the sections that follow below: the nature of error, the obscurity of human identity, the residual force of magic, the wayward energies of language, the uncanny power of objects, the tension between religion and the marketplace and the experiences of time and of marriage. Criticism has taken an interest, too, in *Errors*'s comic world, its juxtaposing of genres and styles and its disparateness of sources and analogues. In this early play,

---

1   See Rowe, 'Some Account of the Life, etc. of Mr. William Shakespeare', in *Works*, 1.xvii, xxii; Jonson, 'To the Memory of my Beloved, the Author Mr. William Shakespeare', in F, sig. A4ʳ.

2   Pope², 1.xxi; sig. B1ʳ.

3   See Baldwin, *Small Latine*; *Structure*.

Shakespeare investigates the range and nature of comic drama. The very locale, magical Ephesus, makes 'an obvious metaphor for the theatre' as 'a place of transformation where people lose their sense of self'.[1] *Errors* has come not only to presage Shakespeare's subsequent interests and achievements but to suggest the possibilities of theatrical comedy.

ERROR AND IDENTITY

The idea of error: 'What error drives our eyes and ears amiss?'

The idea of error fascinated Renaissance thinkers.[2] The humanist movement attacked what it perceived as empirical, philological and epistemological errors, from Lorenzo Valla's debunking of the forged Donation of Constantine and Erasmus's corrections of medieval translations of the Bible to Francis Bacon's critique of erroneous methods of proof. Accusations of heretical errors typified the raging Protestant–Roman Catholic controversies of the sixteenth century. No wonder that *The Faerie Queene*'s definitive monster, lodged deep in the 'wandring wood', is Errour (Spenser, *FQ*, 1.1.13). It takes the emblematic shape of half loathsome woman and half horrible serpent, with a vast, knotty tail – '*Errours* endlesse traine' (1.1.18) – and it spews forth papers and books of false Roman Catholic doctrine. (For one image of Error, see Fig. 2.) Redcrosse, the knight errant ('wandering'), finds himself afflicted by error ('deception', 'misconception') in the maze of fairy land. Error helps to drive romance, as in Ariosto's *Orlando Furioso* or Spenser's *The Faerie Queene*, and it frequently drives dramatic comedy. Renaissance humanists embraced the medieval commentary of Evanthius (or Donatus) on Plautus and Terence that made error

---

1   Betteridge & Walker, 8.
2   See Rigolot, 1220; Shelburne, 138.

Inextricabilis error.
Error is inextricable.

2   Error. From Claude Paradin, *Heroical Devices* (1591)

central to comic plot.[1] Thus, comic characters traditionally become entwined in Evanthius' 'knot of errors', with mistakes compounded on each other – the kind of bind that makes Viola throw up her hands: 'too hard a knot for me t' untie' (*TN* 2.2.41).

Of the various definitions of the noun 'error', three pertain especially to *The Comedy of Errors*: (1) 'The action of . . . wandering' (*OED n.* 1); (2) 'Something incorrectly done through ignorance' (*OED* 4a); and (3) 'the holding of mistaken notions or beliefs' (*OED* 3a).[2] In *Errors*, wandering applies to both the physical and the mental domains. Physically, it refers

---

1   Evanthius, in *De fabula* (attributed to Donatus in the Renaissance), describes the epitasis of comedy as the 'development and enlargement of the conflict and, as it were, the knot of all the errors' (305). See pp. 62–3.

2   The word derives from the Latin verb *errare*, which, according to the *OLD*, collects several meanings: aimless movement ('to wander'; 'to float or drift'); uncertainty ('to be in doubt'); and departure from reason or rectitude ('to think or act in error'; 'to stray from the path of virtue').

to the movements of characters, pre-eminently Syracusan Antipholus, the comic version of the knight errant, who scours the Mediterranean world for his lost brother. His role is reprised in a potentially tragic key by his wandering father (whose threatened execution poses an alternative ending to both his adventure and his son's).[1] Father, son and others circulate in a world of restless human displacement and travel (see pp. 52–4). These wanderers are at loose ends in the world, essentially lost, homeless.

Mentally, wandering indicates a straying from truth that, in *Errors*, can transform into a causal chain whereby each blunder generates a successor. Two such forms of error are misidentification (as when Adriana mistakes Syracusan Antipholus for her husband) and faulty inference (as when the Courtesan concludes that Ephesian Antipholus is mad). Such errors have a way of making an 'endlesse traine'. The Courtesan's inferential error, for example, derives partly from Syracusan Antipholus' attempt to exorcize her, that error from his own false assumption about witchcraft in Ephesus, and that one from his first misrecognition of Ephesian Dromio. Likewise, the Courtesan's error arises from Ephesian Antipholus' tale of being locked out of his house, and that from Adriana's admitting the wrong Antipholus into it. Error, by nature, multiplies and spreads, such that Syracusan Antipholus feels as if his confused soul 'wander[s] in an unknown field' (3.2.38).

Error is most damaging in the form of self-perpetuating misconceptions and faulty habits of mind. In *Errors*, such mistakes differ from those deriving from the trickery found in most Roman comedies or in the prototypical Italian comedy, Ariosto's *I Suppositi* (1509), where error is induced and sustained by the ruses of conniving servants or desperate lovers. Rather, these errors possess agency. 'What error drives our

---

1   *Errors*'s structuring into the plot of an alternative, tragic ending is a device that Shakespeare will exploit elsewhere, as in *A Midsummer Night's Dream*.

eyes and ears amiss?' (2.2.190), asks Syracusan Antipholus, pondering the claim of Adriana and Luciana to know him. He feels himself ensnared in a dream, perhaps magically transformed. Later, convinced that Luciana must be a goddess or siren, he finds his understanding 'Smothered in errors, feeble, shallow, weak' (3.2.35). Antipholus envisions error as a hostile and disabling force, an immaterial version of Spenser's monster.

Antipholus may grasp the power of error, but he misrecognizes its origin, for the play's crucial errors are generated not externally but internally, from a character's interpretive framework or set of prior assumptions. At its most profound, error is not misidentification but misconception. Errors flow from biases and passions that reflect a particular sense of self or world[1] – a territory that Shakespeare will chart in comic characters such as Bottom and Dogberry and in tragi-comic plays such as *The Winter's Tale*. Antipholus' conceptual error is to believe that Ephesus is rife with witchcraft (see 1.2.97–103). He has some biblical warrant for that view (see pp. 50–1), which is abetted by his impressionability and excitability. Once asserted, the misinterpretation becomes entrenched, impervious to mounting evidence that the city might contain exactly the lost twins the Syracusans seek. Every encounter, such as with the Courtesan, reinforces the *idée fixe*. The counterpart for the Ephesians, befitting their mercantile decorum, is the conviction that the resident Antipholus is mad; it generates knots both of plot errors and of binding rope. Error rises from the psyche, whence it further colonizes the mind and invades Ephesus like a virus, operating beyond the mix-ups typical of farce.[2] Error so experienced approximates to Henri Bergson's sense of the comic as something mechanical encrusted upon the living, here the compulsion 'to mould things on an idea of one's own,

1   See Griffiths, esp. 298–9.
2   See Shelburne, 141–2.

instead of moulding one's ideas on things' (179). As illustration, the play materializes error in the chain, or 'carcanet' (see 3.1.4 and n.), which circulates among characters and whose links suggest a potentially 'endlesse traine' (see pp. 35–8), and again in the knotted ropes, the 'knot of errors', that Doctor Pinch tightens around Ephesian Antipholus and Dromio.

Renaissance writers conceived of error as a dominating idea or paradigm that leaps from a small particular to a vast conclusion and then overwhelms the mind: various of Shakespeare's tragic heroes, such as Othello, suffer from it, as do all of Marlowe's. It feels involuntary even when fundamentally volitional.[1] The origins of such error remain obscure: 'They say this town is full of cozenage' (1.2.97), muses Syracusan Antipholus, as he summons forth the false explanation that will drive his actions. That phrase, 'They say', hints at the self-perpetuating power of slander (see e.g. 3.1.100–6), the very model of error. '*Inextricabilis error*', reads a Latin emblem-book motto in Claude Paradin's 1591 *Heroical Devices* (see Fig. 2). The motto derives from a line in Virgil's *Aeneid*, a work that hovers in the background of *Errors*'s first scene: 'Error is inextricable', or, we might say, one cannot extricate oneself from error.[2]

Yet perhaps one can. Errors must be addressed empirically, of course, and in the denouement the Duke functions as a rational, proto-scientific investigator. Syracusan Antipholus attempts to bring the Duke's sorting out of misidentifications to a conclusion: 'And thereupon these errors are arose' (5.1.388). But, in a memorable phrase, the Abbess insists upon error's weird, communicative power: 'this sympathized one-day's error' (397), the adjective suggesting both the day's uncanny

---

1 'Renaissance high culture seems to have foregrounded the involuntary character of error, with its uncanny origin and often disastrous consequences' (Rigolot, 1223).

2 See *Aen.*, 6.27: '*hic labor ille domus et inextricabilis error*', a reference to the house of the Minotaur, an inextricable labyrinth built with great labour.

sharing of experiences and the working of mysterious agency (see p. 30, and 5.1.397n, on *sympathized*). Characters have lived out each other's lives, commanded each other's servants and suffered for, or profited by, each other's deeds. The Abbess speaks from levels of knowledge different from her son's, those of a mother impossibly reunited with her fractured family and of a nun intuiting the miracles of Christian providence. In Renaissance magic, sympathy indicates a psychic ability to work material effects at a distance; the Abbess's sympathized error bespeaks a harmonizing of happenstance that looks very much like the action of grace. The 'endlesse traine' becomes the golden chain, and wandering turns out to be the way home.

Dim inwardness: 'if that I am I'

Likeness and doubleness of character attracted Shakespeare, in *Errors* as in *Dream* and *Twelfth Night* (he was himself the father of twins).[1] *Errors* questions whether the self should be understood as a presumably authentic yet only dimly knowable inwardness or instead as a recognizable but potentially deceptive outwardness.[2] The play ultimately takes a mediating position, that character 'is not co-extensive with its outward marks, but neither is it ' "that within that passes show" ':[3] it is something of both, in-betweenness.

Syracusan Antipholus establishes the paradoxical instability of identity:

> He that commends me to mine own content
> Commends me to the thing I cannot get:
> I to the world am like a drop of water
> That in the ocean seeks another drop;

---

1 Mistaken identity fascinated Elizabethans. In a letter of 10 July 1590, the traveller Sir Henry Wotton described meeting in Florence someone 'so like me as we are saluted in the street for one another', 'the spirit of myself' (Wotton, 1.282).

2 On inwardness, see Maus.

3 Lanier, 'Character', 317.

> Who, falling there to find his fellow forth,
> Unseen, inquisitive, confounds himself.
> So I, to find a mother and a brother,
> In quest of them, unhappy, lose myself.
>
> (1.2.33–40)

That is, as Antipholus seeks wholeness in reunion with his lost mother and brother, he forfeits his selfhood; the family both gives and denies. Further, Antipholus imagines himself as without the 'content' of a stable identity, liable to lose form, 'confound[ed]', no more than a mirror-effect. Given his sense of precarious selfhood, Antipholus will necessarily dread Ephesian necromancers: 'Dark-working sorcerers that change the mind, / Soul-killing witches that deform the body' (1.2.99–100). From a psychoanalytic perspective, Antipholus represents 'identity confusion and ego loss in adolescence, attendant on a break away from filial identifications and into adult identity' (Kahn, 201–2). He must give up his 'narcissistic mirroring' of family and seek fulfilment in a separate other – his future mate, Luciana (Kahn, 202). Conceived differently, Antipholus' frightening ocean image may signify the threat of 'overwhelming' maternal 'reabsorption', against which Antipholus will seek union with his twin brother as 'alter ego' (MacCary, 530, 528). Filial identification can be threatening; fraternal identification, possibly salvific. Yet Antipholus embodies qualities at odds with those of his brother (and others): he is the unstable and transformable Syracusan, difficult to reconcile with the hierarchical and proprietary Ephesian.[1] Antipholus experiences a shifting, contrary pull of outward and inward forces: his attraction to the rather straight-laced Luciana may promise a clash of those incompatible sensibilities, or it may hint at their reconciliation.[2]

---

1   See Freedman, *Gaze*, 84–8.
2   On recent performances of Luciana as 'Edwardian' and 'prim', see Rutter, 457.

The experience of identity in *Errors* diverges from that of the so-called 'humanist subject', who perceives himself as autonomous, self-unified and coherent. Many Renaissance humanists, such as Montaigne, recognized the variableness of the self. Inwardness in *Errors* takes a particular form, for characters regularly sense that they are somehow each also a second person, someone other.[1] If, in the classical ideal, male friendship consists of two bodies but one mind, as in *Two Gentlemen*,[2] the reverse occurs in *Errors*, where the brothers constitute, in effect, one body but two minds. Twinness confuses autonomous identity, and the play's events cause each Antipholus to experience aspects of the life of the other, the Syracusan progressively enjoying his brother's home and objects, the Ephesian enduring their loss. Sometimes one *doppelgänger*-brother even seems psychically immanent in the other. Adriana can exert an imaginative pull on Syracusan Antipholus partly because he wonders if he has been 'married to her in [his] dream' (2.2.188), her 'mist' manifesting in him an anterior self, the genius-presence of his brother. Likewise, the marked antagonism that the exorcist Doctor Pinch evokes in Ephesian Antipholus provides a displaced outlet for the fear and anxiety that his Syracusan twin feels about demonic possession.

Yet other moments of being beside oneself are more blurry and less referential than those just mentioned and do not always seem confined to the effects of having a sibling twin:

> how comes it,
> That thou art then estranged from thyself?

> (2.2.125–6)

---

1 See Freedman, *Gaze*, 89–92.
2 See Carroll, *Two Gentlemen*, 3–19.

I am transformed, master, am I not?
I think thou art in mind, and so am I.

(2.2.201–2)

Known unto these, and to myself disguised?

(2.2.220)

if that I am I

(3.2.41)

Call thyself 'sister', sweet, for I am thee.

(3.2.66)

I am an ass, I am a woman's man, and besides
myself.

(3.2.75–6)

Hath almost made me traitor to myself.
But lest myself be guilty to self-wrong

(3.2.167–8)

The fellow is distract, and so am I

(4.3.43)

To make of him a formal man again.

(5.1.105)

In these statements, the vague possibility of otherness – a self disguised to the self, or become animalistic or inchoate – intrudes in interrogatives, hypotheticals, speculations and surprised declarations. Notions of self-loss and self-estrangement can yield to the idea of a second self, standing, as it were, beside the speaking self, differently constituted or unrecognizable, possibly traitorous to the first. The threat to identity occurs here as the self's displacement by a mysterious other, a secret sharer. That dimly intuited, penumbral self

17

registers in the alienated identity that characters experience when they fear that they are enchanted. When the Courtesan sees Ephesian Antipholus trembling in his 'ecstasy' (4.4.52), she identifies precisely that sense of being 'beside oneself' (*OED* ecstasy *n*. 1).

Although G.R. Elliott observes that 'Real horror attaches to the notion of the *complete* identity of two human beings' (57), the two Antipholuses differ in character. The fact of twinness will later prove more uncanny in *Twelfth Night*, where Viola's insistence on keeping the image of her drowned brother alive through her disguise in effect calls him back from the sea. But *Errors* has its own unsettling mysteriousness, for the language of multiple selves reaches out subtly but suggestively. In Plato's *Gorgias*, Socrates tells Callicles that he would prefer to be at odds with others 'rather than that I myself, who am but one man, should be out of tune with myself and contradict myself' – a moral idea of unified self-identity (*Gorgias*, 265, par. 482c). In phenomenological terms, however, the very fact of self-consciousness implies a double self, the 'I' who is the object of self-commentary and the 'I' who comments. Beyond that, *Errors* hints at one's possession of another, opaque self, intuited from outward encounters yet deeply within and barely knowable, potentially engulfing, dangerous.

Deceptive outwardness: 'reverend reputation'

The second self is hinted but not fully realized; more straightforward is the concept that identity derives from social relations.[1] As Ephesian Antipholus loses the evidence of his social standing – he is locked out of his home by his wife and servants, arrested for debt and finally captured, bound and

---

1 Findlay argues that *Errors* 'is almost obsessively concerned with the minutiae of social decorum' because '[r]itualized interactions which endow the self with proper respect – make the self a sacred thing – are the essence of . . . social order' (338, 352).

imprisoned as a lunatic – he becomes enraged, almost mad with fury (see 5.1.169–77), suggesting the contingency of material status-markers and the anxiety of owning them.[1] Similarly, her husband's neglect makes Adriana feel degraded in selfhood (see 2.1.86–100). To a considerable degree, characters know themselves in the mirroring that others give them. In this proto-capitalist, credit-dependent economy, a stable public image of oneself and others acquires economic value.[2] When Ephesian Antipholus denies his debt to Angelo, the goldsmith responds, 'Consider how it stands upon my credit' (4.1.68). Angelo will later describe Antipholus as

> Of very reverend reputation, sir,
> Of credit infinite, highly beloved,
> Second to none that lives here in the city;
> His word might bear my wealth at any time.

$$(5.1.5-8)$$

Financial credit itself stands upon reputation, the avatar of identity (see 3.1.86, 100–6). When a character's behaviour deviates from reputation, others respond either by denying the anomaly (e.g. by labelling odd actions as 'merry' or mad) or by redescribing the character in question (as we shall see). Both misconceived responses expose the difficulty that society faces in analysing idiosyncratic behaviour. When someone acts 'out of character', the observer can be left grasping after lame explanations in a momentary crisis of identity about others and the self.[3] The conundrum derives from the characters' need to have their expectations reflected back to them in the responses of their intimates and acquaintances; otherwise, the world turns whimsical or lunatic.

---

1 See Lanier, 'Character'.
2 On emotional responses to the credit system in early modern England, see Leinwand, esp. 42–80.
3 See Lanier, 'Character', 307–10.

The social and economic entrenchment of identity shows in the close relationship of selfhood to property. If we know Egeon as a pauper, we know Ephesian Antipholus as a wealthy member (apparently a merchant) of the bourgeoisie. Antipholus will suffer subtraction of property and its rights until he finds himself dispossessed and confined rather than playing the expansive host among the luxury goods in his impressive home. If identity is attached tightly to one's property, then being severed incomprehensibly from it can bring rage and near-madness. Thus, Antipholus' reported fiery attack on Doctor Pinch expresses not only his brother's fear of sorcery but his own displaced violence against whatever force has conjured away the evidence of who he is (see 5.1.238–46).[1] His twin enjoys the opposite, of course, an influx of wealth that leaves him wondering if he knows himself. By the play's end, social identities and bonds will be re-established only when debts are paid and possessions returned to their owners (see 5.1.377–92).

Bacon expresses a Renaissance notion of the communal dimension of the self when he writes, 'There is formed in every thing a double nature of good: the one, as every thing is a total or substantive in itself; the other, as it is a part or member of a greater body' (246). Shakespeare puts to the test that matter of public identity, or what Nancy Selleck calls 'interpersonal' identity.[2] The Ciceronian, humanist trope of a friend as 'another self' became 'ubiquitous' in literary works of the 1590s (Selleck, 35), as in *Two Gentlemen*, and it expanded from friendship to include love and marriage (see pp. 46–9). The trope occurs twice in *Errors*, the first time enunciated by Adriana, the second by Syracusan Antipholus. Adriana's speech

---

1 Antipholus' reported singeing of Pinch's beard (see 5.1.170–1) suggests the further degradation of symbolic emasculation.
2 Discussing Bakhtin, Selleck comments, 'In this model, the self not only counters and responds to the other, it emerges through the conceptual framework of the other' (4); see Selleck, 1–20.

to Antipholus about love and marriage (2.2.116–52) constitutes the most emotionally authentic, intellectually probing and affecting speech in *Errors*. In it, she employs the same drop of water image used by Antipholus in 1.2.35–9 – by him for sibling and filial, by her for marital, shared selfhood:

> For know, my love: as easy mayst thou fall
> A drop of water in the breaking gulf,
> And take unmingled thence that drop again
> Without addition or diminishing,
> As take from me thyself, and not me, too.

> (2.2.131–5)

Adriana pushes this image to an extreme so literal that it challenges credibility, for she argues that when her husband commits adultery, she herself is thereby 'possessed with an adulterate blot' (146), that her blood is mingled with lust, her flesh poisoned and herself 'strumpeted by [his] contagion' (150) (with 'blot' and 'contagion' probably alluding to venereal disease). Adriana claims an instant, mystical transference of physical elements and moral qualities between partners. Her passionate sincerity is moving but her proposition dubious. She has driven her argument beyond the figurative level of mutuality[1] and down to the concrete level of bodily fluids and moral attributes communicated magically, where it collapses. That problem is aggravated when, imagining her husband as the sturdy elm and herself as the winding vine (180–6), Adriana fastens on his sleeve and apparently attempts to wrap her arms (or more) around him. The incident is often acted with such exaggeration (as by Judi Dench in the Nunn production) that it provokes audience laughter, as if earnestness had morphed into its parody. 'Oneself-as-another' compels as a trope, but, when pushed

---

1 See Selleck, 36–7.

21

towards literalism, risks becoming ridiculous. Even worse, Adriana rhapsodizes about inalienable, mutual identification to the wrong person (Syracusan rather than Ephesian Antipholus). At Antipholus' response, 'Plead you to me, fair dame?' (153), spectators chuckle. Her claim to an inward physical union (and her hope for a spiritual one) is belied by the fact that she knows her husband only via the system of observable markers – physical characteristics, clothes, companions – that she shares with everyone else.

Syracusan Antipholus employs language similar to Adriana's in wooing Luciana: 'It is thyself, mine own self's better part' (3.2.61). Adriana's self-as-another imagery has invaded his consciousness. Yet Antipholus evokes neither the poignancy nor the comedy of Adriana: the trope has become the less authentic for being the more used. Antipholus (paralleling Adriana) claims fusion with a beloved who believes that he is someone else. If his importunings move Luciana (as they seem to), with whom is she entertaining mutual selfhood: her brother-in-law, as she presumes, or a complete stranger? For his part, Antipholus thinks that he shares selfhood with someone who might be a 'mermaid' or 'siren' (45, 47). The idea of oneself-as-another may have become current by the 1590s, but, regarding love and marriage, *Errors* parodies as much as affirms it.

Identities destabilize further as characters describe each other and then revise their descriptions, as Adriana does in relation to her husband, Ephesian Antipholus. She worries that Antipholus' attentions are being distracted by another woman, and Ephesian Dromio's wild story of Antipholus' 'mad' refusal to come home for dinner confirms to her that Antipholus is consorting with alluring 'minions' (2.1.56, 86). His behaviour, she claims, has ruined her beauty, discourse and wit. Later, more harshly and extremely, Adriana depicts her husband as 'estranged', 'licentious', 'adulter[ous]' and 'lust[ful]' (2.2.126, 137, 146, 147). Next, believing that Antipholus has attempted to seduce her sister, she unleashes a torrent of abuse:

He is deformed, crooked, old and sere,
Ill-faced, worse bodied, shapeless everywhere;
Vicious, ungentle, foolish, blunt, unkind,
Stigmatical in making, worse in mind.

(4.2.19–22)

Moments later, however, she equivocates – 'I think him better than I say' (25) – leaving her views unfixed.[1] Is Ephesian Antipholus an adulterer with the Courtesan? He declares his innocence to Angelo and Balthazar (3.1.111–13), but Adriana's ever-worsening redescriptions of him are so insistent and cumulative as to make it impossible quite to know the truth. Under pressure, public identity proves a fragile thing, evanescent, a little watery. Other characters suffer redescription, as well, including the innocuous Officer, reimagined as a hellish monster (see e.g. 4.2.32–40), and Doctor Pinch, reconceived as a villainous and pernicious scoundrel (5.1.238–46). No characters endure such vicissitudes more than the Dromios. In 1.2, as Syracusan Antipholus' anger rises towards Ephesian Dromio, his terms descend: 'trusty villain' (19), 'sir knave' (72), 'slave' (87). We are reminded of the truth-power of slander and the in-betweenness of identity.

Metamorphosis: 'Transform me'

The extreme version of character-change in *Errors* is metamorphosis.[2] Early in the play, Syracusan Antipholus takes lodging at an inn aptly named the Centaur and expresses fear of Ephesian mind-changing sorcerers and 'Soul-killing', body-deforming witches (1.2.100); later, he will imagine Luciana as a supernatural being with the power to 'Transform'

---

1 In these speeches, argues Piesse, Adriana 'acknowledges the inadequacy of a single way of seeing' (159).
2 On the Renaissance fascination with metamorphosis, see Carroll, *Metamorphosis*, 3–40.

him (3.2.40); by the end, the Duke will wonder if those around him 'have drunk of Circe's cup' (5.1.271). Characters fear or suspect metamorphosis. It might involve the transformation of the human body into an animal or into a thing while the mind remains human, the effect of Circe's potion. Such change is epitomized in Ovid's *Metamorphoses*, a central influence on Shakespeare.[1] In *Errors*, metamorphosis can have different meanings: the body changed or the mind changed instead of the body. (For Bottom in *Dream*, both effects occur.) The Syracusans continually fear that they are being transformed; certain touches of dialogue indicate that they might even desire it, as when Antipholus imagines himself seeking dissolution of the self into another drop of water or when he invites Luciana to 'create me new' (3.2.39). Antipholus' language sometimes shadows forth a self-negating melancholy, despair's kinsman (see 1.2.20; 5.1.79–80), recalling Egeon's hopelessness. At such moments, subjectivity weighs like a burden to be escaped through transformation.

The language and imagery of Circean metamorphosis saturate *Errors*, and its possibility haunts the characters. Behind their fears lies a cultural anxiety about the instability not only of identity but of borders between humans and animals.[2] Characters in *Errors* often imagine themselves as animals. Although Adriana and Luciana compare women to horses and asses (2.1.13–14), and Adriana speaks of her husband as a 'too-unruly deer' (99), only the Dromios suffer persistently the comparison to objects, insects and fauna – footballs, gnats, slugs, snails, apes, dogs, sheep – and to none more than to beasts of burden. 'I am an ass', says each Dromio (2.2.207, 3.2.75, 4.4.30). Ephesian Dromio accepts the label of ass because his master calls him one and beats him as if he were; the self-description expresses recrimination towards himself

---

1 See Bate.

2 See Boehrer; also Maisano.

and, more strongly, antagonism towards his oppressor: 'I should kick, being kicked . . . beware of an ass' (3.1.17–18; see also 4.4.30–3). Asinine metamorphosis might lead to revenge. Syracusan Dromio comes closer to thinking himself an actual ass. Embracing enchantment, he imagines himself 'transformed' (2.2.201) by the Ephesian women-fairies into an ape and then an ass: ''Tis true: she rides me, and I long for grass. / 'Tis so, I am an ass' (206–7). Dromio carries to comic extreme the Syracusans' fear of being degraded through sorcery. Presiding over this dimension of *Errors*, Circe stands for the power to change, if not men's bodies, then their minds.[1]

If, by the end, the light of empiricism dispels the 'mist' of enchantment, so that no one becomes an ape or ass, transformations of some sort nonetheless take place. Syracusan Antipholus enters willingly into the 'mist' or 'fallacy' or 'dream' (2.2.222, 192, 188) proffered by Adriana – this willingness itself constituting a change in him – and it is in that receptive attitude that he discovers Luciana as a goddess or siren whom he can love, another change. Like *Dream*'s Demetrius, Antipholus remains love-enchanted at the end, even if he hopes that he no longer dreams. By contrast, Ephesian Antipholus acts with a rage and apparent irrationality that convince others that he is mad:

COURTESAN [*to Adriana*]
    How say you now? Is not your husband mad?
ADRIANA
    His incivility confirms no less.
    . . .

---

1 Circe was a widely applied Renaissance image. Gosson's *The School of Abuse* (1579) links Circe to poetry's transformational power: 'These are the Cuppes of Circes, that turne reasonable Creatures into brute Beastes' (sig. A3ᵛ): Shakespeare may be alluding to anti-theatrical arguments. In *Errors*, Roberts sees the expression of Renaissance 'anxieties' over 'seduction, rebellion, subversive enthrallment of men by women, loss of male rationality' and ultimately fiction's power to destabilize truth ('Circe', 203; see 194–206).

LUCIANA

    Alas, how fiery and how sharp he looks!

COURTESAN

    Mark how he trembles in his ecstasy.

                                  (4.4.46–7, 51–2)

After Antipholus and Dromio are captured and bound, Dromio recommends that they might go mad in earnest: 'Will you be bound for nothing? Be mad, good master: cry "The devil!"' (128–9; see Figs 3 and 4). Later, Antipholus' reportedly

The COMEDY OF ERRORS. Act 4. Sc. 9.

3   Doctor Pinch subduing Antipholus of Ephesus (4.4). Drawn by Francis
    Hayman, engraved by Hubert-François Gravelot, from Thomas Hanmer
    (ed.), *The Works of Shakespear*, vol. 1 (Oxford, 1743)

4 Doctor Pinch subduing Antipholus of Ephesus (4.4). Drawn by John
   Gilbert, engraved by the Dalziel brothers, from Howard Staunton (ed.),
   The Plays of Shakespeare, vol. 1 (1858)

murderous attack on Pinch (5.1.168–77) and his threat to
disfigure Adriana (182–3) argue that the Ephesian has
undergone moments of transformation indistinguishable from
madness and possession.

Other transformations, deep if muted, also occur. Some
characters learn adaptability, despite their reliance on fixed
explanations for aberrant events. Adriana, at first jealous, then
clingy, finally turns self-critical (although some commentators
consider her change a surrender to patriarchal values). By the
end, transformation shades into rebirth. Adriana finds herself
able to move beyond jealousy; Egeon recovers his family and
presumably his hope; Luciana and Syracusan Antipholus
appear bound for the altar; Ephesian Antipholus and Adriana
gain the possibility of reconciliation; and two pairs of twins

recognize that they look like each other but may differ, too.[1] As the Abbess says, applying the Pauline image that replaces enchantment, 'such nativity!' (5.1.406). While the conclusion is not exactly tidy and the future not exactly clear, the ending yet embraces the possibility of transformation.

THE CULTURAL WORLD

Magic: 'Dark-working sorcerers'

The two Syracusans attribute the errancy they experience to black magic, a motif launched early by Antipholus:

> They say this town is full of cozenage –
> As, nimble jugglers that deceive the eye,
> Dark-working sorcerers that change the mind,
> Soul-killing witches that deform the body,
> Disguised cheaters, prating mountebanks,
> And many such – like liberties of sin.

> (1.2.97–102)

What the Syracusans ascribe to magic, the Ephesians blame on madness, conceived as demonic possession. Magic becomes the presumed nexus generating all the misadventures. On the level of plot, the denouement would seem to untie the knots of error and dispel misapprehensions. Satan may be the author of confusions, but reason and material evidence are the harbingers of truth. Yet the play concedes residual power to the idea of magic. Magic saturated biblical Ephesus (see pp. 50–1, and 1.2.97n., on *this town*), and *Errors* brims with related imagery: sorcerers, jugglers, fairies, fairy land, goblins, sprites, mermaids, sirens, enchanting mists, misleading illusions,

---

1   On the ending, Altman comments: 'as each individual's practical understanding increases through the collective testimony . . . so also does his concept of self, seen now in all its relations' (174).

devils and totems, Circe, genius-spirits and, pre-eminently, witches. Characters experience magic with an emotional intensity that makes it difficult entirely to dismiss. Individuals testify, in effect, to an enormous human susceptibility to possession by occult or demonic forces. When it apparently happens, they express outsized responses – trepidation, certitude, anger – and understandably so, since bewitchment and possession were feared in the early modern world as capable of spreading contagiously. The imaginative and psychological power of magic exceeds the ending's explanatory reach.

The play itself creates uncanny effects, in the form of words, thoughts or experiences that drift from one character to another. An example occurs in Syracusan Antipholus' use of the famous 'drop of water' image to describe his unformed selfhood (1.2.35–8) and Adriana's subsequent application of exactly the same image to marriage (2.2.131–5) (see pp. 14–15, 21). That convergence may encourage Antipholus in wondering whether a 'mist' of enchantment swirls about him (222). Likewise, certain echoes carry from *Errors*'s first scene, in which Egeon receives a sentence of death, to the second, in which his peripatetic son arrives in Ephesus.[1] Those echoes work at the level of language, with the repetition of words and phrases ('mart[s]', 'goods', 'confiscate', 'dispose[d]', 'thousand', 'too soon', 'five', 'inquisitive', 'quest', 'travel[s]'),[2] topics (risk, wealth, time) and tonalities (melancholy, weariness).[3] The third scene, in which Adriana frets over her husband's tardiness, also echoes the first, here in its topics and images (weeping, liberty or its loss, time as men's master, the sea) and diction ('woe[s]',

---

1 See Brooks, 'Themes'.
2 See: 'mart[s]', 1.1.17, 1.2.27, 74; 'goods', 1.1.20, 42, 1.2.2; 'confiscate', 1.1.20, 1.2.2; 'dispose[d]', 1.1.20, 83, 1.2.73 (and 'undisposed', 80); 'thousand', 1.1.21, 1.2.81, 84; 'too soon', 1.1.60, 1.2.2; 'five', 1.1.100, 132, 1.2.26; 'inquisitive', 1.1.125, 1.2.38; 'quest', 1.1.129, 1.2.40; 'travel[s]', 1.1.139, 1.2.15.
3 See Elliott, 61–2; Cartwright, 'Language', 337–8.

'adverse'/'adversity', 'bound[s]', 'burden[ed]', 'helpless'[1]). A general wash of words, feelings and images from character to character and from scene to scene typifies *Errors*. Words are repeated in other plays, of course, but the phenomenon differs here by happening in an aura of magic and in a plot-structure of mysterious repetitions and displacements. From outside the play, such matters may appear as structural harmonies that provide unity, but from within the play, they suggest an uncanniness that permeates Ephesian life, its effects wandering from scene to scene. Indeed, exactly this quality of experience must obtain to create the full force of the Abbess's meaning when she exclaims upon the 'sympathized one-day's error' (5.1.397), for 'sympathy' in Renaissance magic expresses the psychic ability of one being to work a long-distance effect on another being or object, and, in the Abbess's usage, it claims a capacity for mysterious, psychic infectiousness.

A related aspect of magic in the play is what can be called 'materialization' or 'manifestation', referring to the power of words or thoughts to call forth objects or actions, to produce real effects.[2] Such materialization intensifies late in the play, as the Ephesian world increasingly seems mad and magical. Syracusan Antipholus' early fear of cozeners and sorcerers eventually becomes manifest in the figure of the conjuror Doctor Pinch, although his conjurations are pursued against the other Antipholus (see Figs 3 and 4). Ephesian Antipholus excoriates Pinch as a 'mountebank' and 'juggler' (5.1.239, 240), repeating terms used by his fearful brother when he imagined Ephesian sorcerers (see 1.2.101, 98), as if the brothers were sharing the same psychic experience (see p. 16). Pinch's scene parallels that in which Syracusan Antipholus has attempted to conjure away the devil-Courtesan. The sorcerer is,

1   See: 'woe[s]', 1.1.2, 27, 108, 2.1.15; 'adverse'/'adversity', 1.1.15, 2.1.34; 'bound[s]', 1.1.81, 133, 2.1.17; 'burden[ed]', 1.1.55, 107, 2.1.36; 'helpless', 1.1.157, 2.1.39.
2   See Cartwright, 'Language', 341–2; Parker, 'Bible', 71; also Cartwright, 'Scepticism', 225–8.

5   Emblem of Death and Father Time. Engraved by William Marshall, from
    Francis Quarles, *Hieroglyphics of the Life of Man* (1638)

in effect, a bogeyman fulfilling the characters' apprehensions of
witchcraft and demonic possession.[1] He exists as both fraudulent
and psychologically real. His appearance has been foreshadowed
by Dromio's fear of fairies: 'They'll . . . pinch us black and
blue' (2.2.198), and it calls forth his counterpart, the Abbess, as
an after-effect. In the last act, another character, Egeon, also
flickers into relief as a kind of materialization, here of the figure
of Time (see Fig. 5). When Egeon refers to 'Time's deformed

---

1   In that regard, he is quasi-allegorical; on the interpenetration of the mimetic and
    allegorical in English Renaissance drama, see Lin, 71–104.

hand' he is speaking, by way of a transferred epithet, of his own age-changed hand and of himself as Time's personification (see 5.1.299 LN). Cumulatively, such moments evoke the potential of the quotidian and the sensible to be crossed unexpectedly with wonder: indeed, the marvellous recombinations of the ending strive for exactly that effect.

Language: 'your words' deceit'

The Comedy of Errors, like Shakespeare's other early comedies, treats language thematically. In *The Two Gentlemen of Verona*, the problematic constancy of linguistic meaning parallels the problematic constancy of the male lovers, qualities amplified in *Love's Labour's Lost*, where the open-ended use of language coincides with the tenuousness of male vows and foreshadows the irresolution of the ending.[1] In *The Taming of the Shrew*, the word-play between Kate and Petruchio in the wooing scene establishes a form of private love- and sex-play. In such instances, a particular use of language becomes a metaphor for aspects of the action. In *Errors*, language likewise responds to its play-world, such as its aura of magic. When Dromio thinks fearfully of a demon, he quasi-chants a list of the totemic items by which a demon works: 'Some devils ask but the parings of one's nail, a rush, a hair, a drop of blood, a pin, a nut, a cherry-stone' (4.3.73–5), as if one image preternaturally generated the next.

Puns, quibbles and word-play help to create the vagrant energy of the Ephesian world. *Errors*'s puns generate a 'linguistic anarchy' that contrasts to its modes of formulaic rhetorical speech (Grennan, 158). Puns embody multiple meanings spoken from different imagined worlds; conversation and thought may, at any moment, turn in a new direction. Quibbling also expresses the classical humanistic value of

---

1   See Carroll, *Two Gentlemen*, 64–7; Woudhuysen, 16–33.

copia, or amplitude and expansiveness. Likewise, word-games bespeak festivity and playfulness, associated most with the Dromios. Linguistic play in *Errors* thus enriches and enlivens, offers new perspectives and seems, on the whole, morally positive. Yet quibbling can get out of hand. The mounting crisis of Act 4 is refracted in Syracusan Dromio's speech about the Officer (see 4.3.16–34 and nn.), composed of puns with multiple meanings piled upon other puns – legal, urban, biblical – such that Syracusan Antipholus takes it as obscure 'foolery' (36) and the audience has little better prospect of understanding. Dromio's speeches to Adriana about the same character a scene earlier (see 4.2.32–40, 44–6 and nn.) have their own hallucinogenic feel, as if that rather mild-mannered sergeant were the demon lurking in Dromio's imagination.

Quibbles and language-play broach another feature of *Errors*: repetition as a form of comic patter. In 2.2, for example, the two Syracusans engage in a mock disputation based on each character's ability to appropriate and reinterpret the other's words: 'sconce', 'basting', 'dry', 'a time for all things', 'fine and recovery' and more (see 35–114). Conversations frequently advance by a listening character's fastening on the words of the preceding speaker and questioning, exploring or reanimating them in a fresh direction. 'How chance thou art returned so soon?', asks Syracusan Antipholus; ' "Returned so soon"? Rather approached too late!', answers Ephesian Dromio (1.2.42, 43). Dromio invests Antipholus' phrase with a different energy and meaning, and then uses it to fashion his own statement (rhetorically, *asteismus*[1]) – and so it goes throughout the play. Such activity enacts repetition-with-difference on the level of language. Sometimes called 'connective repetition',

---

1   In *Errors*'s first scene alone, Shakespeare draws freely from the Renaissance's rich inventory of rhetorical forms of repetition, using *polyptoton* (see 1.1.38n., on *hap*), *antimetabole* (see 1.1.49n.), *diacope* (see 1.1.66–7n.), *anadiplosis* (see 1.1.70–1n.) and *epanalepsis* (see 1.1.84n.).

this device is part of the ancient art of theatrical improvisation and of the Italian tradition of slapstick *commedia dell'arte* that informs *Errors*. Connective repetition involves shifts of thought, of tone and even of genre, in *Errors*'s spirit of spontaneity and unpredictability.

The Dromios often employ connective repetition for a further purpose: self-defence. In 4.4.24–40, Ephesian Antipholus, beating Ephesian Dromio, calls him a 'senseless villain'; Dromio captures the adjective and sends it back at Antipholus with a changed signification and an implicit accusation: 'I would I were senseless, sir, that I might not feel your blows.' Antipholus next calls Dromio 'an ass', to which the servant retorts, 'I am an ass, indeed', and proceeds to detail the folly of his service – in his best speech in the play. The Antipholuses may dominate their slaves physically, but they cannot overpower them with wit. In the economy of such farcical moments, the Dromios' clever rejoinders confirm their superiority to their circumstances and provide a measure of revenge.

Finally, language problems in *Errors* often occur as ones of context – predictably, in a play about characters misidentifying each other. After listening carefully to Adriana, who has mistaken him for her husband, Syracusan Antipholus claims that he lacks the wit 'one word to understand' of her long, heart-felt plea (2.2.157); later, he will ask Luciana to explain 'The folded meaning of your words' deceit' (3.2.36). Luciana will report to Adriana that Antipholus has wooed her 'With words that in an honest suit might move' (4.2.14), but she distrusts his protestations because she mistakes Syracusan Antipholus for Adriana's husband. Some of the play's most moving speeches lose their effectiveness because they are not expressed within the bounds of a comprehensible relationship. In Aristotelian rhetorical terms, these attempts lack 'ethos', the sense of a rhetor's credibility. Words fail when characters do not know the speakers, understand the context of communication or trust the petitioner's intentions. A play concerned with location, *Errors* illustrates the degree to which contextual dislocation can make verbal communication impossible.

Objects: 'The chain, unfinished'

Just as words can circulate, so can objects, pre-eminently the chain, which functions as both an error-compounding property and a metaphor for the linkages among characters.[1] The 'chain' – or necklace or carcanet – is 'promised' to Adriana by her husband (2.1.105), presumably as a means of marital appeasement; his tardiness for dinner results from watching the chain being crafted. When Adriana locks him out of his house, Ephesian Antipholus angrily reassigns the chain to the Courtesan (for a courtesan, see Fig. 6). Meanwhile, the goldsmith delivers it to the wrong Antipholus. Later, when the goldsmith attempts to collect payment, the other Antipholus denies the debt and suffers arrest for it. Syracusan Antipholus' subsequent withholding of the chain from the Courtesan encourages her to judge him mad and to inform Adriana, who then has Ephesian Antipholus 'pinched', bound and incarcerated as demonically possessed. Finally, Syracusan Antipholus' wearing of the chain almost leads to a duel with the Second Merchant, who confronts him as a liar. The chain binds characters ever more firmly and contentiously to each other.

The carcanet (or chain) – a conspicuous ornamental necklace or collar wrought from gold, often with filigreed metalwork and gems (see Fig. 7, and 3.1.4n.) – constitutes a luxury commodity and signifies Ephesian Antipholus' prosperity. It is linked with both the domestic mercantilism and the international trade that characterize the playworld, since the goldsmith must collect payment for the chain in order to settle accounts with a merchant

---

1   Objects accompany farcical action. *Errors* features a chain, a ring, a key, two purses of coins and a rope's end, each passed once or more times among characters; in *Love's Labour's Lost*, multiple letters circulate from scene to scene.

6 An Italian courtesan. From Giacomo Franco, *Habiti delle donne Venetiane* (Venice, 1610)

bound for Persia. As it wanders through the play, the chain becomes an object of desires, expectations, obligations and perceptions of good fortune or injustice; it hoops together not only baffled characters but their spiralling misprisions and farcical violence. It also exemplifies 'materialization', for it emblematizes the ideas of linkage and bondage, and so connects to the play's ropes and bonds. The chain stands figuratively for certain domestic values (marriage or its betrayal) as well as economic ones (the paradoxical abundance and scarcity of wealth).[1] More abstractly, the chain expresses the concept of

1 See Bruster, 75–7.

7   Lady with a chain. Engraved by Giacomo Franchi, from Fabrizio Caroso,
   Il Ballarino (Venice, 1581)

'the finding of one's self by losing one's self and the freeing
of one's self by binding one's self', especially in marriage
(Henze, 35).

   In Renaissance drama, a stage property can gather 'an
uncanny aura because of how its movement from hand to hand
in the play links characters in ways they are unable to
understand' (Yachnin, 112). *Errors*'s chain is such an object. It
is being 'forged as the action is proceeding', thus evolving into
a figure for the plot's dynamic development. Further, the chain
becomes 'mystif[ied]' by Syracusan Antipholus' treatment of
it as a golden gift (see 3.2.188), associated with Ephesian
witchcraft and sorcery. Although the 'delusive, magical potency

of the chain' may undergo demystification in the course of the play, it remains 'a powerfully associative object' expressing the deep feelings of personal bonds (Dawson, 141, 142). It is a figure *in* the play and *of* the play.

The marketplace and religion: 'redemption – the money in his desk'

Greeted by friendly Ephesians who would loan him money or sell him commodities, Syracusan Antipholus conjectures that 'Lapland sorcerers' (4.3.11) must inhabit the city. What Antipholus takes as magic, the audience understands as mercantilism, the marketplace's power to multiply things almost by legerdemain. According to one critic, *Errors*'s 'process of doubling, exchange and possession, wherein people, things, identities and even attributes endlessly circulate' reflects a fantasizing of the 'nightmarish threat of the market' (Raman, 193). The play's mysterious circulation of words and objects is matched by the market economy's circulation of obligations and goods. *Errors* is saturated with merchants (for a merchant, see Fig. 8); the comedy's backdrop is a trade war; a luxury commodity plays a key role in the plot; and an international trader's urgency to collect a debt spurs the action into crisis. The idea of 'debt' assumes not only financial but religious, emotional, moral and social connotations that help to structure the play. Adriana wants her husband, Ephesian Antipholus, to pay the marriage debt (see 2.1.105–7); he is detained for financial debt, while he wishes to remunerate Adriana, by beating her, for the debt of humiliation he has suffered at her hands (see 4.1). Egeon awaits death 'Hopeless[ly]' (1.1.157), deficient of the money needed to settle a state-imposed fine.[1] The ending takes the form of the repayment of a debt of time as

---

1   Egeon the merchant's world-weariness cannot be separated from 'the uncertainties of his mercantile estate' (Perry, 42).

8 A merchant. From Cesare Vecellio, *Habiti Antichi, et Moderni di tutto il Mondo* (Venice, 1598)

well as of forgiveness of debt, or redemption, a term of financial and equally religious power. These effects exceed a modern sense of impersonal, balance-sheet accounting.

Market circulation reformulates the play's larger question of whether agency is a function of the self or of outside forces (recalling the problem of identity). Here *Errors* vacillates between 'a traditional view of commerce as a subset of ethics, in which the appetitive subject assumes moral responsibility for his or her transactions' and 'an emergent conception of commerce as an amoral, global system to whose demands the subject and the nation have to submit'.[1] In the background of *Errors* is the capacity of market exchange to reduce people to objects. Illustrating the extreme case, the Dromios are essentially chattel, vulnerable to physical abuse like spurned footballs. Ephesian Dromio's intermittent hostility towards his master reflects that dark side of the brothers' existence: they are slaves ('Dromo' was a slave's name in Terence), 'bought' from their mother to serve Egeon's sons (1.1.57). The true status of the 'servant' becomes clear from Shakespeare's primary source text, Plautus' *Menaechmi*, where the slave Messenio is eventually manumitted for helping to sort out the identities of the twins. When a Dromio is called a 'slave', the word is more than an epithet.[2] Often regarded as attendants, though beaten as slaves, the Dromios illustrate conditions of 'de facto enslavement' that could exist in Elizabethan England; thus their representation may constitute 'social commentary' (Hunt, 40, 38). In particular, Ephesian Dromio's marked ambivalence towards his master – evidenced by occasional sarcasm and hostility and by his vivid speech about his years of being beaten (4.4.31–40) – invites audience sympathy for him in his enslavement. Yet, unlike *Menaechmi*'s Messenio, the Dromios can apparently never receive or buy out their freedom.

For others, wealth can tighten or loosen domestic knots. Ephesian Antipholus would proffer Adriana a showy chain, instead of the show of love that she desires (see 2.1.105–7), and he will display his anger at her by investing his jewellery in her rival, the Courtesan. If money can negotiate relationships and confer status, then impecuniousness means adversity. Egeon must forfeit his life less for being a Syracusan than for lacking

---

1   Harris, 30. Harris argues further that the tension between internal and external causal forces mirrors 'later sixteenth-century medical discourse', raised in *Errors* by allusions to venereal disease.

2   See 1.2.87, 104; 2.1.1, 74, 77; 2.2.2, 175; 4.1.96, 107.

a thousand marks (see 1.1.18–25). *Errors* achieves its denouement not when the Abbess frees Egeon's bonds (at 5.1.339–40) but when Ephesian Antipholus' purse of ducats finally makes its circuitous way to the Duke as pawn for his father (at 389). Only with the financial forfeiture placed before him does the Duke respond, 'It shall not need' (390). The Duke's sympathy notwithstanding, clemency seems most possible when the merchant's exchange value has been confirmed and the money put on the table. Yet tones constantly shift, for the play locates its final sentiment in the affectionate restoration of brotherhood by the two characters who are the most used by, and the most excluded from, the market economy: the Dromios.

Contrastingly, *Errors* also brims with religious language, sometimes politically charged. Words such as 'jugglers', 'sorcerer' and 'mist' were often employed in attacks on Roman Catholicism for practices that include exorcism, veneration of the Host and intercessory prayers for souls in purgatory. With 'nimble jugglers' (see 1.2.98 and n., on *nimble jugglers*), Syracusan Antipholus invokes a loaded noun frequently used to derogate Catholic priests as tricksters and would-be magicians, as in Reginald Scot's *The Discovery of Witchcraft* (1584). In its anti-Catholicism, 'jugglers' recalls earlier stage history. Nicholas Udall's *Jack Juggler* (*c.* 1556), based on Plautus' *Amphitruo*, employs two presumably identical characters to discredit indirectly the Roman Catholic doctrine of transubstantiation on the grounds that Christ cannot have two bodies and be in two places (heaven and the Host) simultaneously. Likewise, *Errors*'s suggestive image of an enchanting 'mist' was marshalled variously in attacks on Catholic superstition and irrationality (see 2.2.222n., on *mist*). *Errors* stages two mock exorcisms, at 4.3.49–80 and 4.4.55–8, the latter memorable for its satire of the bogus, slightly creepy conjuror Doctor Pinch. Against Ephesus's presumed demons and fairies, Syracusan Dromio would reach for his rosary beads, recite paternosters and cross himself manically (see 2.2.194 and nn.), in comic allusion to Roman Catholic practices. Such freighted images and incidents pepper the play.

Those moments of satire strike in scatter-shot fashion, more opportunistic and local than systematic. Other bursts of nonce topical satire – references to Henry of Navarre's French wars, jokes about venereal disease, jabs at Spanish imperialism, slighting allusions to Gabriel Harvey – find their way into *Errors* and are typical of earlier Tudor drama generally. Notwithstanding, anti-Catholic thrusts constitute the most persistent of the play's topical references, extending from 'jugglers' to the Duke's 'Circe's cup' – the enchantress Circe being a figure frequently associated by Protestant reformers with the Roman Catholic Church (see 5.1.271n.). Yet even regarding Catholicism the play's attitude can vary. The Abbess, in 5.1, arrives from England's pre-Reformation world. She has implicitly displaced the pagan goddess Diana of New Testament Ephesus as a representative of authority, and her remedies are not Pinchian exorcisms but the humane administration of 'wholesome syrups, drugs and holy prayers' (5.1.104) after the 'charitable duty of [her] order' (107). At astute psychology, rational analysis, skilled rhetoric and the restoring of social cohesion, the Abbess surpasses the Duke. She is, in sum, both Catholic and exemplary (despite her dust-up with Adriana, suggestive of that between a wife and a mother-in-law). Indeed, she resembles other well-meaning Shakespearean figures of the Roman Catholic cloth, such as Friar Lawrence in *Romeo and Juliet* or Friar Francis in *Much Ado About Nothing*.

The Comedy of Errors has been seen as enacting a movement from a pagan to a Pauline Christian ethos. It directs us '*away* from the farce of a world of men who are foolish in their pursuit of fortune and family when they forget about God and *toward* a sense of comedy . . . as providential confusion' leading to 'rebirth' in the form of 'reuniting' (Kinney, 'Kinds', 33). The experience of 'reuniting' signifies a Pauline quickening of new life, as expressed, for example, in the New Testament Epistle to the Ephesians, ch. 2. The incipient imagery of Christ at the play's end emphasizes 'the precise moment of that catastrophic change [from the pagan world to the Christian] as the Elizabethans always perceived it – at the moment of the nativity' (Kinney, 'Kinds', 32). That argument rightly claims the salience of the play's religious imagery and biblical allusions, but it leans heavily towards seeing the play in the context of medieval religious theatre. While one may not wish to turn *Errors* into a religious play, its sense of reuniting and rebirth acquires considerable power from its aura of spiritual mystery.

The idea of rebirth also responds to the play's inchoate sense of the 'apocalyptic' (Kinney, 'Kinds', 34) (the apocalypse being doomsday as foretold in the New Testament Book of Revelation). That notion helps to organize *Errors*'s copious but seemingly disparate biblical allusions to Genesis, Psalms, Proverbs, Ecclesiastes, Matthew, Mark, Acts, Romans, Corinthians and especially Ephesians.[1] *Errors* begins 'heavy with the sense of impending end' represented by the law's condemnation of Egeon, while its later acts 'are filled with fragments of allusion to the biblical interim of waiting for redemption . . . before a final Doom' (Parker, 'Bible', 57). In that waiting's 'dilation' (its expanding quality of delay), as it deepens towards the apocalyptic, there emerges the possibility of recovery, reunion and redemption. Yet such readings are in danger of over-allegorizing *Errors*, for the play never quite surmounts the 'disjunction of contexts and discourses' between its portentous allusions and its 'mundane' marketplace setting (77, 78).

The world of biblical apocalyptic time and the world of the market resist easy assimilation to each other, even when they overlap linguistically. The play applies religiously charged

---

1   See Parker, 'Bible'.

9   An angel coin. Illustration by Frederick William Fairholt, from James O.
Halliwell (ed.), *The Works of William Shakespeare*, vol. 3 (1854). 'The
Angel, or the *Noble Angel*' is 'so called because *St. Michael* the Archangel
slaying the Dragon, is on one side . . . and on the other side, a *Ship* with
one *Mast* and *Tackles*, and an Escochion with *France* and *England*
quarterly' (Randle Holme, *The Academy of Armoury* (Chester, 1688))

words such as 'redeem' and 'redemption' in a monetary sense:
to release Ephesian Antipholus from arrest, Dromio asks
Adriana for 'redemption – the money in his desk' (4.2.46).
Monetary angels function as religious ones (for an angel coin,
see Fig. 9). Similarly, Ephesian merchants are condemned to
death, says the Duke, because they lack 'guilders to redeem
their lives' (1.1.8). Paul's Epistle to the Ephesians is filled with
the language of redemption: 'redemption through his blood'
(1.7); 'redemption of the purchased possession' (1.14); 'the day
of redemption' (4.30); and 'redeemying the time' (5.16). Such
biblical language fits the commercial world of *Errors* without
shedding its Pauline Christian colouring. Indeed, Paul's epistle
is notable for its 'physical, even mercantile metaphors' that
'negotiate between visions of capital acquisition and those of
salvation', so that 'the marketplace becomes an image of
Christ's actions' (Finkelstein, 328, 329). Thus, in *Errors*, the
mercantile and the salvific converge in the talismanic power of

gold to effect quasi-mystical redemptions.[1] Yet the potential brightness of the play's ending still leaves lingering the dark doomsday tones of its middle, which evoke fears deeper than can be reached by exorcisms, comic reunion or marriage. In those elements beyond reconciliation, such as the apocalyptic with the mercantile, the play signals the tensions in an 'early modern shift' from a religious episteme towards a more secularized one (Parker, 'Bible', 81).

Errors expresses a further tension, that between Protestantism and Roman Catholicism. While Donna B. Hamilton, for example, sees the play as a 'reworking' of the religious–political conflicts involving Elizabethan Church establishmentarians and Puritans,[2] Aaron Landau argues that the play's scepticism towards strict rationality, as in the Abbess's 'sympathized one day's error', reflects a Roman Catholic Counter-Reformation reassertion of wonder. That argument, in effect, musters the religious reading of the play in service of a polemical position within Renaissance religious debate. But if the play indeed valorizes a religiously tinged wonder, it also employs anti-Catholic code words such as 'jugglers' and parodies Roman Catholic superstitions. In the end, *Errors* does not align easily with one confessional position over another.

Time and marriage: 'a time for all things'

Luciana connects time not only to business but to marriage when she attempts to excuse Adriana's husband from dinner because 'Time' is the 'master' of men of affairs (2.1.8) – and thus wives must wait. Time shapes *Errors*'s plot and orchestrates its sense of immediacy and speed, since events transpire in one day, with all narrative lines converging at 5 p.m., the time scheduled for Egeon's execution. Like his classical predecessors, Shakespeare employs the 'unity of time' as a source of narrative

---

1   See Finkelstein, 334, 336–7; also Freedman, *Gaze*, 100.
2   Hamilton, 61; see 58–85.

anxiety and suspense. *Errors* mentions the advancing hours repeatedly and contains more time references than any other of Shakespeare's comedies (Salgādo, 83), references not only to specific hours but to temporal urgency, lateness and earliness: 'soon', 'day', 'ere the weary sun set', 'till', 'hour', 'dinner-time', 'then', 'Soon at five o'clock', 'afterward', 'till bedtime', 'present . . . now' – all of that in just the first thirty lines of the second scene. Farcical speed disrupts the characters' experience of time and sequence. Whether there is a time for all things is the subject of the Syracusans' mock disputation in the second act (2.2.66–114), while Adriana will wonder confusedly if time is running backwards (4.2.54). Her comment crystallizes an aspect of farcical time in *Errors*, its sense of repetition and recurrence. Against the compressed, topsy-turvy time of farce stands a more expansive sense of time. It occurs in the apocalyptic images in Act 4; in the decades-long, slowly unfolding family narrative that encloses the farcical action (see Salgādo); in the metaphoric sense of cyclical death and rebirth that defines the Egeon family; and in the romance-time delay, that suspended temporal bubble, created by the Duke's postponement of execution, within which the play's action unfolds. Expansive Christian or romance time and compacted or precarious farcical time resolve in the biblical and narrative idea of redeeming the time: the ecstatic reunion of the Egeon family returns the romance narrative to its starting point, reclaims the family's past, enables the characters' futures and reorders and restarts time: 'After so long grief, such nativity!' (5.1.406).[1]

Something lost and partially recovered or newly found through time is marriage. In *Errors*, marriage participates in both the urgency of farce and the broader arc of comic and romance teleology. In the last act, the Abbess reveals herself as

---

1 On the Abbess's doorway, through which characters exit in 5.1, as representing a final convergence of time and space, see Low, esp. 80–7.

Emilia, Egeon's long-lost wife, and frees the merchant from his fetters (5.1.339–40). This is a comic high moment, since it comes entirely unlooked for by the audience, happens outside the goal of fraternal reunion and often becomes, onstage, a delightful sartorial transformation in identity as the Abbess removes her nun's habit and reveals herself underneath in full secular garb (much as *Measure for Measure*'s Duke steps out of his robes). The aged and estranged Egeon receives the antidote of fresh perspective and domestic embrace. Accordingly, marital reunion arrives as something both comic (can a nun so easily cast off her 'habit'?) yet also deeply redemptive. Irony afflicts other potential marital relations: neither Syracusan Antipholus nor Luciana quite knows who the other is, while Ephesian Antipholus can only wonder but never ask what transpired between his brother and his wife.

The play puts the very nature of marriage under debate: is the husband the master, according to the traditional view defended by Luciana (2.1.15–25), or do married partners share some kind of equality and even mutuality, according to the newly emerging vision of Protestant 'companionate marriage' as held by Adriana?[1] (Shakespeare visits similar themes in *Shrew*, where Kate changes from a position somewhat like Adriana's early views to a final one rather like Luciana's.) Luciana's male-mastery speech sounds stuffy and bookish, and Adriana legitimately mocks her inexperience. Later, Luciana argues that Adriana's husband should conceal his adultery by means of deception (3.2.1–28). Given both her theory of male mastery in marriage and the apparent fact of male infidelity, Luciana understandably remains unwed, fearing 'troubles of the marriage bed' (2.1.27).

By contrast, Adriana declares herself for female liberty and 'sway' (2.1.28), defending the idea of approximate female

---

1   On English ideas of companionate marriage in the sixteenth century, see Wayne. On the play as advocating a companionate view, see Strier.

equivalency in marriage. Yet the husband persists still as first among equals, for Adriana makes her beauty, discourse and wit dependent upon her mate's favourable views (87–97); later, she pictures herself as the clinging vine to his stout elm (2.2.179–82). Despite the earnestness of her speech to Syracusan Antipholus (2.2.116–52), Adriana pushes the idea of a Pauline union between man and wife to such an extreme in terms of the body (e.g. the magical transference of sin) that it becomes physiologically incomprehensible (see pp. 21–2). She imagines marriage as a Pauline oneness of flesh but casts it in negative terms: 'stained skin', 'adulterate blot', fleshly 'poison' and 'contagion' (2.2.142, 146, 149, 150).[1] It is unclear how much the idea of spiritual or psychological mutuality explains Adriana's view of marriage, for her desire to have some 'sway' and her sense of her vulnerability to her husband's neglect (but not vice versa) remain not quite reconciled to her argument that to her mate she is 'undividable, incorporate, . . . thy dear self's better part' (128–9).[2]

That Adriana (like others) could be deceived by the outward signs of identity shows the vulnerability of her doctrine of marriage. Indeed, the revulsion that Syracusan Dromio expresses towards Nell's physicality makes evident a shared male distaste for the very flesh with which, according to Pauline doctrine, man would be one. Yet Adriana wants more than bodily union. For her, marriage creates a debt not just of the marriage bed but of love. That debt cannot be paid by flattery, as Luciana would have it, nor by golden carcanets, as her husband would prefer (see 2.1.105–7). Adriana longs for the restoration of a romanticized past in her marriage (see

---

1   According to Luxon, humanist thinkers reserved the oneness of souls largely for male friendship; see above, pp. 20–2.

2   Adriana's complicated views may reflect some ambivalence in emerging Protestant ideas of marriage; see Matz, 'Introduction'.

2.1.105–11, 2.2.118–24), but that bygone time, if it existed, can never be fully redeemed, nor can the marriage debt of love ever be fully paid. In the end, the carcanet is restored to Ephesian Antipholus, but what will be restored to Adriana? The playtext gives the Ephesian couple no lines of reconciliation or understanding. Likewise Luciana: although Syracusan Antipholus declares his intentions, the dialogue gives Luciana no reply. Instead, as events decelerate, attention turns to the restoration of personal property, the sorting out of confusions, the reunion of the Egeon family and the comic communion of the servant twins. Luciana and Adriana exit separate from, and prior to, the Antipholuses: the nuances in these relationships must be determined in performance, despite the ending's jubilant and restorative air. Final questions of heterosexual bonds are elided, and the denouement narrows to celebrate re-established male kinship and fraternal equality. Comedies typically end with the possibility of joyful marriage, and that prospect can swell the genuine and well-earned euphoria of reunion and closure. Joy dominates *Errors*'s conclusion, yet, as in later plays such as *Twelfth Night*, *Measure for Measure* and *All's Well That Ends Well*, Shakespeare leaves, towards marriage, a sense of business unfinished. Only time will tell.

POETIC GEOGRAPHY, TRAVEL, DARK EPHESUS

Although constructed from real places (see Fig. 1), *The Comedy of Errors*'s world exists as a 'poetic geography' of layered frames of historical references and figurative meanings.[1] Place operates in *Errors* as a metaphor and a 'palimpsest of perspectives owned by more than one culture'[2] to a degree

---

1 On poetic geography, see Gillies, esp. 1–7; also Sullivan.
2 See Martin, 'Artemis', 366.

greater than in Shakespeare's other early comedies, such as *The Two Gentlemen of Verona* or *The Taming of the Shrew*. The play's locale exudes both familiarity and exotic disorientation, and invites questions: why Ephesus? what values does the play's geography call forth?

Plautus' *Menaechmi* is set in Epidamnus, but *Errors* shifts the action to Ephesus, with *Menaechmi*'s site remembered in the name Epidamium (see 1.1.41n., on *Epidamium*, and 1.1.41 LN), which is mentioned seven times. Epidamnus was an ancient Hellenic commercial seaport on the north-eastern coast of the Adriatic in an area (now Albania) that was once known as Illyria or Illyricum (after the Indo-European Illyrii tribes; *Twelfth Night* takes place in Illyria).[1] References to Epidamium lend *Errors* a vaguely Hellenistic aura, but Ephesus (where Plautus located *Miles Gloriosus*) was preferable as a setting, because it would have been better known than Epidamnus and would have evoked complex associations.

Ephesus, a Greek commercial city in Asia Minor (now in modern Turkey), is mentioned in the New Testament and was legendary for its wealth. Situated on the eastern Mediterranean coast, at the convergence of travel routes, the city thrived on international trade between east and west. In classical times, it housed a great temple of Diana (or Artemis), one of the Seven Wonders of the World. Famous for its mercantilism and pagan sorcery, ancient Ephesus was visited by the Apostle Paul in the first century AD and eventually became a centre of Christianity. The New Testament describes how, on his first, two-year visit, Paul won converts and performed miracles (see Acts, 19.1–41). His sojourn made Ephesus notorious for magic and idol-worship as well as for greed and sharp mercantile practices. In Acts, craftsmen do good business selling silver shrines of

---

1   Baldwin speculates that Shakespeare might have had in mind a second ancient Epidamnus in Ionia near Ephesus (see *Genetics*, 113–14, 149–50), but for a trade route to Sicilian Syracuse the Illyrian city makes the better sense.

Artemis, apparently to pilgrims and tourists. When Paul denounces pagan idolatry, the outraged artisans nearly riot (19.23–41), inducing him to depart (20.1). The Geneva Bible's marginal commentary emphasizes the Ephesian merchants' covetousness and preference for profit and worldliness over religion, likening them to Roman Catholics ('Papistes'). Paul also converts various Ephesian magicians, upon which they burn their magic books, valued at 'fiftie thousande peeces of siluer' (19.19); perhaps echoing Acts, *Errors*'s Ephesus houses 'Dark-working sorcerers' (1.2.99). In addition, Paul's Letter to the Ephesians contains an influential discussion of marriage to which *Errors* alludes (see e.g. 2.1.7–25n.; 2.2.116–52n., 125–52n.).

According to legend, Ephesus was the site of the Virgin Mary's Assumption into heaven, and the home of St John the Evangelist, the author of the Book of Revelation. In AD 431, Ephesus hosted a famous Church council that repudiated Nestorianism, the doctrine that Christ is two distinct persons, a witting or unwitting association for *Errors*. The miraculous healing in the Apollonius of Tyre tale also occurs in Ephesus; the story was adapted by John Gower and Lawrence Twine and known to Shakespeare (see pp. 87–9). In Shakespeare's time, Ephesus was held by the Turks, although the city had become largely uninhabited (Seltzer, 581). Shakespeare mentions Ephesus only in *Errors*, but Falstaff later uses the epithet 'Ephesian' to suggest 'roisterer' (*2H4* 2.2.150, *MW* 4.5.18); in *Errors*, Ephesus carries a hint of Asian luxuriance and sensuality. While Ephesus as a place possesses a number of associations, its most important ones for *Errors* are with eastern mercantilism and Paul's biblical encounter.

Ephesus's rival city was Syracuse, Sicily's metropolis, 'in the olde tyme of a meruailous renowme in strength and rychesse' (Cooper, *Thesaurus*, sig. Q3ʳ). Syracuse is imagined, like Ephesus, as one of a series of city-states in the Greek-dominated classical Mediterranean. In the fourth century BC,

Syracuse was the seat of the Greek tyrant Dionysius, well known in the Renaissance and dramatized in Richard Edwards's humanist play *Damon and Pythias* (1564) (see p. 91). Ruled by Spain when *Errors* was written, Syracuse was an important commercial port and a departure point for Spanish naval excursions against the Ottoman empire, aspects that reinforce the play's emphasis on trade and implicit contrast of west and east.[1]

Asia provides *Errors*'s geographical theatre.[2] The Syracusans, from the western Mediterranean, have arrived in Ephesus across the sea, with western restraint putting eastern pleasure and magic into subtle relief. The play's narrative arises out of the misadventures of travel. Travelling home from Epidamium, Egeon, his wife, their twin sons and their twin boy-slaves were shipwrecked (see Fig. 10) and separated, presumably near the Gulf of Corinth (see Parks, 93). The father, one son and one boy-slave were rescued, and eventually returned to Syracuse. The mother and the other two children were picked up by men from Epidamium, and the boys were subsequently kidnapped; all of them found their way to Ephesus

---

1 Two other cities, Epidaurus and Corinth, receive seven mentions in *Errors*'s opening and concluding scenes; they enhance *Errors*'s sense of Hellenism, biblical times and modern commerce. On Epidaurus, see 1.1.93 LN; on Corinth, see 1.1.87, 93n.

2 Shakespeare probably derived his geographic knowledge for *Errors* from 'the leading atlas of its time' (Parks, 97), Abraham Ortelius's *Theatrum Orbis Terrarum* (Antwerp, 1570), the 1579 edition, one of whose maps features Epidamnus and Epidaurus on the eastern Adriatic coastline. The '*Nomina . . . Antiqua*' in Ortelius lists 'Ephesus', 'Epidium', 'Epidamnus' and 'Epidaurus' one below the other in a column. Ortelius's *Theatrum* contains a map of Paul's New Testament peregrinations that might have brought Ephesus and Corinth to mind; no other single source provides so many of *Errors*'s geographic details, especially concentrated close to each other in entries and maps (Parks). Shakespeare also could have consulted Solinus Polyhistor's *Collectanea Rerum Memorabilium*, to which the opening line of *Errors* alludes, and which mentions Epidaurus and Ephesus in separate places; or Cooper's *Thesaurus*, which contains dispersed entries on Ephesus, Corinth and Epidamnus but not on Adriatic Epidaurus.

10 The rescue of the mother (Emilia) by fishermen of Corinth (narrated
    in 1.1). Painted by F. Wheatley, engraved by J. Neagle, from George
    Steevens (ed.), *The Dramatic Works of Shakespeare*, vol. 2 (1802)

in Asia Minor. Egeon, in search of his sons, has roamed 'farthest
Greece' and 'the bounds of Asia' (1.1.132, 133) before arriving
in the Ephesian harbour. A sense of movement across the
Mediterranean infuses *Errors*'s action.

Apprehended in Ephesus, Egeon is sentenced to death
because of an inter-urban trade war. Syracusan Antipholus and
Dromio then turn up, accompanied by a travelling merchant.
Later, an Ephesian merchant prepares to depart for Persia, and
the Syracusans book passage on one of the many outbound

ships. The other Antipholus has resettled from Corinth to Ephesus and has soldiered (presumably abroad) with Duke Solinus in his wars. Much of the business of Ephesus is international trade.[1] Before their intended departure, the Syracusans even stock up on valuable oil, balsamum and *aquavitae*, as if they were themselves traders (see 4.1.85–92). The action's predominant location is 'the mart'. The fictive world connotes displacement and relocation, along with commercial bustle and constant voyaging among the coastal cities of the Mediterranean.

In this atmosphere, differences between west and east blur, and the play's locales become curiously undifferentiated. The places mentioned are urban and suggest a 'larger Hellenistic world, at once far-flung and homogeneous' (McJannet, 92). Ephesus and Syracuse, apparently sister cities, are now fighting an 'intestine' (i.e. internal) and presumably temporary war, prompted by a trade dispute (see 1.1.11 and n.) but not reflective of nationalistic or religious antagonisms. Incipient violence, such as the kidnapping or ransoming of shipwrecked survivors, is business by another name. Ottoman Ephesus hints at a fantasy version of Elizabethan mercantile life: its friendly merchants ply Syracusan Antipholus with luxury goods and offers of loans (see 4.3.1–9); a finely crafted chain and an expensive ring circulate among characters; prosperity seems abundant even as debts pile up; and a merchant readies himself for a trade expedition to the interior of Persia (as if referring to Queen Elizabeth's interest in cultivating trade relations with the Turk). That exotic world is synecdochally evoked in Ephesian Antipholus' reference to a Turkish tapestry covering a desk at home that contains a purse of ducats (4.1.103–5). Ephesus is so affluent, affable and seeming-generous that Syracusan Dromio

---

1 *Errors*'s goldsmith Angelo may recall the Ephesian silversmiths of Acts who become enraged against Paul.

could imagine remaining there and 'turn[ing] witch' (4.4.157). Ephesus ultimately occurs for him as a fantasy version of the world he already knows.

But Ephesus also has a nightmare aspect. Shakespeare's comedies, such as *A Midsummer Night's Dream* or *As You Like It*, often develop a contrast between city and country, or between the stiff and artificial court world and the more metamorphic and unmediated green world, with the action moving from the entanglements of the former to the resolutions of the latter.[1] *Errors* lacks such contrasts of locale; it has no Forest of Arden as refuge for characters from the court. Instead, its mundane, workaday world and its magical green world co-exist as different dimensions of the same place. Rather than distinct realms geographically separated and diachronically experienced, these two interfused domains are encountered simultaneously. *Errors* was Shakespeare's first such experiment, and remains his most fully developed.[2] The simultaneity of the ordinary and the magical makes possible *Errors*'s uncanniness. The play's bourgeois environment intersects with an unnerving Ephesian potential: despotic execution, pagan sorcery, Turkish carnality. Shakespeare's audience might have been bothered by Ephesian death threats and money demands, recalling vexatious Turkish acts of kidnapping and piracy and of the ransoming of English seamen and travellers (Degenhardt, 42). Elizabethans, of course, would have known Ephesus's alarming reputation for sorcery from the New Testament (see 1.2.97n., on *this town*). Ephesus's ancient temple of Diana was a central symbol of heathen fertility-cultism, and its associations with matriarchy and female sensuality colour the play's women characters, Luciana, Adriana, the Courtesan, Nell and even the Abbess

---

1 On the green world, see Frye.

2 In *The Taming of the Shrew*, Shakespeare locates the values of the mundane and the madcap in one character, Petruchio.

Emilia, whose priory displaces Diana's temple.[1] Male nightmarish fears about engulfment by females prompt Syracusan Dromio's cartographic description of Nell's gargantuan body, imagined as multiple countries, nasty extrusions and bad airs (see 3.2.115–44). Such is the flip-side of the comfortable Ephesus of pan-European trade and Pauline conversion. But sorcery and tyranny finally dissipate; the Courtesan, for example, turns out to be not the 'devil's dam' (4.3.53) but a kindly businesswoman. The dangers of Ephesus emerge, in the end, as more psychological than real; Dark Ephesus resides largely in the mind's predispositions, desires, fears and imaginings.

At the outer edge of Ephesus, however, lies a hazardously real (if ultimately providential) geography: the sea, the grand image of upheaval and change. At the margin of the bourgeois city built by the seaways of trade waits this dimly evoked, watery place in all its danger, 'alienating, threatening, and vast' (Mentz, 40). Trade thrives upon the sea, but the sea's perils divide members of the Egeon family and hurtle them in opposite directions that will define their identities. Egeon's physical deterioration is an index to the toil of voyage. Sea travel has eroded his will to live, and in the play's recognition scene he appears so sea-changed with grief – wrinkled face, dimmed eyes, cracked voice, deformed presence – as to be unrecognizable as himself (see 5.1.298–318). Yet for a moment, life returns from the sea. A reknitting of a family after it has roamed and changed almost beyond knowing; a reunion sanctified by suffering, profoundly desired and joyously fulfilling: Shakespeare would come back to such moving scenes of loss and recuperation over the course of his playwriting life.

It is a truism that every Shakespearean city is always, to some degree, London, and so with Ephesus. Its characters' unintentional 'misidentifications' can be compared to the

---

1   See Martin, 'Artemis', and Hart.

11   A jailer or officer. From Geffray Mynshul, *Essays and Characters of a Prison and Prisoners* (1618)

intentional misidentifications, or larcenous tricks, exposed by Robert Greene and others in the cony-catching pamphlets of 1590s London, for the city was a place where urban selfhood had to be established largely by outward material signs.[1] Shakespeare alludes to pamphlets by Greene and Thomas Nashe and to the then-roiling dispute between Nashe and Gabriel Harvey (see e.g. 4.4.44n., and pp. 92, 319–21). The Officer (see Fig. 11) who detains Ephesian Antipholus hails from contemporary London's urban literature and evokes the fear of debtor's arrest that troubled many citizens (including Inns of Court students) (see e.g. 4.2.32–40n.). Various Christian

---

1   See van Elk, 'Misidentification'.

references also pull the play's sense of locale towards contemporary England (see e.g. 2.2.194nn.), as do its English household names: 'Maud, Bridget, Marian, Cic'ly, Gillian, Ginn!' (3.1.31), and, of course, Nell. Such present-world allusions emerge distinctly in Act 4, as the stage community enlarges to catch more and more city character-types in the whirligig of confusion. These evocations of London fill out Dark Ephesus: the Officer, in Syracusan Dromio's imagination, constitutes a demonic figure capable of carrying poor souls to hell (see 4.2.40n., on *hell*).

Although *Errors* is anchored to actual places with histories and reputations, its poetic geography has nonetheless the character of a borderland, altering according to perspective, difficult to fix – properties consistent with the play's sense of movement, change, juxtaposition and surprise. Even more, Ephesus becomes a place where virtually all the characters lose control, and experience powerlessness and even helplessness, sometimes benign, sometimes not. The play begins, of course, with Egeon 'Hopeless and helpless' (1.1.157). The Antipholus brothers and the Dromios progressively lose control of situations; so does the wooed Luciana; so do minor characters such as the goldsmith and the Courtesan. Adriana struggles throughout the play to assert authority, only to yield it to the Abbess. The incipient chaos that overtakes and disempowers characters is embodied in the exorcist Pinch and adumbrated by the play's preternatural suggestion of magic. As it will turn out, of course, 'helpless' is not necessarily 'hopeless', for Ephesus is also a place of transformations.

GENRE AND STYLE

Different generic hats

Errors's fun comes partly from its different generic hats, doffed or donned with a mime's ease. Comedy is a capacious genre, and especially so in *Errors*: Plautine farce, romance of familial separation, even potential tragedy. Some critics have claimed *Errors* as a 'problem play' and a 'tragi-comedy'.[1] Farce dominates the middle sections, framed by the Egeon romance of the first and last scenes, while darker tonalities sift through the entire action. Mode and tone can pivot in a moment: entering at 4.2.28.1 as the *servus currens*, the conventional running servant of Plautine comedy, Syracusan Dromio suddenly breaks into an Elizabethan-pamphlet fantasia about demonism (32–40). *Errors*'s formal register shifts easily, surprising auditors and generating suspense.[2]

Coleridge called *Errors* 'pure farce' (1.99). A subgenre of comedy, farce thrives on certain conventions: misinformation and error; complicated plots (the mix-ups arising from two sets of twins); adulterous possibilities (the dinner between Adriana and Syracusan Antipholus); misdirected, circulating objects (the chain, the rope's end, the purse of coins); comic near-misses (the 'lock-out' of 3.1); speed and acceleration (the running Dromios and the increasing momentum of Act 4); violence without injury (the beatings of the Dromios); physical exertion (the binding of the 'madmen' and the chase of 4.4); and an absurd world with its own logic (sets of identical twins born in the same night in the same inn). '[W]onderfull Intricacie of mistakings', wrote a seventeenth-century reader in a copy of the First Folio, near the beginning of Act 5 (Yamada, 31). Farce depends on recurrent accidents (an Antipholus encounters the wrong Dromio in the street) that multiply throughout the plot. Its actions are so improbable and fantastical that they force characters into fabricating explanatory narratives that presume disreputable motives or diabolical agents and that generate subsequent actions.[3] Over a third of

---

1 Kehler, 229; King, 5–8.
2 See Cartwright, 'Surprising'; van Elk, 'Genre', sees the play's generic strains of romance and farce as in competition with each other.
3 See Witmore, 62–81.

Errors's lines are taken up with characters' declaring their versions of prior events:[1] such 'stories about past actions are themselves actions' that can produce further confusions (Witmore, 73). The narrative has a quality of machine-like repetition, amusing and a little manic.

From a Freudian perspective, farce offers a fantasy of wish-fulfilling aggression and violence, and it indulges us vicariously in other pleasures that conventional life generally denies.[2] Farce lets spectators, for example, 'savor the adventure of adultery . . . without taking the responsibility or suffering the guilt' (Bentley, 229). Conversely, farce typically employs a 'paranoid' plot to heighten 'anxiety and menace', signified by a convention, the chase, that propels the action towards absurdity, as in *Errors*.[3] The absence of meaning so typically attributed to farce 'is intrinsic to the genre' because it privileges 'the humorous acceptance of normally unacceptable aggression'.[4] Farcical laughter can put us in a state of sustained 'euphoria' (Bentley, 234). Yet farce's 'structure of absurdities' can also paradoxically reveal complex meanings, for '[t]he heaping up of crazy coincidences in farce creates a world in which the happily fortuitous seems inevitable' (245). In *Errors*, such farce transforms finally into providentialism, while anger and paranoia yield to communion and wonder.

Those concluding values evoke the genre of romance. A form difficult to define, romance involves elements such as quests, multiple and interrupting story-lines, marvels, magic and extended time.[5] A common activating circumstance of romance is an error that leads to wandering (see pp. 9–11).

---

1 Salgādo, 82; see also Witmore, 66.
2 Farce is often set in motion by a mischief-maker who embodies the form's spirit; the role of *Dream*'s Puck or *Twelfth Night*'s Sir Toby is here fulfilled by error.
3 Freedman, *Gaze*, 105.
4 Freedman, 'Farce', 234.
5 On defining romance, see Fuchs, 1–11; on romance as a medieval and Renaissance form, see Cooper, *Romance*, 1–44.

Romance's pattern of quest, furthermore, allows for both the seeking of a particular end and its postponement, the purposeful journey whose completion is relentlessly deferred.[1] As romance complications widen, the unexpected intervenes, and narrative threads multiply. To such a form, error as wandering and mistaking is fundamental.[2] By its very name, then, *The Comedy of Errors* puts farce's compactness in tension with romance's expansiveness.[3]

Romance motifs colour Egeon's opening narrative of the shipwreck at sea that splits the family and leads to the father's and son's arduous searchings for reunion. Such is the stuff of the genre from the Apollonius of Tyre legend to Sidney's *Arcadia*, both of which, along with the *Aeneid*, the first scene evokes. The play's beginning not only retells the merchant's mishaps and wanderings but opens up another romance-like space of roaming and deferred resolution, as Egeon is allotted a day to enquire throughout Ephesus for the ransom to redeem his life.[4] It is inside this space of delay that the rest of the play unfolds. As it proceeds, *Errors* continues to employ romance themes: the intention of the traveller Antipholus to 'wander' (1.2.31) through the city, as his father is doing; the correspondence between the money needed for Egeon's ransom and the amount in Antipholus' possession; the sea motif echoed in a variety of images; the metaphorical 'divorce' of the Egeon family replayed in the estrangement of the Ephesian husband and wife; the emphasis on encroaching time; and the final convergence of manifold story-lines.[5] The romance elements of *Errors* largely contain its tragic potential, but that potential also reaches rather beyond them, as in the

1   See Parker, *Romance*, 4.
2   See Parker, *Romance*, 16–44. According to Dolven, romance has a 'generic habit of subjecting settled ideas to the disruptions of error and marvel' (135).
3   See Shelburne, 139.
4   See Parker, 'Bible', 56–61.
5   See Parker, 'Bible', 60.

apocalyptic strains of the middle section (see pp. 43, 45). Likewise, the bleakness of Gower's Apollonius of Tyre story occasionally breaks through (see pp. 87–9), as in Egeon's humiliated and pathetic self-descriptions in 5.1 (298–301, 307–16).

As a comedy as well as a romance, *Errors* makes particular structural use of a term derived from *errare*: 'errand'. The plot of *Errors* stays in motion partly because the Antipholus brothers and Adriana keep sending the Dromios on errands. Those errands, although intended as missions, often turn into wanderings, as the agent reaches the wrong destination. Other characters pursue ineffectual missions, too. In 1.2, for example. Syracusan Antipholus sends his Dromio with a cache of money to an inn. The First Merchant then chats with Antipholus and departs on an errand. Moments later, Ephesian Dromio enters, having been sent by Adriana, whose household now springs into imaginative life. Antipholus, his temper rising with his confusion, strikes Dromio, who runs away, back to Adriana's house (subsequently, Adriana will chase him forth again). Antipholus worries that Dromio has been enchanted and sets off himself to find Dromio and his own money: the action has become self-perpetuating. From here forward, the Dromios will continue to criss-cross and interweave the story-lines. The device of errant errands creates not only continuation in the action but structure in the scene. In 1.2, the early departure of one Dromio and the later entrance of the other provide symmetry and contrast. Twice the stage is partially cleared, allowing Syracusan Antipholus to soliloquize alone, the first time about his desire to discover family and identity, the second about his fear of losing identity. In such manner, errant entrances and exits will continue to produce internally balanced scenes of parallels and oppositions.

Comedy, like romance, has a generic association with error. The well-known essay *De fabula* (often appended to Renaissance editions of Terence), attributed to the fourth-century AD grammarian Aelius Donatus but probably written by Evanthius of Constantinople, lays out the three major parts of comedy: protasis, epitasis and catastrophe.[1] The epitasis, or middle section, involves 'the increase and progression of the turbulations, and the whole, as I might say, knot of error' (Evanthius, in Baldwin, *Structure*, 33). Schoolboys were undoubtedly familiar with the theories of Evanthius and Donatus and are likely to have known the Donatian analysis of Terence's *Andria* in terms of error, with the tightening 'knot of error' signifying rising confusion, tumult and comic peril.[2] In *Errors*, Shakespeare virtually allegorizes that theory by writing a cleverly paradigmatic comedy driven by self-compounding errors that are materialized in the knotted ropes that bind Ephesian Antipholus and Dromio. More broadly, knotting different modes and tones together constitutes a characteristic of comedy. *Errors*'s metadramatic self-awareness makes the play a celebration of comic form itself.

Farce and romance conjoin in the comic wonder of the close. To be sure, the denouement leaves relationships precariously open.[3] Although Ephesian Antipholus volunteers ransom for his father and expresses 'much thanks' to the Courtesan for her 'good cheer' (5.1.392), he remains verbally reticent, even silent, towards his wife and brother, while Adriana must attempt to be patient when confronted with the news that her husband accepted a ring from the Courtesan.[4] Perhaps, too, Egeon will never fully recover from his world-weariness. Yet the ending's dominant emotions are the joy of reunion (and prospective

---

1 For Evanthius' 'On drama' and Donatus' 'On comedy', see Preminger *et al.*, 301–9; also Baldwin, *Structure*, 28–52; Herrick, *Theory*, 58–60, 106–29. See also p. 9, and p. 9, n. 1.

2 See Baldwin, *Structure*, 34–44; Burrow, 140–1.

3 Shakespearean comedies, according to Ghose, raise pertinent social issues and employ differing perspectives but leave 'didactic import' unclear (122; see 117–23).

4 See Martin, lx.

marriage) and the wonder of the impossible truth of twinness. Phenomenologically, wonder constitutes a state of suspension, the simultaneous experience of what is and what is not, a liminal ground between empirical materialism and continuity, on the one hand, and sceptical faith and discontinuity, on the other.[1] Rationality supports both. While the empirical facts have been sorted out, the mystery of the day's 'sympathized' events remains beyond the power of explanation. In the reknitting of the family, time has miraculously 'turn[ed] back' (see 4.2.55). We sometimes associate wonder with the reunions in which romance specializes, but in *Errors* it also asserts the climactic possibilities of farce. The ending's wonder reformulates the expectation of closure into the discovery of new beginning, wherein the secular goes hand in hand with the sacramental.[2] 'Such nativity': that definitive exclamation comes from a character, the Abbess, who stands for rebirth, who herself has been reborn into the narrative and who joins together the lay and the holy.[3] A final, surprising congruity emerges between loose ends and revealed bonds, deferred reconciliations and new relationships, and wanderings and wonderings.

Verbal shape-shifting

Besides varying generically, *The Comedy of Errors* also shifts verbal styles as it alters in tone and action, to the increase of the play's dramatic energy. From rhymed pentameters to 'tumbling verse' to prose, from soliloquies to duelling stichomythia, from blank verse to couplets to quatrains, from Egeon's epic tone to the Dromios' domestic colouration, the play's stylistic

1 See Bishop, esp. 73.

2 See Bishop, 88–92.

3 *Errors*'s Abbess and Hermione in *The Winter's Tale* are the only figures in Shakespeare believed dead by other characters and the audience until they re-emerge in the denouement.

modes succeed each other in tune with changing events, conflicts and personalities. Shakespeare's theatre-goers appreciated such orchestration of sound and rhythm, since many of them were schooled in the rhetorical principles of Quintilian and Cicero, and shared in a tradition of verse drama. '[H]ighly patterned speech was congenial' to Shakespeare's audience, and Elizabethans customarily encountered '[r]hyme and meter' and other 'rhetorical devices . . . in public places'.[1] Accordingly, early treatises on English poetry coach would-be poets in metrical virtuosity to enable them to move their hearers. As George Puttenham's *The Art of English Poesy* (1589) explains, 'the heart by the impressions of the ear shall be most affectionately bent and directed' (98): or, as Puttenham's editors put it, 'the ear is the essential gateway to the mind' (44). Shakespeare's playhouse emphasized that aural experience: the resonant, voice-amplifying, cylindrical wooden Elizabethan playhouse offered 'the largest, airiest, loudest, subtlest sound-making device fabricated by the culture of early modern England'.[2]

The play proceeds overwhelmingly in verse. Of its 1,787 lines of dialogue, 13% are prose and 87% verse, with some 25% of those verse lines rhyming.[3] In a predominantly verse play, rhyme becomes a key tool for differentiation. *Errors*'s default verse form is iambic pentameter. Its first scene begins almost perfectly in that form (except for the trochaic 'Merchant',

---

1 Wright, *Metrical*, 95.
2 Smith, *Acoustic*, 207–8; see 206–45.
3 Spevack, 1.361; *TxC*, 96. Spevack separates out 22 split lines; those are treated here as verse; cf. *TxC*, 96, whose verse numbers derive from Chambers, *ES*, 2, App. H. *Errors*'s high quotient of verse lines compares closely with percentages for *The Taming of the Shrew* (82%), *2 Henry VI* (84%), *Romeo and Juliet* (87%) and *A Midsummer Night's Dream* (80%). The high degree of rhyming verse underscores *Errors*'s connections to *Romeo and Juliet* (18% of whose verse lines rhyme) and *Richard II* (19%); see Chambers, *ES*, 2.398. For comparison, 52% of *Dream*'s verse lines rhyme, as do 66% of *Love's Labour's Lost*'s (Chambers, *ES*, 2.398).

3), with the first two lines end-rhymed and those ensuing in blank verse:[1]

EGEON

> Pro**ceed**, So**li**nus, **to** pro**cure** my **fall**,
> And **by** the **doom** of **death** end **woes** and **all**.

DUKE

> **Mer**chant of **Syra**cu**sa**, **plead** no **more**:
> I **am** not **par**tial **to** in**fringe** our **laws**.

$$(1.1.1–4)$$

That opening establishes the work's dominant verse form (and initiates what John Hollander calls the 'metrical contract' with the audience about what style to expect (181)). From here on, *Errors* presupposes a play-listener's discerning ear for aural shifts, as it ranges through blank verse, heroic couplets, quatrains of alternating rhyme, tumbling verse (containing a fairly regular number of stressed syllables, most commonly 4–6, and an irregular number of unstressed ones), hexameters, short lines, stichomythia and shared lines (i.e. lines divided between two or more speakers) – with occasional passages of prose interspersed. Movement among verbal forms illuminates differences. Lower-status figures such as servants (the Dromios) gravitate towards tumbling verse (associated with popular forms) or prose, while higher-status speakers express themselves in blank verse, heroic couplets and quatrains, although servants may also employ blank verse in talking to those above them in station, and masters and mistresses can use prose according to the situation and the addressee. Sometimes a speaker will adapt his or her style tellingly to the tone of a scene in a way that diverges from his or her normal form.[2] Rhymed couplets can

---

1   In a pentameter line, stresses will vary in emphasis; often four syllables are noticeably stressed, as in the first line here, where 'to' would be stressed lightly, at best. The fewer the heavy stresses, the more a line invites speed in delivery.

2   Adherence of a speaker's style to the form of a scene constitutes the 'law of dominant mood' (Vickers, *Artistry*, 8).

elevate the tone, encapsulate an idea memorably or mark the beginning or ending of an argument, episode or scene. Alternating rhyme is associated with wooing and expressions of romantic love (as at 3.2.1–52); its quatrains replicate the pattern of the Shakespearean sonnet. Tumbling verse shows a shift into colloquialism, while prose, the next step towards informality, facilitates fast-paced punning, *double entendres* and verbal momentum. Tumbling verse derives from an older tradition of farcical drama typified in plays such as *Gammer Gurton's Needle* (*c.* 1553). It appears especially in the topsy-turvy 'lockout' scene (see 3.1.11–85 and n.), where the Dromios and others engage in mirror-like tumbling exchanges. Here the equality of stresses and the steady cadence of unstressed syllables lend all the speeches a frenzied speed and rhythmic sameness, submerging the characters' individual identities in 'acoustic anarchy'.[1] Shakespeare orchestrates an antiphonal mob scene that displays the characters' bewitchment by errors and that marks a climax in the play – accomplished through tumbling verse. Yet in that scene, as elsewhere, one form gives way to another: 3.1 begins in, and returns to, iambic pentameter and ends in a couplet. *Errors* progresses by means of rhythmic metamorphosis.

A word or phrase may alter in meaning and import by being reiterated: repetition-with-variation. During *Errors*'s denouement, the Abbess wraps up much of the action with a key speech. Within the space of three iambic pentameter lines, she twice uses the term 'nativity' (5.1.404, 406); the second occurrence constitutes her climactic last word in the play. Some editors have judged the duplication of 'nativity' to be a compositorial error and have emended the second instance to 'felicity' or 'festivity'. But the two occurrences entail different pronunciations, initially as three syllables, 'na-**tiv**'-ty', and then more fully and emphatically as four, 'na-**tiv**-i-**ty**', with a

1 O'Donnell, 407; see 403–8.

secondary stress on the last syllable (see 5.1.404, 406n.).[1] The same word pronounced differently: scansion suggests not erroneous typesetting but doubling and varying in a way that initially acknowledges specific births but then celebrates the ending's inclusive sense of rebirth. Another kind of repetition-with-variation occurs when Ephesian Dromio insists that his master has beaten him, despite Antipholus' denial. Dromio's line scans thus: 'Say **what** / you **will**, sir, // but **I** / know **what** / I **know**' (3.1.11). This two-clause line is iambic pentameter, with an epic caesura (a foot, typically the second, containing three syllables – unstressed, stressed, unstressed – before a pause). The line repeats Dromio's assertive 'I know', but the iambic stress moves, the second time, from 'I' to 'know' so as to elevate Dromio's outraged certainty.[2] Even a name can change meaning through repetition, as evidenced by Luciana's 'Dromio, thou *Dromio*, thou snail, thou slug, thou sot' (2.2.200), where the second iteration turns Dromio's name into an epithet. (Petruchio likewise reformulates Kate's name in *The Taming of the Shrew* (see 2.1.185–90).) Adriana repeats words and phrases to build pathos: 'How comes it now, my husband, O, how comes it' (2.2.125). As that scene progresses the word 'come' is reiterated, with different meanings and increasing urgency as the women attempt to force the action to their will: 'Come, come, no longer will I be a fool' (209); 'Come, sir, to dinner' (212); 'Come, sister' (217); 'Come, come, Antipholus, we dine too late' (225). A question, a declaration, an enticement, a command, an exhortation: doubling a term registers the unfolding emotional drama. Repetition-with-variation, however subtle, contributes to *Errors*'s crispness and dynamism.

---

1   Syncopation of the unstressed medial vowel in 'nativity' retains 404 as pentameter; full syllabification would make it hexameter.

2   An alternative scansion would be to treat the last six syllables as two anapaestic feet (see O'Donnell, 405), although the phrase's second iteration would again call for increased emphasis. The parallel 'what' constructions link the line's two halves and sharpen the opposition: what Antipholus says; what Dromio knows.

In long speeches, sound devices can organize the narrative and also open it to changing meanings. Shakespeare's early dramatic verse is sometimes faulted for too frequently using end-stopped lines, as in the blank verse of the first scene:

> At length another ship had seized on us,
> And, knowing whom it was their hap to save,
> Gave healthful welcome to their shipwrecked guests,
> And would have reft the fishers of their prey
> Had not their bark been very slow of sail;
> And therefore homeward did they bend their course.

> (1.1.112–17)

When employed as units of thought, such end-stopped lines can manage lengthy and complicated sentences, here a six-line, fifty-word sentence with two main clauses (one with three co-ordinate verbs, a modifying participial phrase and a subordinate clause). Despite that syntactical complexity, each line plants in the final iambic foot a stressed verb, noun or pronoun – 'us', 'save', 'guests', 'prey', 'sail', 'course' – that delivers narrative content emphatically. Shakespeare uses the end-position to make meaning and to register effect; in Puttenham's terms, 'the cadence which falleth upon the last syllable of a verse is sweetest and most commendable' (169).

Likewise in the first scene, recurrent alliterations and embedded rhymes or near-rhymes create continuity as well as contrast. Alliterations draw attention to phrases – '*d*oom of *d*eath' – or link action across a series of lines: '*P*roceed . . . *p*rocure . . . *p*lead . . . *p*artial' (1–4). Similarly, 'meaner' (54) and 'meanly' (58) connect aurally but refer differently; 'bought' and 'brought' (57) catch the ear by their proximity; 'weepings' (70) and 'Weeping' (71) offer a near-repetition that underlines pathos; and 'Was carrièd' (87) and 'Was carried' (109) duplicate words but contrast in pronunciation. Even the doubling of a phrase – 'Corinth, as we thought' (87, 111) – amplifies its implication. In Egeon's story of familial joy dashed by shipwreck, a certain syllable, *hap*, is repeated: in 'happy' (37, 138), 'hap' (38, 113), 'mishap[s]' (120, 141), 'Hapless' (140). Those *hap-* words introduce repetition-with-variation as they register the twists of narrative, and they add an echoing power to their near cousins in Egeon's closing lines, when his haplessness has left him 'Hopeless and helpless' (157). The floating phoneme *hap* may even hint at a possible alternative, happier narrative.[1]

Tonal shifts can arise through incomplete lines, metrical variations and rhymes. In a line early in the first scene, a syllable seems missing after 'me': 'And by me, had not our hap been bad' (1.1.38). Some editors have inserted a word into that empty space, but the missing syllable creates a rhetorical pause that acknowledges a break in the narration, as Egeon's haps start to shift from good to bad. Another short line occurs later: 'We came aboard' (61).[2] Its brevity makes rhetorical sense, for it invites a pause, a sigh, a deep draught of air before Egeon begins to relive the details of his shipwreck and family separation.[3] Later in the scene, one more short line occurs after the Duke (in a headless nine-syllable line at 155) instructs the Jailer to take custody of Egeon, and the Jailer responds with only the single line 'I will, my lord' (156). It could be prose, but prose occurs nowhere else in the scene; the 'law of dominant mood' (see p. 66, n. 2) urges verse, the compactness of which clears room for a disruptive physical action as the Jailer takes forceful control of the merchant. Altered metre or intrusion of rhyme can also shift the tone. Towards the end of the scene, the Duke must proceed dutifully against the prisoner, despite his growing sympathy. He demonstrates his resolve with two

---

1   On that alternative narrative, see Miola, *Comedy*, 24–5.
2   The line is inferred by editors: in F, 60 and 61 are printed as one improbably long heptameter line.
3   Shakespeare also sometimes uses short lines to end long speeches (Bowers, 78).

assertive trochees: '**There**fore, **mer**chant' (150). The scene finishes with its fourth couplet: 'Hopeless and helpless doth Egeon wend, / But to procrastinate his lifeless end' (157–8). Such couplets have power: 'wend' captures the sense of wandering inherent in error as *errare*; 'end' cuts short Egeon's travels and travails in the finality of prospective execution. The two together foreshadow the play's long day of happenstance and the final convergence of all the lines of action at sundown.

Stichomythia (single lines alternating between speakers, sometimes also with rhyme in *Errors*) can enhance the dynamism of an argument, as in the exchanges between the wife Adriana and her sister Luciana in 2.1. They are debating male and female prerogatives in marriage. In the first set of stichomythic lines, 10–15, in iambic pentameter couplets, Luciana completes Adriana's rhyme at 15. That topping-off momentarily gives Luciana the upper hand, and launches her into a defence of her views. Although Luciana again bests Adriana by means of stichomythic rhyme at 31, Adriana fights back rhetorically not only with her rebuttal at 32–41 but with her take-over of the rhyming position at 86 and again at 102, each triumphing rhyme catapulting her into a sustained speech. Notwithstanding, Luciana gets the final rhyme and the final word, 'jealousy' (115), defining the scene's concluding perspective on Adriana. Rhyming stichomythia arbitrates the sisters' rhetorical contest.

Brief statements can elsewhere function confrontationally. One example occurs when Ephesian Antipholus and Angelo the goldsmith discuss the delivery of the chain intended for Adriana (4.1.40–68); each assumes that the other has it. Questions and accusations bounce back and forth in speeches of only one to three lines, with the word 'chain' repeated eight times. These speech-volleys function as the rhetorical counterpart to the missing object, tossed like a hot potato between the contestants. The scene's mounting aggression is defused by Syracusan Dromio at 85–92, when he bursts in to notify the wrong

Antipholus, in a lyrical speech, that their 'fraughtage' (baggage) has been neatly stowed on a trim ship departing for Epidamium that only awaits a merry wind. The lyrical intrusion stops short the tennis match of accusations, the shift in perspective achieved by a shift in poetic form.

In 2.2, changing aural effects again amplify action. The scene begins in blank verse as Syracusan Antipholus first soliloquizes and then argues heatedly with, and climactically strikes, Syracusan Dromio. From there the agitated Dromio shifts into prose and the tone of the scene moves from physical conflict to a wit-combat, in which the servant, speaking in a form well suited to him, equals, perhaps betters, his master. Prose, Dromio's idiom, carries the speed of verbal thrust and parry and communicates spontaneity; it facilitates witty puns and comically realistic banter wherein the underclass is allowed to excel. (Later, in 3.2, Syracusan Dromio's anti-romantic prose will serve as the counteragent to Antipholus' rhyming love-duet with Luciana.) Amidst this prose, a few lines of verse intrude, 45–9: first blank verse from Antipholus and then rhymed tumbling verse from Dromio as a mocking response (47–8). The tone and action change again after 114.1 with the entrance of the aggrieved Adriana, who addresses Antipholus (mistakenly) with moving earnestness and elevates the tone further (beginning at 177) with the rhymed couplets that will dominate the scene until 194. She even has a dignified hexameter at 124 that summarizes the points of her preceding lines. Adriana's movement into couplets captivates Antipholus and Dromio, for they adopt couplets, too, as if entranced, the rhyme corresponding verbally to Antipholus' sense of being enfolded in a strange 'mist' cast by the women (222). The verbal forms in this scene shift their shape with the action.

Errors's stylistic juxtapositions produce continuing surprise. They complement the juxtapositions of genres – farce, near tragedy, romance – that characterize *Errors*. Such shifts contribute to the play's experiential meaning as they evoke the fictive world's openness to change and possibility. The fatalism of Egeon in the first scene is subtly counterbalanced by hints of a mysterious and unifying order, embedded even in a syllable such as *hap*, behind the apparently random events that threaten his ruin. Such point and counterpoint have a special force in comedy, where the audience is frequently in a position of knowledge greater than that of the characters and where the playwright may wish to prevent that knowledge from turning into complacency. The sound effects of *Errors* point to a mysterious dimension of its providentialism – a latent volatility, a receptiveness to newness and possibility, as in a second 'nativity' – that may be close to the heart of Shakespeare's comic vision.

Technicalities in scansion

George Gascoigne, in the first treatise on English poetry, 'Certayne Notes of Instruction' (1575), identifies the predominance of iambic pentameter in English verse and explores techniques for regularity, concerns echoed by William Webbe in his *Discourse of English Poetry* (1586) and by other writers. Gascoigne observes that, in a well-conceived iambic line, words should receive their 'natural *emphasis* or sound', yet he also defends 'poetical licence', which allows the skilful poet to cover 'many faults in verse' by making 'words longer, shorter, of more syllables, of fewer, newer, older, truer, falser'.[1] The poet is granted an arsenal of techniques for compressing or expanding words, including, for compression, elided vowels ('t'admit', ''tis'), suppressed consonants ('e'en') and syncopated unstressed syllables ('rig'rous', 'threat'ning',

---

1 Gascoigne, 'Notes', 164, 168. Likewise, Aristotle, in *Poetics*, had defended the 'lengthenings, abbreviations and alternations of words' in drama for the production of 'heightened effect' (57). Elizabethan poetic thinkers considered 'meter as a *pattern artificially imposed* on the words' (Berry, 'Prosodies', 117).

'nativ'ty'); and, for expansion, contiguous vowels pronounced as disyllables ('-i-on', 'fa-ir') and *-ed* suffixes given syllabification ('sympathizèd').[1] Because actors learned a part overwhelmingly by studying its language, rhythm assisted them with memory and embedded hints for performance.[2]

Within iambic pentameter, certain metrical variations or substitutions were conventional, including the trochaic foot, feminine ending, epic caesura, headless foot (missing its initial unstressed syllable), double onset (two unstressed syllables preceding a stressed one) and the like.[3] Essentially, the iambic line integrated systematic non-iambic substitutions that allowed the poet flexibility and that served for variety or emphasis. In *Errors*, lines generally conform to iambic pentameter and its recognized variations. Of course, no actor in the theatre is required to sound an *-ed*, elide a vowel or employ other compensations in the service of an abstract metrical exactitude; the demands of expression and action necessarily take precedence. The Folio text, however, offers enough examples of verbal compression or expansion in verse lines to indicate that metre was a consideration. Numerous irregular lines occur – Shakespeare's dramatic verse is always more open in form than his lyric or narrative poetry – but they often serve a dramatic purpose, such as creating a breach in the dialogue for pauses or stage actions. Elizabethan verse theatre assumes a poetical contract with the audience and makes a metrical toolbox available to performers, always keeping as its primary consideration the drama of character, action, emotion and thought.

1 See Wright, *Metrical*, 149–59. *Errors* has comparatively high instances of disyllabic *-ion* and stressed *-ed* (Tarlinskaja, 28, 135).
2 See Stern, *Rehearsal*, 61–76.
3 See Wright, *Metrical*, 160–84.

SOURCES AND INFLUENCES

Since *The Comedy of Errors* ranks among Shakespeare's most derivative works, it invites specific attention to its sources, the understanding of which can affect how we experience the play. Shakespeare sometimes worked close to a prior text, as with Plautus' *Menaechmi*, adapting, cutting, altering or expanding it, whether for local incidents or the play's overall plan. *Errors* also expresses more broadly generic influences, such as the traditions and conventions of comic writing, as are found in sixteenth-century Italian drama. It draws, too, on narrowly specific and local sources, such as earlier English comedies or the Elizabethan pamphlet literature of Nashe and Greene prominent in Act 4. Sources range eclectically: Shakespeare is like a juggler tossing up both footballs and teacups. The play's richness reflects the sources' variety and the directness or indirectness of their use; sensing them in the background brings shadows and echoes to the reading or spectating experience.

Plautus

For *The Taming of the Shrew*, *The Merry Wives of Windsor*, *Twelfth Night* and pre-eminently *The Comedy of Errors*, Shakespeare drew liberally on the comedies of the classical Roman playwright Plautus.[1] He found his main source for *Errors* in *Menaechmi*, with which he amalgamated elements from Plautus' *Amphitruo* – a process that Renaissance rhetoricians called *contaminatio*, the combining of multiple sources.[2] The Latin plays of Plautus and his successor Terence were widely taught in Elizabethan grammar schools for their linguistic richness, eloquence and moral examples,

---

1   See Miola, *Comedy*.
2   Traill argues that *Errors* 2.1, the marriage debate between Luciana and Adriana, shows the influence of a related scene (2.2) in Plautus' *Casina*; she also finds other correspondences.

and Shakespeare undoubtedly studied them.[1] Elizabethan schoolboys performed Roman drama for training in elocution and self-presentation, and universities frequently staged Terence and especially Plautus. Annotated editions of their works were widely available in the sixteenth century, and those of Terence typically included commentaries by the medieval writers Donatus, Evanthius and others.[2] The first English translation of *Menaechmi*, by William Warner, was published in 1595, although the manuscript, the printer's letter tells us, had previously been in circulation (it was entered into the Stationers' Register on 10 June 1594). Shakespeare could have seen Warner's manuscript, especially since Warner's patron was Henry Carey, Lord Hunsdon, the Queen's Lord Chamberlain, whose theatre company Shakespeare had joined in 1594. Warner's 'Argument' refers to *Menaechmi*'s 'Much pleasant error' (13), a phrase that could have influenced Shakespeare's title (Bullough, 1.4). Warner, like Shakespeare, turns *Menaechmi*'s bracelet ('*spinter*') into a 'chain' (see *CE* 2.1.105 and n.), has Erotium accused of being a witch (absent in Plautus), as is Shakespeare's Courtesan, and resembles *Errors* in certain words and phrases.[3] Shakespeare may have read Warner, though no evidence exists of significant reliance.[4] One striking difference is that Warner omits *Menaechmi*'s prologue, while Shakespeare adapts details from it. Likewise, certain name-forms in F, especially 'Antipholus Sereptus' and

---

1 See Baldwin, *Structure*, 667–9. On Shakespeare's grammar-school training, see Baldwin, *Small Latine*; also Riehle.

2 See pp. 9, 62–3. Baldwin argues that *Errors* reflects Shakespeare's acquaintance with Dionysius Lambinus's 1576 edition of Plautus, whose marginal commentary to *Menaechmi* identifies instances of error by characters; see *Structure*, 667–81, 691–4. Riehle sees insufficient evidence that Shakespeare used Lambinus (90); Miola accepts Baldwin's position (*Comedy*, 21).

3 For verbal comparisons, see Foakes, xxv–xxvi; Riehle, 279–83; *Var.*, 307.

4 Riehle's argument that Shakespeare used Warner rests largely on inconclusive tonal and thematic matters.

'Antipholus Erotis' (or 'Errotis'), prove Shakespeare's acquaintance with the Latin version (see List of Roles, 3n. and 4n.). If Shakespeare used Warner's version, he probably kept it side by side with a Latin edition of *Menaechmi*, upon which he clearly drew.[1]

Shakespeare was attracted to a Latin comedy that many in his audience would have known (perhaps even acted in), and whose presence in the public imagination would add a layer of intertextual enjoyment to *Errors*.[2] Both Everard Guilpin and John Manningham, apparently referring to *Errors*, identified it by its resemblance to Plautus (see pp. 110; 110, n. 3; 111). Renaissance commentators generally praised Plautus' theatrical sense above Terence's (Terence was admired for moralism and elegant Latin): Plautine comedy's knowing playfulness would have attracted Shakespeare.[3] *Menaechmi* delights in alliterations, assonances, rhymes, puns and colloquialisms, as does *Errors*. In *Menaechmi*, Plautus also 'marr[ies] the personae and story-lines of New Comedy directly to familiar Italian traditions of autoschediastic [i.e. extemporaneous, improvisational] entertainment' (Gratwick, 14–15), an influential characteristic of his drama. Shakespeare, too, cultivates the impression of spontaneity, as characters in wit-games snatch up each other's words and hurl them back with new inflections (as at 2.2.47–114; see pp. 33–4). In Plautus, improvisational moments point towards the play's self-consciousness of its own theatricality (metatheatre), which might be manifested variously, as in metaphors of life as theatre, or in addresses to the audience that allude to the play's fictional status.[4] In *Errors*, the Syracusans turn to the audience to wonder what kind of

---

1   On the scholarly consensus for this position, see Miola, 'Play', 4–10.
2   On intertextuality, see Miola, 'Intertextuality', and Marrapodi, 1–2.
3   On the relationship between Shakespeare and Plautus, see Miola, *Comedy*, and Riehle.
4   On Plautine metatheatre and improvisation, see Slater, esp. 1–14.

world they are in, and riffs such as Syracusan Dromio's on Nell's body (3.2.85–151) constitute overt bids to amuse spectators. Shakespeare also borrowed from *Menaechmi*'s comic dialectic: in Erich Segal's famous argument, *Menaechmi* 'presents the conflict of *industria* and *voluptas*, holiday versus everyday, . . . the reality principle versus the pleasure principle' (44). That contrast is represented on Plautus' stage by the two opposed houses: the wife's, or *matrona*'s, standing for domestic, social and legal obligations; and the prostitute's, or *meretrix*'s, betokening pleasure and escape from daily responsibilities. *Menaechmi*'s action 'takes place in a magnetic field between personifications of restraint and release' (Segal, 43). Shakespeare echoes that dialectic in Adriana's and the Courtesan's residences. A related polarity, bewildering dispossession versus carnivalesque bounty, further structures *Menaechmi* and *Errors*.

Menaechmi's contrasts play out in the unwitting collision of the twin Menaechmus brothers, separated in childhood by abduction. The play opens in Epidamnus, where the comfortable citizen Menaechmus, at odds with his overbearing wife, seeks relief at the house of the prostitute Erotium. Attached to Menaechmus is Peniculus, his ever-peckish parasite, while Erotium's household contains a cook and a maid – all typical residents of 'Plautopolis'. When the Syracusan brother (Sosicles Menaechmus) arrives, with his loyal slave Messenio, in search of his lost twin, the delightful chaos of mistaken identity breaks loose. Sosicles Menaechmus is mistakenly 'wined, dined, and concubined' by Erotium; citizen Menaechmus is called to account by his wife for stealing her possessions and giving them to Erotium; and the husband (or rather his twin) is taken for mad by two other Plautopolisians, the *senex* father-in-law and the *medicus*, or doctor. Eventually Messenio (smarter than his master) grasps the mix-up and manages the reunion in exchange for his freedom from bondage. The embattled wife is divorced, and the reunited brothers sail off happily for Syracuse.

One impecunious brother wins the lottery – food, sex, money – while the bourgeois other watches himself being nightmarishly divested.[1]

Shakespeare adapts ambitiously. *Errors* recirculates *Menaechmi*'s protagonist twins and its basic situation and thematic structure, and likewise observes the classical unities of place and time (i.e. one day). But Shakespeare also strives to trump his celebrated predecessor, in the emulative manner of Renaissance authors, by appropriating one of the ancients' best plays and multiplying its effects. Enter a second slave, or 'servant', Ephesian Dromio, twin to Syracusan Dromio, escalating the possibilities for errors of misrecognition. Exit the *senex*, *parasitus* and *coquos*, and enter the sister Luciana, who takes over the father-in-law's patriarchal sentiments and serves as Adriana's sounding-board, only to turn into a romantic love-interest herself. The wife becomes the normative centre of the play. Exit the prologue and enter the affecting, aged Egeon (also a father-in-law), who narrates the backstory; enter, too, his wife, for one more marital couple at the play's end. (Egeon's sadness may be influenced by *Menaechmi*'s prologue, which mentions the grief-induced death of the twins' father.) Exposition now occurs through dramatic dialogue. Exit the reasonable, if overconfident, *medicus* and enter the dubious exorcist Doctor Pinch, along with the Duke, a new locus of rationality, and, for colour, assorted merchants, a goldsmith and the fantastical maid Luce/Nell (who displaces Erotium's *ancilla*). Tensions are heightened by the addition of a trade war between city-states and a new setting in Ephesus, evocative of mercantilism, magic and religion (see pp. 50–1), to replace

---

1 *Menaechmi*'s action contains seven distinct errors or misrecognitions and follows the classic stages of exposition, complication, reversal, resolution and recognition (see Gratwick, 16–30).

Plautus' Epidamnus. With these, the possibilities for mayhem skyrocket.[1]

Shakespeare cleverly turns the classical unity of time into a plot problem by giving the condemned Egeon one day to find ransom. That lugubrious backdrop puts the farcical mishaps in relief. To launch the confusions early, Shakespeare shifts the initial perspective from Plautus' resident twin to *Errors*'s traveller, Syracusan Antipholus, who mistakes the other Dromio for his servant and trembles over Ephesian sorcery. The dreamy traveller Antipholus, now the romantic lead, has been made over from the scampish traveller Sosicles Menaechmus, just as the carefree resident Menaechmus turns into the irascible resident Antipholus. Shakespeare additionally shifts the domestic centre from the prostitute Erotium's house to the wife Adriana's, foregrounding marriage as an issue. The traveller Antipholus' romance with Luciana now substitutes for the Menaechmus–Erotium dalliance. With Adriana and Syracusan Antipholus, Shakespeare introduces the possibility for character change and growth more deep-reaching than in farce. Adriana makes for potentially the most sympathetic character in the play, a far cry from Plautus' one-dimensional *matrona*.

Shakespeare's doubling of twins and reorientating of interests employ Plautus' contrasts, but they also facilitate a mirroring of scenes and episodes definitively greater than in the model.[2] For example, *Errors* begins with parallel arrival scenes, the first (1.1) by the Syracusan father, the second (1.2) by the son. Adriana and Luciana have two scenes of debate about Adriana's husband (2.1 and 4.2), each interrupted by the entrance of a Dromio (though different ones). Exorcisms

---

1 Rouse counts fifty instances of error in *Errors*, against the seventeen he sees in *Menaechmi* (xiv). Notwithstanding, in a complex action in which one character can experience the same confusion repeatedly, what counts as an error becomes murky.

2 Robert Hornback sees such effects as especially typical of Terence (private conversation, 1 July 2013).

happen twice, once when Syracusan Antipholus attempts to exorcize the devil-Courtesan (4.3.49–89), and again when Doctor Pinch undertakes to expel the demons from the other Antipholus (4.4.55–8). Syracusan Antipholus' wooing of Luciana (3.2.1–70) reverses Adriana's wooing of him (2.2.116–224) and is parodied by Nell's reported wooing of Syracusan Dromio (3.2.75–160). Adriana's lock-out of her husband in 3.1 is re-enacted in the Abbess's lock-out of Adriana from her husband in 5.1, sparking Adriana's moment of self-recognition. In 3.1, Shakespeare puts the Dromio twins plus Ephesian Antipholus onstage together for a potential resolution – derailed because they talk to each other through or across a closed door. Instead of mutual recognitions, the confrontation produces angry domestic misrecognitions that send the comic confusions spiralling outward. The scene becomes a 'false denouement' (Williams, 'Correcting', 96), which must be rectified by the real denouement of 5.1. (The idea of the climactic 'lock-out' scene apparently amused Shakespeare, for he also employs it in *Shrew*, drawing probably from Gascoigne's adaptation of Ariosto's *I Suppositi*.) Ephesian Antipholus and Adriana's angry accusations and counter-charges in 4.4 fail to get sorted out, perhaps because presided over by the quackish Doctor Pinch, and wait to be rehearsed and resolved before the real authority figure, the Duke, in 5.1. *Errors* is chock-a-block with such internal parallels, large and small. Repetitions-with-difference create the sense of uncanny surprise, the aura of a magical world recycling itself in mad combinations.

Errors's 'lock-out' scene draws not from *Menaechmi* but from Plautus' *Amphitruo*, which might also have inspired Shakespeare's use of twin slaves.[1] Shakespeare probably knew the play in Latin, since no English translation was published until 1694 (although the Tudor interlude *Jack Juggler* was

---

1 Miola calls *Amphitruo* one of Plautus' 'errors plays' (*Comedy*, 18); Whitworth sees its farcicality as influencing *Errors* (25–7).

based on it). In *Amphitruo* the gods Jupiter and Mercury impersonate the Theban general Amphitryon and his slave Sosia, respectively. Jupiter has fallen in love with the general's wife, Alcumena, whom he sleeps with just as Amphitryon arrives home from war (their offspring will be Hercules). When Sosia attempts to enter Alcumena's house as a messenger, he is blocked by Mercury, who insists that he himself is Sosia (*Amph.*, 341–462), leading to farcical fisticuffs. Later, when Amphitryon would enter his house to see his wife, Mercury-as-Sosia locks him out and taunts him from the roof (1009–34). Those scenes, compressed together, inspired *Errors* 3.1, wherein Adriana orders her door barred, Syracusan Dromio guards it against, and hurls taunts at, the Ephesian master and his Dromio, and Adriana later adds insults from the balcony. The 'lock-out' scene parallels the Mercury–Sosia scene in its emphasis on the competition to claim the servant's identity.[1] Given the shortness of *Menaechmi* (1,162 lines), Shakespeare's addition of the lock-out device from *Amphitruo* allowed him to amplify the misidentifications in *Errors* and to introduce a hilariously climactic false denouement with its consequent restarting of the action.

Amphitruo gave Shakespeare a pious and dignified wife, Alcumena, who, without knowing it, sleeps with an impostor husband. Such a wife combines with *Menaechmi*'s less appealing *matrona* to engender the complexly comic Adriana – jealous, errantly seductive, misguided in goodwill, yet capable of self-recognition. Likewise Shakespeare augments *Amphitruo*'s 'rhetoric of accusation and protest between husband and wife' and its 'latent violence' (Miola, *Comedy*, 30, 32). Amphitryon's astonishment at the wonder-filled birth of the half-divine Hercules possibly encouraged Shakespeare to introduce into *Errors* his own providential wonder at the

---

1 The parallel may extend to *Errors*'s reiteration of 'face' and 'name' (Whitworth, 26).

reunion (imaged as 'nativity') of the entire Egeon family. Shakespeare's addition of such romance values typifies Renaissance practice. At a performance of *Menaechmi* in 1526 before Cardinal Wolsey, for example, the play was preceded by a pastoral procession (including Henry VIII) and was followed by courtly orations, decorous dancing and a pageant featuring Venus: Plautus' 'world of satirically observed realities' was enclosed by the court's 'world of romantically imagined ideals' (Smith, *Ancient*, 137). Shakespeare's 'magnifying [of] the spectacle and heightening [of] the love interest' speak to the temper of his times (Miola, *Comedy*, 7).

In Shakespeare's comedy, errors double and darken, ethics intrude and *eros* turns into romance. Certain Plautine elements are sacrificed. Shakespeare abandons the guileful servant, the *servus callidus*, who often, as in the brilliant *Pseudolus*, saves the clueless youthful lovers and outwits his master. Likewise, Shakespeare forfeits that familiar Roman comic volte-face, the prostitute discovered to be well-born. And he loses, too, the pleasure of watching various Plautine characters improvise their way out of tight social situations – an effect that he replaces with word-play and comic set-pieces. Nonetheless, Shakespeare has altered the classical comic idea of error from a matter of misinterpretation or trickery to something more intrinsic and potentially darker.[1] As Robert S. Miola deftly states, if 'Plautine comedy begins and ends as a comedy of doors', Shakespearean comedy 'is a comedy of thresholds, of entranceways into new understandings and acceptances' (*Comedy*, 38).

Italian cinquecento comedy

Shakespeare's reworkings of Plautus occur in a European humanist culture where, especially in Italy, rediscovered

---

1   On error in classical comedy, see Riehle, 102–4, and Salingar, 76–128.

Roman comedies and tragedies were being newly performed, translated, adapted and refashioned.[1] Roman and Italian drama had exerted an influence on Tudor theatre well before Shakespeare began to write, as witnessed, in comedy, by *Terence in English . . . Andria* (*c.* 1520); by school-play imitations of Plautus and Terence such as *Thersites* (*c.* 1537), *Gammer Gurton's Needle* (*c.* 1553), *Ralph Roister Doister* (*c.* 1553), *Jack Juggler* (*c.* 1556) and *July and Julian* (1570); by Inns of Court plays such as Gascoigne's *Supposes* (1566), a translation of Ariosto's *I Suppositi* (itself a *contaminatio* of plays by Plautus and Terence), and John Jefferes's (?) *The Bugbears* (*c.* 1566) (a free adaptation of Grazzini's *La Spiritata*, in *contaminatio* with other sources); by educational 'Christian Terence' plays such as *Misogonus* (1571); by Anthony Munday's *Fedele and Fortunio* (1585), adapted from Pasqualigo's *Il Fedele*; and, more generally, by the comedies of Lyly, especially *Mother Bombie* (1591). From Italian drama arose what Louise George Clubb calls 'theatergrams' – in essence, conventions of character, situation, action, tone and the like. Such shared conventions reflect the practice of borrowing and adapting from previous works, including medieval romances, *commedia dell'arte*, Plautus, Terence and early Italian comedies. That technique 'demanded the interchange and transformation of units, figures, relationships, actions, *topoi*, and framing patterns' into a shared repository of conventions both efficient for playmaking and 'weighty with significance from previous incarnations' (Clubb, *Italian Drama*, 6).

In Clubb's analysis, *Errors* shares so many features with late sixteenth-century Italian comedy that a fundamental resemblance cannot be denied. From the first half of the cinquecento to the second, Italian comedy changed significantly from buffoonishness to the more tragicomic *commedia grave*

---

1   See Miola, *Comedy*, 1–18; Herrick, *Italian Comedy*; Clubb, *Italian Drama*; Clubb, *Pollastra*.

(*Italian Drama*, 49–63). Characterizing this change were increased seriousness in aesthetics, morality and emotion; didactic support for marriage and the Church; ethical debates (e.g. on love vs. honour); and heightened emotional tensions, deepened characters, imperilment and sadness: 'a mixture of sentiment, pathos, and danger with lively comic action' (55). Even a stock figure such as the Courtesan could become relatively respectable. *Commedia grave* featured intricate knots of error arising from misunderstandings and character misidentifications, all structured according to protasis, epitasis and catastrophe. A frequent motif was supposed magic, often linked to the theme of madness; another was the ultimate subsuming of fortune, chance and accident under the power of providence. Thus, according to Clubb, although *The Comedy of Errors* may not be indebted to any particular *commedia grave*, it betrays an Italianate form that exceeds its predecessors:

> The addition of pathos and a hint of tragedy; the moral de-emphasizing of the courtesan's role to play up the wife Adriana and her sister; the dialogue of these two on the topos of jealousy in marriage; the weaving of multiple sources into a newly complicated pattern of errors with something like a unifying theme in the thread of feared madness and sorcery; Aegeon's evaluation of 'the gods' at the beginning, proved false at the end, when the maddening errors and nearly fatal sentence become instruments to reunite families and confirm loves . . . It cannot be proved that Shakespeare read Italian plays, or saw commedia dell'arte troupes or Italian amateurs perform *commedie gravi* at Elizabeth's court, or heard about them from a friend . . . It is next to certain, however, that the brilliant upstart crow knew something about the latest Continental fashion in comedy.

> (62–3)

The model here is 'intertextuality', a language of shared conventions by which plays borrow from, and 'talk to', one another, reflective of the methods of *imitatio* and *contaminatio* that were central to Renaissance humanism.

However, it remains difficult to grasp how numerous, highly specific theatergrams from late cinquecento *commedia grave* could have spread, in a few short decades, into English artistic or cultural awareness. Furthermore, Shakespeare's comedies differ from Italian comedy or tragicomedy in many respects. The streets and houses of the Italian urban stage set, for example, bespeak a familiar world of stable values, while the indefinite and open space of the Elizabethan stage accommodates more abstract and conflicting values (see Pressler). Likewise, Italian Renaissance comedy develops a sexual frankness and bawdiness – as in the barely offstage love-making scene (3.10) in Bibbiena's *La Calandra* (1513), or Lelia's teasing of Isabella and their same-sex kiss (2.6) in *Gl'Ingannati* (1532), or that same play's matter-of-factness about sexual assault – missing from Shakespearean comedy. Italian comedy is frequently unromantic and even cynical (e.g. Machiavelli's *La Mandragola* (1518)) beyond anything in Shakespeare. *Errors* also lacks the *beffa*, the elaborate trick, usually by a servant, that accounts for much of the action in Italian comedy.

Nonetheless, scholars have argued that 'between Italian and English theatres . . . some sort of contact must have occurred' (Pressler, 107), and some general influence can be claimed. English actors toured the continent; *commedia dell'arte* troupes visited London; Italian novellas were widely translated; and some English travellers and readers knew Italian plays. Shakespeare himself, according to Jason Lawrence, learned Italian in the 1590s, eventually well enough to read plays in the original.[1] Yet *Errors* lacks any known Italian ancestor. The case for shared theatre conventions between Italian comedy and Shakespeare

---

1 See Lawrence, 118–76.

is attractive, but it implies concrete vehicles of transmission and a familiarity on Shakespeare's part for which evidence remains elusive.

Apollonius: Gower and Twine

The tale of Apollonius of Tyre, well known in the Renaissance, figures as a source for certain incidents in *Errors* and also influences its tone and genre. Shakespeare might have adapted the Apollonius story from two sources: Book 8 of John Gower's medieval *Confessio Amantis* (1393; printed in 1483, 1532 and 1554); and Lawrence Twine's *The Pattern of Painful Adventures*, entered into the Stationers' Register in 1576 but surviving in no edition earlier than 1594. Gower's version, in tetrameter couplets, derives from Geoffrey of Viterbo's Latin verse *Pantheon*; Twine's romance, in prose, descends from a French translation of the Latin *Gesta Romanorum*.[1] Thus, the story as it came to Shakespeare had dual lineages, with its 'unbroken popularity' and 'almost unchanging plot' maintained 'from the fifth century to the seventeenth and beyond' (Archibald, 3). The story engaged Shakespeare, for he would return to it much later in writing *Pericles*.

In each version, Apollonius, Prince of Tyre, suffers shipwreck, washes up on the shore of Pentapolis, distinguishes himself and marries Lucina, the king's daughter (she goes unnamed in Gower).[2] As they voyage back to Tyre, Lucina apparently dies while giving birth to a daughter, Tharsia, and her coffined body is commended to the sea. The casket drifts to Ephesus, where Lucina is discovered alive and revived; she becomes a nun at Diana's temple. Apollonius, believing Lucina dead, mourns *in extremis* (especially in Gower). Grief-stricken, he leaves his daughter in Tharsus to be raised by a trusted couple. Later, returning for her, he is told that she, too, is dead,

---

1 On the history of the Apollonius tale, see Archibald.
2 Names in this summary follow those in Twine.

and his suffering increases. Apollonius eventually arrives at the city of Machilenta, where he is miraculously reunited with Tharsia – who has endured threats to her life and maidenhood but who is now beloved of the city's prince. Advised in a dream to go to Diana's temple, Apollonius sails to Ephesus and is movingly reunited there with Lucina.

The Apollonius tale involves wandering, shipwreck, harrowing loss, suffering and miraculous recovery – the stuff of romance. Shakespeare refashioned these events into Egeon's framing narrative.[1] Adapting the Apollonius ending, *Errors*'s denouement spectacularly reveals the Abbess of the Ephesian priory to be Egeon's wife, Emilia, not known to be alive. In Gower, the wife is an 'abbesse' at the temple (1849),[2] in Twine a 'nunne' (e.g. Ch. 10, par. 96). In both works, as in *Errors*, it is the wife who recognizes the husband. In Twine's version (but not in Gower's), when Lucina identifies her husband, she rushes to him, embraces him and attempts to kiss him, at which Apollonius, not yet perceiving who she is, takes offence and pushes her away. That detail may have been reworked by Shakespeare into Egeon's poignant recognition of Antipholus and Dromio (of Ephesus), which they deny (see 5.1.283–329). The Apollonius story accounts for important differences between *Errors* and Plautus' *Menaechmi*: the family romance that gives context to the day's adventures; the shock of the Abbess's unexpected return from presumptive death; Egeon's abiding sadness from loss, transformed into joyous recovery; the mysterious sense of a redemptive providential order governing the tides and winds. For these effects, both Apollonius sources, rather than one alone, probably influenced Shakespeare. Twine's version attends more than Gower's to physical details, such as the beauty of Lucina's pseudo-corpse; on the other

---

1   Twine's name for Apollonius' wife, Lucina, perhaps influenced Shakespeare's naming of the sister in *Errors* as Luciana (see List of Roles, 8n.).

2   Line numbers here refer to excerpts in Bullough, 1.50–4.

hand, Gower more strongly registers Apollonius' near-despair; and the reunion of husband and wife in Gower draws towards its close with the same rhyme on 'wende' and 'ende' (1883–4) that forms Egeon's concluding couplet in *Errors*'s first scene (1.1.157–8). Twine's version has more surface play of emotion, Gower's more depth. Both sources emphasize moralism, however, while *Errors* avoids enunciating any moral as such.

The Bible: Acts and Ephesians

Errors refers frequently to the Bible and, as noted (see pp. 42–4; 50–1; 52, n. 2), especially to the New Testament Acts of the Apostles and Epistle to the Ephesians. Those writings, with the Apollonius story, provided inspiration to locate *Errors* in Ephesus. According to Acts, the Apostle Paul evangelized for two years in Ephesus in the mid-first century AD and a decade later wrote (from Rome) the Epistle to the Ephesians. From Acts, 19.1–41, Shakespeare drew on pre-Christian Ephesus's reputation for mercantilism and pagan sorcery and on specific incidents such as Paul's sensational encounters with false exorcists and heathen icon-sellers, material familiar to his audiences. Paul's Epistle to the Ephesians forms a background to the debate in *Errors* 2.1 about mastery in marriage, for Paul advises wifely obedience, a view contested by Adriana but defended by Luciana (see 2.1.7–25 and n., and p. 47). Likewise, in Ephesians, 6.5, Paul commands slaves to obey their masters. On both topics, however, he calls for mutuality, and he models human relationships on the love between Christ and his Church. Ephesians's sense of new beginning in Christ (4.22–4) is alluded to at 3.2.39, and the epistle's famous armour-of-God language (6.11–17) is invoked by Syracusan Dromio moments later at 3.2.150. More generally, Ephesians's vivid description of the sin-dead soul made quick through Christ (2.1–6) adds resonance to the Apollonius story. Ephesians imagines Christ's followers, once strangers and foreigners, as putting away contentiousness and assuming the forgiveness that allows them to become citizens in the household and temple of the Lord (2.19–22, 4.31–2), not unlike the concluding spirit of *Errors*. Passages from Paul's epistle would have been read aloud in Church of England services between 25 August and 30 October 1594, when Shakespeare might have been working on *Errors*.[1] Extensive references from other parts of the Bible also range across the drama. Sometimes they evoke a sense of the apocalyptic that darkens the play, or make problematic the differences in marriage between the union of the flesh and the union of the spirit. They also foreground the tension, and overlap, between mercantile and religious ideas. The New Testament lends *Errors* complexity in tone and content.

Tudor drama

The Comedy of Errors follows a Tudor practice in modelling itself on Roman comedy (the latter is a model also for Italian cinquecento comedy). *Gammer Gurton's Needle*, a Cambridge University student play and one of the best pre-Elizabethan dramas, adopts Plautus' farcical mode, including a mischievous 'bedlam' character, rampant irrationality among villagers, a mock exorcism (and much Roman Catholic parody) and the eventual arbitrating of partial and conflicting truths by the magistrate Bailly, who in function closely resembles the Duke in *Errors*. Nicholas Udall's *Ralph Roister Doister*, adapted from Plautus and Terence, offers a send-up of Ralph the braggart soldier as he is manipulated by the parasite MerryGreek. *Jack Juggler*, another school play, probably by Udall, refashions Plautus' *Amphitruo*. Here the Vice Jack dresses like the shiftless servant Jenkin Careaway and insists to Jenkin that he (Jack) is

---

1   See Whitworth, 224.

Jenkin. Jenkin becomes confused and suffers beatings. The epilogue discusses the impossibility of something being in two places at once, parodying the Roman Catholic doctrine of transubstantiation (Jack may also represent Catholic bullying). Thus, Shakespeare's farcical doubles and anti-Catholic satire have precedent in earlier Tudor plays based on Roman comedy. Doubling also occurs in another Tudor school play, *Tom Tiler and his Wife* (*c.* 1561), whose theme is marriage between a shrewish wife (named Strife) and a wimpish, wife-beaten husband (Tiler). Tiler's friend, Tom Taylor, impersonates Tiler and subdues Strife. Foolishly, Tiler admits the ruse to her and loses the upper hand, so that she pummels him again. *Tom Tiler* provides an early instance of doubles in drama connected to the theme of marital mastery.

Richard Edwards's humanist court melodrama *Damon and Pythias* has elements of Roman comedy, such as witty servants. It features two outsiders who arrive in a foreign city, Syracuse, ruled by a tyrant, who threatens the life of one of the friends. The play strongly develops the theme of oneself-as-another (see pp. 20–2). In *Errors*, the First Merchant's mentioning of the condemned Egeon (1.2.3–7) resembles the servant Stephano's story in *Damon* of having seen in the street a man condemned by the tyrant (7.12–19). Gascoigne's *Supposes*, which influenced *The Taming of the Shrew*, might have suggested the war of city-states that figures in *Errors*'s plot, for in *Supposes* a trade war between Siena and Ferrara makes it impossible for any Sienese to reveal his identity in Ferrara. *Supposes*'s action proceeds by a series of false surmises, or 'supposes', that Gascoigne identifies in the margins of the printed text. Gascoigne illustrates how humans build conjectures upon imperfect knowledge in their efforts to 'construct a reasonable world' (Altman, 165). Shakespeare strips away the characters' trickery and magnifies their 'supposes'.

Shakespeare also learned from John Lyly, his predecessor Elizabethan comic playwright. Lyly's *Mother Bombie*, a children's play for popular audiences, may have given Shakespeare the name Dromio, since there it belongs to a clever servant descended from Roman comedy (see List of Roles, 5, 6n.). *Mother Bombie* emphasizes farcically complicated action and resembles Plautus in its 'dramatic and comic use of language' (Riehle, 21). The plot involves two fathers blocking the romance of their respective son and daughter, and two other fathers attempting to deceive each other so as to marry off their mentally challenged respective son and daughter. Those latter two children, in Roman comic fashion, turn out to have been exchanged at birth for the former two. The carefully constructed action employs paired characters along with paralleling and contrasting scenes, and relies heavily on 'discrepant awareness' (the audience's superior knowledge to that of the characters) – a feature shared with *Errors*. *Mother Bombie* also hosts a prophetic 'cunning woman' (its titular character) and, theatrically, employs two stage houses for the fathers, in the spirit of Roman comedy and *Errors*.

Allusions: Elizabethan urban writings

The Comedy of Errors's allusions to Elizabethan urban pamphlets influence the atmosphere late in the play. Scenes 2–4 of Act 4 make various references to contemporary London, especially to bailiffs who arrest individuals for debt and to London debtors' prisons, both fodder for popular pamphlets and ballads. Those scenes refer to pamphlet skirmishes between Nashe and Harvey (see e.g. 4.4.44n.) and evoke contemporary London more than any other sequence in the play; in these scenes of conflict, confusions whirl beyond control, characters' emotions boil over, paranoia heightens, and chases and violent actions ensue, all lending a nightmarish realism.

Syracusan Dromio's fantastical descriptions of the Officer, transformed in his imagination from a rather harmless functionary into a demonic predator, and Dromio's accompanying allusions to London's harrowing debtors' prisons, draw upon the writings of Greene, Luke Hutton and others.[1] The real-life Elizabethan horrors of arrest, imprisonment and persecution for debt cast a shadow over 4.2–3. (Arrest for debt will come up again in *The Merchant of Venice* and imprisonment in *Measure for Measure*.) Dromio's references to the Officer's metal-buttoned coat and to the Prodigal Son, along with the Officer's likeness to a bass viol, suggest affinities with William Fennor's *The Compter's Commonwealth*,[2] the fullest and most famous contemporaneous account of arrest and incarceration for debt. But, problematically, *The Compter's Commonwealth* was not published until 1617, more than two decades after Dromio was first frightened by the Officer. Given Dromio's fractured and barely comprehensible descriptions, in contrast to Fennor's detailed narrative, *Errors* could hardly have been a source for *Commonwealth*. The explanation may be that certain images and formulations for arrest and incarceration had so entered the popular imagination that they were reiterated through a body of writing. Allusions to debt, detention and imprisonment reflect shared public fantasies that would have heightened the realism and emotional register of Act 4. Built upon the humanist traditions of Roman drama, the latest fashions of Italian theatre, the narratives of medieval romance and the vulnerable impecuniousness of Londoners, *Errors* may be short in length, but it possesses depth and reach.

STAGING

The Comedy of Errors presents few staging problems and adapts easily to different imaginative settings. A distinctive feature of the play is its implied stage houses, after the model of

---

1 See e.g. 4.2.32–40n., 34n., 37n., on *shoulder-clapper*, 37n., on *countermands*, 40nn.
2 See 4.2.34n.; 4.3.17–18n., 23n.

12   A comic stage set. From Terence, *Comoediae* (Lyon, 1493)

Roman comedy (for a Roman comic stage scene, see Fig. 12; for a Renaissance version, see Fig. 13). Plautus' *Menaechmi* envisions a streetscape with two houses: one, on the left, belonging to the resident Menaechmus and representing civic and familial duty; the other, on the right, belonging to the Courtesan Erotium and representing holiday, sensuality and indulgence. Similarly, modern productions of *Errors* often feature the house of Ephesian Antipholus and Adriana (the Phoenix) on one side of the stage, the house of the Courtesan (the Porpentine) on the other, with the abbey upstage between them. On the Elizabethan bare stage, curtained booths could have been thrust out, but they are unnecessary, since the main rear opening and the typical theatre's two side-doors would have served the play's needs well, with the same doorway even serving for different locales at different moments, as practised in productions at modern replica theatres such as Shakespeare's Globe in London or Blackfriars in Staunton, Virginia.

13 The comic scene (*Scena comica*). From Sebastiano Serlio, *Libro Secondo, Tutte l'Opere d'Architettura* (Venice, 1584)

The 'lock-out' scene (3.1)

One scene, involving a house, poses special problems in staging: 3.1, the so-called 'lock-out' scene, in which Ephesian Antipholus and Dromio arrive home at the Phoenix for noon-time dinner only to discover that they have been locked out of their home by Adriana and, as it seems, themselves.[1] The Ephesians have been displaced by the Syracusans, the master

---

1 See Williams, 'Correcting'; Cartwright, 'Staging'; Ichikawa, 'Staging'.

now dining in an upper chamber with Adriana and the servant guarding the street door to ensure privacy. The mannered hospitality of the arriving party deteriorates into the shouted threats and insults from either side of the Phoenix's door. The disturbance requires Syracusan Dromio, Luce and Adriana to speak their lines (some twenty of the episode's fifty) from within the fictional residence, presumably the stage façade. The problem is whether they are hidden together behind the door or somehow visible to the audience.

Errors assumes an Elizabethan bare stage, with two side-doors, a central discovery space and a balcony above containing an opening (see Appendix 2, pp. 343–6),[1] as in an Elizabethan public playhouse. At the end of 2.2 the exiting Adriana has instructed Syracusan Dromio to 'play the porter well' and to 'keep the gate' (217, 212), that is, the door to Adriana's residence.[2] The playtext, like *Taming of the Shrew* at 1.2.5–19, implies an urban street door, i.e. a door in the stage façade, which entails the question of Syracusan Dromio's positioning. At the end of 2.2, there is no SD for Dromio's exit; rather, Adriana orders Dromio to guard the door: 'if any ask you for your master, / Say he dines forth, and let no creature enter' (215–16). Reasonably then, one might insert a stage direction, as Bevington does, for Dromio to remain onstage, '*visible to the audience but not to those approaching the door*' (SD at 218, Bevington[4]; 225 in this edition). Some modern productions import a free-standing door (fixed in a frame or held by extras) to give Syracusan Dromio visibility and to put him physically

---

1 For a debate on the nature of Elizabethan stage entryways, see Gurr, 'Stage doors'; Fitzpatrick & Millyard; Gurr, 'Gulf'; Gurr & Egan.

2 The multiple references to 'door' and 'gate' argue that a real wooden door is indicated. Antipholus' 'my door is locked' (3.1.30) suggests that he tries the door, even rattles it. Later Ephesian Dromio encourages him to 'knock the door hard' (58).

close to the opposing Ephesian party.[1] In Clifford Williams's 1962 production (see pp. 122–4), Dromio simply drew a door in the air and played behind it. A production might also employ an open-framed arcade house (as possibly used for the tomb scene in *Romeo and Juliet*).[2] Still, the action hardly requires a free-standing door or an arcade house. As the eighteenth-century editor Nicholas Rowe imagined, at the end of 2.2 Dromio could follow Luciana, Adriana and Antipholus through a doorway in the façade (probably the centre one),[3] after which – so as to 'let none enter' (224) – Dromio might linger in the opening.

When 3.1 begins, the opposite set of twins, Ephesian Antipholus and Dromio, enter with Angelo and Balthazar. Finding the door locked, Antipholus orders Dromio to 'Go bid them let us in' (30), launching the scene's central fifty-odd lines of heated dialogue between insiders and outsiders.[4] Syracusan Dromio apparently delivers his ripostes from just inside the 'locked' door that he is guarding. F supplies him with no entrance direction because, in effect, he has never exited, a condition that requires conceiving of the playing space as extending backwards behind the façade.[5] Soon Dromio is joined in his badinage – '*Enter* LUCE' (47.1) – and, in turn, those two are joined by the wife – '*Enter* ADRIANA' (60.1).

A character can '*enter*' yet still remain backstage, behind the *frons scenae*. Ichikawa cites examples in *Romeo and Juliet*, *Measure for Measure* and other contemporary plays of

---

1   *The Comedy of Errors* at the Shakespeare Theatre in Washington, DC, in 2005 did exactly that, to great comic effect.
2   See Hotson, 69, 76–7; also Dessen, 176–95.
3   Gurr argues that early stages such as the first Globe and the Rose had central openings that were probably fitted with hinges that allowed doors to be lifted in or out ('Stage doors'). Such a central opening with doors was used effectively as the entrance to the Phoenix in the 2006 *Errors* at Shakespeare's Globe in London.
4   On how actors onstage and backstage were able to hear each other's dialogue and cues, see Stern, 'Arras'.
5   See Ichikawa, *Entrances*.

characters being directed to '*enter*' while remaining behind stage doors (*Entrances*, 130–2). Luce might then '*enter within*' by joining Syracusan Dromio behind the door (Jorgensen inaugurates this emendation).[1] Alternatively, Luce might enter on to the balcony (as in Cam). Notwithstanding, because she begins by addressing Syracusan Dromio, partners with him in retorts (even shares a rhyme) and appears to the outsiders as able instantly to let them in (see 49), she may well '*enter*' to Dromio behind the stage door.[2]

But that approach presents the problem of a previously unintroduced character participating extensively in dialogue while still remaining behind the façade, invisible to the audience.[3] Luce might perhaps be sighted partially or fleetingly (without undercutting Syracusan Dromio's imaginative description in 3.2). According to Andrew Gurr and Egan, '[t]here is strong evidence . . . for doors giving access to the stage having grilles or grates cut into them' (139). Salisbury in *1 Henry VI* describes himself as looking through such a 'grate' (1.4.60).[4] Although references to grates in Renaissance plays are more likely to be 'fictional' than 'theatrical',[5] enough instances of characters speaking from behind bars occur to keep open the possibility of grated doors.[6] Thus, Dromio and

---

1   On '*within*' as a SD, see Dessen, 72–3, 238–9; Ichikawa, 'Acting', 126–34. Ichikawa provides evidence for '*within*' used in relation to offstage speech, probably sometimes from the upper level, and she demonstrates that some characters located '*within*' may be fleetingly visible to the audience.

2   If Luce is the same character as Nell the kitchen wench, an entrance on the lower stage level conforms to her place in the household.

3   Shakespeare pointedly names Luce (at 49) after her first speech, and Syracusan Dromio repeats the name (at 53), so that spectators could associate her voice with a name.

4   The Gunner has earlier described the grate: 'a secret grate of iron bars' (*1H6* 1.4.10); for commentary on staging this scene, see Burns, 1.4.10n., 21.1n. and 59n. Burns locates the action on the balcony.

5   See Dessen, 55–9; Dessen & Thomson, 104.

6   See e.g. Ichikawa 'Acting', 136–8.

Luce might have been visible through a grille or grate in the stage door (or grilles in double doors).

This problem of visibility introduces the enigmatic line that Syracusan Dromio addresses early in the scene to his brother: 'Either get thee from the door or sit down at the hatch' (3.1.33). A 'hatch' might be a 'half-door . . . with an open space above', or 'the lower half of a divided door' (*OED n.*[1]).[1] *Errors*'s reference to a 'hatch' may evoke the proverb 'It is good to have a hatch within the door', a figurative cautioning of someone, here Ephesian Dromio, to be silent (see 3.1.33n.). But 'sit down at the hatch' sounds literal ('sit down') as well as metaphorical ('and be quiet').[2] These considerations suggest that F envisions Luce to be partially and occasionally visible behind either a grille or a fleetingly opened upper half-door. She and Dromio, of course, could also rapidly open and close the door(s) in taunt. Such staging encourages comic near-misses and visual jokes that complement the dialogue's rhymes, rapid pacing and shared lines.

Finally, Adriana. 'Who is that at the door' making 'all this noise', she asks on entrance (3.1.61). Ephesian Antipholus responds, 'Are you there, wife? You might have come before' (63). Antipholus' 'there' and 'come before' might suggest that Adriana has joined Dromio and Luce behind the stage door.[3] Notwithstanding, some editors (e.g. Bevington, and Mowat and Werstine) fix Adriana on the balcony, alone or with Luce, presumably because Adriana had proclaimed in the previous scene to her presumed husband that she would 'dine *above* with you today, / And shrive you of a thousand idle pranks'

---

1   'Hatch' is used to refer to the lower half of a divided door in *KJ* 1.1.171, 5.2.138; *MW* 2.2.19; *KL* 3.6.73.

2   The interchangeability of 'gate' for 'door' is also suggestive, for 'gate' can denote 'a framework of wood or iron' with 'bars or 'gratings' (*OED* gate *n.*[1] 6a) – in effect a grille. Shakespeare employs such an image of 'gates of steel' in *Son* 65.8.

3   Ichikawa prefers this location for Adriana (see 'Staging', 10–11).

(2.2.213–14; emphasis added). Productions sometimes signify Adriana's dining and 'shriving' with remnants of food and dishevelled articles of clothing flying from the balcony, 'above'.[1] A balcony location for Adriana allows for a widening ripple of comic disruption, while the lower-level location associates her less appropriately with Dromio and Luce's fishwives' joking. The balcony positioning also makes the scene's dialogue triple-directional and physically two-tiered, and it multiplies the possibilities for changes in characters' orientations and for related stage gags and near-sightings. Such staging would fit the notion of the 'lock-out' scene as a comic failed ending – a 'false denouement' – at *Errors*'s mid-point. The scene radiates with invigorating theatricality.[2]

Visually for the spectators, the balcony occupies the same vertical plane as the 'gate' or 'door': the plane of the stage façade. Thus, if Adriana enters on to the balcony, she would be speaking, in terms of the fictional moment, from inside her house to other characters likewise inside. On the other hand, Adriana stands forth theatrically on the façade's exterior balcony even though she is fictionally inside the dwelling, so that the *frons scenae* represents simultaneously both the interior and the exterior of the house. That interpenetration of spaces allows for Adriana and her husband almost, but not quite, to

---

1 Adriana and Syracusan Antipholus are sometimes visible dining above at the beginning of the scene, turning Ephesian Antipholus' comments about the insufficiency of his fare for his dinner guests into delicious irony.

2 Productions at the American Shakespeare Center in 2005 and Shakespeare's Globe in London in 2006 located the inside characters – Syracusan Dromio, Luce and Adriana – on the balcony, imagined as '*within*', while the outsiders shouted towards the doorway below. That approach puts the opposing sets of characters onstage simultaneously and makes them visible to the audience, but it also creates distance between the insiders and outsiders and forces character groups to direct their lines away from each other. In the Globe production, the two Dromios used a speaking tube running from the doorway to the upstairs level, such that when one Dromio yanked the tube, the other was jerked forward.

make eye-contact, a fictional impossibility but a theatrical danger that becomes part of the fun.

To double actors or not

A major divide occurs between productions that employ four different actors for the two Antipholuses and the two Dromios and productions that employ one actor for both Antipholuses and one for both Dromios. Doubling these major roles solves the presumed problem of finding two sets of actors who look credibly like each other – although costumes, wigs and make-up can go a long way, and some productions, such as Tim Supple's (1996), simply ignore the problem. Doubling the twins can create potential confusions for the audience that a production may attempt to solve by emphasizing props, sometimes associated with the characters (e.g. the chain and ring), or by distinguishing characters through clothing articles or caricatured body movements. Doubling underscores the actors' virtuosity and thus draws audience attention towards performance *per se* and away from narrative.[1] That approach turns the last part of Act 5 into the 'big' moment, anticipated with suspense, when both sets of twins are onstage together: how will the actors manage the impossible? Overall, productions that double the major parts tend to stress farce and showcase acting; those that employ different actors leave more room for *Errors*'s romantic and dark elements to emerge. Both approaches can be highly successful. (For other possible doublings, see Appendix 3.)

Pacing

Errors moves masterfully from Egeon's dignified, tragical and oratorical speeches in the opening scene, to the comic encounters involving two or three characters of 1.2–2.2, to the crowded, contentious 'false denouement' of 3.1, to the

---

1   For an appreciative view, see Hartley, 168–74.

expansive chaos that ties issues and characters in knots in Act 4, towards the flurry of entrances and exits and the grand convergence of Act 5, with its decompression in the final, affecting chatter of the Dromios. Steadily, individual scenes and the play as a whole incorporate more and more characters and more and more movement, reaching a climax in the chase of 4.4. In the beginning, chaos is narrated; in the climax, it is experienced. The play's pacing, its building of momentum and its capacity for varied tones and surprises constitute a gift of masterful stagecraft to any company that would undertake a production.

EARLY PERFORMANCES

In June 1594 the London playhouses, having been closed for most of the preceding year and a half because of plague outbreaks, reopened. The assorted playing companies of 1592, damaged by the closure, were now reorganized into two: the Lord Admiral's Men, led by Edward Alleyn, and the Lord Chamberlain's Men, led by Richard Burbage, with Shakespeare as a member. Shakespeare appears to have belonged previously to Pembroke's Men (and before that perhaps to Lord Strange's Men).[1] Pembroke's Men had been forced by London's plague to tour in the provinces and in the summer of 1593 had broken up from financial failure while on the road. Under the terms of the 1594 reorganization, the Lord Admiral's Men received permission to perform at the Rose Theatre in Southwark, south of the Thames, while the Lord Chamberlain's Men were approved for the Theatre, to the city's north.[2] The reopened companies faced a demand for plays, both revived and new. Since it is improbable that it could have been commissioned

---

1 On Strange's Men and Pembroke's Men, see Gurr, *Companies*, 258–77.

2 The Chamberlain's Men subsequently played at the Curtain, near the Theatre, after 1597 when their lease on the Theatre expired.

specially for a performance at Gray's Inn in December 1594, and since it was probably written late in the 1593–4 period, *Errors* is likely to have been among the new plays performed by the Chamberlain's Men at the Theatre during the latter half of 1594 (see Appendices 1 and 2).

The original 1594 shareholders of the Lord Chamberlain's Men were George Bryan, Richard Burbage, John Heminges, Will Kemp, Augustine Phillips, Thomas Pope, William Shakespeare and probably Will Sly (Gurr, *Company*, 13). These men would have formed the core acting company for *The Comedy of Errors*. Additional, hired players for the first season may have included John Holland, Humfrey Jeffes and John Sinkler (or Sincler or Sinklo).[1] Burbage would have played Syracusan Antipholus, the leading role, with Kemp probably as Syracusan Dromio, the principal comic part. Sinkler makes sense for Doctor Pinch, since Sinkler was known to have played small, lean, sharp-faced characters, and his name appears in other plays of the Chamberlain's Men from this period; the part may have been written with him in mind. The actor playing Pinch might also have doubled for Egeon,[2] or Shakespeare himself might have taken the part (Foster, 133).[3]

Errors was apparently performed at Gray's Inn, late at night, on Holy Innocents' Day, 28 December 1594. (For the Great Hall of Gray's Inn, see Fig. 14.) The Master of the Revels'

---

1 On Holland and Jeffes, see Gurr, *Company*, 231. On Sinkler, see Gurr, *Company*, 241; Gurr, *Companies*, 72–3; Marino.

2 See 5.1.295n. and 337n., on *ghost*; on doubling, see Appendix 3.

3 Foster bases this claim on computer analysis of words from the role that reappear in Shakespeare's plays subsequently to a degree disproportionately high in comparison to words from the play's other roles. According to tradition, Shakespeare performed Adam in *As You Like It* and the Ghost in *Hamlet*. Foster argues that Shakespeare also played the Chorus and the Friar in *Romeo and Juliet*, King Henry (after 1596) in *1 Henry IV*, King Henry (after 1598) in *2 Henry IV*, Brabantio (after 1604) in *Othello* and Albany (after 1605) in *King Lear*. The list, if correct, suggests that Shakespeare specialized in older characters. Egeon constitutes the play's most poignant, least comic, figure; he is also a storyteller.

14   The Great Hall of Gray's Inn, from the east end

accounts indicate, however, that Shakespeare, Will Kemp and Richard Burbage received payment on behalf of their company for a performance at Court that same day. E.K. Chambers hypothesizes that the Revels records should have read 27 December instead of 28, and his explanation has been generally accepted; the alternative would be to imagine that the company played twice on the same day in different locales, once before the Court and again in the evening at Gray's Inn.[1] Holy

1   See Chambers, *ES*, 4.56, 164–5.

Innocents' Day remembers Herod's slaughter of children in his vain search for the infant Jesus, but nothing about *Errors* or the Gray's Inn celebration pertains to that feast day. The revels lasted altogether from 20 December 1594 to 4 March 1595 and consisted of daily festivities plus some dozen interspersed major events.[1] The general spirit of the revels was to observe social and legal hierarchies and protocols by inverting and lampooning them, with the whole presided over by the elected mock regent, the Prince of Purpoole, and his court. The success of 'the first grand Night' (20 December), filled with comic proclamations and elaborate dancing, raised the stakes for the next, scheduled for 28 December. We can follow the account from the *Gesta Grayorum* (the only surviving record, published in 1688):[2]

> There was the Conclusion of the first grand Night, the Performance whereof increased the Expectation of those things that were to ensue; insomuch that the common Report amongst all Strangers was so great, and the Expectation of our Proceedings so extraordinary, that it urged us to take upon us a greater State than was at the first intended: And therefore, besides all the stately and sumptuous Service that was continually done the Prince, in very Princely manner; and besides the daily Revels, and such like Sports, which were usual, there was intended divers grand Nights, for the Entertainment of Strangers to our Pass-times and Sports.

> (Nelson & Elliott, 2.395)

That language suggests that before 20 December the Grand Nights had not been planned out fully, or perhaps had not been

---

1   See Nelson & Elliott, 2.364.
2   On the 28 December Gray's Inn festivities and *Errors*, see Henning, *Var.*, 519–24.

planned at all, which might partially explain the disorganization, confusion and impromptu quality of the 28 December event. The details are murky:

> The next grand Night was intended to be upon Innocents-Day at Night; at which time there was a great Presence of Lords, Ladies, and worshipful Personages, that did expect some notable Performance at that time; which, indeed, had been effected, if the multitude of Beholders had not been so exceeding great, and thereby there was no convenient room for those that were Actors; by reason whereof, very good Inventions and Conceipts could not have opportunity to be applauded, which otherwise would have been great Contentation to the Beholders. Against which time, our Friend, the Inner Temple, determined to send their Ambassador to our Prince of State, as sent from Frederick Templarius their Emperor, who was then busied in his Wars against the Turk. The Ambassador came very gallantly appointed, and attended by a great number of brave Gentlemen, which arrived at our Court about Nine of the Clock at Night.

> (2.395)

The ambassador from the Inner Temple and his entourage were received with great mock solemnity by the Prince of Purpoole, though the Temple retinue may have been larger than expected, since the author in one sentence complains about the too-great number of beholders and describes in the next the entrance of the Inner Templarians, as if to explain the 'exceeding great' multitude and the resulting disorder.

> When the Ambassador was placed, as aforesaid, and that there was something to be performed for the

Delight of the Beholders, there arose such a disordered Tumult and Crowd upon the Stage, that there was no Opportunity to effect that which was intended: There came so great a number of worshipful Personages upon the Stage, that might not be displaced, and Gentlewomen, whose Sex did privilege them from Violence, that when the Prince and his Officers had in vain, a good while, expected and endeavoured a Reformation, at length there was no hope of Redress for that present. The Lord Ambassador and his Train thought that they were not so kindly entertained, as was before expected, and thereupon would not stay any longer at that time, but, in a sort, discontented and displeased. After their Departure the Throngs and Tumults did somewhat cease, although so much of them continued, as was able to disorder and confound any good Inventions whatsoever. In regard whereof, as also for that the Sports intended were especially for the gracing of the Templarians, it was thought good not to offer any thing of Account, saving Dancing and Revelling with Gentlewomen; and after such Sports, a Comedy of Errors (like to Plautus his Menechmus) was played by the Players. So that the Night was begun, and continued to the end, in nothing but Confusion and Errors; whereupon, it was ever afterwards called, The Night of Errors.

(2.396–7)

Because there exists no other play from *c.* 1593–4 performed by a professional company based on Plautus' *Menaechmi* and entitled 'Comedy of Errors', that description must constitute a record of the first known performance of Shakespeare's play. Apparently the 'Actors' referred to early in the narrative were not the same as the 'Players' later mentioned, since the former were unable to perform; most likely the 'Actors' were members of Gray's Inn who had rehearsed a 'notable Performance', perhaps a mock ceremony along the lines of that at the first Grand Night or a masque or other entertainment. So crowded were the dignitaries on the 'Stage' that the Prince's court could not proceed with the 'good Inventions' and 'Sports' intended to honour the Inner Templarians. Thus, after some dancing and revelling, *The Comedy of Errors* was enacted by the Lord Chamberlain's Men, probably late in the evening. Although the performance of *Errors* must have been part of the makeshift plan for the Grand Night, it was not the main event but rather a diversion to round out the 'Inventions', 'Sports', dancing and revelling.

Yet the play left a strong enough impression that the members of the Inns seized upon it spontaneously to reimagine the whole evening.[1] Because of the great confusion of the 'Night of Errors', the Prince of Purpoole conducted a parodic inquiry on the following night at which the 'Disorders' were blamed on 'Sorceries and Inchantments; and namely of a great Witchcraft used the Night before' (Nelson & Elliott, 2.397). On the next evening following, a public Judgement was read

> . . . against a Sorcerer or Conjurer that was supposed to be the Cause of that confused Inconvenience. Therein was contained, How he had caused the State to be built, and Scaffolds to be reared to the top of the House, to increase Expectation. Also how he had caused divers Ladies and Gentlewomen, and others of good Condition, to be invited to our Sports; also our dearest Friend, the State of Templaria, to be disgraced, and disappointed of their kind Entertainment, deserved and

---

1 On affinities between *Errors* and the revels, see Rhatigan.

intended. Also that he caused Throngs and Tumults, Crowds and Outrages, to disturb our whole Proceedings. And Lastly, that he had foisted a Company of base and common Fellows, to make up our Disorders with a Play of Errors and Confusions; and that that Night had gained to us Discredit, and it self a Nick-name of Errors. All of which were against the Crown and Dignity of our Sovereign Lord, the Prince of Purpoole.

(2.397–8)

That account suggests the power of the witchcraft motif in *The Comedy of Errors*, as if the enchantment felt in Ephesus had registered strongly enough upon the play's beholders that, like Adriana's mist, it beclouded the imagined principality of 'Graya'. In a delightful bit of spontaneous, high-handed humour and comic fantasy, all the events and mishaps of the Night of Errors are reconceived as wrought by a powerful 'Sorcerer or Conjurer', his diabolical work including the foisting of 'a Company of base and common Fellows' (i.e. the professional players) to complete and mirror the night's 'Disorders' and 'Confusions'. The Prince and his court behaved as did the confused and disordered characters in *Errors*: Doctor Pinch has triumphed. Shakespeare's play may not have been entirely lost, after all, upon the assemblage.

The *Gesta Grayorum* mentions the stage and the scaffold for spectators erected for the occasion. The playing space probably stood in the middle of the long Gray's Inn Hall (70 feet × 34 feet 8 inches, or 21.3 × 10.5 metres), between the dais, where the Prince of Purpoole held state and where the high table was located, and the temporary scaffolds (Knapp & Kobialka). The stage was thus 'wide and shallow, with the audience seated on at least two, and possibly all four, sides' (Knapp & Kobialka, 438). In these crowded quarters, the use of booth-like structures, even modest ones, for Ephesian Antipholus' house or the abbey is doubtful.[1] Rather, the actors would have provided nonce solutions that appealed to the spectators' imaginations. The account of the Gray's Inn performance supports the view that *Errors* was written to be conformable to a variety of venues.

An apparent allusion to *Errors* in 1598 offers 'evidence' that it was 'revived in 1597–98':

> Persuade me to a play, I'le to the *Rose*,
> Or *Curtaine*, one of *Plautus* Comedies,
> Or the *Patheticke Spaniards* Tragedies

(Everard Guilpin, 'Satire V')[2]

Those lines may well refer to both *The Comedy of Errors*, staged by the Lord Chamberlain's Men at the Curtain, and *The Spanish Tragedy*, from the Admiral's Men at the Rose (this latter is confirmed by Henslowe's Diary; see Knutson, 62–3).[3] Francis Meres's reference to *Errors* in 1598 (see Appendix 1, p. 314) likewise implies its public performance after 1594, perhaps in the 1597–8 season, as Roslyn Lander Knutson proposes. In addition, the anonymous *Birth of Hercules* (published *c.* 1598), a play based on Plautus' *Amphitruo*, contains a witty servant named Dromio whose name may derive from *Errors*, strengthening the conjecture that *Errors* was revived in 1597–8.[4]

---

1 Booths would have crowded the stage and compromised sight lines for spectators. They were probably not part of the scheme for the evening's earlier entertainments and thus would have required setting up immediately before *Errors* commenced, a disruption that would hardly have been permitted.

2 From Guilpin's *Skialetheia*, recorded in the Stationers' Register on September 1598; Knutson, 62.

3 The identification of 'one of *Plautus* Comedies' as *Errors* is strengthened by Manningham's subsequent likening of *Errors* to *Menaechmi* and suggests the comparative and generic perspective that certain spectators might have brought to the play.

4 See Henning, *Var.*, 524.

The vitality of *Errors* in the public imagination was such that, in February 1602, John Manningham could remember it when seeing another Shakespearean play, *Twelfth Night*, performed at another Inns of Court establishment, the Middle Temple, as his diary records: 'At our feast wee had a play called "Twelfth night, or what you will"; much like the commedy of errores, or Menechmi in Plautus' (Manningham, 48). Since Manningham was not admitted to the Middle Temple until 1598 and was apparently studying at Cambridge in 1594, he, too, might well have seen *Errors* in revival in 1597–8.

On 28 December 1604, *The Comedy of Errors* – the 'Plaie of Errors' by 'Shaxberd' – was performed by Shakespeare's company, now recommissioned as the King's Men, before the newly crowned King James as part of the Court's Christmastide celebrations, ten years to the day after its performance at Gray's Inn (Chambers, *ES*, 4.171). Perhaps the play was recommended to the King by Sir Francis Bacon, who had written considerable material for the 1594 Gray's Inn revels and who may have remembered *Errors* from that occasion.[1] If not recommended by Bacon, *Errors* might have come to the Court because it was being performed in revival as part of the King's Men's 1604–5 season. Knutson observes that around 1594 there had been a 'flurry of interest' in plays related to magic, such as *Doctor Faustus*, *The Wise Man of West Chester* and *A Midsummer Night's Dream* (143). *Errors*, with its hilarious and slightly disconcerting treatment of magic, could have reasonably been included. Likewise, around 1602–3, 'another such flurry' arose (143); a reappearance of *Errors* at that time might well have been part of a renewed interest in plays dealing with magic. Thus, the early performance history of *Errors* argues for

---

1 In *The Advancement of Learning* (1605), Bacon refers to 'some comedies of errors, wherein the mistress and the maid change habits' (Bacon, 247). The mismatch between his example and *Errors*'s plot suggests the degree to which Shakespeare's title had become a generic term.

its firm place in the public theatre, its persistent appeal and its memorability.

AFTERLIFE: IMAGE, STAGE AND SCREEN

Image

When Nicholas Rowe, the first named editor of Shakespeare, published the collected plays in 1709, *The Comedy of Errors* was no longer being presented in the London commercial theatre, although, much cut, it may have been performed privately (see p. 115). Rowe's frontispiece illustration (see Fig. 15) represents the climactic scene, derived from reading but visualized as theatre; it constitutes one of the 'earliest direct responses' to *Errors*.[1] The illustration combines events synchronically that happen sequentially: a puzzled Syracusan Antipholus and Dromio in the left foreground; the Second Merchant on the right, about to duel with Antipholus but restrained by Adriana (or Luciana) and a bystander; the condemned Egeon bareheaded in the left middle ground; the Abbess (or perhaps Adriana) at centre supplicating the Duke on bended knee;[2] and the Duke's guards forming a horizontal line across the background before the dark, recessed abbey entrance. Shadows bespeak late afternoon. The illustration brings together multiple dimensions: the framing set itself may reflect Sebastiano Serlio's notion of a tragic stage setting, but the scene's energy and confusion evoke comedy, and the abbey portal, which centres the scene's triangular geometry, points towards the romance of family reunion and its concluding

---

1 Sillars, 11. The illustration was designed by François Boitard and engraved by Elisha Kirkall. On the frontispiece, see Sillars, 13–17.

2 Sillars argues reasonably that the kneeling figure is the Abbess, given her gown, suggestive of a nun's habit (14), although the play specifies that Adriana kneels before the Duke (see 5.1.129).

15   Act 5. From Nicholas Rowe (ed.), *The Works of Shakespear* (1709), vol. 1.
      Probably designed by François Boitard and engraved by Elisha Kirkall

'gossips' feast' (5.1.405; Sillars, 13–17). The visual arrangement of characters and episodes thus moves inward and
towards the play's resolution, with a 'metatheatric' sense of
the whole (Sillars, 16).

   The Rowe frontispiece holds diverse, potentially conflicting,
aspects of the play in balance: bafflements at apparently magical
events; farcical confusions and violence; marital troubles;
familial sufferings; threats of death; mystical reconciliations.
By contrast, few stage productions manage to balance such

issues equally, and many choose to stress only some of *Errors*'s dimensions to the exclusion of others. Commonly, productions ramp up the farce, strip out material about identity and marriage, stereotype characters, de-emphasize the family romance, add visual and physical gags and turn the Dromios into the *de facto* stars. The late-seventeenth-century acting versions of the play – for example, the Smock Alley promptbook – distil the play into fast-moving farce. Such productions are facilitated by *Errors*'s overt symmetries, its multiplication of mistakes and its progressive recombinations of different characters illustrating the permutations of misprision. A few productions – most famously Theodore Komisarjevsky's at Stratford-upon-Avon in 1938 – give *Errors* a decidedly abstract *mise en scène*, overturning realism, mixing styles of dress and acting, inserting music and saturating the play with comic, generic and cultural allusions. Such productions can shade from 'interpretation' to 'adaptation', as exemplified by Thomas Hull's late eighteenth-century adaptation or by Abbott, Rodgers and Hart's 1938 *The Boys from Syracuse*. Here politicized issues – for example, *Errors*'s exploration of marriage – often undergo revision. At the other end of the spectrum, bare-stage versions of *Errors* have been successfully mounted, from William Poel's important 1895 Elizabethan-revival production to contemporary ones at Shakespeare's Globe in London. Stagings that avoid big production values open the door to exploring *Errors*'s language and its shifting and complex tones, and those – such as RSC productions by Clifford Williams in 1962 or by Tim Supple in 1996 – come closest, although in different ways, to realizing *Errors*'s rich multivalence, as evoked by the Rowe frontispiece. The historical adaptability of *The Comedy of Errors* expresses the play's multidimensionality.[1]

---

1   On the play's adaptability and its history of productions, see Miola, 'Play', 28–37; see also Ford.

Stage: the Restoration and the nineteenth century

Although *Errors* went largely unproduced during the Restoration, extant promptbooks indicate that it may have been performed at the Smock Alley Theatre in Dublin, *c.* 1670; possibly at the Barbican 'Nursery' in London, a training company for young actors, *c.* 1672; and in Douai, France, perhaps for the English Roman Catholic college, *c.* 1694.[1] John Ashbury's Smock Alley promptbook (a mark-up of part of a copy of the Third Folio of 1664) is representative; it cuts Shakespeare's shortest play by a remarkable 30% (Evans, 8.75), possibly with student or amateur actors in mind. The first scene, for example, loses some forty lines of Egeon's recounted grief and tragic narrative detail. Syracusan Antipholus' ruminations in 1.2 about Ephesian magic disappear, as does almost all the debate between Luciana and Adriana about marriage in 2.1 (see Evans, 3.2). The ensuing cuts systematically strip out *Errors*'s darker tonalities and its human and social concerns; what remains assumes the brevity, speed and punch of a Plautine romp.

In the first half of the eighteenth century, *Errors* was adapted as a stage farce under the titles *Everybody Mistaken* (1716) and *See If You Like It* (1734).[2] In the second half of the century, it was largely replaced by the actor-writer Thomas Hull's adaptation, which theatre historians believe was first performed in 1762 at Covent Garden (*Var.*, 525). With various alterations, Hull's *Errors* was revived regularly – and with increasing frequency – during the eighteenth century and into the nineteenth. Hull's version was popular enough to be printed twice, privately in 1770 and again, revised, in 1793, holding the stage for some fifty years (*Var.*, 525–6, 542). Hull's influential

---

1   See Evans, 3.1.3–12; Shattuck, 67; *Var.*, 525.
2   See Hogan, 1.98, 99; *Var.*, 539; Odell, *Shakespeare*, 1.228.

1793 text sentimentalizes the relationship between Syracusan Antipholus and Dromio, deepens Adriana's pathos, fills out the recognition events in Act 5 and eliminates the closing conversation between the Dromios. In Hull's opening scene, for example, the hints in Egeon's narrative of encompassing nature and providential order recede, along with his fatalism; the scene moves economically, despite added sympathetic interruptions by the Duke, but forfeits its cosmic implications. Similarly, in 1.2, Syracusan Antipholus' fantasia about Ephesian witchcraft disappears, replaced by a lament over the lost comforts of a father's love, with magic ebbing as a theme. In 2.1, Hull retains the women's debate on marriage but adds lines to Luciana's defence of female forbearance, re-enforcing patriarchal values against Adriana's egalitarian revisionism. The byplay between Syracusan Antipholus and Dromio in 2.2 drops out, presumably on account of its bawdiness. Ephesian Dromio's lament at being beaten in 3.1 is likewise cut, leaving violence against servants unquestioned. To Adriana's advances, Syracusan Antipholus responds decorously and coldly, all hint of sexual misadventure deleted. Hull's *Errors* is Syracuse to Shakespeare's Ephesus: attitudes are conventionalized, music is introduced, rough edges filed away, sentimentality increased, Dark Ephesus brightened. Such complacency has its satisfactions – George Odell, for example, prefers Hull's adaptation to Shakespeare's original – but it forfeits the tragicomic dimension.[1]

In December 1819, Frederick Reynolds premiered an English operatic version, close in its script to Hull's, with the addition of music; it was performed, apparently with great

---

1 See Odell, *Shakespeare*, 2.48. In 1780 the Theatre Royal in Edinburgh saw a three-act farcical version of *Errors*, called *The Twins, or Which is Which*, by W. Woods, and in 1786, Vienna enjoyed an operatic adaptation, *Gli Equivoci*, in the spirit of *opera buffa*, by Stephen Storace (a friend of Mozart), with libretto by the famed Lorenzo Da Ponte (Dean, 94, 100).

success, twenty-seven times.[1] Reynolds adorned *Errors* with a cornucopia of ' "Song, Duets, Glees, and Chorusses, Selected entirely from the Plays, Poems and Sonnets of Shakespeare" ' (Odell, *Shakespeare*, 2.131). Reynolds's lavish staging included a hunting scene with snow-capped mountains and a 'grand bacchanalian revel' at Balthazar's house, while the finale 'blaze[d] up' with a medley taken from *The Tempest* and *A Midsummer Night's Dream* (2.132, 134). In New York, a version of *Errors*, probably Hull's adaptation, appeared on the stage in 1804,[2] while in 1845 a trimmed, farcical *Errors* was launched at Niblo's Garden by the twins Thomas and Henry Placide. The Placides, as the Dromios, dominated the play with their banter, antics and stage business, such as Syracusan Dromio's use of a horseshoe to repel magic – and they kept doing it for twenty years (*Var.*, 527). Stripped down to a farce at Smock Alley, sentimentalized by Hull, overwhelmed with music and operatic values by Reynolds or turned into a vehicle for the Dromios: stage renderings of *Errors* had preferred limited visions of the play to the complexities of Rowe's frontispiece.

That condition changed when, at London's Sadler's Wells Theatre in 1855, Samuel Phelps substantially restored *Errors*. Phelps was part of a theatrical vanguard advocating a return to Shakespeare's playtexts – especially to Shakespeare's language. Phelps cut a relatively modest 234 lines (e.g. some forty lines from Egeon in 1.1, the punning on Time in 2.2 and part of the Dromios' reunion (*Var.*, 553)) and retained a few of Hull's additions. The Courtesan, 'Lesbia' in Hull, makes a return. Phelps's version, performed twenty-eight times at Sadler's Wells over five seasons, was the closest that the London stage had come to Shakespeare's *Errors* in 250 years; audiences laughed heartily, although critics carped (see Allen, 314–15,

---

1 See Odell, *Shakespeare*, 2.131–5.
2 See *Var.*, 526; Odell, *Annals*, 2.204.

222). In 1858, a blackface minstrel adaptation was staged in New York (see Wells, *Burlesques*) and there, too, the J.S. Clarke interpretation (1864), in the spirit of Victorian realism, emphasized the mercantile aspects of the play with its elaborate staging of a market scene in 4.3 (*Var.*, 553–4). In 1878, W.H. Crane and Stuart Robson began their decade-long success as the Dromios in a scenically overstuffed version of *Errors*, with features (in 1885) such as a vast pageant of priests, priestesses and acolytes of the goddess Diana. America lacked a transformational Phelps. In London, the return of 'original' Shakespeare reached an important point in 1895 with a December performance of *Errors* in the Great Hall of Gray's Inn, directed by William Poel (see Fig. 16). The performers wore sixteenth-century costumes, played before the hall screen without set or interval and attempted to capture period acting values, while spectators sat at the hall's long tables. G.B. Shaw

16   William Poel's 1895 production of *The Comedy of Errors*, Act 5, Scene 1, 'Not One Before Another'; photograph by Russell & Sons

termed it 'delightful'.[1] This production honoured the playtext and its implicit scenic fluidity.

Stage: four twentieth-century productions and an adaptation

On 12 April 1938, at the Shakespeare Memorial Theatre in Stratford-upon-Avon, the Russian director Theodore Komisarjevsky launched undoubtedly the most famous modern production of *The Comedy of Errors*. Komisarjevsky, who emigrated from Russia to England in 1919 because of Lenin's hostility to theatre, introduced British audiences to Chekhov's plays and built a reputation for innovative directing.[2] His *Errors* rejected Victorian scenic realism and Poel's bare stage in favour of abstraction, a dream-like Ephesus of colourful, off-scale 'toy-town' houses and of mixed period costumes (plumed bowler hats of different colours, sailors in US naval uniform, Viennese Keystone Cops, top hats and frock coats, modern handbags, Elizabethan farthingales, futuristic garb) that defied identification with any particular time or place (see Fig. 17).[3] Consequently, the set took on a 'haunting, almost hallucinogenic quality' (Berry, 'Komisarjevsky', 81). This Ephesus evoked the 'proper scene of eternal pantomime and harlequinade. Its citizens appear as puppets and playboys bound to no especial century, but heirs of a timeless invention. In a moment we are enraptured.'[4] A clock in a central tower struck the hours, with its hands whirling around to catch up – a witty response to the play's interest in time. All was colour, brightness, merriment and physical inventiveness, with evocations of the Marx Brothers, *The Mikado* and Mae West (from the Courtesan). *Errors*'s dark opening with the Syracusan merchant was quickly

1 See Speaight, *Poel*, 109–10; Shaw, 1.269, 275.
2 On Komisarjevsky as a director of Shakespeare, see Berry, 'Komisarjevsky'.
3 Berry, 'Komisarjevsky', 81; see 81–2; see also Kennedy, 131–2.
4 Ivor Brown, *Observer*, 17 April 1938, quoted in Berry, 'Komisarjevsky', 82.

17 Act 5, Scene 1, in Theodore Komisarjevsky's production for the Royal Shakespeare Company, Stratford-upon-Avon, 1938

forgotten as the action gave way to inventive farce. The Duke was accompanied by a servant who mimicked his gestures and facial expressions. The pink of the Dromios' bowlers was echoed in the Abbess's clothing. Citizens were liable to outbreaks of singing and dancing; it was an 'operatic, balletic diversion' (Trewin, *Shakespeare*, 179). At the end of the first act, Ephesian Antipholus' line – 'This jest shall cost him some expense' – was repeated chorally by others to the music of Handel. Conversely, long speeches were divided among different speakers, creating a 'collectivization of response' reminiscent of a Victorian glee club (Berry, 'Komisarjevsky', 82). The atmosphere was both carnivalesque and dream-like, as if the world really had turned topsy-turvy. Komisarjevsky's influential *Errors* transformed this previously undervalued play into a theatrical *tour de force*.

Some seven months after Komisarjevsky's production, and across the Atlantic, *Errors* figured in another signal theatrical event. On 23 November 1938, at the Alvin Theatre in New York, the musical *The Boys from Syracuse* opened, with book by George Abbott, music by Richard Rodgers, lyrics by Lorenz Hart and choreography by George Balanchine. It was a smash hit. *Boys* introduced songs that became standards, and it still retains its capacity to delight.[1] With *Boys*, *Errors* became the first Shakespeare play adapted for a musical in the American theatre, and the production 'introduced' to Broadway the 'organic musical', in which music, lyrics and dance became 'integral to the plot and advanced its development'.[2] *Boys* gives a political twist to certain of *Errors*'s incidents and otherwise

1　As indicated, for example, by revivals in New York in 1963, 1997 and 2002, London productions in 1963 and 1991, a rollicking version at Baltimore's CenterStage in 2006–7, a semi-staging by the Shakespeare Theatre in Washington, DC, in 2011, and a Singapore production in 2012. In 1940, it was made into a now-dated movie starring Allan Jones, Irene Hervey and Martha Raye.

2　Dash, 48, 2; on *Boys*' relationship to *Errors*, see Dash, 10–48; the comments here draw substantially from Dash's discussion.

creates contemporary interest. Its opening scene of a mob calling for execution, its emphasis on the irrational criminalizing of a person's birthplace and its attention to the Syracusans' urgency to hide themselves all allude to political events in Nazi Europe. *Boys* also develops *Errors*'s tensions about marriage. Adriana and Luciana no longer debate marital hierarchy; rather, the two, especially Luciana, become romantic principals – although, ironically, their music is sometimes fitted out with anti-romantic lyrics. *Boys* considerably expands Luce's role and displaces the real criticism of marriage on to the lower-class characters, as in Luce's song 'What Can You Do with a Man?' The Courtesan, with her associates, takes on a larger and franker role in *Boys* than in *Errors*. Likewise, the division of Ephesian Antipholus' attention between two women is made concrete and illustrated in a *pas de trois*, with one woman wearing ballet shoes, the other tap. Syracusan Antipholus' concern in *Errors* about identity becomes realized in *Boys*, not by him, but by the Dromios in a mirrored dream-dance and song, 'Big Brother'. The plebs gain sympathy over the toffs. *Boys* also features a comic 'lock-out' scene that, expanding on *Errors*'s fear of scandal, turns into a public near-riot of music and dance (see Fig. 18). *Boys* constitutes a brilliant reading of *Errors*.

Meanwhile, back at Stratford-upon-Avon, it would be twenty-four years before the RSC, in 1962, again undertook *The Comedy of Errors*, this time as an after-thought (a substitute for a cancelled play) but with revelatory effect.[1] Directed by Clifford Williams, this production succeeded because it both emphasized the ensemble quality of the play and brought out not only its farcical humour but its complex tonalities. Williams's version was the closest expression to date of the values perceived in the Rowe frontispiece. The set was

---

1   As Ford points out, the 'Williams production' actually went through re-stagings in 1963, 1964 (for television) and 1972 (15–16).

18   'Let Antipholus In'. *The Boys from Syracuse*, New York, 1938

restrained, with three performance tiers and a ramp that facilitated the flow of action. Before the start of the play proper, the actors filed out, dressed in similar grey tops and jeans, and showed themselves to the audience, heightening metatheatrical awareness. The performance added colour as it proceeded, and it likewise paid attention to the play's varied emotional and generic tones. Egeon's soulful opening narrative made audiences feel 'genuinely concerned'; Syracusan Antipholus reacted to events 'like someone imprisoned in a Kafkaesque nightmare'; and Adriana exhibited 'a genuine core of feeling'.[1] The staging of 3.1 was addressed by Syracusan Dromio's air-drawing of a door, behind which he could hide. Although the production was bright with music, mime and *commedia dell'arte* touches, it also showed 'dark and disquieting forces at work' (Billington, 488). Its power and memorability thus arose

---

1   Speaight, 'Williams', 485; Billington, 487.

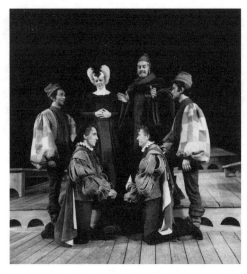

19 Act 5, Scene 1, directed by Clifford Williams for the Royal Shakespeare Company, 1962

from a sensitive engagement with the playtext. The company's complementary ensemble acting also made the production a definitive statement of the RSC style (see Fig. 19). The cast blended 'superlative team-work' with 'physical slickness' and 'complete understanding of comedy's vocal nuances' (Gardner, 481). Characters were sharply etched, and humour was not imposed but arose through situation.

Williams's comprehension of both the hilarity and the disquieting mystery of *Errors* encouraged subsequent explorations. Trevor Nunn's 1976 *Comedy of Errors* for the RSC managed to combine aspects of Williams's production with those of American musical comedy. (This production can be seen in DVD format.) Guy Woolfenden wrote the music and Nunn the lyrics, with Gillian Lynne choreographing. The nine original musical numbers, using lines of dialogue as points of departure, displayed 'a variety of styles, from rock to Greek',

20 Act 4, Scene 4, directed by Trevor Nunn for the Royal Shakespeare
    Company, 1976. Doctor Pinch (Robin Ellis) preparing for his examination
    of Dromio (Nickolas Grace) and Antipholus of Ephesus (Mike Gwilym)

with 'zappy choral songs' adding 'pace and lift' (Emerson,
498). Doctor Pinch exorcized Ephesian Antipholus by singing
and dancing (see Fig. 20); Syracusan Antipholus and Luciana
wooed each other in a duet, and Ephesian Dromio crooned and
danced away his beatings, so that the songs advanced the action,
although sometimes with a loss of darkness and critical impact.
Nunn's Ephesus was a cluttered Turkish marketplace catering
to tourists, with people wearing straw hats, women of dubious
honour leaning from balconies, men hanging around in outdoor
bars and gangsters styled after the 1930s. The Duke was a
dictator with big epaulettes, and Syracusan Antipholus had a
touch of 'gum-chewing sleaziness'.[1] While Emerson calls
Nunn's version 'rollicking fun' (497), Warren objects that the
song and dance turned characters into 'puppets' and blunted
their personalities, especially compared to Williams's

1   Emerson, 498; see also Warren.

production (500) – a comment that hints at both the opportunities and the sand-traps of *Errors*.

If Nunn's *Errors* 'managed to keep Aegeon credibly pathetic' (Trewin, 'Britain', 216), no production has explored pathos so much as Tim Supple's for the RSC in 1996 at The Other Place in Stratford-upon-Avon. Miola captures its tone:

> At the outset we see a glum, shackled old man, who eventually tells his woeful story without gimmickry or distracting stage business, conveying real anguish at his losses and his plight. At the end Emilia appears as a serious woman who has suffered and found strength and peace in the spiritual life, instead of as the usual cartoon in a nun's costume. Their reunion is poetic and moving, though they forgo the customary joyful embrace, that easy solution yielding to the delicate and wary uncertainty of spouses who are now strangers.
>
> (Miola, 'Play', 34–5)[1]

Supple offered no Plautine houses or colourful toy-town; rather, his set was stark, dark and simple, with central double doors and a few windows fixed in a brick façade. In front of it were ramps and a grille to which, before the play began, the audience saw the dirty, ragged Egeon chained. Mystery, strangeness and wonder saturated this production rather than pantomime and double-takes. The casting was multi-ethnic. Unfamiliar middle-eastern instruments played eerie Turkish music; bells sounded, prompting action; the breaking of ocean waves could be heard in the distance. As part of the soundscape, the verse was realized subtly, and with effect, as when Solinus listened intently to Egeon's words. Magic and witchcraft were real, disturbing possibilities in this Ephesus, and Syracusan Antipholus reacted with apt superstition and amazement. At the end, characters faced the future with a sense of uncertainty. Notwithstanding,

1   See also Smallwood, 215–19.

21 Act 2, Scene 2, directed by Tim Supple for the Royal Shakespeare Company, 1996. Antipholus of Syracuse (Robert Bowman, right) to Dromio of Syracuse (Dan Milne): 'Yea, dost thou jeer and flout me in the teeth? Think'st thou I jest? Hold, take thou that, and that!' (2.2.22–3)

the central scenes were farcical and active (see Fig. 21), so that the drama generated both boisterous humour and emotional profundity. This production 'treated the play with deep respect and with a thoughtful, affectionate delight in the story' (Smallwood, 217). Supple's production was a signal achievement, even deepening the insight suggested by the Rowe frontispiece.

From Komisarjevsky's hallucinogenic farce, to Rodgers and Hart's exuberant musical adaptation, to Williams's textual sensitivity and *commedia dell'arte* touch, to Nunn's stuffed, good-natured musical romp, to Supple's haunting essay on wonder: the range latent in *The Comedy of Errors* becomes self-evident. The problem of identity and otherness has resilient appeal, while the play's abstract patterning, its oppositions and its varied and elastic tonalities allow for stretching, compressing, decorating and recolouring without forfeiting the dramatic

127

core. Justly so, since these interpretations of *Errors* have continued the tradition of revision that Shakespeare brought to Plautus.

Stage: other modern productions and adaptations

Under the influence of such varied explorations, *The Comedy of Errors* has now become an often-performed play. Its adaptability and its multiple valencies invite experimentation with all sorts of modes and settings: sunny Italian coastal town, Turkish bazaar, nostalgic Edwardian England, 1930s cubist metropolis, London inner-city neighbourhood, 'post-consumerist present' (Rutter, 459), gangster-land New Jersey, carnival or bare stage. It can be played as a madcap farce, as a balance of romance and comedy, or as something darker; music is often added, and circus motifs and allusions to early twentieth-century film comedies frequently recur. It also lends itself to political or cultural commentary. In 1923, the Ethiopian Theatre of Chicago produced a jazz version of *Errors* performed by African-American actors – perhaps, in its own way, a response to the nineteenth-century minstrel *Errors* (see p. 118). An Edwardian-styled production (2011) became a commentary on pre-1918 class divisions and cultural values.[1] In 2012, St Louis's Repertory Theatre set the play in New Orleans, with jazz-era standards woven nostalgically into the narrative. Adrian Noble's immensely popular 1983 RSC version of *Errors* featured jazz, ragtime music, carnival tunes and dance steps in a production with circus themes, slapstick gags and costumes and make-up that, in Brechtian style, constituted the set. His Dromios wore plaid trousers and beeping red noses; the Antipholus brothers' faces were bright blue, Doctor Pinch's saffron; Luciana's hair looked like an ice-cream cone; and the

---

1 See Rutter, 457–8.

Courtesan rose out of a trapdoor wearing red face-paint and a red leotard. Going a step further, in 1987 the Flying Karamazov Brothers premiered a *Comedy of Errors* in which all the Ephesians shared an odd characteristic: they were all 'nimble jugglers' (*CE* 1.2.98). The townsfolk included tightrope walkers, sword-swallowers, tumblers, fire-eaters and a baton-twirling Adriana.

By contrast, in 2004, Joe Banno's Folger Shakespeare Theatre production was 'Mafia-chic', with the opening scene set in a Brooklyn-style Italian-American restaurant where a godfather-Duke interrogated Egeon across a checked tablecloth with breadsticks and dining items used to illustrate the backstory. The women were sex-starved, the goldsmith looked like a rapper, and Syracusan Dromio turned into a stand-up comic. The next year the Shakespeare Theatre of Washington, DC, produced Douglas Wager's surrealist *Errors* with a Salvador Dali melting clock and an M.C. Escher stairway. The two Dromios were played by African-American actors, so that their beatings by white Antipholuses had political resonance and their reunion a profound air of special recognition (black Dromios were first introduced in John Philip Kemble's *Comedy of Errors* in 1780). As the two Dromios spoke the closing lines (5.1.417–26), they began to remove parts of their costumes and make-up, and their tone of voice softened from the 'theatrical' to the conversational, as if their human identities were being revealed under the confusion and superficiality of costumes. In 2006, Shakespeare's Globe in London demonstrated the play's solid dramatic structure with a bare-stage, minimum-prop version, infused with visual and sound gags but emphasizing easy transitions and ensemble acting, although the characters did acquire a caricatured quality. In 2012, the British comedian Lenny Henry starred (as Syracusan Antipholus) in a National Theatre production of *Errors* directed by Dominic Cooke. This acclaimed staging had a modern, edgy, urban-industrial feel, brightened by Henry's comic acting and by Adriana and

Luciana's hipness as they swirled martinis on their condo balcony. By contrast, the summer 2013 production in New York's Central Park, directed by Daniel Sullivan, set the play in 1940s Damon Runyonesque upstate New York, with one of the Dromios suffering abuse by spaghetti but with the ending 'unexpectedly' achieving 'some of the emotional heat' of the recognition scenes in later Shakespeare (Isherwood).

Explicitly political, a 1950s South African production of *Errors* 'subvert[ed] and interrogate[d] official culture' and became a Bakhtinian 'communal refusal to be bound by the rigid strictures of theatrical norms developed by white culture' (Quince, 549), reminiscent of effects in Komisarjevsky's version. Subsequent South African productions used *Errors* for socio-cultural satire and carnivalesque purposes and adaptations were enacted not only by whites but by Asians and black South Africans. In 2012 the award-winning actress-director Corinne Jaber directed a *Comedy of Errors* set in Kabul, performed by Afghani actors and spoken in Dari, as part of the Globe Theatre's World Shakespeare Festival. *Errors*'s tale of broken families bore echoes of war-torn Afghanistan, and the reunion of Egeon and Emilia at the end was as deeply moving as the flirtation between Luciana and Syracusan Antipholus was delightful (see Fig. 22). Likewise in 2012, Palestinian director Amir Nizar Zuabi's production for the RSC used the conflict between Syracuse and Ephesus to allude to contemporary middle-eastern strife, with a shipping-port setting, machine-gun-toting guards and torture of illegal immigrants.[1]

The most noted late twentieth-century adaptation of *Errors* was *The Bomb-itty of Errors* (New York, 1999), a comic, hip-hop, rap operetta, in the tradition of, but a far cry from, *The Boys from Syracuse*. *Bomb-itty* employs 'rap to mime the verbal texture of early Shakespearean comedy, the regular beat,

---

1 On *Errors* in Germany, see Walch; for Japan, see Milward; and on a 1983 *Errors* in Stockholm with political implications, see Ring.

22 Act 5, Scene 1. Roy-e-Sabs production, directed by Corinne Jaber at Shakespeare's Globe, London, 2012. Performed by Afghan actors speaking in Dari, with Afghan music and dance. Farzana Sayed Ahmad as Rodaba (Luciana) and Abdul Haq as Arsalan (Antipholus of Syracuse)

alliteration and rhyme, density of wordplay and metaphor', while it 'incorporates elements of African-American verbal culture that suggest analogies to Shakespeare' (Lanier, *Popular*, 78). In 2001, Yasunari Takabashi created a Japanese adaptation, *The Kyogen of Errors*, which combined elements of Japanese Kyogen (akin to *commedia dell'arte*) and Noh drama.[1] The adaptability and broad appeal of *The Comedy of Errors* appear to be inexhaustible.

Screen

The Comedy of Errors has infiltrated cinema and television in localized and liberally adapted forms. Laurel and Hardy's

1   See Burt, 2.767.

1936 film *Our Relations* echoes *Errors* in its multiple pairs of twins and plot motifs.[1] The 1981 Mexican film *Los Gemelos Alborotados* transposes the action to a rural Mexican town with sombrero-wearing good and evil twins. The celebrated Bollywood Hindi comedy *Angoor*, directed in India by Gulzar in 1982, makes the play into a domestic farce set in a modern Indian city, with the travellers getting the resident's household high on opium-laced aubergine snacks. The traveller-protagonist's reading of crime novels generates his misperceptions of the locals. *Angoor* is one of several Indian films based on *Errors*. The 1988 American film *Big Business*, starring Lily Tomlin and Bette Midler, uses the twin motif to comment on corporate rapacity: *Errors*'s symmetries provide attractive opportunities for social satire. For television, a 1984 BBC production (available on video), directed by James Cellan-Jones, forfeits some comic voltage in favour of close-ups that attend to the characters' inner lives.

Over three hundred years after the Rowe frontispiece, those productions and many others confirm *The Comedy of Errors*'s enduring vitality, its range of tones and generic values, its emotional depth and mystery and its adaptability. The play's central trope of doubleness and its pattern of repetition-with-difference lend all its aspects multivalency and reach. The play's concerns – identity, debt, religion, time, marriage, language, genre – radiate prismatically from the sense of multiplicity that overwhelms Ephesus, that workaday centre of commerce and, simultaneously, enchanted world. *Errors*'s very nexus of doubled, paradoxical values and tones has made the play delightfully open to different critical and theatrical interpretations. It has become the paradigm: every comedy is a comedy of errors.

1   On film adaptations, see Burt, 1.144–7.

THE COMEDY
OF ERRORS

LIST OF ROLES

EGEON, Merchant of Syracuse   *father to the Antipholuses and husband to the Abbess, though separated from all*

Solinus, DUKE of Ephesus

ANTIPHOLUS OF SYRACUSE ⎫
ANTIPHOLUS OF EPHESUS ⎬ *twin brothers, sons to the Merchant of Syracuse and the Abbess but unknown to each other*

DROMIO OF SYRACUSE ⎫ *twin brothers, slaves to the*   5
DROMIO OF EPHESUS ⎬ *two Antipholuses*

ADRIANA   *wife to Antipholus of Ephesus*
LUCIANA   *sister to Adriana*
Emilia, an ABBESS at Ephesus   *wife to Egeon*

JAILER   10
FIRST MERCHANT   *friend to Antipholus of Syracuse*
ANGELO   *a goldsmith*
BALTHAZAR   *a merchant*
LUCE (or Nell)   *kitchen-maid in Adriana's household*
SECOND MERCHANT   *creditor to Angelo*   15
OFFICER
COURTESAN
Doctor PINCH   *a schoolmaster and conjuror*
MESSENGER

Attendant to the Duke, three or four Attendants to Doctor Pinch,   20
Headsman, other Officers

LIST OF ROLES In the first published list of roles, Rowe (1709) grouped characters by sex. The present list modifies Rowe's order but retains the gist of his descriptions. Main characters are listed first, in order of appearance, except with the twins paired. Secondary characters, starting with the Jailer, are presented in order of appearance.

1   EGEON Although the Folio entry SD (TLN 2) and the Duke's address (TLN 7, 1.1.3) identify this character as the '*Merchant of Siracusa*', editors since Rowe have employed the SP 'Ægeon' or 'Egeon'. The name *Egeon* (1.1.157) arises from the character's wandering through, and weathering by, the Aegean Sea in search of his lost son (see 1.1.132–6). That sea takes

134

its name from the mythical King Aegeus, the father of Theseus (see 7n.). Aegeus, long separated from his son, failed at first to recognize him at reunion, and later drowned himself in the mistaken belief that Theseus had perished. Additionally, Riehle argues, 'Egeon' may partly derive from the Latin verb *egere* (*egeo* in the first-person present indicative), 'to be poor, destitute, in need of something' (177; see also King, 12, n. 2), and thus reflects the character's circumstances in the first scene. F's generic SP, treating Egeon as essentially a merchant, eventually breaks down. In Act 5, the Folio SP changes from '*Mar.Fat.*' (for '*Merchant Father*', at TLN 1671) to '*Fa[ther]*.' (TLN 1762+), as Egeon's familial identity asserts precedence (see 5.1.195–6n.).

2   DUKE 'Duke' functions as a generalized term for ruler (*OED n.* 1a), more king than governor. The Duke's name, Solinus ('So-lie-nus'), occurs once, at 1.1.1. It probably derives from Gaius Julius Solinus, a third-century AD Roman writer. Solinus was the author of *Polyhistor* ('multi-history'), translated in 1587 by Arthur Golding as *The Excellent and Pleasant Work of Julius Solinus Polyhistor*. Originally published in Latin in Venice, 1473, *Polyhistor* is a compendium of historical geography, sometimes exotic; it was often consulted in the Middle Ages and later. The early occurrence of Solinus in *CE* may alert the spectator to be prepared for the 'diversities of customes of unknown nations' and even for the fabulous (Solinus, Dedicatory Epistle). Contrastingly, Dutton argues that the name Solinus evokes contemporary Turkish rulers – Suleiman, Selim or Selimus (316). An Athenian character named Solinus appears in 4.1 of John Lyly's *Campaspe* (pub. 1584).

3, 4 ANTIPHOLUS The name Antipholus ('An-tif-o-lus') is given to each of the twin masters, enabling much of *CE*'s comic confusion. In Plautus' *Menaechmi*, the twins are distinguished at birth as Menaechmus and Sosicles; after the former is stolen as a child, the latter is memorially renamed Menaechmus (see

4n.). Shakespeare may wish the audience to assume a like explanation in *CE*. 'Antipholus' is preferable to 'Antipholis' (although both spellings occur), because it rhymes with another *-us* word, *ruinous* (3.2.2, 4) (Wright, 1.518). Of the name's sources, Foakes observes candidly, 'we do not know where Shakespeare found it' (2, n. 1). Sidney's *Arcadia* makes for the best candidate (Cuningham), with Terence, Lucian and Rich as other possibilities. Both the old and the new *Arcadia* contain the story of the Princess Erona (the name suggestive of 'error'), who, after foolishly scorning Cupid, falls madly and unsuitably in love with her nurse's son, the unworthy Antiphilus. Initially, their marriage is prevented; later Antiphilus betrays her, and by the end Erona comes to stand for wrongheaded and unrequited love. Variants of the name also appear in Roman comedy. A romantic heroine named Antiphila figures in Terence's *Heauton Timorumenos* (the servant name Dromo also occurs there; see 5, 6n.); a lover called 'Antipho' figures in Terence's *Phormio*; and his *Eunuchus* contains a friend of that same name (see Baldwin, *Genetics*, 101). More recently, Dutton has argued that 'Antipholus' derives from a famous classical essay by Lucian, *Calumnia non temere credendum* ('On not believing rashly in slander'), widely translated in the 15th and 16th centuries. The only proposed source that connects a variant of the name Antipholus with the city of Ephesus, *Calumnia* contains an anecdote about Antiphilis slandering Apelles of Ephesus. Slander functions as an important subtheme in *CE* (see Dutton, 309, 310–13). A hitherto unnoticed possible source is Barnabe Rich's prose romance *The Adventures of Brusanus, Prince of Hungaria* (1592). The romance's main hero is Antipholus, Prince of Illyria, a valorous knight who sets out to find and recover his eloped sister, Moderna. In composing *Twelfth Night*, Shakespeare drew from a tale in *Rich's Farewell to the Military Profession* (1581).

3   ANTIPHOLUS OF SYRACUSE This twin brother's home city corresponds to that of

the twins in Plautus' *Men.* (on Syracuse, see pp. 51–2). Oddly, Antipholus of Syracuse is identified in two of F's entry SDs as '*Antipholis Erotes*' (TLN 162) and '*Antipholis Errotis*' (TLN 394). The Latinate but unknown terms *Erotes/Errotis* may imperfectly recollect some form of the Latin *errare* (*erratus* in the nominative past participle); Foakes speculates that the two cognomens are a corruption of *erraticus* (Latin 'wandering'), although they are difficult to account for (xi–xii, xxvi–xxvii). The echoes of *erraticus* recall Plautus' itinerant Menaechmus (just as the echoes of *surreptus* in the SDs for Ephesian Antipholus recall Menaechmus' stolen brother; see 4n., and also Foakes, xxvii). The Latin infinitive *errare* means not only 'to wander' but 'to float or drift', 'to be in doubt', 'to go astray', 'to think or act in error' or 'to stray from the path of virtue' (*OLD errare*). Many, perhaps all, of those definitions apply to Antipholus of Syracuse.

4   ANTIPHOLUS OF EPHESUS On Ephesus, see pp. 50–1. F names Antipholus of Ephesus as *Antipholis Sereptus* (TLN 273). The cognomen *Sereptus* recalls the Latin nominative past participle for 'stolen', *surreptus*, and undoubtedly refers to the brother in Plautus' *Men.* who was abducted and carried off to Epidamnus when the twins were children: '*alitus ille surrepticius*' (*Argumentum*, 7). In *Men.*, after the boy was stolen, his father died 'because of his grief' (Prologue, 35–6) and his grandfather decided to change the remaining son's name to that of his lost brother, Menaechmus. Throughout the Argument and Prologue in *Men.*, where the backstory is told, forms of *surripere* ('to steal', 'to snatch') appear multiple times in various conjugations. Shakespeare may have remembered the lost brother as 'Menaechmus Surreptus' and brought that mnemonic into *CE* for its analogous character (Warner's translation of *Men.* has nothing comparable). According to Clark & Glover, the stolen Menaechmus was commonly distinguished in the 16th century as 'Surreptus' (1.462; see also Foakes, xxvi).

5, 6 DROMIO The proximate source for the name Dromio (almost always pronounced as two syllables, Dròm-yo), is Lyly's farcical *Mother Bombie*, probably performed *c.* 1590 and published in 1594 (see Lyly, *MB*, 9). There, a character named Dromio is one of several prominently featured witty servants who seek to outscheme their masters and win freedom from indenture. With its identity tricks and surprise revelations of birth, *Mother Bombie* shows a debt to Roman comedy. The servant name Dromo occurs in several of Terence's plays (*Andria*, *Heauton Timorumenos* and *Adelphoe*); the dialogue of Plautus' *Asinaria* also mentions a servant named Dromo. In Greek, *dromos* means 'running track' or 'race-course'. Thus, 'Dromio' might suggest 'runner', recalling the stock 'running servant' or *servus currens* of Latin comedy (see 2.2.200n., on *Dromio, thou snail*). The connection is made specifically when Syracusan Dromio enters out of breath from *running fast* (4.2.30) (see also 3.2.70.1).

7   ADRIANA The name probably alludes to the Adriatic Sea, which lies to the east of Italy, just as 'Egeon' recalls the Aegean Sea (see 1n.). Adriana repeats Antipholus of Syracuse's sea-image of the drop of water (see 2.2.131–5 and n.), and she is linked variously to water by her weeping (see 2.1.114 and n.). The name also hints at a negative stereotype: Petruchio in *TS* says that he would not fear a shrewish wife were she as 'rough' as 'the swelling Adriatic seas' (1.2.73, 74). For a less obvious source, the stem of 'Adriana', *adro*, derives from an Italian variant of 'dark', facilitating a dark/light contrast with Luciana (see Feldman, 119; Levith, 69). Other associations have been proposed: for example, that the name is a variant spelling for the classical character Ariadne, alluded to elsewhere by Shakespeare and known for her weeping complaint at Theseus' abandonment of her (as at *TGV* 4.4.167–8; see Riehle, 179–81); and that 'Adriana' recalls the Roman emperor Hadrian who refounded Ephesus, first settled by Amazonian women who refused male domination (see Maguire, 369, 364–5).

8 LUCIANA The first syllable of 'Luciana' suggests Italian *luce*, or 'light' (Latin *lux*), supporting the idea of a light/dark contrast in the appearances of Luciana and Adriana (see 7n.). Comparable pairings occur in other of Shakespeare's early comedies (see *Var.*, 6). Syracusan Antipholus refers to Luciana as a *fair sun* with *golden hairs* (3.2.56, 48). More complicated derivations include the possibility that 'Luciana' may recall 'Lucina' in Lawrence Twine's prose translation (*c.* 1576) of the Apollonius of Tyre story and that the character, to the extent that she exposes folly, may allude to the Roman satirical essayist Lucian (see Riehle, 183–97). Like 'Adriana', 'Luciana' is Italianate. In F, '*Luciana*' appears consistently except for one entrance SD (TLN 786), where she is called '*Iuliana*', and the subsequent SP (TLN 787) where she is identified as '*Iulia.*'. For these exceptions, no satisfactory explanation has been found.

9 ABBESS The Abbess's name, Emilia (in F, '*Æmilia*' at TLN 1828, 1831, 1838), also occurs in *Oth*, *WT* and *TNK*. That last play dramatizes Chaucer's *The Knight's Tale*, in which Emilia is the beloved of two rival cousins. The name carries the aura of romance narrative.

10 JAILER See 16n.

11 FIRST MERCHANT To F's *Marchant* (TLN 162), Dyce added 'First' in order to distinguish the character from the other merchant who appears in Act 4 (see 4.1.0.1n.). F's SPs initially use *Mer.* and subsequently *E.Mar.*, with *E.* presumably signifying 'Ephesian'. On this character's lone appearance, see 1.2.26n., on *five o'clock*.

12 ANGELO The goldsmith's name evokes gold, since in Elizabethan times an 'angel' was a gold coin (introduced in 1465), worth 10 or 11 shillings and stamped on one side with the image of St Michael (and on the other with an Elizabethan galley; see Fig. 9, p. 44). F introduces the character as '*Angelo*' (SD at TLN 617), but after 3.1., his SPs name him as '*Gold*[*smith*].', his identity absorbed into his type. Shakespeare also gives the name Angelo to the hypocritically righteous deputy in *MM*.

13 BALTHAZAR The name Balthazar has an association with feasting, fitting for a prospective dinner guest in 3.1, the character's only scene. Balthazar (i.e. Belshazzar) was the pagan King of Babylon, named in Daniel, 5.1, who 'made a great feast' and 'dranke wine before the thousand' of his princes, using gold and silver vessels that his father had taken as spoils from the Temple. Voragine, in *The Golden Legend*, also gives 'Balthasar' as an alternative name for one of the three magi (1.79). The name recurs for servants or attendants in *MA*, *MV* and *RJ*.

14 LUCE The name (pronounced as one syllable) appears only in 3.1. Critics have generally accepted the argument that the kitchen-maid whom Syracusan Dromio describes in 3.2 as Nell is the same character as Luce (see 3.2.110n.). Later Dromio will refer to her as Dowsabel (4.1.110). 'Luce' shares a syllable with 'Luciana'; perhaps to avoid confusion, Shakespeare switched to 'Nell' in 3.2, where the character functions as Luciana's parodic double (see 3.2.75–149n.). Maguire (369–70) associates 'Nell' with other sexually forward females in Shakespeare, such as Helena in *MND* and Helen of Troy in *TC*, with a sexual pun on Luce/loose (for 'loose' as 'unchaste', see Williams, *Glossary*, 193–4). Wells cites Bland's suggestion that 'Luce' refers topically to a famous London brothel-keeper, Lucy 'Negro' Morgan (see Bland, 94).

15 SECOND MERCHANT This character's entrance SD in F (TLN 981) reads '*a Merchant*'. As early as 1741, the stage role was identified as 'Second Merchant' (Scouten, 3.942), and it appeared again in Thomas Hull's 1793 adaptation. The editorial 'Second' was subsequently introduced by Dyce to distinguish this merchant from the one in 1.2 (see 1.2.0.1–2 t.n.).

16 OFFICER The Officer (or *sergeant*; see 4.2.55, 60) is introduced in 4.1 in relation to debt collection (see 4.1.6n., on *officer*). Later, in 4.4, with Ephesian Antipholus under arrest, F identifies him as a *Iailor* (TLN 1280; see 4.4.0.2, 110, 143), the term perhaps following the character's changed function. In Act 1, a *Jailer* guards Egeon

(1.1.0.2). That Jailer and the Officer of Act 4 are sometimes treated in production as the same character, thus linking the story of Egeon to that of the Antipholuses.

18 DOCTOR PINCH Pinch's name reflects his pinched, sour, *lean-faced* look (5.1.238), a key to his humourless and zealous character. Pinch is also described as *hungry*, *threadbare* and *needy* (5.1.238, 240, 241), so that he is 'pinched' in both face and pocket (see *OED* pinch *v*. 10c). Doctor Pinch engages in 'pinching' when he binds Ephesian Antipholus and Dromio. Syracusan Dromio has feared that Adriana and Luciana, as witches, will 'suck our breath or pinch us black and blue' (2.2.198); that fear comes true in his encounter with Adriana's agent, Doctor Pinch. Pinch was probably played by John Sinkler (or Sincler or Sinklo), a character actor notable for his thinness. See 4.4.40.2n., 5.1.238–42n. and Appendix 3, pp. 352–3.

THE COMEDY OF
ERRORS

1.1   *Enter* [Solinus,] *the* DUKE *of Ephesus, with*
[EGEON,] *the* Merchant of Syracuse, Jailer
and other Attendants.

EGEON
Proceed, Solinus, to procure my fall,
And by the doom of death end woes and all.
DUKE
Merchant of Syracusa, plead no more:
I am not partial to infringe our laws.
The enmity and discord which of late   5

1.1 The Folio playtext begins with *Actus primus, Scena prima*, although F's Act 1 contains no subsequent scene divisions; the same is so for Acts 3, 4 and 5, while Act 2 lacks any scene designation. Theobald established the now-traditional scene 'changes'; Capell added the numbers. The location is unspecified; Theobald envisioned a formal chamber of the Duke's palace, as do most productions; Capell imagined a 'public place'.

1 **Proceed** 'institute and carry on a legal action' (*OED v.* 2c); or simply 'continue' (*OED* 4a); the scene opens in mid-conversation (cf. *TGV* 1.1.1).
Solinus See List of Roles, 2n.
procure 'bring about, cause, effect' (*OED v.* 4a); often used in a legal sense (see e.g. *OED* procurator *n.*[1] 7). The Duke both prosecutes and judges.

1–2 **fall . . . all** Here and again at 26–7, 94–5 and 157–8, Egeon employs couplets. The first begins and the last ends the scene, but

the middle two suggest premature closures, as if he did not want to continue.

2 **doom of death** sentence of death; a phrase echoed widely elsewhere, e.g. *Tit* 3.1.24, *H5* 3.6.44. The concrete, monosyllabic Anglo-Saxon *doom* and *death* jolt against the more abstract, polysyllabic and Latinate *Proceed* and *procure* (1), the two lines referring differently to the same eventuality.
woes i.e. my woes; repeated at 27; cf. 5.1.310 and n.

3, 36 **Syracusa** common, if slightly archaic EM spelling. On Syracuse, see pp. 51–2.

4 **partial** inclined (*OED adj.* 5), with the secondary suggestion of appearing *partial* towards a party in a controversy (see *OED* 4a)
infringe transgress, contravene

5–10 'The hostility [between Ephesus and Syracuse] that recently arose from the spiteful violence of your duke (who, with his cruel laws, has executed fair-dealing merchants of our city because they could

---

1.1] *(Actus primus, Scena prima.)*; ACT I. SCENE I. *Rowe*   0.1 Solinus] *Collier*   0.2 EGEON] *Capell (Rowe subst.)*   Syracuse] *Collier*[4]; *Siracusa F*   1+ SP] *Capell (Rowe subst.); Marchant., Mer., Merch. F*
1 Solinus] *Salinus F2*   3+ SP] *(Duke., Duk.)*   3 Syracusa] *Syracuse F4*

Sprang from the rancorous outrage of your duke
To merchants, our well-dealing countrymen,
Who, wanting guilders to redeem their lives,
Have sealed his rigorous statutes with their bloods,
Excludes all pity from our threatening looks;   10
For, since the mortal and intestine jars
'Twixt thy seditious countrymen and us,

not pay his fines), rules out any pity that might make me reduce my sentence against you.' This speech, along with 4, establishes the Duke's internal conflict, for he will become progressively more sympathetic; see 142–54; 5.1.390. The plot device of inter-city war recurs in *TS* (see 4.2.81–5); see also *TN* 3.3.25–9. Gascoigne's *Supposes* (1566) offered a possible model; see p. 91.

5   **enmity and discord** rhetorical *synonymia*, the same idea repeated in different words

6   **Sprang** modernized from F's 'Sprung'. Shakespeare employs both past tense variants of 'to spring' (e.g. 'sprang'st', *3H6* 5.7.31; 'sprung', *2H4* 1.1.111).
     rancorous outrage ranc'rous; malicious and violent injury (*OED* rancorous *adj.* 3, first citation, applied to an action)
     duke ruler (*OED n.* 1a)

8   **wanting** lacking
     guilders gold or silver coins current in the Netherlands and Germany; also a general term for money (again at 4.1.4), occurring only in *CE*. This is the first of many references to measures of economic value, including *angel*, *bond*, *carat*, *ducat*, *mark*, *note*, *present money* and *rag* (see Fischer, 170). One need not be overly precise about the worth of *CE*'s currencies.
     redeem ransom (*OED v.* 3; also at 4.4.84), initiating the play's Christian resonances

9   **sealed . . . bloods** 'ratified his tyrannical laws with the forfeit of their lives', with a play on 'seal' as 'to place a seal upon (a document)' (*OED v.*[1] 1a) and perhaps as

'to decide irrevocably (the fate of a person or thing)' (*OED* 1g; *OED* does not record this use before 1810, but cf. 'seal'd up my expectation', *2H4* 4.5.103). Red sealing-wax was used on Elizabethan documents (Wells).
     rigorous rig'rous; harsh, cruel
     bloods blood

10   **Excludes** exclude. In EM English, co-ordinated singular nouns, such as *enmity and discord* (5), are often viewed as one and given a singular verb ending, *-s* (Hope, 2.1.8a; Abbott, 333); cf. 87 and n., on *Was*; 1.2.76.

11   **intestine jars** quarrels between the two cities; i.e. internal to the region (see *OED* intestine *adj.* 1); Shakespeare's only other use of *intestine* refers to civil warfare (*1H4* 1.1.12). Ephesus and Syracuse are independent city-states, but *intestine* posits them as both within the Greek political sphere (Wells). Because Syracuse was ethnically Dorian and Ephesus Ionian, some tension between the two Greek strains may be implied. According to Herodotus, Dorians were given to wandering, while the Ionians were more settled (1.56) – like the play's Syracusans and Ephesians.

12   **seditious** 'factious with tumult; turbulent' (Johnson, *Dictionary*), a broader meaning than the modern one: engaged in inciting 'revolt against constituted authority' (*OED adj.* 1a). Together, *intestine* (11) and *seditious* imply some affinity between the two cities.

6 Sprang] *Oxf*[1]*;* Sprung *F*

It hath in solemn synods been decreed,
Both by the Syracusans and ourselves,
To admit no traffic to our adverse towns.   15
Nay, more: if any born at Ephesus
Be seen at Syracusan marts and fairs;
Again, if any Syracusan born
Come to the Bay of Ephesus, he dies,
His goods confiscate to the Duke's dispose,   20
Unless a thousand marks be levied
To quit the penalty and ransom him.
Thy substance, valued at the highest rate,
Cannot amount unto a hundred marks:
Therefore, by law thou art condemned to die.   25

13 **synods** councils or assemblies; typically used in a religious or ecclesiastical sense, e.g. 'heavenly synod' (*AYL* 3.2.150)
14 ***Syracusans** modernized from F's '*Siracusians*' (here and subsequently). The *-an* form was used in the 16th and 17th centuries and takes the same metre as the *-ian* spelling (see *OED adj.* and *n.* Derivatives).
15 to 'allow no trade between our hostile towns' (Ard²); perhaps 'T'admit'
adverse opposing, actively hostile (*OED adj.* 1a); 'adverse town' occurs in *TN* 5.1.84; cf. *KJ* 4.2.172.
16 **any** anyone
Ephesus See pp. 50–1.
17 ***at Syracusan** for F's 'at any *Siracusian*'. To regularize the verse, Pope dropped 'any'. The compositor may have inserted a gratuitous 'any' because of the visual attraction of the word in the lines before and after, the phenomenon of 'eye-skip'.
marts public marketplaces (*OED n.³* 1a); see 1.2.27n. The play mentions *marts* and *mart* 11 times; most of its action will occur in the main Ephesian mart.
18 **Again** in return (Crystal & Crystal *adv.* 1)
any Syracusan born anyone born in Syracuse

20 **confiscate** confiscated (see *OED adj.* 1); here pronounced with the accent on the second syllable, though not so at 1.2.2
dispose disposal (*OED n.* 3); cf. 'undisposed' at 1.2.80 (and see n.).
21 **a thousand marks** The mark, a common 16th-century European coin, was worth two-thirds of a pound sterling in early modern England (*OED n.* 2a). '[O]ne thousand marks is a large sum' (Fischer, 93). Cf. e.g. *TS* 5.2.34, *2H6* 5.1.79. See also 1.2.81 and n., 4.1.21 and n.
levied levièd; collected, as of a debt (*OED levy v.* 1b)
22 **quit** remit (*OED v.* 4); cf. *MV* 4.1.381.
***and ransom** F reads 'and to ransome'; F2 removed 'to' presumably as metrically disruptive. The F compositor might have inserted it to create a parallelism with *To quit*.
23 **substance** possessions, wealth; secondarily, one's being or essence (see *OED n.* 2, 1), implying an equivalence between a sum of money and a human life. In Shakespeare, *substance* often refers to a person's embodied self; e.g. *TGV* 4.2.123, *1H6* 2.3.38.

14 Syracusans] *Pope; Siracusians F*   15 To admit] T'admit *F2*   17 at] *Pope;* at any *F*   17, 18, 28 Syracusan] *Pope; Siracusian F*   22 and] *F2;* and to *F*

EGEON

> Yet this my comfort: when your words are done,
> My woes end likewise with the evening sun.

DUKE

> Well, Syracusan, say in brief the cause
> Why thou departed'st from thy native home,
> And for what cause thou cam'st to Ephesus.   30

EGEON

> A heavier task could not have been imposed
> Than I to speak my griefs unspeakable.
> Yet that the world may witness that my end
> Was wrought by nature, not by vile offence,

---

26 **this** this is

27 **woes** See 2n., on *woes*.

evening sun the first of the play's many time markers (and perhaps an oblique reference to Egeon's agedness; cf. *weary sun*, 1.2.7). As in classical drama, the action will occur during one day, with all the plot-lines converging at Egeon's scheduled execution time, five o'clock. See 150–5; 1.2.26n., on *five o'clock*; and 5.1.118 and n., on *dial . . . five*. See also 100n., on *five*. On time, see pp. 45–6.

28 **say . . . cause** 'briefly tell the reason', quibbling on *brief* as 'writing issued by legal authority' (*OED n.* 1) and on *cause* as both motive (*OED n.* 2) and 'matter before a court' (*OED* 7, 8). The Duke invites Egeon to defend himself judicially (cf. 30; see *OED* cause *n.* 3), just as his *Well, Syracusan* prolongs the action and prepares for his sympathetic day's reprieve.

31–2 These two lines (employing rhetorical *adynaton*, a stringing together of impossibilities) were compared by Theobald to the exordium of Aeneas' speech to Dido: '*Infandum, regina, iubes renovare dolorem*' ('Beyond all words, O queen, is the grief

thou bidst me revive') (*Aen.*, 2.3; *infandum*, meaning 'monstrous' or 'unspeakable', figures importantly in *Aen.*). See 94 and n., on *came – . . . more*. Both Egeon and Aeneas tell stories – of losing a wife, wandering over the seas and suffering shipwreck in a storm – to the ruler of the place where they have landed. On *CE* and *Aen.*, see Baldwin, *Small Latine*, 2.485–7. Egeon's sentiment was also quasi-proverbial: 'The revealing of griefs is a renewing of sorrow' (Tilley, R89).

32 **Than I** 'than for me'; EM English sometimes substituted 'I' for 'me' (Hope, 1.3.2a); cf. e.g. 'no child but I', *AYL* 1.2.17. **griefs** Cf. 2 and n., on *woes*.

33 **my end** Elizabethans often used 'mine' instead of 'my' before a word beginning with a vowel, but practice was changing (*CE* employs both); *my* 'carries emphasis' (Hope, 1.3.2a); cf. 1.2.14.

34 **by nature** either 'by a natural event, by the course of providence' (Hanmer) or 'by natural affection' (Malone), i.e. for his lost son. Hanmer's notion of the providential squares with *Fortune* (105), *misfortunes* (119) and Egeon's fatalism. Cf. 2.2.75, 107.

---

26 this] 'this' *(Walker, Versification)*   29 home,] *Rowe subst.;* home? *F*   34 nature] fortune *Collier² (Collier, Notes)*

142

I'll utter what my sorrow gives me leave.   35
In Syracusa was I born, and wed
Unto a woman, happy but for me,
And by me, had not our hap been bad.
With her I lived in joy; our wealth increased
By prosperous voyages I often made   40
To Epidamium, till my factor's death,
And the great care of goods at random left,
Drew me from kind embracements of my spouse;
From whom my absence was not six months old
Before herself (almost at fainting under   45

36–139 Egeon's exposition replaces the Prologue in *Men*. Directors uneasy about its length have often cut lines, employed mimes (e.g. National Theatre, 2012) or had the merchant illustrate the story with props. Nonetheless, the unaided speech stands up well. Shuffled objects and miming can distract from the section's rhetorical values, Egeon's descent into sorrow and the Duke's growth in sympathy.

37 **happy . . . me** 'happy except in having me as a husband'. Egeon sees himself as dogged by misfortune; *happy* means 'joyous' (see 39), while its punning second sense, 'fortunate', prepares for *hap* in 38, dual meanings that *CE* explores; *hap* and its derivates function importantly in this scene (see 38, 113, 120, 138, 140, 141), suggesting an agency that is more than accidental. See also 1.2.40 and n., on *unhappy*; 5.1.60 and 284 and nn., on *Haply*. See also p. 70.

38 **by me** through me (Folg²). Egeon means either (1) happy except for the effect of my presence and my agency (making him the instrument of his wife's unhappiness); or (2) happy in her life with me except for misfortune. Both read awkwardly.

me, The line is one syllable short. F reads 'me;', the partial stop after *me* perhaps suggesting a dramatic pause (for a tonal change) that takes the place of a stressed syllable; F2's 'too' after *me* was followed by editors for two centuries.

hap fortune or luck, playing on *happy* (37); rhetorical *polyptoton*, the repetition of a word using the same root but a different stem (see also n., and 130–1 and n.); on *hap-* words, see 37n.

41 **Epidamium** with *-ium* monosyllabic. The name alludes to Epidamnus, the location of Plautus' *Men.*; see p. 50. On F's *Epidamium* instead of Pope's influential emendation, 'Epidamnum', see LN.

factor's mercantile agent's; cf. *R3* 3.7.134.

42 **care** Egeon uses forms of *care* three more times in this scene (78, 84, 124) and *cares* at 5.1.310.

at random 'in a neglected or untended condition' (*OED* random *n.* P2b)

43 **Drew me** i.e. to Epidamium

45 **herself** she; the reflexive pronoun could function as an emphatic personal pronoun (Blake, 3.2.2.3).

at to the point of; *at* can 'indicate a point reached' (Blake, 5.4.2).

38 me,] *Cam;* me; *F;* me too, *F2;* me, – *Ard²;* me happy, *Oxf (Hills)*   39 our] oür *Keightley*
41 Epidamium] *Epidamnium* / *Rowe; Epidamnum* / *Pope;* Epidamnus *Oxf¹*   42 the . . . care . . . left]
Theobald; he . . . care . . . left *F;* he . . . store . . . leaving *F2*

The pleasing punishment that women bear)
Had made provision for her following me,
And soon and safe arrived where I was.
There had she not been long but she became
A joyful mother of two goodly sons, 50
And, which was strange, the one so like the other
As could not be distinguished but by names.
That very hour, and in the self-same inn,
A meaner woman was delivered
Of such a burden, male twins, both alike. 55
Those, for their parents were exceeding poor,
I bought, and brought up to attend my sons.
My wife, not meanly proud of two such boys,
Made daily motions for our home return.

46 **pleasing punishment** i.e. pregnancy, expressed as an oxymoron; child-bearing pains were considered women's punishments inherited from Eve at the Fall: 'In sorowe shalt thou bring forthe children' (Genesis, 3.16).

47 **following** foll'wing

48 **arrived** arrivèd

49 **had . . . became** The repetition of *she* with the reversed subject–verb order reflects rhetorical *antimetabole*.

50 **goodly** handsome; echoed in *pretty* at 72; cf. *fair* at 5.1.343.

52 **As** i.e. that they; sometimes used as a relative pronoun (Hope, 1.4.2)
names which we never learn

54 ***meaner** of inferior social class. F's 'mean' is emended here to Delius's unobtrusive *meaner*, regularizing the metre. The sense remains unchanged, since Shakespeare sometimes uses *meaner* non-comparatively as a synonym for *mean*, indicating lower class standing, as in *TS* 1.1.205.
delivered deliverèd

55 **burden . . . alike** The 'meaner woman was delivered' of the same burden, identical

male twins, as was Egeon's wife. F2's punctuation, 'burthen, Maletwins', is preferred here over F's 'burthen Male, twins' because *male twins* creates the sharper sense, while 'burden male' was not a familiar collocation (Oxf[1]). Associated with pain and birth, *burden* will return resonantly at 5.1.343 (see n., on *at a burden*), 402; cf. also 2.1.36. Cf. 107 and n., on *burdened*.

57 The alliteration and rhyme of *bought* and *brought* add rhetorical artfulness. Other repetitions or echoes in 1.1 include *meaner*, *meanly* (54, 58); *did*, *Did* (66, 67); *weepings*, *Weeping* (70, 71); *fastened*, *Fastened* (79, 85); and *Was carried*, *Was carried* (87, 109); see 66–7n., 70–1n., 84n. For related examples, see 1.2.47–50 and n.; 4.4.30–40 and n.; 5.1.404, 406 and n.
attend wait upon as servants

58 **not meanly** not moderately, i.e. greatly (*OED* meanly *adv*.[1] 2); contrasted to *meaner* (54) for the rhetorical effect of *antistasis*

59 **motions** suggestions, proposals (*OED* n. 13a); cf. *TS* 1.2.278, *MW* 1.1.54.

54 meaner] *Delius (Walker, Critical);* meane *F;* poore meane *F2;* mean-born *Oxf;* mean young *Oxf[1]*
55 burden, male twins] *F2 (*burthen, Maletwins*);* burthen Male, twins *F*   twins,] *Capell;* twins *F*

Unwilling, I agreed. Alas! too soon   60
We came aboard.
A league from Epidamium had we sailed
Before the always wind-obeying deep
Gave any tragic instance of our harm.
But longer did we not retain much hope,   65
For what obscured light the heavens did grant
Did but convey unto our fearful minds
A doubtful warrant of immediate death;
Which, though myself would gladly have embraced,
Yet the incessant weepings of my wife,   70
Weeping before for what she saw must come,

60–1 *These two lines constitute one extra-metrical line in F. This edition, like most, follows Pope's division, yielding a two-foot line at 61 that invites a pause to raise narrative suspense for Egeon's long exposition of catastrophe (cf. 38 and n., on *me,*). Shakespeare may be imitating Virgil's famous half-line (e.g. *Aen.*, 2.66, 233), which some Renaissance commentators viewed as a poetic device to excite emotion. Short lines occur often and variously in Shakespeare; cf. e.g. 1.2.16. Alternatively here, some portion of the text may have been omitted in the typesetting process.

60 **too soon** echoed at 1.2.2 (see n., on *goods too soon*)

62–95, 98–120 The shipwreck story is inspired by the Apollonius of Tyre tradition and by biblical and romance narratives (see pp. 87–9). The image of shipwreck engaged Shakespeare's imagination, as in *3H6*, a play rife with sea and shipwreck images (e.g. at 5.4.3–38), or in later plays such as *MV, TN, Oth, Per, WT* and *Tem.*

62 **A league** about three miles; the term typically occurs 'in poetic or rhetorical statements of distance' (*OED n.*[1]); see also 100, and e.g. *MND* 1.1.159.

63 **wind-obeying** a complex phrase in a rare

pre-modifying position; cf. 'cormorant devouring Time' (*LLL* 1.1.4), 'too hard-a-keeping oath' (*LLL* 1.1.65) and 'ne'er-yet-beaten horse' (*AC* 3.1.33) (Hope, 1.2.9). **deep** i.e. deep sea (*OED n.* 3a)

64 **instance** evidence; sign (*OED n.* 7) or omen, with *tragic* functioning as a transferred epithet (or *hypallage*): 'evidence of tragic harm', subtly elevating the tone

66 **obscured ... heavens** obscurèd ... heav'ns

66–7 **did ... Did** Repetition of words in close proximity (rhetorical *diacope*) can express heightened emotion (see 57n.); cf. 2.2.125 and n. A chiasmic *d*-alliteration continues in *doubtful* and *death* (68).

68 **doubtful warrant** dreadful proof (*OED* doubtful *adj.* 3; warrant *n.*[1] 5a)

70–4 Lines 70 and 72 are parallel in grammar and in sense; after each comes a line of amplifying explanation (rhetorical *aetiologia*) that builds suspense for the climactic change at 74 (*Forced . . . delays*).

70–2 On the image of a soul crying in adversity, cf. 2.1.34–41.

70–1 **weepings ... Weeping** repetition for effect, rhetorically close to *anadiplosis*; see 57n.

71 **before** beforehand. The homonymic *before for* slows the line.

60–1] *Pope; one line F*   60 agreed. Alas!] *F4 subst.;* agreed, alas, *F*

And piteous plainings of the pretty babes,
That mourned for fashion, ignorant what to fear,
Forced me to seek delays for them and me.
And this it was, for other means was none: 75
The sailors sought for safety by our boat
And left the ship, then sinking-ripe, to us.
My wife, more careful for the latter-born,
Had fastened him unto a small spare mast
Such as seafaring men provide for storms;   80
To him one of the other twins was bound,
Whilst I had been like heedful of the other.
The children thus disposed, my wife and I,
Fixing our eyes on whom our care was fixed,
Fastened ourselves at either end the mast,   85

72 **plainings** utterances of grief (*OED n.*), perhaps as a tragic archaism; *plainings* contributes to the line's three alliterating plosives; cf. the softer *w* alliterations in 68–71.

73 **for fashion** i.e. in imitation of their mother; cf. *AYL* 3.2.255.

74 **delays** postponements of the looming disaster

75 **And ... ¹was** 'and this is what happened'. The stock phrase heightens anticipation as it delays the narration; cf. *R3* 1.1.62 (Ard²).

76 **sought ... boat** i.e. sought to save themselves by taking to the ship's small boat (cf. *TN* 1.2.9–11)

77 **sinking-ripe** ready to sink, like water-laden ripe fruit (*OED* ripe *adj.* 1d). Gerund + *ripe* occurs similarly elsewhere in Shakespeare: as in 'weeping-ripe' in *3H6* 1.4.172, *LLL* 5.2.274 (Ard²); cf. the proverb 'Soon ripe, soon rotten' (Dent, R133).

78–82 The wife fastened her younger son and a slave twin to one end of a small unused mast, or 'jury-mast' (Oxf¹); Egeon did the

same at the other end with the remaining two children; cf. *TN* 1.2.14.

78 **careful** See 42 and n., on *care*.
latter-born i.e. second-born; the wife takes traditional maternal care for her younger child. Because Egeon later says that he kept his *youngest boy* (124), some editors have emended F's *latter* to 'elder'.

81 **bound** the first occurrence of this narratively and metaphorically important word, used variously; see 1.1.133; 4.1.3, 33; 4.4.95, 128, 147; 5.1.127.2, 145, 291, 294, 305, 338, 339. Also associated with *bond*; see 4.1.13n.; 5.1.339n., on *bond*.

82 **like** likewise
other i.e. other two twins

84 exemplifying rhetorical *polyptoton* (see 38n., on *hap*) and *epanalepsis* (repetition at the end of the clause of the word with which it begins); *Fixing, Fastened* (85) and *floating* (86) create a rhetorical unit that conveys the action; see 57n.
care See 42 and n.

75 was, for] *Rowe;* was: (for *F*   none:] *Ard¹;* none) *F;* none. *Rowe*   77 sinking-ripe] *(*sinking ripe*), F2*
78 latter-born] *(*latter borne*), Steevens²*   79 fastened] *(*fastned*)*   85 Fastened] *(*Fastned*)*

And floating straight, obedient to the stream,
Was carried towards Corinth, as we thought.
At length the sun, gazing upon the earth,
Dispersed those vapours that offended us,
And by the benefit of his wished light   90
The seas waxed calm, and we discovered
Two ships from far, making amain to us:
Of Corinth that, of Epidaurus this.
But ere they came – O, let me say no more!
Gather the sequel by that went before.   95

DUKE

Nay, forward, old man; do not break off so,

---

86 **straight** immediately (*OED adv.* C2a); also
at 3.2.190; 4.1.102; 4.2.62; 4.4.57, 141.
87 **Was** with *wife and I* (83) as its subject; see
10n.
carried carrièd
87, 93 **Corinth** Corinth, in the Peloponnese,
was an ancient Greek city and a major trading centre: 'it was the greattest marte towne
in all the worlde' (Cooper, *Thesaurus*, sig.
G1ʳ). Corinth was also the base for St
Paul's early missionary activities in Greece
and Macedonia (see Acts, 18.1–18).
88 **At length** in time; repeated at 112
gazing staring (*OED v.* 2); forms of 'gaze'
occur seven times in *CE*; cf. especially
3.2.57 and n.; also 1.2.13; 3.2.56; 5.1.53,
244.
89 **vapours . . . us** mists that assailed us (by
obscuring the light, as at 66) (see *OED*
vapours *n.* 2a); see also *VA* 184, *1H4*
1.2.202–3. Cf. the obscuring *mist* at
2.2.222.
offended vexed, annoyed (*OED v.* 5b); or
attacked or assailed (*OED* 6a), emphasizing
the sun's beneficent intervention (note
benefit, 90)
90 **wished** wished for
91 **discovered** discoverèd
92 **amain** at full speed (*OED adv.* 2)
93 With his deictic *that* and *this*, Egeon enters

imaginatively into his retelling of the providential rescue, intensifying his collapse
in the next line.
Epidaurus probably the Epidaurus on the
coast of the eastern Adriatic, rather than
the southern Epidaurus on the Aegean near
Corinth in the Peloponnese; see LN and
p. 52, nn. 1, 2. If the ship cited by Egeon
were travelling from Aegean Epidaurus,
then it would be coming from the same
direction as that from Corinth, whereas
Egeon's *that* and *this* imply different
directions. Geographical exactitude, however, is not essential.
94 **came – . . . more** Egeon breaks off
(rhetorical *aposiopesis*), overcome as he
re-experiences his sorrow, confirming his
inability 'to speak my griefs unspeakable'
(32); see 31–2n. His change in sentence
form exemplifies rhetorical *anacoluthon*.
O a 'crypto-direction', not so much a
specific word or sound as a signal to the
actor 'to sigh, groan, gasp, roar, weep' or
'make whatever noise was locally appropriate' (Honigmann, 123)
95 **sequel** after-consequence (*OED n.* 3)
that that which; cf. *TGV* 2.4.10.
96 **old man** The Duke's address has become
more personal, as opposed to 'Merchant of
Syracuse' (3).

---

93 Epidaurus] *F2; Epidarus F*   94 came – O,] *Rowe³ subst.;* came, oh *F*

147

For we may pity, though not pardon thee.

EGEON

O, had the gods done so, I had not now
Worthily termed them merciless to us;
For ere the ships could meet, by twice five leagues,   100
We were encountered by a mighty rock,
Which being violently borne upon,
Our helpful ship was splitted in the midst;
So that, in this unjust divorce of us,
Fortune had left to both of us alike   105
What to delight in, what to sorrow for.
Her part, poor soul, seeming as burdened
With lesser weight, but not with lesser woe,
Was carried with more speed before the wind,
And in our sight they three were taken up   110
By fishermen of Corinth, as we thought.
At length another ship had seized on us,

---

97 **pity . . . pardon** Shakespeare adopts a rhetorical technique – two words paralleled alliteratively and grammatically (rhetorical *isocolon*) but contrasted in meaning – made popular by Lyly; for similar examples, see 106, 108, 124, 128. The Duke's pity provides a model for emotional response to Egeon's story and explains his desire to hear the rest of the narrative.

98 ^{2}**had** would have (see Blake, 4.3.6)

99 **Worthily** deservedly, justly (*OED adv.* 3)

100 **ere . . . leagues** i.e. before the two ships could intersect with us, being a great distance away; *twice five leagues* is best taken poetically, since it is about 30 miles; on *leagues*, see 62n.

five This number recurs in *CE* regarding distance, time and amount, helping subtly to link aspects of the play. See 132; 1.2.26 and n., on *five o'clock*; 4.1.10; 4.4.13; 5.1.118. See also 27n., on *evening sun*.

101 **encountered** assailed, confronted

102 ***borne upon** thrust or pushed against (*OED* bear *v.*[1] III).

103 **helpful ship** i.e. the floating mast to which they clung, *helpful* because it saved their lives

splitted a common form; the word splits the line metrically; cf. 5.1.308 and n.; *2H6* 3.2.411.

104 **unjust** recalling *merciless* at 99

106 See 97n.

107 **as** as if

burdened burdenèd; recalling 55, but here the burden of woe

108 See 97n.; *lesser weight* because the wife weighs less than Egeon

111 **of Corinth** presumably the ship from Corinth sighted in 93

112 **another ship** the second ship, coming from Epidaurus

seized on taken possession of by force (*OED* seize *v.* 9a, 6a). Hints of aggression also occur in *reft* and *prey* (115). If the

---

102 upon] *Pope;* vp *F;* up upon *F2*   103 helpful] *(*helpfull*);* helpless *Rowe;* hopeful *Hudson^2 (Jervis)*

And, knowing whom it was their hap to save,
Gave healthful welcome to their shipwrecked guests,
And would have reft the fishers of their prey   115
Had not their bark been very slow of sail;
And therefore homeward did they bend their course.
Thus have you heard me severed from my bliss,
That by misfortunes was my life prolonged
To tell sad stories of my own mishaps.   120

DUKE

And for the sake of them thou sorrow'st for,
Do me the favour to dilate at full
What have befall'n of them and thee till now.

survivors had to pay for their rescue (see 113n.), their saviours would be only a little removed from pirates. In Shakespeare's time, piracy, kidnapping and prisoner-taking were common in the Mediterranean, where Spaniard vied with Englishman, and Turk with Christian.

113 **knowing . . . save** i.e. knowing that they had luckily saved a wealthy merchant capable of rewarding them; on *hap-* words, see 37n.

114 **healthful** health-giving

115 **reft . . . prey** The Epidaurian sailors would have 'robbed' (*OED* reave *v.*¹ 1) the Corinthians of their *prey*, Egeon's wife and children; alternatively, *reft* may mean 'rescued' (*OED* 6b); cf. *Reft* at 128. Cf. 2.1.40 and n.

116 ***bark** a small sailing vessel; sometimes applied to a Spanish fishing ship common in the Mediterranean (*OED n.*²); see also 3.2.155; 4.1.85, 99; 4.3.39. The image of the adventurous sea-tossed *bark* appears in *RJ* 3.5.130–7, *MV* 2.6.14–19.

118 **heard . . . bliss** 'heard how I was cut off from my happiness', but *heard me severed* may recall Egeon's threatened execution.

bliss supreme delight; heavenly joy (*OED n.* 2a, b), a powerful emotional expression about one's family that anticipates the play's ending

119 **That** 'so that' or 'such that'
misfortunes See 34n.

120 anticipating Richard's desire to 'tell sad stories of the death of kings' (*R2* 3.2.156; see Forker, 3.2.156 LN). Egeon's spared life now consists of retelling, Ancient Mariner-like, the pitiful tale of his misadventures; cf. e.g. *3H6* 1.4.160, *RJ* 5.3.309.
mishaps sufferings of misfortune (*OED n.* 3); cf. *mishap* (141); on *hap-* words, see 37n.; *mishap(s)* and *Hapless* (140) apply in *CE* exclusively to Egeon.

122 **dilate** 'relate, describe, or set forth at length; enlarge or expatiate upon' (*OED v.*² 4). In Shakespeare, *dilate* connotes delay, deferral and protraction of time (*OED v.*¹).

123 **What . . . of** 'what has become of' (see *OED* befall *v.* 6b), i.e. what things have happened to. *What* takes a plural verb because it refers to the fates of several people.

114 shipwrecked] *(ship-wrackt)*   116 bark] *F2*; backe *F*   121 sake] sakes *F2*   123 have] hath *F2*   thee] *F2*; they *F*

149

EGEON

My youngest boy, and yet my eldest care,
At eighteen years became inquisitive   125
After his brother, and importuned me
That his attendant, so his case was like,
Reft of his brother, but retained his name,
Might bear him company in the quest of him;
Whom whilst I laboured of a love to see,   130
I hazarded the loss of whom I loved.
Five summers have I spent in farthest Greece,

124 See 97n.
　　youngest boy Cf. 78, where the younger
　　twin is assigned to the care of the wife;
　　youngest rather than 'younger' presumably
　　to parallel the emphatic *eldest*.
　　care See 42 and n.
125 **inquisitive** Cf. 1.2.38 and n., on *Unseen,
　　inquisitive*.
126 **importuned** perhaps importunèd; solicited
　　pressingly and persistently (*OED v*. 3)
127 **attendant** i.e. Dromio of Syracuse. On the
　　Dromios' status, cf. *villain* (1.2.19 and n.,
　　96), *servants* (4.1.113) and *slave* (1.2.87
　　and n., on *slave*); see p. 40.
　　so ... like 'so much was his situation
　　like mine'. F2 emends *so* to 'for', but
　　Blake notes that *so* commonly occurred as
　　a conjunction in clauses of comparison
　　(5.3.2.9[a]; see also *OED* so *adv*. 9).
128 See 97n.
　　Reft robbed, deprived; see 115 and n.
　　retained his name The remaining brother
　　memorializes the lost brother by taking his
　　name, as in *Men*. (Prologue, 41–3).
129 **company** probably comp'ny
130 **Whom** i.e. the son lost with the wife
　　I ... love i.e. I was troubled [or burdened]
　　from my love (*OED* labour *v*. 15). Egeon's
　　loving desire to see his long-lost son was
　　a physical pain or burden suggestive
　　of childbirth; cf. 45–6; 5.1.400–6.

Shakespeare's male characters sometimes
express emotion in terms of maternal
feelings; see e.g. *WT* 4.4.666–7; also cf.
Sidney, *A&S*, 1.12.
130–1 **love ... loved** rhetorical *polyptoton*
　　(see 38n., on *hap*)
131 **whom** i.e. the remaining son
132–4 This speech is adapted from Plautus'
　　Men., where the slave Messenio announces
　　that for six years Sosicles Menaechmus
　　and he have searched for the stolen
　　brother: 'We've sailed round the people
　　near the Danube, the Spaniards, the people
　　of Marseille, the Illyrians, the entire
　　Adriatic, Sicily, and all Italian shores,
　　wherever the sea reaches' (*Men*., 235–8).
　　In *CE*, by contrast, Egeon's travels couple
　　farthest Greece with *Asia*, where Ephesus
　　is located, as opposed to *Men*.'s itinerary
　　of Adriatic and western Mediterranean
　　coastlines; *farthest Greece* recalls
　　Messenio's '*Graeciamque exoticam*' (236;
　　translated by de Melo as 'Sicily' but
　　literally 'and foreign Greece'). '*Graecia
　　exotica*' referred to classical Greek
　　settlements in southern Italy; in Warner's
　　translation, the phrase becomes 'all high
　　Greece' (17).
132 **Five summers** i.e. five years, a
　　synecdoche; on *Five*, see 100n., on *five*;
　　5.1.309 and n.

127 so] for *F2*

150

Roaming clean through the bounds of Asia,
And coasting homeward came to Ephesus,
Hopeless to find, yet loath to leave unsought   135
Or that or any place that harbours men.
But here must end the story of my life;
And happy were I in my timely death,
Could all my travels warrant me they live.

DUKE

Hapless Egeon, whom the fates have marked   140
To bear the extremity of dire mishap:
Now, trust me, were it not against our laws,
Against my crown, my oath, my dignity,

---

133 **clean** entirely (*OED adv.* 5c); cf. *JC* 1.3.35; perhaps recalling '*omnis*' in '*orasque Italicas omnis*' ('and all Italian shores') (*Men.*, 237).
bounds 'territory situated on or near a boundary' (*OED* bound *n.*[1] 3a); Egeon has roamed Asia's coastal areas. Cf. *bound* at 2.1.17 and *AYL* 3.5.107. See also 81n.
Asia trisyllabic ('Asïa'), as in Tamburlaine's famous line 'Holla, ye pampered jades of Asia!' (Marlowe, *2 Tamburlaine*, 4.3.1) and Pistol's garbled memory of it, 'And hollow pamper'd jades of Asia' (*2H4* 2.4.164)

134 The line recalls the Apostle Paul's arrival at Ephesus: 'Paul passed through the vpper coastes, and came to Ephesus' (Acts, 19.1). Paul's ministry took him throughout Asia Minor. In Twine's *The Pattern of Painful Adventures* (1594), Apollonius of Tyre instructs his captain to 'coast towards Ephesus' (sig. K2ʳ).
coasting Where possible, ships generally travelled by going from coastal city to coastal city, keeping land in sight; cf. *LLL* 5.2.554. One could not coast, however, from Ephesus to Syracuse in Sicily.

135 **Hopeless** See 151n.
unsought unexplored (*OED adj.* 3)

136 **Or ... or** either ... or; a familiar Elizabethan usage (Blake, 5.3.1.c),

recalling Latin's *aut ... aut* (see e.g. *Men.*, 211, 373); cf. 4.2.4, 5.1.84.
[1]**that** i.e. Ephesus
harbours accommodates (cf. *KJ* 2.1.262); evoking coastal cities as ports full of itinerant travellers

137 **the story ... life** Cf. *Oth* 1.3.129, *Tem* 5.1.305.

138 **timely** seasonable, well-timed

139 **travels** punning on 'travails' and connoting both journeys and hardships; cf. *travel* at 1.2.15. 'Travail' often takes the place of ME 'travel' in 16th-century travel-book titles.
warrant assure (*OED v.* 5); cf. 4.4.3 and n., on *warrant thee as*.

140 **Hapless** unfortunate (*OED adj.*); on *hap-* words, see 37n.
Egeon See List of Roles, 1n. That the merchant's name first occurs here suggests that the Duke now sees him in personal terms; it recurs similarly at 5.1.337 (see n.).

141 **extremity** extreme degree (*OED n.* 3); also extreme penalty (*OED* 3b)
mishap misfortune (*OED n.* 1); cf. *mishaps* (120); on *hap-* words, see 37n.

142–5 The Duke's compassion conflicts with his sworn promise to uphold a rigorous law, as happens with dukes in other Shakespearean comedies, such as *MND*, *MV* and *MM*. See 5.1.390 and n.

143 **dignity** high office (Ard[2])

Which princes, would they, may not disannul,
My soul should sue as advocate for thee.   145
But, though thou art adjudged to the death,
And passed sentence may not be recalled
But to our honour's great disparagement,
Yet will I favour thee in what I can.
Therefore, merchant, I'll limit thee this day   150
To seek thy hope by beneficial help.
Try all the friends thou hast in Ephesus;
Beg thou or borrow to make up the sum,
And live. If no, then thou art doomed to die.
Jailer, take him to thy custody.   155

144 **would they** 'even if they wished to'
disannul 'cancel', 'bring to nothing',
'annul' (*OED v.* 1), applied comprehens-
ively and not only to *laws* (142). Theobald
relineated 143–4.
145 **sue** plead (*OED v.* 10); a legal term, like
advocate
146 **adjudged** adjudgèd; sentenced
147 **passed** passèd
148 **our** making clear that the Duke speaks
from his official position; cf. *I* (149).
disparagement 'dishonour', 'disgrace'
(*OED n.* 2)
150 **Therefore, merchant** The two trochaic
feet here mark the Duke's climactic
'transition from comment to decision'
(Ard²). The formal *merchant* now replaces
the familiar *Egeon* (140).
limit appoint (*OED v.* 1a)
151 *hope emended from F's 'helpe' to avoid
circularity: to seek 'help' by means of
help. Collier²'s *hope* squares with the
dialogue; the original 'helpe' may have
occurred because of metathesis from its
second occurrence in the line. Egeon had
declared himself *Hopeless to find* his son
at 135; thus, the Duke's *To seek thy hope*

addresses Egeon's near-despair in a like
image of searching. The Duke's *hope* cues
Egeon's subsequent demurral, *Hopeless
and helpless* (157). In 151, *hope* refers not
to a feeling of expectation but to the thing
hoped for (*OED n.*¹ 4c); that is, the ransom
money (cf. 'But if thou catch thy hope,
turn back to me', *Son* 143.11).
152 **friends** See 5.1.284n., on *friend*.
154 **If no** 'if you are unsuccessful'; or 'if you
do not'. In EM English, 'no' could replace
'not' as an adverb of negation (Blake,
5.1.3.6 [ii]).
155 The thrust of this nine-syllable line is
trochaic (technically, trochaic pentameter
catalectic), creating a tone of aggressive
finality (Shakespeare uses catalectic forms
elsewhere, such as in *MND*, *Mac*). Cf. 150
and n., on *Therefore, merchant*. Alternatively, with a pause after *Jailer*, the line
becomes regular; a missing unstressed
syllable following a caesura (creating a
short foot) is a familiar variant within the
blank verse form (Wright, *Metrical*, 102).
Although some editors have added one-
syllable words before or after *Jailer* (see
t.n.), no correction is necessary.

143, 144] *lines transposed in Theobald*   151 hope] *Collier² (Collier, Notes);* helpe F; life *Rowe³;* fine
Singer²; pelf *Ard¹;* health *Cam¹*   154 no] not *Rowe*   155 Jailer,] Jailer, now *Hanmer;* So, jailer, *Capell;*
Jailer, go *Ard (anon., per Cam)*   custody.] custody. *Exeunt Duke, and Train.* / *Theobald*

JAILER
I will, my lord.
EGEON
Hopeless and helpless doth Egeon wend,
But to procrastinate his lifeless end.   *Exeunt.*

[**1.2**]   *Enter* ANTIPHOLUS [OF SYRACUSE], [First]
         Merchant *and* DROMIO [OF SYRACUSE].

1 MERCHANT
Therefore, give out you are of Epidamium,
Lest that your goods too soon be confiscate.
This very day a Syracusan merchant
Is apprehended for arrival here,

157 **Hopeless and helpless** The opening
trochee and the alliteration and rhetorical *antisthecon* (*Hopeless*/*helpless*) lend
emphasis and resonance. For *helpless*, cf.
2.1.39 and n.
Egeon The third-person reference adds
detachment to Egeon's resignation.
157–8 **wend . . . end** Egeon completes this
blank verse scene with a rhyming couplet,
a common practice in Shakespeare. Here
wend/*end* recapitulates the themes of
wandering and loss. Shakespearean
comedies often begin in melancholy (see
e.g. *MV*, *TN*, *AW*). Anglo-Saxon *wend*
means 'to go off, depart' (*OED v.*¹ 10), but
it also suggests altering or reversing
direction (*OED* 1, 6). With its archaic and
formal tone, *wend* occurs elsewhere in
Shakespeare only twice (*MND* 3.2.372,
MM 4.3.145). See pp. 71, 89.
158 **procrastinate** postpone; Shakespeare's
only use of this word
lifeless end i.e. his end in lifelessness

1.2 The setting is the Ephesian mart, as
indicated by *from the mart* (74; also at
2.1.5, 2.2.6; see also *at the mart*, 3.1.12).
0.1 *ANTIPHOLUS OF SYRACUSE See List of
Roles, 3n.
0.1–2 ***First Merchant** See List of Roles, 11n.
1 **Epidamium** See 1.1.41n. The mention of
Epidamium links this scene to the previous
one, and the Merchant's speech recalls that
scene's action.
2 **goods too soon** with *too* probably referring
adverbially to *goods*, i.e. 'also'; but cf. *too
soon* at 1.1.60, one of the scene's numerous
verbal echoes with the first; see p. 29.
confiscate cònfiscàte; confiscated; cf. *goods
confiscate* (1.1.20 and n.), with different
stress.
3–7 The Merchant's strange awareness of the
first scene's events evokes both the pressure and plasticity of time in *CE*.
4 **for arrival** because it is a crime for *any
Syracusan born* (1.1.18) to enter Ephesus
(see 1.1.11–22), although Antipholus is not
precisely *Syracusan born*

156] *verse as Wells*   157 Egeon] *F2; Egean F*   **1.2**] *Pope (*SCENE II.*)*   0.1 ANTIPHOLUS] *(Antipholis),*
Malone   OF SYRACUSE] *Rowe; Erotes F*   0.1–2 First Merchant] *Dyce; a Marchant F;* a *Merchant* of Ephesus
Kittredge   0.2 OF SYRACUSE] *Capell subst.*   1+ SP] *Dyce; Mer., E.Mar. F; 1. E. Mer. Riv*   1 Epidamium]
Epidamnium / Rowe; Epidamnum / Pope; Epidamnus *Oxf*¹   3 Syracusan] *Pope; Syracusian F*   4 arrival]
*F2 (*arrivall*);* a riuall *F*

And, not being able to buy out his life,   5
According to the statute of the town
Dies ere the weary sun set in the west.
[*Offers a purse to Antipholus.*]
There is your money that I had to keep.
ANTIPHOLUS OF SYRACUSE [*to Dromio, giving the purse*]
Go, bear it to the Centaur, where we host,
And stay there, Dromio, till I come to thee.   10
Within this hour it will be dinner-time;
Till that, I'll view the manners of the town,

---

*arrival F's splitting of *a*-words (here 'a riuall') is 'not uncommon' (Ard²); cf. F's 'A lots' for 'Allots' (*TS* 4.5.41).

5   **buy out** ransom, redeem (*OED* buy *v.* 8a)

7   **weary sun** recalling the time appointed for Egeon's execution (see 1.1.27 and n., on *evening sun*; 150); one of the scene's several time references. The sun's personification as *weary* recollects Egeon's age and world-weariness (see also 1.1.26–7; cf. *R3* 5.3.19, *KJ* 5.4.35); *weary* also occurs at 15.

8   **your money** The Merchant hands Antipholus' money back to him implicitly as protection in case of arrest, thereby displaying a possible means for Egeon's redemption; cf. 5.1.389 and n. That the Merchant held Antipholus' funds goes unexplained, although his costume may include a secure-looking pouch. The visual emphasis on money prepares for Antipholus' concern about it later in the scene; *money* occurs 26 times in *CE* (Oxf¹), the most in any Shakespearean play. The incident reflects *Men.*, where, shortly after arriving, Sosicles Menaechmus demands the wallet of money from his servant, Messenio (265–72).

9   **Go, bear** Cf. *Men.*, 385–6, 435–6.
    the Centaur an inn, identifiable by its sign of a centaur (a Greek mythological creature having a man's head, arms and trunk but a

horse's body and legs); no contemporary London inn so-named has been discovered. The name recurs at 2.2.2, 5.1.410. *Centaur* suggests a being either uniting opposites or caught between two natures (traditionally the civil and appetitive). In Ovid's *Met.*, drunken centaurs try to abduct the bride at a wedding feast, provoking a bloody battle (12.209–26), an event to which Shakespeare alludes in *Tit* 5.2.203, *MND* 5.1.44. The *Centaur* offers the first of several animal-named places: the *Phoenix* (75), the *Tiger* (3.1.95) and the *Porpentine* (3.1.116). *Phoenix* and *Tiger* recur as ships' names in *TN*.
    host lodge (*OED v.* 2); a rare usage in Shakespeare; cf. 5.1.410, *AW* 3.5.94.

11 **dinner-time** Dinner (the largest meal of the day) occurred between 11 a.m. and somewhat past noon for the better-off classes; servants and labourers dined afterwards (Breton, sig. F2ʳ⁻ᵛ) (Cam¹). Elizabethan merchants took dinner around noon (Harrison, 144). It is now about 11 a.m. in Ephesus (Boswell–Malone). Dinner will be a recurrent motif in *CE*.

12 In Richard Edwards's *Damon and Pythias*, Damon and Pythias, newly arrived in Syracuse, plan to 'view this town' and 'consider the people's manners' after dinner (7.82–3).

7 SD] *Capell subst.*   9+ SP] *(Ant.)*   SD] *Capell subst.*   11–12] *lines transposed in F2*

Peruse the traders, gaze upon the buildings,
And then return and sleep within mine inn;
For with long travel I am stiff and weary.   15
Get thee away.

DROMIO OF SYRACUSE

Many a man would take you at your word
And go indeed, having so good a mean.   *Exit.*

ANTIPHOLUS OF SYRACUSE

A trusty villain, sir, that very oft,
When I am dull with care and melancholy,   20
Lightens my humour with his merry jests.

---

13 **Peruse** 'examine or scrutinize in the course of travelling' (*OED v.* 5a)
   traders suggestive of Ephesian mercantilism, as with *merchants* at 24
   gaze See 1.1.88n., on *gazing*.
14 **mine** See 1.1.33n.
15 **travel** F's 'trauaile' means here primarily *travel* and secondarily 'travail' or 'labour'; see 1.1.139n., on *travels*; 5.1.400 and n., on *travail*. In the 17th century, 'travel' and 'travail' became distinguished from each other in usage (Oxf[1]).
   weary See 7n.
16 another speech-ending half-line, perhaps here followed by a verbal pause filled with stage action; see 1.1.60–1n.
17–18 'Many a servant [*man*] would take literally your command to go and would abscond with the money [the *mean*].' The speech suggests Dromio's trustworthiness and, indirectly, his desire for release from servitude.
18 **mean** i.e. means, instrument (*OED n.*[3] 2a); also perhaps a trick (*OED* 2c) or an 'opportunity' (Ard[2], citing *Luc* 1045)
19 **A . . . sir** Antipholus may be responding to a show of alarm from the Merchant at Dromio's threat. The epithet *villain* means both low-born 'rustic' and 'scoundrel' (*OED n.* 1c), although the latter here only

playfully; subsequently (e.g. 96, 2.2.169) it is used more harshly. It perpetuates a series of varying descriptors (e.g. *attendant, slave, servant*) for the Dromios; see 1.1.127n., on *attendant*, and pp. 23, 40. Antipholus' mode of address to Dromio will deteriorate as his anger increases: *sir* (53), *sir knave* (72), *slave* (87), *villain* (96).
20 **dull** sluggish, enervated; gloomy (Norton, citing *OED adj.* 4)
21 According to ancient and medieval science, the body contains four types of fluids or humours (blood, phlegm, yellow bile and black bile) that correlate with the elements (air, water, fire and earth, respectively) and with emotional dispositions (sanguine, phlegmatic, choleric and melancholic, respectively). An excess of heavy, earthy black bile in the human system produces melancholy. Dromio's merry jests thus infuse Antipholus with airy sanguinity and 'lighten' him. Shakespeare's early plays often invoke humoural theory: see e.g. *RJ* 1.4.12. See also 58; 2.2.7 and 64, 69n.; 4.1.27, 57; 4.4.82. *Lightens* additionally suggests colour: Dromio brightens Antipholus' countenance, which had been darkened by black bile (cf. *LLL* 1.1.231–4) (Ard[2]).
   merry jests i.e. good-natured pranks; *merry* occurs here and elsewhere as a

---

15 travel] *(trauaile)*   17 SP] *(Dro.)*   18 mean] meanes *F2*   SD] *(Exit Dromio.)*

What, will you walk with me about the town
And then go to my inn and dine with me?

1 MERCHANT

I am invited, sir, to certain merchants,
Of whom I hope to make much benefit;   25
I crave your pardon. Soon at five o'clock,
Please you, I'll meet with you upon the mart,
And afterward consort you till bedtime;
My present business calls me from you now.

ANTIPHOLUS OF SYRACUSE

Farewell till then. I will go lose myself,   30
And wander up and down to view the city.

---

convenient explanation for inexplicable behaviour; see 69, 79; also 2.2.7, 20; 3.2.183; 4.1.27; 4.3.60. Overall, *merry* occurs eleven times in *CE*. See also *jest(s)* at 62, 68. Practical jokes run through Renaissance comedy, but in *CE* characters perceive *jests* that never occur.

23 **my** See 1.1.33n.

25 **Of** from (*OED prep*. 9a)
    benefit 'pecuniary advantage, profit' (*OED n*. 3d)

26 **crave** 'ask earnestly' (*OED v*. 2a, b)
    Soon at at nearly, at about (Boswell–Malone); see also 3.2.179; *MV* 2.3.5.
    five o'clock the hour set for Egeon's execution (5.1.118); *five* has received emphasis in *twice five leagues* (1.1.100) and *Five summers* (1.1.32), and will reappear later, e.g. *Five hundred ducats* (4.4.13) (see also 1.1.27n., on *evening sun*, and 1.1.100n., on *five*). Five o'clock will be the time appointed for Ephesian Antipholus to meet Angelo (4.1.10). It corresponds to supper-time (see 3.2.179), which was five o'clock (or between five and six) for Elizabethan students, gentry and nobility (six o'clock for merchants (Harrison, 144)). The hour will ultimately mark *a gossips' feast* (5.1.405). 1.2 establishes the

possibility for story-lines to converge providentially (although the First Merchant will not return in the finale: the actor was probably needed for another role). On *five o'clock* as a possible meta-theatrical reference, see Appendix 1, p. 318; on time, see pp. 45–6.

27 **mart** See 1.2n., 74, 2.2.6, 3.1.12; and see also 1.1.17n., on *marts*. The mart was a common setting for Roman comedy (although not *Men.*).

28 **consort** 'keep company with' (*OED v*. 1); treated ironically at *RJ* 3.1.46. The Merchant uses refined diction.

30, 40 **lose myself** get lost; submerge myself or forget myself (*OED lose v.*[1] 5d), multiple meanings relevant to the action; *lose* could also mean destroy (*OED* 2a; see *Ham* 3.2.195). Antipholus will fear losing himself by magical transformation (e.g. 99–100, 2.2.201–2), yet he will also wish for it from Luciana as siren (e.g. 3.2.40). See also *TGV* 2.6.20, *AC* 1.2.117.

31 **wander** a key word associated with Syracusan Antipholus; see List of Roles, 3n. See also 2.2.3 and n., on *wandered*; 3.2.38 and n., on *wander*; 4.3.44 and n., on *wander*. His intention recalls the predicament of his father at the end of 1.1.

24 merchants] merchants' *Oxf*[1]

1 MERCHANT

Sir, I commend you to your own content. [*Exit.*]

ANTIPHOLUS OF SYRACUSE

He that commends me to mine own content
Commends me to the thing I cannot get:
I to the world am like a drop of water   35
That in the ocean seeks another drop;
Who, falling there to find his fellow forth,
Unseen, inquisitive, confounds himself.

32 **commend** deliver, entrust (*OED v.* 1)
32, 33 **content** contentment. At 32 *content* suggests 'pleasure', at 33 a more inward state of 'satisfaction' (see *OED n.*² 1); also perhaps the 'thing contained', as in the substance of a conception (*OED n.*¹ 4).
35–40 Antipholus likens himself to a drop of water that falls into the ocean in search of another drop but whose resulting dissolution and absorption make the quest impossible, since it erodes his sense of identity; see pp. 14–15. The proverbial figure 'As lost as a drop of water in the sea' (Dent, D613) signifies likeness to others and, here, disintegration (35–6). Later, Adriana will use this simile to describe marriage; see 2.2.131–5 and n. The image develops from 'Egeon's account of his shipwreck and parallels his story of searching by sea' (Ard²). Water references punctuate *CE*; see e.g. 3.2.45–52 and n. On water-dissolution, see also *TGV* 3.2.6–8, *R2* 4.1.260–2, *AC* 4.14.9–11. The comparison may recall Messenio's observation on the Menaechmi's likeness: 'water isn't more similar to water anywhere . . . than he is to you and you in turn to him' (*Men.*, 1089–90). For related images, see Plautus' *Miles Gloriosus* (551–2), which Shakespeare knew, his *Amphitruo* (601), a source play for *CE*, and his *Bacchides* (Fragments v), a comedy that features twin sisters and mentions Ephesus.

37 **Who** the prior *drop* (35); 'who' in Shakespeare often refers to a personified inanimate object (Ard²).
falling Cf. 'fall' at 2.2.131 (see n.).
find . . . forth find out (*OED* forth *adv.* 8); *forth* occurs likewise at 4.4.96, 98.
38 **Unseen, inquisitive** modifying *Who* (37). F encloses the two adjectives in parentheses, as if qualifying the same object, necessarily *Who*, since *inquisitive* could hardly apply to *fellow* (37). *Unseen* refers to the drop-as-Antipholus rather than to the drop-as-object of the search: because he has become invisible, Antipholus cannot find his mother and brother. *Unseen* might also suggest 'unknown' or 'unnoticed' (Ard²), as in *LLL* 5.2.358, *Son* 118.3. For *inquisitive*, cf. 1.1.125.
confounds himself both defeats and confuses himself. Various meanings of 'confound' pertain: (1) 'defeat utterly, bring to ruin' (*OED v.* 1a); (2) 'throw into confusion of mind or feelings' (*OED* 4); (3) 'waste' (*OED* 1e); and (4) 'mix up or mingle so that the elements become difficult to distinguish' (*OED* 6). By this last definition, *confounds himself* means 'loses his sense of identity'; cf. *lose myself* at 30, 40. Shakespeare often uses 'confound' reflexively to mean 'confuse' (e.g. *R3* 4.4.262), but he employs it variously (see e.g. *Tit* 4.2.6, *LLL* 5.2.397, *R2* 5.3.86).

32 SD] *Rowe subst.; Exeunt* F   37 falling] failing *Oxf*¹   38 Unseen, inquisitive,] *(*(Vnseene, inquisitiue)*)*

So I, to find a mother and a brother,
In quest of them, unhappy, lose myself.   40

Enter DROMIO OF EPHESUS.

Here comes the almanac of my true date.
– What now? How chance thou art returned so soon?

DROMIO OF EPHESUS

'Returned so soon'? Rather approached too late!
The capon burns, the pig falls from the spit;
The clock hath strucken twelve upon the bell;   45

40 **quest** associated in Arthurian romance with knights errant who undertake a journey to achieve an exploit (see *OED n.*[1] 6)
unhappy both 'unfortunate, ill-fated' and 'wretched in mind', the first suggesting an outward, the second an inward, condition (*OED adj.* 2); *unhappy* modifies *myself* rather than *them*. It recalls the *hap-* words of 1.1; see 1.1.37n.
lose myself completing the self-revelation begun with *lose myself* (30) and echoed in *confounds himself* (38). Antipholus' self-estrangement makes him psychologically vulnerable to subsequent challenges to his sense of identity.

41 **almanac ... date** calendar of my own birth date (and age); see 1.1.53–5. Antipholus can identify something *true* about himself by looking at Dromio (here the wrong Dromio but the right inference). An *almanac*, commonly used for agricultural purposes, was a book of tables containing months and dates, anniversaries, seasonal information, records of previous years and astronomical and astrological calculations and predictions (see *OED* almanac). Cf. 'calendars of their nativity' (5.1.404 and n.).

42 **chance** 'does it happen that' (see *OED v.* 5); cf. *MW* 5.5.218.

43 **'Returned so soon'** Dromio appropriates and re-inflects Antipholus' phrase, a practice typical in *CE* (see e.g. 32–3), deriving from *commedia dell'arte* (see pp. 33–4). 'Mistiming' – as in *so soon, too late* – 'is a feature of the sequence of "errors" in the play' (Ard[2]). Stage Dromios often enter this scene running and breathless (see 53, 63), launching the Roman comedy motif of the *servus currens*, the 'running slave' (e.g. 4.2.28.1; see also List of Roles, 5, 6n.).

44–8 Dromio's imagination conjures forth a scene of realistic, seeming-simultaneous domestic bustle; cf. 97–102 and n.

45–6 Cf. 2.1.48 and n.

45 **strucken** struck; a past participle form of 'strike' used in northern England and Scotland (see *OED* strike *v.*); 45–6 offers further time references.
twelve ... bell Time has elapsed with preternatural speed since the scene began (see 11n.). Productions of *CE*, e.g. Komisarjevsky's in 1938 (see pp. 119–21), often feature a large public clock. In Shakespeare's time, urban clock towers displayed a city's status; elaborate public clocks might include a mechanical effigy with a hammer striking a bell at set intervals.

40 them, unhappy,] *Rowe*[3]*;* them (vnhappie a) *F;* him (unhappie) *F2;* them, unhappier, *Cam*[1] *(Cam);* them unhappy, *Cam*[2]*;* them (unhappy), ah, *Riv*   43+ SP] *Malone subst. (Dro. E.); E.Dro. F*   43 'Returned so soon'] *this edn;* Return'd so soone *F*

My mistress made it one upon my cheek.
She is so hot because the meat is cold;
The meat is cold because you come not home;
You come not home because you have no stomach;
You have no stomach, having broke your fast. 50
But we that know what 'tis to fast and pray
Are penitent for your default today.

ANTIPHOLUS OF SYRACUSE

Stop in your wind, sir; tell me this, I pray:
Where have you left the money that I gave you?

46 **one** i.e. one blow and one o'clock. Beating a servant resembles the striking of a clock.

47–50 The repetition of words or clauses, typically from one line to another (rhetorical *anadiplosis*), often appears in a sequence of lines that builds towards a rhetorical climax, as at 52. The comic repetition invites a speed of delivery and a change of tone that contrast to Antipholus' preceding meditative speech. On repetition, see 1.1.57n.; also e.g. *R3* 5.3.193–5; *AYL* 5.2.32–7; Kyd's *ST*, 1.3.33–8. Dromio's *anadiplosis* evokes a concrete, offstage domestic world of actions and things.

47 **hot** figuratively, angry; literally, overheated, from an excess of yellow bile, characteristic of the choleric humour; accordingly, *hot* can describe a bad-tempered person (*OED adj.* 8b). Cf. 21n.

49 **stomach** 'appetite or relish for food' (*OED n.* 5a); perhaps also 'courage' (*OED* 8a), i.e. courage to face his wife

50 **broke your fast** i.e. eaten; the phrase's religious connotation sets up Dromio's images in 51–2 (see *OED* fast *n.*[1] 1).

51 Dromio imagines poorly fed but devout servants praying for succour. Fasting and prayer occur together only a few times in the Bible; here Shakespeare may be recalling Jesus on exorcism: 'Howebeit, this kynde [of devil] goeth not out, but by prayer and fastyng' (Matthew, 17.21).

For two mock exorcisms, see 4.3.69 and n., on *conjure*; 4.4.55–8 and n. On *pray*, cf. 90. On prayer and fasting, cf. *LLL* 1.1.300–3.

51–2 **pray . . . today** Dromio underscores his complaint with a climactic end-rhyme; it will be echoed by Antipholus to assert his own perspective: *I pray* (53).

52 **penitent** undergoing penance; that is, fasting on behalf of, or in sorrow for, or (ironically) because of Antipholus (see *OED adj.* 2, 3). Dromio cannot eat until his master has dined.

default absence; *default* often suggests a legal failure to act (*OED n.* 3a) or a culpable neglect of duty, and was sometimes used in a religious sense (see *OED* 4a); another meaning was 'lack of food' (*OED* 1b); *fault* in the sense of 'default' (*OED* 5a) occurs at 65.

53 **Stop . . . wind** 'stop talking', 'be quiet'. *Stop in* means 'block up' (*OED* stop *v.* 10); *wind* refers to 'breath' in speaking (*OED* wind *n.*[1] 11b). Figuratively, *wind* connotes vain or empty talk (see *OED* 15); Dromio may also be breathing heavily (see 43n.).

your Antipholus switches from the familiar *thou/thee* used towards servants (as at 10, 16 and 42) to the more distant *you/your*, expressing his growing annoyance; see Hope, 1.3.2b.

54 For this relationship reversed, see 4.3.13 and n.

DROMIO OF EPHESUS

O, sixpence that I had o'Wednesday last   55
To pay the saddler for my mistress' crupper?
The saddler had it, sir; I kept it not.

ANTIPHOLUS OF SYRACUSE

I am not in a sportive humour now;
Tell me, and dally not: where is the money?
We being strangers here, how dar'st thou trust   60
So great a charge from thine own custody?

DROMIO OF EPHESUS

I pray you, jest, sir, as you sit at dinner.
I from my mistress come to you in post;
If I return, I shall be post indeed,
For she will score your fault upon my pate.   65

55–7 Dromio remembers receiving from Ephesian Antipholus, days earlier, the modest sum of sixpence to pay to the saddle-maker.

56 **crupper** 'A leathern strap buckled to the back of the saddle and passing under the horse's tail, to prevent the saddle from slipping forwards' (*OED n.* 1)

58 **sportive** 'inclined to jesting or levity' (*OED adj.* 1; first cited from Thomas Nashe's *Christ's Tears over Jerusalem*, 1593)

humour See 21n.

60–1 **trust . . . custody** 'give up your duty regarding such an important responsibility [as taking care of the money]' (see *OED* charge *n.* 13a); *charge* also means 'material load' (*OED* 1), here the *money* (54) or *gold* (70).

62 **jest** joke; amuse yourself (*OED v.* 4a, b); cf. *jests* at 21, 68.

63 **in post** in haste, as a courier (*OED* post *n.*³ P4); *post* occurs also at 3.2.152.

64 **return** i.e. return without Antipholus

post a wooden post; esp. 'doorpost on which the reckoning at a tavern was kept'

by scoring (*OED n.*¹ 6); figuratively, a whipping post; see 65n.

65 **score** Although F's 'scoure' could mean 'scour', its primary meaning here is *score*, because it completes the image of scoring on a *post* (64); that is, recording a debt by making marks or grooves upon a wooden piece used for a tally (*OED v.* 10a); cf. *1H4* 2.4.27–8. Dromio fears that Adriana will record Antipholus' debt (his *fault*, or *default*; see 52n., on *default*) by striking Dromio upon his *pate* (the crown of the head: *OED n.*¹ 1a); she has already 'made it one upon [his] cheek' (46); cf. 82, 2.1.77, 2.2.72, *1H4* 5.3.31. Dromio complains that he must pay for Antipholus' transgressions. Additionally, *score* can refer to inflicting marks, cuts or bruises to the skin (*OED v.* 1a); Dromio elaborates the tally upon him at 82–4 (Adriana makes specific threats of pate-breaking at 2.1.77, 2.2.224). Secondarily, F's 'scoure' suggests (1) cleansing by means of abrasion (*OED v.*² 1a), as in 'scouring' or cleaning away a fault; and (2) beating or scourging (*OED* 9); cf. *H5* 2.1.56–7.

55 o'Wednesday] *Capell subst.;* a wensday *F*   56 crupper?] *F4;* crupper: *F*   65 score] *Rowe;* scoure *F*

Methinks your maw, like mine, should be your clock
And strike you home without a messenger.

ANTIPHOLUS OF SYRACUSE

Come, Dromio, come, these jests are out of season;
Reserve them till a merrier hour than this.
Where is the gold I gave in charge to thee?   70

DROMIO OF EPHESUS

To me, sir? Why, you gave no gold to me!

ANTIPHOLUS OF SYRACUSE

Come on, sir knave, have done your foolishness,
And tell me how thou hast disposed thy charge.

DROMIO OF EPHESUS

My charge was but to fetch you from the mart
Home to your house, the Phoenix, sir, to dinner;   75

66–7 *maw ... messenger i.e. you should, like me, tell time by your hunger, which will draw you home for dinner without requiring a messenger. The *maw* is the jaws or mouth of an 'insatiably hungry person' (*OED n.*[1] 3a). Dromio, like other servants, is associated with hunger and eating; cf. Launcelot, *MV* 2.5.46. Dromio's speech recapitulates the struck clock-bell image from 45–6.

67 **strike you home** The general idea is proverbial: 'The belly is the truest clock' (Tilley, B287a); and 'My stomach has struck twelve' (Dent, S872) (Ard²). In his transitive *strike* Dromio combines intransitive uses: (1) to strike the hour (*OED v.* 41); (2) to make one's way (*OED* 1); and (3) to strike home, 'to make an effective thrust with a weapon or tool' (*OED* 80, as in *Tit* 2.3.117, *MM* 1.3.41), all contributing to Dromio's urgency about hunger.

68 **jests** anticipated in 21 (see n., on *merry jests*); cf. 62 and n.
out of season untimely, inopportune, inappropriate (*OED* season *n.* 16a); cf. 2.2.47 and n., 4.2.57 and n.; perhaps with a pun on *season* as 'seasoning' (*OED* 19).

69 **merrier** See 21n., on *merry jests*.

70 **gave ... thee** entrusted to you (*OED* charge *n.* 13b); *charge* recurs at 73, 74 (see n.).

72 **knave** 'base and crafty rogue', here used playfully but condescendingly (*OED n.* 3; see also 19n.)

73, 74 **charge** See 61, and 60–1n.; Dromio uses *charge* to mean a task (*OED n.* 12); cf. 70 and n.

74 **mart** See 27n.

75, 88 **the Phoenix** Ephesian Antipholus' house is named after the red- and gold-plumed, eagle-like bird of classical mythology (see Ovid, *Met.*, 15.391–407), which, after living five or six hundred years in the Arabian deserts, burns itself to ashes on a funeral pyre and then rises, reincarnated, with renewed youth to repeat the cycle (*OED n.* 1). It symbolized constant love, as in *PT* (1601). *Phoenix* suggests Adriana's fidelity and perhaps the rich beauty of her home (*OED* 2). More distantly, *Phoenix* may recall the near-death history of Egeon's family. In London, a 'Phoenix in the pelican's nest' was the sign for a Lombard Street shop referred to in Heywood's *The First Part of King Edward*

66 your clock] *Pope;* your cooke *F;* you cooke *F2*

161

My mistress and her sister stays for you.

ANTIPHOLUS OF SYRACUSE

Now as I am a Christian answer me
In what safe place you have bestowed my money,
Or I shall break that merry sconce of yours
That stands on tricks when I am undisposed.   80
Where is the thousand marks thou hadst of me?

DROMIO OF EPHESUS

I have some marks of yours upon my pate,
Some of my mistress' marks upon my shoulders,
But not a thousand marks between you both.
If I should pay your worship those again,   85
Perchance you will not bear them patiently.

ANTIPHOLUS OF SYRACUSE

Thy 'mistress' marks'? What 'mistress', slave,
    hast thou?

IV (1599) (17.29; see Sugden, 409). The shop sign *Phoenix* may indicate that Ephesian Antipholus is a merchant (Cam[1]). The scene's second mythological animal place-name (cf. 9 and n., on *the Centaur*), *Phoenix* occurs again at 2.2.11; see also e.g. *3H6* 1.4.35, *Son* 19.4, *PT*.

76   **sister** casually introducing the woman with whom Antipholus will fall in love (Oxf[1])
     stays See 1.1.10n.

77   **as . . . Christian** To promise 'as a Christian' to beat someone sounds ironic; see 92 SDn.

79   **break . . . sconce** 'crack your merry head'; *sconce* is a jocular synonym for head (*OED n.[2]*), possibly derived from *sconce* as a lantern (*OED n.[1]*) or a small fortification (*OED n.[3]* 1a); cf. 65 and n., 2.2.34–8 and n., 3.1.77 and n.
     merry See 21n., on *merry jests*.

80   'which [i.e. your head] insists on practising tricks when I am not in the mood'; *stands on* means 'insists on doing' (*OED* stand *v.* Phrasal verbs 'to stand on' 1); and *undisposed*, 'not inclined or willing' (*OED*

undisposed adj. 6), with an historical (if not etymological) association with 'disposition' as humour (*OED* disposition *n.* 7b). Cf. *dispose* at 1.1.20.

81   **thousand marks** the same amount as Egeon's ransom; see 1.1.21 and n., on *a thousand marks*.

82–4   **marks** bruises; see 65n.

82   **pate** See 65n.

85–6   hinting at resentment and aggression. Dromio's shift from subjunctive (*should*) to declarative (*will*) adds imminence to his implied threat. Cf. Ephesian Dromio at 3.1.15–18, 4.4.30–40.

85   **pay** i.e. repay by beating (*OED v.[1]* 12c), punning on the idea that servants' wages are paid in bruises

86   **patiently** perhaps recalling 51–2. The motif of patience and impatience occurs repeatedly in *CE*, especially in relation to Adriana and Ephesian Antipholus; see 2.1.9, 32, 34–41, 85; 3.1.94; 4.2.16; 4.4.18–19; 5.1.87–8, 102, 174; and related nn.

87   [2]**mistress** While Dromio means the female head of household (*OED n.* 2a), Antipholus

---

87 'mistress' marks'] *this edn;* Mistris markes *F*   What 'mistress'] *this edn;* what Mistris *F*

DROMIO OF EPHESUS

Your worship's wife, my mistress at the Phoenix;
She that doth fast till you come home to dinner,
And prays that you will hie you home to dinner.   90

ANTIPHOLUS OF SYRACUSE

What, wilt thou flout me thus unto my face,
Being forbid?   [*Strikes Dromio.*]
                                 There, take you that, sir knave.

DROMIO OF EPHESUS

What mean you, sir? For God's sake hold
    your hands!
Nay, an you will not, sir, I'll take my heels.   [*Exit.*]

ANTIPHOLUS OF SYRACUSE

Upon my life, by some device or other   95
The villain is o'er-raught of all my money.

understands 'female sweetheart' (*OED* 6a) – or worse (see *OED* 7). In *Men.* (265–71), Sosicles Menaechmus reclaims his wallet from Messenio because he fears that Messenio, as 'a great lover of the ladies' (269), will be delinquent with the money.

slave a harsh epithet; it recurs at 104; 2.1.1, 74, 77; 2.2.2, 175; 4.1.96, 107; 5.1.242. Cf. 1.1.127n., on *attendant*.

89, 90 **home to dinner** rhetorical *antistrophe*, the repetition of a word or phrase at the ends of successive lines, here underlining the action that Dromio encourages

90 **prays** Cf. 51 and n.
hie hasten, go quickly (*OED v.*[1] 2a); also at 3.2.152, 4.3.93, 4.4.57

91 **flout** 'mock, jeer, insult' (*OED v.* 1)

92 SD Cf. Dromio's 'you beat me at the mart' (3.1.12). The Elizabethan 'Homily on Matrimony' insists that it is 'a great shame for a man to beat his bondservant' (*Homilies*, 544).

93–4 **hold . . . heels** Dromio's *take my heels*

for 'run off' is colloquial (see Dent, H394). Its paralleling with *hold your hands* constitutes rhetorical *isocolon* (successive phrases of similar length and structure) and marks the climax of the episode. Antipholus apparently beats with both *hands*.

95 **device** trick (see *OED n.* 6), often signifying the kind of ingenious scheme typical in comedy (see e.g. *TGV* 2.1.139, *TS* 1.1.193)

96 mirroring Sosicles Menaechmus' fear; see *Men.*, 265–9.
villain repeated from 19 but now in earnest. Antipholus will review this episode at 2.2.17–19. See 1.1.127n., on *attendant*.
***o'er-raught** i.e. overreached; outwitted, cheated (*OED* overreach *v.* 5b); *raught* or 'wrought' (as in F) are archaic past participles of 'reach' (*OED* reach *v.*[1] form 2a). Spenser uses 'ouerreach' to describe a fiendish spirit outwitting a human (*FQ*, 4.2.10; cited in *OED*), as Antipholus may imagine here.

92 SD] *Capell subst. (after* you*)*   93 God's] *Theobald*[2]; God *F*   94 an] *(*and*)*   SD] *F2; Exeunt Dromio Ep. F*   96 o'er-raught] *Hanmer;* ore-wrought *F;* o're wrought *F4*

They say this town is full of cozenage –
As, nimble jugglers that deceive the eye,
Dark-working sorcerers that change the mind,
Soul-killing witches that deform the body,   100

97–102 Shakespeare's catalogue emphasizes witchcraft and charlatanism. By contrast, *Men.*'s Messenio highlights 'hedonists and drinkers', 'impostors and cajolers' and 'prostitutes' (258–64). Warner translates, 'full of Ribaulds, Parasites, Drunkards, Catch-poles, Cony-catchers, and Sycophants', as well as 'Curtizans' (17). Antipholus' anxiety moves him to imagine, in an extended fantasia, a profusion of threatening agents (rhetorical *amplificatio*). A similar rhetorical manner typifies Ephesian Dromio's catalogue (44–8), so that the two speeches establish Ephesus as a place of the most normal domesticity and, contradictorily, the most dangerous deception and witchcraft. Antipholus feels threatened here; later he will welcome transformation by the presumed goddess Luciana; see 3.2.39–40 and n. On Ephesian transformation, cf. 2.2.201–8. On error in judgement, see pp. 11–13, 2.2.190 and n.

97 **this town** perhaps with a meta-dramatic reference to Elizabethan London. On Ephesian magic, see pp. 28–9, 50–1.
   cozenage cheating, deception or fraud (*OED n.* a); cf. *MW* 4.5.63, *Ham* 5.2.67. Cozenage was a main theme of Robert Greene's London cony-catching pamphlets in the early 1590s, e.g. *A Notable Discovery of Cozenage* (1591); see Kinney, *Rogues.*

98 **As** such as

98–100 **nimble ... body** rhetorical *isocolon*; see 93–4n. Here the parallelisms suggest a self-perpetuating rhythm of thought.

98 **nimble jugglers** evoking criminal deception, foolery, magic, demonism, papistry and more. 'Juggler' often meant a cheater (cozener), magician or illusionist (*OED n.* 2). A juggler, being *nimble* in sleight-of-hand, might cozen money or goods from

a gull by physical deception. More darkly, 'juggler' denoted a magician, wizard, sorcerer or conjuror (*OED* 2); cf. the *juggler* and *conjuror* Doctor Pinch (5.1.240, 243). Protestant reformers applied 'juggling' derogatorily to the Catholic Mass and other Catholic practices, and 'juggler' was a demeaning term for a Catholic priest. The word 'juggler' could also denote an entertainer employing buffoonery or tricks (*OED* 1); Elizabethan actors used juggling deceptions to create realistic effects. On 'juggler' and 'juggling', see Caputo; Axton, 18–20; Butterworth, 3–4, 7–25; White, 126–8.

99 **Dark-working** (1) invoking the powers of darkness; (2) darkening (i.e. clouding or confusing) the mind; and perhaps (3) working in the dark (Steevens[4]). In *The Discovery of Witchcraft*, Scot calls attention to witchcraft's capacity to alter human judgements and emotions (Scot, 6; see also *Malleus Maleficarum*, 99). According to the *Malleus Maleficarum*, the devil 'can incite the fancy and inner sensory perceptions of a man by apparitions and impulsive actions' (50). The *Malleus* also describes how the devil can 'darken' one's 'understanding' (55); cf. Sidney, *A&S*, Fifth song, 77–8.

100 *Soul-killing* exaggerates the hypothetical power of witches. Scot acknowledges the somewhat more limited belief that witches can 'bring trembling to the hands', 'kill whom they list with lightening and thunder', 'make a woman miscarrie', 'with their looks kill either man or beast' and 'deprive men of their privities' (6). On *deform*, cf. 4.2.19, 5.1.299. The term 'witch' is applicable to either sex (*OED n.*[1], *n.*[2]); cf. 3.2.161 and n.; 4.4.148, 157 and n.

97 cozenage –] *this edn;* cosenage: *F*   99 Dark-working] *(*Darke working*);* Drug-working *Warburton;* Soul-killing *(Johnson)*   100 Soul-killing] Soul-selling *Hanmer;* Dark-working *(Johnson)*

Disguised cheaters, prating mountebanks
And many such – like liberties of sin.
If it prove so, I will be gone the sooner.
I'll to the Centaur to go seek this slave;   104
I greatly fear my money is not safe.   *Exit.*

2[.1]   *Enter* ADRIANA, *wife to Antipholus* [*of Ephesus*],
                    with LUCIANA[,] *her sister.*

ADRIANA

Neither my husband nor the slave returned
That in such haste I sent to seek his master?
Sure, Luciana, it is two o'clock.

LUCIANA

Perhaps some merchant hath invited him,
And from the mart he's somewhere gone to dinner.   5

---

101 **Disguised** disguisèd
    prating chattering (*OED* prate *v.* 2a); cf.
    2.1.80, 2.2.199.
    mountebanks charlatans who sold
    medicines in public places, often using
    entertainment to attract a crowd (*OED n.*
    1a); from the Italian *monta in banco*,
    'climb on a bench'; recurring at 5.1.239.
    See also Jonson, *Volpone*, 2.2.
102 **such – like liberties* The dash, editorially
    introduced, signals that Antipholus breaks
    off his catalogue of cozeners at *such* and
    shifts his thought to a comparison of *this*
    town (97) to sinful *liberties*. Editors have
    typically accepted either 'such-like
    liberties' (with *liberties* referring to sinful
    activities) or 'such-like libertines'; see LN.
    A 'liberty' was 'an area of local admin-
    istration distinct from neighbouring territory
    and possessing a degree of independence'
    (*OED* liberty *n.*¹ 6c(a)). Thus, a London
    precinct established as a liberty might
    permit 'sinful' bawdy houses or playhouses

while remaining immune from the city's
legal sanction (see e.g. Mullaney, 20–5).
As with *this town*, *liberties* may refer meta-
dramatically to Elizabethan London. Cf.
liberty at 2.1.7, 10, 15; 4.3.20; 5.1.53, 340.
104 **I'll to** 'I'll go to'. 'Omission of a verb of
    motion [e.g. 'go'] may occur after modal
    auxiliaries, especially *will* or *shall*' (Blake,
    6.3.2.3); cf. *3H6* 4.3.3.
    the Centaur See 9n., on *the Centaur.*
    slave See 87n., on *slave.*
2.1 Pope places this scene inside Antipholus'
    house; White, in an inner courtyard; and
    Dyce, in front of the home.
0.1 **Antipholus of Ephesus* See List of Roles,
    4n.
1   **slave** used derisively, as at 1.2.87 (see n.,
    on *slave*); for a parallel missing slave, cf.
    2.2.2.
3   **two o'clock** another time marker; cf.
    twelve and *one* (1.2.45 and n., on *twelve . . .*
    bell; 1.2.46 and n.).
5   **mart** See 1.2n.

---

102 such – like] *this edn;* such like *F;* such-like *Dyce*   liberties] libertines *Hanmer*   **2.1**] *Rowe* (ACT II.
SCENE 1.); *Actus Secundus.* F   0.1 Antipholus] (Antipholis), *Verplanck (after Malone)*   of Ephesus]
Collier; Sereptus F   1+ SP] (Adr., Adri., Ad.)   2 master?] Master: *F4;* master! *Pope*   4+ SP] (Luc., Luci.)

Good sister, let us dine, and never fret.
A man is master of his liberty;
Time is their master, and when they see time
They'll go or come: if so, be patient, sister.

ADRIANA

Why should their liberty than ours be more?   10

LUCIANA

Because their business still lies out o'door.

ADRIANA

Look when I serve him so, he takes it ill.

7–25 reflecting Ephesians, 5.22: 'Wyues, submit your selues vnto your owne husbandes, as vnto the Lorde' (see 5.22–4) (Ard²). At 3.2.5–28 (see n.), Luciana takes a more deceptive approach to marriage.

7 The line sounds proverbial, but no match has been found; cf. Dent, A88; Tilley, M474 (Ard²).

 man In EM English, *man* could act as a plural when used as an indefinite pronoun to form part of a universal truth: 'man . . . their' (7–8) and 'Man . . . Are' (20–4); see Blake, 3.3.2.7, 6.1.14.

 liberty unrestrained freedom to act (*OED n.*¹ 2a); cf. *liberties*, 1.2.102 and n. On *liberty*, see 7–25 and n.; 10 and n., on *liberty*; 4.3.20 and n.; 5.1.53, 340.

8–9 **Time . . . come** 'Time governs men, who, when faced with its demands, will go or come accordingly'. Luciana's *see time* may mean (1) encounter or accompany time (*OED see v.* 12a); cf. *MW* 4.6.36; or (2) apprehend time mentally (*OED* 3a). The thought flows awkwardly in 7–9 (Wells), where man is first master of his liberty but then a subject of time. In Trevor Nunn's 1976 production, Luciana carried a large book, apparently of proverbs, from which she read these lines.

9 **patient** The Abbess will later repeat Luciana's imperative to Adriana; see 5.1.102 and n.; the Officer will similarly counsel Ephesian Antipholus (see 4.4.18

and n.). On patience and impatience, see 1.2.86n.

10–41 Adriana and Luciana engage in a verbal duel by stichomythia, i.e. alternating, combative single lines, here with competing end-rhymes and mixed with longer homiletic speeches; see also 85–115, 3.2.53–60, 4.4.69–80, 5.1.58–61 and related nn., and p. 71. The style probably derives from Lyly's *Euphues* (Ard²) and illustrates the play's penchant for alternative 'double-truths' (Cam²). Ephesian Dromio, entering (at 42.1), disrupts the pattern with his punning, colloquial prose and irregular verse.

10 **liberty** probably not just freedom of movement (cf. 7) but entitlement to move freely (see *OED n.*¹ 3a, 2c); *liberty* can denote 'improper licence' (Crystal & Crystal, *n.* 1) (see e.g. *1H4* 5.2.71), similar to the Abbess's use at 5.1.53; cf. 1.2.102 and n.

 more greater (Blake, 3.2.3.4)

11 **still** continually, always (*OED adv.* 3a); cf. 4.4.45, 157; 5.1.67, 386.

 out o'door outside (*OED* door *n.* 5); 'away from home'. Cf. 'God hath made the man to travaile abroad, and the woman to keepe . . . for the mans pleasure is most abroade, and the womans within' (Smith, *Marriage*, sig. E2ʳ, 55).

12 **serve him so** 'treat him in the same way', i.e. by going *out o'door* (11), presumably

---

8 master] mistress *Oxf*   11 o'door] *(adore)*   12 ill] *F2;* thus *F*

LUCIANA

O, know he is the bridle of your will.

ADRIANA

There's none but asses will be bridled so.

LUCIANA

Why, headstrong liberty is lashed with woe.   15
There's nothing situate under heaven's eye
But hath his bound in earth, in sea, in sky.
The beasts, the fishes and the winged fowls
Are their males' subjects and at their controls.

unattended; *serve* may imply sarcasm (see *OED* serve *v.*[1] 8a).

*ill F2's *ill* corrects F's 'thus'; the rhyme pattern suggests a compositor's mistake.

13 **bridle** curb or restraint, referring to the headgear with bit and rein used to control horses or similar animals (see *OED n.* 1, 2); a Renaissance iconographic symbol of restraint, temperance or control over the will or passions (see Whitney, 6, 'Temeritas'). A 'scold's bridle' was used in some parts of England for the public punishment of talkative or scolding women (see Boose, esp. 196–213). It consisted of a cage placed over the head, with a flat metal piece that projected backwards into the mouth to repress the tongue.

14 **asses** Adriana refuses to be made into a beast of burden; such transformational possibilities will occur elsewhere, however; see 2.2.205 and n.

15–25 Luciana's homology of man's dominion over animals and women defends hierarchy as producing restraint and, by implication, harmony. It draws on the Bible and other religious writings; see LN. This set-piece peroration features couplets, alliterations (*liberty/lashed*; *fishes/fowls*, etc.), near-rhymes (*wide/wild*), personification and balanced phrasing (e.g. 'in earth, in sea, in sky'). The alliterated likening of *females* (24) to *fish* and *fowls* may lightly undercut the florid argument. Luciana's bookishness establishes an identity from which she can develop. Cf. Katherine's speech, *TS* 5.2.136–79.

15 **liberty** Cf. 1.2.102 and n.

lashed scourged (as with a whip), so that liberty will be punished by woe (*OED v.*[1] 6); cf. *KL* 4.6.161, 'those who refuse the bridle must bear the lash' (Steevens); Luciana accuses Adriana of behaving as a beast. Although *lashed* suggests 'castigated in words' (*OED* 6c, first citation), Ephesian Antipholus will later procure a rope in order to beat ('lash') Adriana; see 4.1.15–18 and n.

16 **situate** situated; probably pronounced as two syllables

heaven's eye the sun, but connoting divine ordination. The personification (as with *liberty* and *woe*) reinforces the speech's sententiousness.

17 **his bound** its boundary, limit; pertaining here to action more than geography (see *OED* bound *n.*[1] 4); cf. 1.1.133 and n., on *bounds*.

18–19 i.e. female beasts, fish and fowls are under the sovereign control of the males of their species

18 **fishes** Shakespeare uses 'fish' or 'fishes' depending on his metrical needs (Hope, 1.3.1).

winged wingèd

18–19 **fowls ... controls** a rhyme (Kökeritz, 422; Cercignani, 225)

19 **at their controls** under their command (*OED* control *n.* 1a, first citation); a unique Shakespearean use of the plural noun *controls*. Cf. *TN* 2.5.66.

Man, more divine, the master of all these,   20
Lord of the wide world and wild watery seas,
Indued with intellectual sense and souls,
Of more pre-eminence than fish and fowls,
Are masters to their females, and their lords:
Then let your will attend on their accords.   25

ADRIANA
This servitude makes you to keep unwed.

LUCIANA
Not this, but troubles of the marriage bed.

ADRIANA
But were you wedded, you would bear some sway.

LUCIANA
Ere I learn love, I'll practise to obey.

ADRIANA
How if your husband start some otherwhere?   30

20 **Man** as in 7; *Man* turns plural in 24 as the complement of *Are masters* (see 7n., on *man*). Genesis uses *man* similarly: God says, 'let us make *man* . . . and let *them* rule' (1.26, emphasis added).

21 **wild watery seas** The extra-biblical emphasis on man's mastery of the seas extends the play's water imagery. Luciana sounds naïve, since Egeon's tale has illustrated the opposite of such mastery. **watery** wat'ry

22 with *intellectual* modifying both *sense* and *souls*, which establish the capacity to understand (*OED adj.* 3a). For Aristotle, humans are endowed – i.e. *Indued* (*OED* endue/indue *v.* 9; F's spelling retains assonance) – with a rational soul, in addition to the sensitive soul of animals and the nutritive soul of plants. Luciana's speech locates human attributes specifically in males. It reflects the Elizabethan 'Homily on Matrimony', which states that a female,

compared to a male, is 'not endued with like strength and constancy of mind' (*Homilies*, 537). For *intellectual*, cf. *H5* 3.7.138.

22–3 **souls . . . fowls** a rhyme (Kökeritz, 482)

23 **more pre-eminence** higher rank

25 **attend . . . accords** 'be subject to their consent'; *accords* implies that male hegemony produces harmony (see *OED* accord *n.* 1a; the plural noun occurs uniquely here in Shakespeare).

26 **servitude** i.e. theory of servitude
keep remain (*OED v.* 39b)

27 Luciana glances at the sexual strife between Adriana and her husband. Folg² compares 1 Corinthians, 7.28: those who marry 'shall haue trouble in their fleshe'.

29 The 1559 *BCP* puts obedience before love: 'wilte thou obey hym and serue him, loue, honour, and keepe him, in sickenesse and in health . . . ?' (sig. O6ʳ).

30 **start some otherwhere** fly off in another direction (Crystal & Crystal, start *v.* 4), i.e.

20–3 Man . . . master . . . Lord . . . souls . . . fowls] Man . . . Master . . . Lord . . . soule . . . fowle *F2*; Men . . . masters . . . Lords . . . soul . . . fowl *Hanmer*; Men . . . masters . . . Lord . . . souls . . . fowls *Steevens*; Men . . . masters . . . Lords . . . souls . . . fowls *Steevens²*   21 wild] wide *F2*

168

LUCIANA
Till he come home again, I would forbear.
ADRIANA
Patience unmoved! – No marvel though she pause:
They can be meek that have no other cause.
– A wretched soul bruised with adversity,
We bid be quiet when we hear it cry;   35
But were we burdened with like weight of pain,
As much or more we should ourselves complain.
So thou, that hast no unkind mate to grieve thee,
With urging helpless patience would relieve me;
But if thou live to see like right bereft,   40

turn unfaithful with another woman; *start* implies an abrupt swerving away, as a horse 'starts' off course (Ard²), continuing the animal imagery. Further, *start* can mean 'desert one's place' (*OED v.* 4c); also, perhaps unintentionally, 'escape' (*OED v.* 14); *otherwhere* = elsewhere (*OED adv.* 1); cf. 103.

31 **forbear** control myself, have patience (Crystal & Crystal, *v.* 3)

32 **Patience unmoved** *Patience*, personified, is emotionally unperturbed. For *unmoved*, see also *Son* 94.4. Cf. Viola: 'Patience on a monument, / Smiling at grief' (*TN* 2.4.114–15). On patience, see 1.2.86n.

32–3 **unmoved! – . . . cause. –** Here *she* (32) indicates that Adriana turns her address away from her sister and probably towards the audience (Wells); the dashes (32, 34) are editorially introduced.

32 **No . . . pause** i.e. it is not to be wondered at that she hesitates (before marrying).

33 'They can be meek who have no cause to act differently'; *meek* means humble and submissive (*OED adj.* 2); and *cause*, ground or reason for action (*OED n.* 3). Adriana's *other* recollects her *otherwhere* at 30; the *other cause* is the 'other woman'.

34–41 The idea that humans can be indifferent to suffering until they experience it themselves is proverbial: see Dent, A124 (Ard²). It occurs elsewhere in Shakespeare, e.g. 'He jests at scars that never felt a wound' (*RJ* 2.2.1); cf. *MA* 5.1.20–3, *Oth* 1.3.212–15. The image of a soul crying (34–5) may recall the weeping narrated by Egeon (1.1.70–2).

34–5 **adversity . . . cry** a rhyme (Kökeritz, 401)

36 **burdened** See 1.1.55n.

38 **unkind** Besides the obvious, *unkind* could also mean 'ungrateful' (*OED adj.* 3a; cf. *AYL* 2.7.175); 'undutiful' (*OED* 3b; cf. *KL* 3.4.71); and 'unnatural' (*OED* 4; cf. *Tit* 5.3.48), all of which might pertain.

39 **helpless** unavailing, not helpful (*OED adj.* 3); cf. 1.1.157; also *R3* 1.2.13, *Luc* 1027.

39, 41 **patience** See 1.2.86n.

39 **would** normally taking 'you', with 'wouldst' taking *thou* (38); the mixed forms reflect the period's linguistic change (see Blake, 3.3.2.1.1).

40 **see . . . bereft** i.e. see yourself bereft of the same right (to the husband's faithful company); *bereft* implies 'forcibly deprived' or 'robbed' (*OED adj.* 1). Cf. *reft* at 1.1.115 and n.; also *right* at 4.2.7.

32 unmoved! – No] *Johnson;* vnmou'd, no *F*   33 cause.] *this edn;* cause: *F*   34 – A] *this edn;* A *F*

This fool-begged patience in thee will be left.

LUCIANA

Well, I will marry one day but to try.

Enter DROMIO [OF EPHESUS].

Here comes your man: now is your husband nigh.

ADRIANA

Say, is your tardy master now at hand?

DROMIO OF EPHESUS   Nay, he's at two hands with me,   45
and that my two ears can witness.

ADRIANA

Say, didst thou speak with him? Knowst thou
    his mind?

DROMIO OF EPHESUS

Ay, ay, he told his mind upon mine ear;
Beshrew his hand, I scarce could understand it.

LUCIANA

Spake he so doubtfully, thou couldst not feel his
    meaning?   50

---

41 'You will abandon this foolish notion of
patience'; *fool-begged* means foolish; 'to
beg (someone) for a fool' means 'to take
him for a fool' (*OED* beg *v*. 5a); cf. 'Let
him be begged for a fool' (Dent, F496).
The phrase derives from a legal strategy for
gaining control of a minor's property by
having him or her declared a lunatic by the
Court of Wards (Johnson, Ard²). See also
Lyly, *MB*, 1.1.41, 4.2.121–2.

42.1 *See LN.

45 **he's . . . me** i.e. he has boxed my ears.
Cam¹ has Dromio enter '*rubbing his head*'.
Dromio here launches a series of quibbles.

48 **told his mind** 'communicated what he
thought', but 'tolled' Dromio on the ears like

a man striking a bell repeatedly (*OED* toll
v.² 2), an image continued from 1.2.45–6.

49 **Beshrew** curse (*OED v*. 3b); cf. *MA* 5.1.55.
scarce could understand Dromio puns
on the sense of *understand* as both
'comprehend' and 'stand under' or, more
specifically, 'endure' or 'withstand'
(Crystal & Crystal, understand *v*. 1); also at
53; cf. *TGV* 2.5.27, *TN* 3.1.79.

50 This 13-syllable line has an epic caesura
with a double feminine ending (or single,
'doubtf'lly'), and a feminine line ending.

50, 52 **doubtfully** at 50, ambiguously or indis-
tinctly (*OED adv*.) (cf. *TGV* 2.1.111, *Tim*
4.3.122); at 52, with the added sense
of 'dreadfully' (*OED* doubtful *adj*. 3);

42.1] *Oxf¹; after* 43 F   OF EPHESUS] *Theobald²; Eph. F*   45+ SP] *(E.Dro., E. Dro., E.Dr., Dro.)*   46 two] *F2;*
too *F*   47] *verse as Steevens⁴*   48–9] *prose Ayscough*   48 Ay, ay,] *Rowe;* I, I, *F;* I? Ay. *Wells*   50–3] *Capell*
lines feel / I / [there]withal / them. /   50] *verse as Oxf*

DROMIO OF EPHESUS   Nay, he struck so plainly, I could
too well feel his blows, and withal so doubtfully that
I could scarce understand them.

ADRIANA
But say, I prithee, is he coming home?
It seems he hath great care to please his wife.   55

DROMIO OF EPHESUS
Why, mistress, sure my master is horn-mad.

ADRIANA   'Horn-mad', thou villain?

DROMIO OF EPHESUS
I mean not cuckold-mad! But sure he is stark mad:
When I desired him to come home to dinner,
He asked me for a thousand marks in gold.   60
''Tis dinner-time', quoth I; 'My gold!', quoth he.
'Your meat doth burn', quoth I; 'My gold!',
    quoth he.
'Will you come home?', quoth I; 'My gold!',
    quoth he.

Antipholus' blows left Dromio fearful but
unenlightened.

feel (1) perceive mentally; (2) experience
through touch (*OED v.* 8, 6). Adriana
applies the first meaning, Dromio the
second.

55 Norton compares 1 Cor., 7.33: 'But he that
hath maryed a wyfe, careth . . . how he
may please his wyfe'.

56 **horn-mad** proverbial (Dent, H628); mad
enough, like a beast, to gore someone with
a horn (*OED* horn-mad *adj.* a). *OED* cites
Nashe, *Have with You to Saffron Walden*
(1596): 'a Bulls roaring and bellowing and
running horne mad at euery one in his way'
(Nashe, 3.27). But also 'mad with rage at
having been made a cuckold' (for a cuckold

was supposed to grow horns on his brows)
(*OED* b, first citation). Dromio means the
first; Adriana hears the second, as Dromio
perceives at 58. Cf. 3.1.72 and n., on
mad . . . buck.

57–8 *See LN.

58 **stark mad** absolutely mad (*OED* stark
adv. 2a); also at 5.1.282

59–70 Dromio recollects both reductively and
hyperbolically. His *quoth I* and Antipholus'
'My gold!' function as *epimone*, or refrain.

60 *thousand F2 corrected F's 'hundred' for
consistency with 1.2.81 (and 1.1.21).
Perhaps the compositor misread 1000 for
100 (see *Var.*).

61–3, 66–7 The repetition of closing words in
successive clauses is rhetorical *antistrophe*.

---

51 struck] *(strooke)*   54–5] *prose White²*   57–8] *Pope;* villaine? / Cuckold mad, / starke mad: / F;
cuckold-mad; / stark mad. / *Collier;* mean, / stark mad. / *Collier³*   57 'Horn-mad'] *this edn;* Horne mad F
60 thousand] *F2 (1000);* hundred F   61 ''Tis dinner-time' . . . 'My gold!'] *Cam (Capell subst.);* 'Tis
dinnertime . . . my gold, F   62 'Your . . . burn' . . . 'My gold!'] *Cam (Capell subst.);* Your . . . burne . . . my
gold F   63 'Will . . . come home?' . . . 'My gold!'] *Cam (Capell subst.);* Will . . . come, . . . my gold, F
come home] *Theobald;* come F

'Where is the thousand marks I gave thee, villain?'
'The pig', quoth I, 'is burned'; 'My gold!', quoth he.   65
'My mistress, sir – ', quoth I; 'Hang up thy mistress!
I know not thy mistress, out on thy mistress!'

LUCIANA   Quoth who?

DROMIO OF EPHESUS   Quoth my master.
'I know', quoth he, 'no house, no wife, no mistress.'   70
So that my errand, due unto my tongue,
I thank him, I bore home upon my shoulders:
For, in conclusion, he did beat me there.

ADRIANA
Go back again, thou slave, and fetch him home.

DROMIO OF EPHESUS
'Go back again', and be new-beaten home?   75
For God's sake, send some other messenger!

ADRIANA
Back, slave, or I will break thy pate across.

---

66 **Hang up** a mild imprecation, from 'hang on a gibbet' (*OED* hang *v.* Phrasal verbs 'to hang up' 3); cf. *LLL* 4.3.52, *RJ* 3.3.57.

67 **out on** another mild imprecation, derived from *out* as 'expel or get rid of' (*OED* out *v.* 1a), i.e. 'to Hell with'

68 Luciana questions Dromio because he has broken the rhythm of *quoth . . .* after each phrase. His vehemence at 66–7 makes her wonder whose sentiments he is reporting (perhaps his own).

70–3 *These lines occur as prose in F, but most editions, as here, have followed Pope's verse layout. Pope also apparently considered 67 and 68 to constitute a short verse line, although they make sense as

prose (see 2.1.57–8 LN). Pope's line-breaks coincide elegantly with full and partial stops in F. The speech comes at the foot of the second column on F's sig. H2ᵛ, where the compositor, apparently running out of room, compressed the verse lines into prose to fit the space.

71 **errand . . . tongue** Dromio's verbal message (the *errand*) called for a verbal response but was returned instead in the form of a beating.

72 *bore** modernized from F's 'bare'. F uses both 'bare' and 'bore'; cf. 5.1.247.

73 **there** perhaps both *shoulders* and *home*

74, 77 **slave** cf. 1.2.87 and n., on *slave*.

77 **pate** See 1.2.65n.

---

64 'Where . . . villain?'] *Knight (Capell subst.);* Where . . . villaine? *F*   65 'The pig' . . . 'is burned'; 'My gold!'] *Cam (Capell subst.);* The Pigge . . . is burn'd: my gold, *F*   66 'My . . . sir – '] *Cam;* My . . . sir, *F* sir –] *Capell;* sir, *F*   66–7 'Hang . . . mistress!'] *Cam (Capell subst.);* hang . . . mistresse. *F*   67 I . . . ¹mistress] Thy mistress I know not *Hanmer;* I know thy mistress not *Ard (Seymour)*   ²thy] my *F2* 69 Quoth] Why, quoth *Hanmer*   70–3 I know . . . there] *verse as Pope*   70 'I know' . . . 'no . . . mistress'] *Cam (Capell subst.);* I know . . . no . . . mistresse *F*   71 errand] *(arrant)*   72 bore] *Oxf¹;* bare *F*   my] thy *F2*   75 'Go . . . again'] *this edn;* Goe . . . againe *F*   77 across] *(a-crosse)*

172

DROMIO OF EPHESUS

And he will bless that cross with other beating;
Between you I shall have a holy head.

ADRIANA

Hence, prating peasant!   [*Beats him.*]
                    Fetch thy master home.   80

DROMIO OF EPHESUS

Am I so round with you as you with me
That like a football you do spurn me thus?
You spurn me hence, and he will spurn me hither;
If I last in this service, you must case me
   in leather.   [*Exit.*]

78–9 Dromio refashions Adriana's threat to break his head *across* (77), i.e. from one side to another, to mean to break it in the form of a cross (*OED* across *adv.* 1). He adds that Antipholus' prospective beating (*OED* bless *v.*[2]) will likewise consecrate (*OED v.*[1] 1a) his head with the sign of the cross (*OED v.*[1] 2a). The result will be a holy head, one both sanctified and full of holes.

80 **prating** See 1.2.101n., on *prating*.
   peasant servant (*OED n.* 1b), but with a further sense, 'ignorant lout' (see *OED* 2); cf. 5.1.231.

80 SD *In the 2006 Shakespeare's Globe production in London, Adriana kicked Dromio, so that he rolled downstage, thus making good his claim to be spurned *like a football* (82).

81–4 Dromio's only recourse against physical violence is wit. Although Dromio is not so *round*, or severe-speaking (*OED adj.* 18a), as Adriana, both she and Antipholus treat him as if he were *round*, or spherical, *like a football*, which they metaphorically kick (*OED* spurn *v.*[1] 2) back and forth between them scornfully (*OED* 3, 6). (Later, Adriana will herself feel spurned; see 2.2.140 and n.) Dromio's *round* also carries

the sense of a swinging blow (*OED adj.* 11a). On foot-spurning, see *MND* 3.2.225, *MV* 1.3.118. Football was a popular lower-class game (cf. *KL* 1.4.86) and a violent one: 'wherin is nothinge but beastly furie, and extreme violence' (Elyot, 109 (Wells)), 'meeter for laming' (James VI/I, sig. T4[r], 143 (Ard[2])). Dromio asks to be 'cased' *in leather*, like the bladder inside a leather football, quibbling on *last* as a verb meaning 'survive' and a noun indicating the wooden model of a foot on which cobblers shape leather pieces into shoes. Cf. Ephesian Dromio's fantasy about Nell as spherical (3.2.116). Dromio riffs again on leather, encasement and survival at 4.2.32–40, 42–5 and, with Syracusan Antipholus, 4.3.13–34 (see 4.3.23n.).

83–4 **hither . . . leather** a rhyme (Kökeritz, 450, 186–7)

84 a 14-syllable line, rhythmically anapaestic tetrameter, perhaps complementing Dromio's rapid exit. The line contains parallel clauses analogous to the prior one (rhetorical *isocolon*), with which it rhymes. Shakespeare counterbalances the Dromios' abuse by giving them lines of rhetorical and poetic virtuosity.

78 And] An *Wells*   80 SD] *Cam*[1] *subst. (opp. home)*   82 thus?] *F4;* thus: *F*   84 SD] *F2*

LUCIANA

Fie, how impatience loureth in your face! 85

ADRIANA

His company must do his minions grace,
Whilst I at home starve for a merry look.
Hath homely age th'alluring beauty took
From my poor cheek? Then he hath wasted it.
Are my discourses dull? Barren my wit? 90
If voluble and sharp discourse be marred,
Unkindness blunts it more than marble hard.

85–115 Luciana and Adriana again share couplets (85–6 and 101–2); see 10–41n. Adriana takes over the rhyming position at 86 and 102, gaining the rhetorical edge, but surrenders the last chiming word to Luciana at 115.

85 **impatience loureth** Cf. *Patience*, 32 and n.; *loureth* means looks darkly and threateningly, i.e. scowls (*OED* lour *v.* 2), looks sullen (Oxf[1]); cf. e.g. *R2* 1.3.235. See 1.2.86n.

86 **do . . . grace** 'give preference to his darlings [i.e. mistresses]'; 'do grace' means 'do honour to' (*OED* grace *n.* P4a). The *minions* are nourished while Adriana must *starve* (87). 'Minion' connotes not only favourite (Crystal & Crystal, *n.* 1) but paramour (*OED n.*[1] 1b) and hussy (Crystal & Crystal, *n.* 2); cf. 'minion' at 3.1.54, 59; 4.4.61; *TS* 2.1.13.

87–98 Adriana represents herself as diminished in physical and mental attractiveness, for which she blames her husband; cf. her subsequent claim that husband and wife are 'undividable, incorporate' (2.2.128).

87 **starve** used figuratively (*OED v.* 4c; first citation); cf. *Son* 75.10, and 'famish'd', *Son* 47.3. Adriana suggests that she is sustained by her husband's 'happy' or 'pleased' (*OED* merry *adj.* 4b) regard.

88–92 Cf. Ephesian Antipholus' reference to the Courtesan's prettiness, discourse and wit at 3.1.109–10 (see n.).

88 **homely age** *age* bringing plainness of appearance (*OED* homely *adj.* 2c); *homely* may play on 'domestic' (*OED* 2a). Age is here personified; cf. 5.1.298–300. The underlying figure of speech is a transferred epithet, rhetorically a form of *hypallage*, in which the modifier is applied to the 'wrong' noun: it is age that is homely-making.

89 **wasted** destroyed (*OED v.* 4a); also squandered (*OED* 9a)

90 **Are . . . dull** 'Is my conversation boring?' Ephesian Antipholus, we shall learn, enjoys the Courtesan's *excellent discourse* (3.1.109). His twin will find Luciana's *discourse*, along with her *presence*, to be *enchanting* (3.2.166 and n.). 'Discourse' suggests conversational power or faculty (*OED n.* 3b).

wit (1) 'power of invention' (Ard[2]); (2) 'talent for saying brilliant or sparkling things', especially amusingly (*OED n.* 7); (3) intellect or intelligence (*OED* 2a); cf. 2.2.84.

91 **voluble** fluent (*OED adj.* 5)
sharp quick-witted, discerning, acute (*OED adj.* 3a); also sharp like a knife and capable of being blunted by a hard object

92 **marble hard** proverbial (Tilley, H311)

90 wit?] *F4;* wit, *F*   92 marble hard] marble-hard *Capell*

Do their gay vestments his affections bait?
That's not my fault: he's master of my state.
What ruins are in me that can be found   95
By him not ruined? Then is he the ground
Of my defeatures. My decayed fair
A sunny look of his would soon repair.
But, too-unruly deer, he breaks the pale
And feeds from home; poor I am but his stale.   100

LUCIANA

Self-harming jealousy! Fie, beat it hence.

ADRIANA

Unfeeling fools can with such wrongs dispense.

---

93 **their gay vestments** i.e. his minions'
showy gowns
affections passions (*OED n.*[1] 1b)
bait entice (*OED v.*[1] 11), with perhaps a
pun on 'bate', diminish (*OED v.*[2] 5a),
referring to Antipholus' lessened affections
towards his wife
94–8 Cf. Adriana's subsequent argument that
husband and wife are one at 2.2.125–52.
94 **he's . . . state** Adriana turns Luciana's
argument for male mastery to her own
advantage (see 15–25, esp. 24).
state (1) condition in life (*OED n.* 1a); (2)
splendour of clothing (as a reflection of her
condition) (*OED* 16): i.e. she lacks *gay
vestments* (93).
95–6 **What . . . ruined** Adriana's condition
and appearance are *ruins* because
Antipholus has *wasted* (89) her beauty; she
hopes for 'repair' (98); *ruins . . . ruined*
exemplifies rhetorical *analepsis*.
96–7 **ground / Of** reason for (*OED* ground *n.*
5c); also base or foundation for (an edifice)
(*OED* 4)
97 **defeatures** ruins (*OED n.* 1); also
disfigurements, defacements (*OED n.* 2).
Cf. 5.1.300 and n., on *defeatures*; *VA* 736;
OED cites these last two as the earliest

instances of 'defeature' as disfigurement.
decayed decayèd
fair beauty (*OED n.*[2] 4); cf. *Son* 18.10.
99 i.e. but, being overly unmanageable (like a
deer in a fenced-in park), he breaks through
the boundary (or fence). For an extended
and erotic version of this image, see *VA*
229–40.
100 **feeds** gratifies (his) sexual desire
(Williams, *Glossary*, 122–3)
stale lover or mistress ridiculed by a rival
(*OED n.*[3] 6), i.e. a laughing stock;
'prostitute' or 'unchaste woman' (*OED n.*[3]
4); also stale food (perpetuating an
association of dining with sex). Halliwell
emphasizes *stale* as a decoy (*OED n.*[3] 3),
the 'ostensible wife' under whose cover
the husband pursues his affairs. Cf. *TS*
1.1.58, 3.1.90. In Warner's translation of
Men., the wife says, 'He makes me a stale
and a laughing stocke to all the world' (30)
(Steevens).
101 **beat** perhaps as she has just beaten
Dromio; personified, *jealousy* can be
flagellated.
102 **with . . . dispense** put up with (*OED*
dispense *v.* Phrasal verbs 'to dispense
with' 8)

99 too-unruly] *(too vnruly)*

I know his eye doth homage otherwhere,
Or else what lets it but he would be here?
Sister, you know he promised me a chain: 105
Would that alone, alone he would detain,
So he would keep fair quarter with his bed.
I see the jewel best enamelled
Will lose his beauty – and though gold bides still
That others touch, yet often-touching will   110
Wear gold – and any man that hath a name

103 **eye** Cf. 5.1.50.
   homage allegiance; the rendering of
   payment in an act of tribute (*OED n.* 1a,
   b); cf. 3.2.43.
   otherwhere See 30n.
104 'Otherwise, what hinders him from being
   here?'; cf. *TGV* 3.1.113.
105 **chain** necklace. The *chain*, or *carcanet*
   (3.1.4), will move from character to
   character, contributing to the confusions.
   In *Men.*, the parallel object is a bracelet
   ('*spinter*', *Men.*, 527) purloined by
   Menaechmus from his wife and given to
   Erotium the courtesan, who mistakenly
   hands it over to Sosicles Menaechmus; in
   Warner's translation, the *spinter* becomes
   a gold chain (23). Shakespeare greatly
   intensifies the object's importance. A chain
   is more easily visible onstage than a
   bracelet and coincides with Elizabethan
   fashion (Ard²). On the chain, see pp. 35–8.
106–7 *'If only he would withhold just that
   [i.e. the chain], provided that he were true
   to his marriage bed' (on *So*, see Abbott,
   133). Awkwardness occurs at *alone, alone*,
   adopted from F2 in place of F's incomprehensible 'alone, a loue'. F2 closes the
   space in 'a loue' and rights *u* to *n*; a turned

n is a common compositorial error.
Adriana occasionally repeats words (e.g.
2.2.126–7), but here the second *alone*
refers differently from the first (rhetorical
antistasis). In delivery, the second *alone*
will receive the greater emphasis. For
alone, alone see also *KJ* 3.1.171, *Luc* 795
(Halliwell and Dyce). Capell treats these
lines as addressed to the audience or to
Adriana herself.
106 **detain** 'keep back, withhold' (*OED v.* 2a)
107 **keep fair quarter** maintain proper
   conduct or relations (*OED* quarter *n.* 17a);
   cf. *KJ* 5.5.20; see also 2.2.151 (Ard¹).
108–12 *'Even the best-enamelled jewel will
   lose its lustre; gold, too, though it can
   withstand touching, will eventually be
   worn away by frequent handling.
   Similarly, a man of good reputation will
   eventually bring shame on it by practising
   falsehood and corruption.' See LN. These
   difficult lines are often cut on stage. On
   reputation, see 2.2.136–52; 3.1.86–8,
   98–106; 3.2.19–20; 4.1.71; 5.1.5; and
   related nn.
108 **enamelled** enamellèd
109 **his** its

103 otherwhere] *(*other-where*)*   106 alone, alone] *F2;* alone, a loue *F;* alone alas! *Hanmer;* alone o' love
Cam¹ (Ard¹); alone a love *Alexander;* alone a toy *Ard² (Kellner);* alone a' love *Riv*   109 his] her *Oxf*
109–12 and though . . . yet often-touching . . . Wear gold – and any . . . By] *this edn;* yet the . . . and often
touching . . . Where gold and no . . . By *F;* and the . . . yet often-touching . . . Wear Gold: and so no . . . But
Theobald; and tho' . . . yet often touching . . . Wear gold: and so no . . . But *Hanmer;* Yet the . . . and often
touching . . . Wear gold, and yet no . . . By *Oxf;* yet the . . . and often-touching . . . Wear gold – and any . . .
By *(Weiss)*   111–12] *om. F2*

By falsehood and corruption doth it shame.
Since that my beauty cannot please his eye,
I'll weep what's left away, and weeping die.   114

LUCIANA

How many fond fools serve mad jealousy!   [*Exeunt.*]

[**2.2**]   *Enter* ANTIPHOLUS [OF SYRACUSE].

ANTIPHOLUS OF SYRACUSE

The gold I gave to Dromio is laid up
Safe at the Centaur, and the heedful slave
Is wandered forth in care to seek me out.
By computation and mine host's report,

---

112 **shame** public dishonour and the painful personal emotion associated with it; *shame* constitutes a powerful form of chastisement in *CE*, as elsewhere in Shakespeare. See 3.2.10, 19–20; 4.1.84; 4.4.68, 81, 106; 5.1.14, 18, 254, 322.

113–15 **eye . . . die . . . jealousy** a scene-ending triple rhyme, with Luciana topping Adriana's couplet (Kökeritz, 454)

114 **weep . . . weeping** Here Adriana may actually weep, an action repeatedly associated with her; see her own reference at 2.2.210; also *weeping sister* (3.2.42), *flood of tears* (3.2.46), *tears and prayers* (5.1.115). The *weep/weeping* repetition is rhetorical *epanalepsis*.

115 **fond** infatuated; silly (*OED adj.* 2); also mad or dazed (*OED* 3), perhaps hinting at the play's emerging theme of madness
      serve provide opportunity to (Crystal & Crystal, *v.* 3)

2.2 Dyce² locates this scene on the mart.

2 **the Centaur** See 1.2.9 and n., on *the Centaur*. Since his last appearance, Antipholus has gone to the inn as he resolved (1.2.104) and has found his gold faithfully deposited by Dromio.
      heedful careful, mindful (*OED adj.*)

slave Cf. 1.2.87n., on *slave*. On a likewise missing slave, cf. 2.1.1.

3 **wandered** strolled without preset route (*OED* wander *v.* 1e), although not aimlessly, since Dromio has *wandered* in search of Antipholus. Antipholus had instructed Dromio to wait for him at the inn (1.2.10), but Dromio instead has gone back to find his master, which Antipholus takes as good service. On *wander*, see 1.2.31 and n.
      in care out of concern (*OED* care *n.*¹ 2)

3–4 ***out. . . . report***, Antipholus concludes, from the innkeeper's report and his own time calculation, that he could not have just spoken with Dromio (1.2.41–94) because Dromio had lacked sufficient time to arrive at the inn, deposit the gold and return for their conversation. Rowe inserted the full stop after *out* and accepted F4's comma after *report* instead of F's full stop. F's punctuation suggests incomprehensibly that Dromio had embarked on his search for his master based on his own calculation and his host's information.

4–6 **By . . . mart** Antipholus' bafflement contributes to his fear of Ephesian enchantment. On 1.2 as set in the *mart*, see 1.2.27n.

---

114 what's left away,] *Pope;* (what's left away) *F*   115 SD] *F2; Exit. F*   **2.2**] *Capell (SCENE* II.*)
(Theobald subst.)   0.1 ANTIPHOLUS] *(Antipholis), Malone*   OF SYRACUSE] *Rowe; Errotis F*   1+ SP]
(Ant., E.Ant., Antiph., Anti., An., Antip.)   3–4 out. . . . report,] *Rowe;* out . . . report. *F*

I could not speak with Dromio since at first   5
I sent him from the mart.

               Enter DROMIO [OF SYRACUSE].

                          See, here he comes.
– How now, sir, is your merry humour altered?
As you love strokes, so jest with me again.
You know no Centaur? You received no gold?
Your mistress sent to have me 'home to dinner'?   10
My house was at the Phoenix? Wast thou mad,
That thus so madly thou didst answer me?

DROMIO OF SYRACUSE

What answer, sir? When spake I such a word?

ANTIPHOLUS OF SYRACUSE

Even now, even here, not half an hour since.

DROMIO OF SYRACUSE

I did not see you since you sent me hence,   15
Home to the Centaur with the gold you gave me.

ANTIPHOLUS OF SYRACUSE

Villain, thou didst deny the gold's receipt,
And told'st me of a mistress and a dinner,
For which I hope thou felt'st I was displeased.

---

6 SD *relocated here from its placement in F
  after the complete line of dialogue; see
  2.1.42.1 LN. A cue for this entrance might
  be *Dromio* (5).
7 **is ... altered** alluding to Ephesian
  Dromio's 'sportive humour' (1.2.58)
7, 20 **merry** See 1.2.21n., on *merry jests*.
7 **humour** See 1.2.21n.
8 **strokes** i.e. being beaten
11 **the Phoenix** See 1.2.75, 88 and n.
  Wast = were
12 ***didst** In EM English, 'to do' was

increasingly used as an auxiliary verb for
emphasis (see Hope, 2.1.1b).
14 SP *F's *E.Ant.* refers to Syracusan Antipholus' cognomen 'Errotis' (i.e. wandering)
  from F's entrance SD: see 0.1 t.n., List of
  Roles, 3n.
14 **here** i.e. the *mart* (6), the scene of 1.2; cf.
  170 and n.
  half an hour another time marker
19 **felt'st** became conscious that (*OED* feel *v.*
  9a), punning on 'experienced physically'
  (i.e. in being beaten, 1.2.92–3) and
  recalling 'feel' at 2.1.50, 52; see n.

6 mart.] *F2 subst.*; Mart? *F;* Mart! *Cam¹* SD] *this edn; after 6 F* OF SYRACUSE] *Rowe; Siracusia F;*
Siracusan F2 9–11 Centaur? ... gold? ... dinner'? ... Phoenix] *Capell ends with raised points to*
denote irony; Centaur; ... gold; ... dinner; ... Phoenix. *Gentleman;* Centaur! ... gold! ... dinner! ...
Phoenix! *Alexander* 10 'home to dinner'] *this edn;* home to dinner *F* 12 didst] *F2;* did didst *F* 13+ SP]
(S.Dro., S.Dr.)

DROMIO OF SYRACUSE

I am glad to see you in this merry vein;   20
What means this jest? I pray you, master, tell me.

ANTIPHOLUS OF SYRACUSE

Yea, dost thou jeer and flout me in the teeth?
Think'st thou I jest? Hold, take thou that [*beating
    Dromio*], and that!

DROMIO OF SYRACUSE

Hold sir, for God's sake! Now your jest is earnest:
Upon what bargain do you give it me?   25

ANTIPHOLUS OF SYRACUSE

Because that I familiarly sometimes
Do use you for my fool and chat with you,
Your sauciness will jest upon my love,
And make a common of my serious hours.
When the sun shines let foolish gnats make sport,   30
But creep in crannies when he hides his beams;

20 **I am** probably 'I'm'
  vein mood (*OED n.* 14b); cf. 4.4.81, *R3*
  4.2.118.
22 **flout . . . teeth** *flout* means mock or insult
  (*OED v.* 1); *in the teeth* means 'to my face'
  (proverbial, Dent, T429): Antipholus takes
  considerable offence. Cf. 45 and n.
23, 24 **Hold** At 23, *Hold* means 'Here, Take
  that!' (see *OED v.* 15b). At 24, Dromio
  reverses its meaning: 'Stop!' (*OED* 27).
23 **take . . . ²that** By contrast, Paul's Epistle to
  the Ephesians (6.9) enjoins masters to be
  mild towards their servants.
24 **earnest** 'serious' (*OED adj.*¹ 1); and,
  punningly, a deposit, typically of money
  (but here of blows), to secure a contract or
  bargain (25), constituting a pledge of
  something that will 'afterwards be received
  in greater abundance' (*OED* earnest *n.*² 1),
  i.e. further beatings. Cf. the proverb 'Leave
  jesting while it pleases lest it turn to
  earnest' (Dent, J46) (Delius).
25 **bargain** Cf. 65 and n.

27 **use . . . fool** i.e. allow you the familiarity
  that a master allows his professional fool
28 **jest upon** trifle with (*OED* jest *v.* 3)
29–32 Antipholus' comment comprehends
  personal, solar and astrological time, and
  sets up Dromio's *out of season* (47), the
  discussion of 'a time for all things' (67) and
  the jokes about Time's baldness. The word
  time occurs 14 times in 2.2.
29 **common** i.e. public property, such as
  common land (see *OED n.*¹ 5a, b)
  (Steevens); cf. *LLL* 2.1.223. Also probably
  referring to a prostitute (*OED n.*¹ 10);
  common is introduced by *sauciness* (28),
  which can connote insolent wantonness
  (Williams, *Glossary*, 268).
  hours At 4.2.55, *hour* quibbles on whore
  (see LN), but in *serious hours* Antipholus
  could be punning only inadvertently.
30–1 Gnats are proverbially worth
  (Tilley, G149); cf. *3H6* 2.6.9, *Tit* 4.4.82.
31 **But** i.e. but let them

21 jest? . . . me.] *Capell*; iest, . . . me? *F*   23 SD] *this edn; & that. Beats Dro. F*   29 common] comedy
Hanmer   hours.] *(howres,)*

179

If you will jest with me, know my aspect,
And fashion your demeanour to my looks,
Or I will beat this method in your sconce.

DROMIO OF SYRACUSE   'Sconce', call you it? So you   35
would leave battering, I had rather have it a 'head'.
An you use these blows long, I must get a sconce for
my head, and ensconce it, too, or else I shall seek my
wit in my shoulders. But, I pray, sir, why am I beaten?

ANTIPHOLUS OF SYRACUSE   Dost thou not know?   40

DROMIO OF SYRACUSE   Nothing, sir, but that I am beaten.

ANTIPHOLUS OF SYRACUSE   Shall I tell you why?

DROMIO OF SYRACUSE   Ay, sir, and wherefore; for, they
say, every why hath a wherefore.

ANTIPHOLUS OF SYRACUSE
'Why' first: for flouting me; and then 'wherefore':   45

---

32 **aspect** aspèct; the favourable or unfavour-
able dispositions of the planets, determined
astrologically by their relative positions
to each other as observed from earth (see
OED n. 4); cf. *WT* 2.1.105–7. With his
metaphors of sun and gnat, planet and
human, Antipholus claims hierarchical
distance from Dromio. Cf. *aspects* at 117.

34 **method** 'instruction' (Warburton)
    in into

34–8 **sconce ... 'Sconce' ... sconce ...
ensconce** As both Dromios do elsewhere,
Dromio reacts to violence by quibbling.
Antipholus' threat (34) to beat Dromio
about the head (*OED* sconce *n.*²) makes
Dromio think of his *Sconce* (35) figuratively as a small fort (*OED n.*³ 1b)
threatened with battering and requiring
a protective screen (37–8) (*OED n.*³ 2;
see also *n.*¹ 1). Dromio will thus need to
ensconce, shelter, himself behind a
fortification (*OED v.* 2) (cf. *Luc* 1515, *Son*
49.9). As a jocular term for head, especially
the crown, *sconce* (at 34; cf. 1.2.79 and n.,
on *break ... sconce*) is associated with
sense and wit (*OED n.*²). Behind

Antipholus' image of knocking knowledge
into the head stands the Elizabethan school
practice of corporal punishment; cf.
4.4.24–7 and 4.4.24, 26n.

35–114 Dromio and Antipholus employ a fast-
paced, arhythmic prose suited to a
wit-contest. They will shift briefly and self-
consciously into verse at 45–9.

35 **So** if only (*OED adv.* and *conj.* 26a)

37 **An** if

38–9 **seek ... shoulders** because beating will
have collapsed his head into his shoulders.
Dromio may also demonstrate his wisdom
by showing his shoulders to Antipholus as
he runs away (Ard¹); cf. *AC* 3.11.7–8. He
may, too, be invoking the proverb 'He has
more wit in his head than you in both your
shoulders' (Tilley, W548) (Ard²).

44 **every ... wherefore** proverbial (Dent,
W331); see also *H5* 5.1.3–4, *Ham* 1.4.57.
Because Dromio uses *why* and *wherefore*
redundantly, Antipholus will make a
double answer (45–6). Cf. 3.1.39 and n.,
on *I'll ... wherefore*.

45–8 *Antipholus mocks Dromio's formulaic
request by responding in iambic

---

35 'Sconce'] *Wells;* Sconce *F*   it? So] *(it? so) Fc;* it so? *Fu*   36 'head'.] *Folg²;* head, *F*   37 An] *(and)*
43 Ay] *(I)*   45–6] *Capell; prose F*   45 'Why' ... 'wherefore'] *Oxf;* Why ... wherefore *F*

For urging it the second time to me.
DROMIO OF SYRACUSE
Was there ever any man thus beaten out of season,
When in the why and the wherefore is neither
   rhyme nor reason?
Well, sir, I thank you.
ANTIPHOLUS OF SYRACUSE   Thank me, sir, for what?
DROMIO OF SYRACUSE   Marry, sir, for this something   50
that you gave me for nothing.
ANTIPHOLUS OF SYRACUSE   I'll make you amends next,
to give you nothing for something. But say, sir, is it
dinner-time?

pentameter, alliterated in 45. Dromio
(47–8) repudiates and parodies Antipholus'
claim with a clever tumbling-verse couplet
(a tumbling-verse line typically has four
strong stresses and an irregular number of
unstressed syllables; see 3.1.11–85n.).
Dromio tops Antipholus by rhyming: *season/
reason*. These two speeches are prose in F,
but Dromio's rhyme suggests verse; also,
in F, Antipholus' prose speech breaks where
a blank verse line break would come.

45 **flouting** See 22n. Folg² sees an allusion in
this exchange to the biblical story of
Balaam and his ass (Numbers, 22.21–34):
the ass queries why he is being beaten, and
Balaam answers, 'Because thou hast
mocked me' (22.29).

46 **urging it** pushing it forward (*OED* urge *v.*
5)

47 **out of season** another oblique time reference. See 1.2.68n., on *out of season*; cf.
66–7 and n., below, and 4.2.57 and n.

48 **neither . . . reason** i.e. neither fitness nor
reasonableness: *rhyme* connotes a correspondence lacking here (*OED n.* 1d). Proverbial (Dent, R98); cf. e.g. *TGV* 2.1.143–4,
LLL 1.1.99. Cf. *reason* at 63, 93, 108.

49 Dromio's ironic politeness justifies maintaining the verse for his half-line, with
Antipholus' next speech completing a

shared verse line. Nonetheless, the speeches
in 45–51 can be shifted back and forth
across the border of prose and verse.

50 **Marry** i.e. by the Virgin Mary, expressing
surprise; a mild oath; also at 71

50–1 **something . . . nothing** recalling the
proverb 'Nothing can come of nothing'
(Dent, N285), although here meaning
'something in payment for nothing'

53 **give . . . something** i.e. Antipholus threatens
to pay him nothing for his services (Ard²).
The reversal of terms is rhetorical
chiasmus.

53–114 **But . . . conclusion** This wit-debate,
or mock disputation, constitutes a set piece
typical in Shakespeare's early plays (see
e.g. *RJ* 2.4.36–100). It re-establishes the
bonhomie and intellectual parity between
master and slave. But the two argue at
cross-purposes: Antipholus insists that
actions be aptly fitted to their circumstances, while Dromio contends that actions
become irreversible and lost to time. The
exchange's   parallelisms,   antitheses,
chiasmuses and puns owe much to Lyly's
snappy dramatic dialogue. The debate
rings comic variations on the play's
concerns: time and timeliness; loss and
recovery; ageing; legal process; evidence
and argumentation; and sexuality. Overall,

47–8] *Rowe³; prose F*   48 reason?] *Rowe³; reason. F*   49] *Ard¹; prose F*   Thank . . . what] *verse Munro*

DROMIO OF SYRACUSE   No, sir, I think the meat wants   55
   that I have.

ANTIPHOLUS OF SYRACUSE   In good time, sir, what's
   that?

DROMIO OF SYRACUSE   Basting.

ANTIPHOLUS OF SYRACUSE   Well, sir, then 'twill be dry.   60

DROMIO OF SYRACUSE   If it be, sir, I pray you, eat none
   of it.

ANTIPHOLUS OF SYRACUSE   Your reason?

DROMIO OF SYRACUSE   Lest it make you choleric, and
   purchase me another dry basting.   65

ANTIPHOLUS OF SYRACUSE   Well, sir, learn to jest in
   good time: there's a time for all things.

DROMIO OF SYRACUSE   I durst have denied that before
   you were so choleric.

ANTIPHOLUS OF SYRACUSE   By what rule, sir?   70

---

the question whether or not 'there's a time for all things' (67) suggests the problems in the play of a life-or-death deadline and, more broadly, the possibility of recuperation.

55–6 prose, as in the surrounding dialogue, even though it scans as iambic pentameter

55 **wants** lacks; also at 157

57 **In good time** 'Indeed!', expressing ironical amazement (*OED* time *n*. P3k(b) (iii)); also at 66–7 (see n.); cf. *TS* 2.1.195.

59 **Basting** a pun: (1) moistening a roast (*OED* baste *v*.[2] 1); and (2) beating (*OED* basting *n*.[3], first citation); cf. Warner, 'basted' (34).

60 **dry** anticipating 65 (see 65n., on *dry basting*)

63 **reason** Antipholus turns the tables on Dromio; see 48 and n.

64, 69 **choleric** angry (*OED adj*. 4a). Choler, or yellow bile (one of the four fluid humours), made men hot and irascible; see 1.2.21n. A food's humoural characteristics (e.g. hot and dry) could produce that humour (e.g. choleric) in an individual: a man's 'temperament or balance of humours depended on his diet' (Ard[2]); cf. *TS* 4.1.169–72.

65 **purchase** obtain (for), acquire (for) (*OED v*. 4a): ironical; cf. *bargain*, 25.
   dry basting a beating that leaves bruises but does not draw blood (*OED* dry *adj*. 12; *OED* basting *vbl*. *n*.[3]). If *basting* is moistening (59n.), then *dry basting* is paradoxical.

66–7 **in good time** 'at the right moment' (*OED* time *n*. P3.k(b) (i)); also at 57 (see n.); cf. 47 and n.

67 **there's ... things** proverbial (Dent, T314); cf. Ecclesiastes, 3.1–4: 'Every thyng hath a tyme, yea all that is vnder the heauen hath his conuenient season . . . A tyme to weepe, and a tyme to laugh'; cf. 105 and n. Lyly similarly alludes to Ecclesiastes in *MB*, 5.3.17–18 (Shaheen, 107). Cf. 4.2.57 and n.

70 **rule** i.e. in logic or dialectic (see *OED n*. 7)

55–6] *verse Theobald*[2]   61–2] *verse Knight*   61 none] not *F2*

DROMIO OF SYRACUSE   Marry, sir, by a rule as plain as
the plain bald pate of Father Time himself.
ANTIPHOLUS OF SYRACUSE   Let's hear it.
DROMIO OF SYRACUSE   There's no time for a man to
recover his hair that grows bald by nature.   75
ANTIPHOLUS OF SYRACUSE   May he not do it by fine and
recovery?
DROMIO OF SYRACUSE   Yes, to pay a fine for a periwig
and recover the lost hair of another man.
ANTIPHOLUS OF SYRACUSE   Why is Time such a niggard   80
of hair, being, as it is, so plentiful an excrement?
DROMIO OF SYRACUSE   Because it is a blessing that he
bestows on beasts; and what he hath scanted men in
hair he hath given them in wit.

71   **Marry** See 50n.
72   **plain** smooth (Onions, plain *n.* 2), i.e.
hairless, bald; see 89–90 and n.
pate See 1.2.65.
Father Time typically depicted as aged,
bearded and bald except for a forelock,
wearing a robe and carrying a scythe.
See Figure 5, p. 31. Time's baldness was
proverbial (Dent, T311). Cf. Whitney, 181,
'In occasionem'. Personifying Time gives
it dramatic presence. Cf. 110–11; 5.1.299
and n. and LN, on *Time's deformed hand*.
75   **that** i.e. who (see Abbott, 262)
by nature naturally; see also 107 and
1.1.34 and nn.
76–7   **fine and recovery** alluding to two legal
manoeuvres that allow a person to convey
to another person an inherited estate that
otherwise might not be transferable
because of legal restrictions (entailments)
on the inheritance. The exchange plays
on *recover(y)* (covering over again;
regaining), and quibbles on *hair* and 'heir',
fine and 'foin' (Ard²). 'Foin' can refer to
fur used to trim gowns (Kökeritz, 107),
and to a sword-thrust (*OED n.²* 1), with

sexual connotations. In both a *fine* (meaning a sham legal suit, *OED n.*¹ 6b) and a
recovery (*OED n.* 2a), the person to whom
the estate is to be conveyed – in the case of
a *fine*, often a married woman who could
obtain the property by no other means
– sues a friendly defendant who admits
the suitor's right to the land, which the
court then records. This complicated legal
strategy is described in *Shakespeare's
England* (1.404–6). Shakespeare alludes
to *fine* and *recovery* in *Ham* 5.1.105–6,
MW 4.2.211.
78   **periwig** highly stylized wig, as worn by
judges and barristers (*OED n.* 1a); the best
were made from human hair; cf. *MV*
3.2.92–6 (Ard²).
79   **recover** The head is 'recovered' with hair
by the wig, effecting the 'recovery' of hair
lost by someone else.
80   **niggard** miser (*OED n.* 1)
81   **excrement** outgrowth, especially hair and
nails; cf. *LLL* 5.1.104, *Ham* 3.4.121.
83   **scanted** given in insufficient quantity
(*OED scant v.* 3a); deprived (of) (*OED* 3b)
84   **wit** intelligence; see 2.1.90.

80 Why] *Pope;* Why, *F*   83 men] *Theobald;* them *F*

ANTIPHOLUS OF SYRACUSE   Why, but there's many a   85
man hath more hair than wit.

DROMIO OF SYRACUSE   Not a man of those but he hath
the wit to lose his hair.

ANTIPHOLUS OF SYRACUSE   Why, thou didst conclude
hairy men plain dealers without wit.   90

DROMIO OF SYRACUSE   The plainer dealer, the sooner
lost; yet he loseth it in a kind of jollity.

ANTIPHOLUS OF SYRACUSE   For what reason?

DROMIO OF SYRACUSE   For two, and sound ones, too.

ANTIPHOLUS OF SYRACUSE   Nay, not sound, I pray you.   95

DROMIO OF SYRACUSE   Sure ones, then.

85–6 there's . . . wit proverbial (Dent, B736).
Men without wit are 'easily entrapped by
loose women', and the consequence of
'lewdness' is 'loss of hair' from syphilis
(Johnson). Allusions to venereal disease
will recur: see nn. at 86, 91–2, 150, 183 (n.
on *possess*), 186 (n. on *Infect*); 3.2.126–7
(126n. on *armed*); 4.3.58 (n. on *light . . .
burn*).

86 hath . . . hair i.e. is clever enough to lose
his hair from venereal disease; cf. 85–6
and n.; *MND* 1.2.97–8. Dromio's reversal
of Antipholus' order of terms, *wit* and *hair*,
constitutes chiasmus.

89–90 Antipholus seeks through puns to catch
Dromio in a contradiction of *hairy* and
plain. His *hairy men* alludes to the hairy
Old Testament figure Esau, who, when
hungry, foolishly (*without wit*) sold his
birthright to his opportunistic brother Jacob
for a mess of potage (Genesis, 25.29–34)
(Shaheen, 107–8). Esau, *hairy* and rightful
'heir' to his father Isaac, satisfied his
immediate need for food but betrayed his
long-term interests. The story served as an
allegory for erring humanity. Esau is *plain*
for being naïve; *plain dealers* means
honest and straightforward persons (*OED*
plain dealer *n.*), but here also people

lacking wit (Ard²; cf. *MV* 3.5.57–8), or
unsophisticated (*OED* plain *adj.*¹ 15). But
if *plain* in one sense, Esau is not in another,
for *plain* can also mean hairless (see 72n.,
on *plain*). In the Bishops' Bible, Esau's
exterior at birth is called 'a hearie garment'
(Genesis, 25.25), and in the Geneva Bible,
Jacob is referred to as 'a plaine man'
(Genesis, 25.27), with *plain* meaning
'smooth', as in clean-shaven. Antipholus
thus accuses Dromio of the biblical
'fallacy' of conjoining *hairy* and *plain*. Cf.
WT 4.4.721–2. The term *plain dealer* is
proverbial (Dent, P381–3). To 'deal' can
also mean to have sexual intercourse (*OED*
v. 11b).

91–2 The plainer . . . lost i.e. the more a man
has sexual intercourse with women, the
sooner he will lose hair through venereal
disease; cf. 85–6 and n.

92 jollity sexual pleasure (*OED n.* 3). Wells
suspects a series of sexual jokes in 93–8:
reason (perhaps punning on testicles as
'raisins'); *two, and sound ones* (healthy
testicles); *thing* (sexual organ); *falsing*
(sexual deception).

93 reason See 48 and n.

95 not sound not valid; also not morally or
physically healthy

---

91 jollity] policy *Ard (Staunton)*   93 reason?] *F2;* reason. *F*   95 sound] sound ones *F2*

ANTIPHOLUS OF SYRACUSE   Nay, not sure, in a thing falsing.

DROMIO OF SYRACUSE   Certain ones, then.

ANTIPHOLUS OF SYRACUSE   Name them.   100

DROMIO OF SYRACUSE   The one, to save the money that he spends in tiring; the other, that at dinner they should not drop in his porridge.

ANTIPHOLUS OF SYRACUSE   You would all this time have proved there is no time for all things.   105

DROMIO OF SYRACUSE   Marry, and did, sir: namely, e'en no time to recover hair lost by nature.

ANTIPHOLUS OF SYRACUSE   But your reason was not substantial, why there is no time to recover.

DROMIO OF SYRACUSE   Thus I mend it: Time himself is   110 bald, and, therefore, to the world's end will have bald followers.

ANTIPHOLUS OF SYRACUSE   I knew 'twould be a bald conclusion.

Enter ADRIANA[*, beckoning to them,*] *and* LUCIANA.

97 **falsing** unreliable; deceptive (*OED* false *v.* 1, 4), only in Shakespeare here. For 'false' as a verb, see *Cym* 2.3.69, and 'falsed', *FQ*, 1.2.30 (Ard¹).

102 ***tiring** dressing, or caring for, his hair (*OED vbl. n.*³). F's 'trying' is probably a compositorial error of transposed letters. **they** i.e. the plain dealer's hairs

103 **porridge** soup, as at *LLL* 1.1.303

104–5 **all . . . all** The repetition of *all* and *time* in reversed order instances rhetorical *antimetabole*.

105 **there . . . things** referring to Ecclesiastes, 3.1; see 67n.

106 **Marry** expressing surprise (*OED int.* 1) ***e'en** corrected from F's 'in' (Capell conj.). Ard² speculates either a scribal

error through sound association (*e'en*/'in') or a confusing Shakespearean spelling of *e'en* as 'in', citing F's 'proclaime it in [e'en?] an howre before his entring' (*MM* F TLN 2279–80; 4.4.8–9) and 'Limbes are in [e'en?] his instruments, / In [e'en?] no lesse working, then are Swords and Bowes' (*TC* F TLN 821–2; 1.3.354–5).

107 **by nature** See 75n.

108 **reason** See 48 and n.

109 **substantial** sound, solidly established (*OED adj.* 10); the word has dialectical and legal connotations (see *OED* 5).

110 **mend** i.e. amend; also at 3.2.106 **Time . . . bald** See 72n.

113 **bald** bare of meaning, trivial (*OED adj.* 6)

114.1 *See 2.1.42.1 LN.

98 falsing] falling *Halliwell (Heath)*   102 tiring] *Pope;* trying F; trimming *Rowe*   106–7 e'en no] *Boswell–Malone (Capell, Notes);* in no F; no F2   113–15] *Capell lines* conclusion. / yonder? /   114.1] *Cam¹; after 115 F*   beckoning to them] *Cam¹ subst.*

185

But soft! Who wafts us yonder? 115

ADRIANA

Ay, ay, Antipholus, look strange and frown:
Some other mistress hath thy sweet aspects;
I am not Adriana, nor thy wife.
The time was once when thou unurged wouldst vow
That never words were music to thine ear, 120
That never object pleasing in thine eye,
That never touch well welcome to thy hand,
That never meat sweet-savoured in thy taste,

115 Antipholus' line has the rhythm of iambic verse, transitional to the ensuing pentameters.

But soft enjoining silence or forestalling haste (*OED* soft *adv.* 8a); cf. 4.1.19.

wafts signals by waving the hand (*OED v.*[2] 2); cf. *MV* 5.1.11. The word is associated with sea-journeys (*OED v.*[1] 1, 2), as at *3H6* 3.3.253, 5.7.41.

116–52 *CE*'s longest speech, earnest and moving not only for its evocation of lapsed love but for its (Protestant) vision of 'companionate marriage' as physical, spiritual and mutual. Such marriage, rooted in Ephesians, 5.21–33, and in the Elizabethan 'Homily on Matrimony', requires its partners to give up stubborn will and self-love; to become understanding, attentive and compassionate; and to achieve together 'one concord of heart and mind' (*Homilies*, 548; see Hennings). Yet Adriana urges the Pauline notion that husband and wife become '*one flesh*' (*Homilies*, 546) in an unsettlingly extreme sense, and the speech variously shifts towards comedy; see p. 48.

116 **look strange** pretend, like a stranger, not to know me; cf. 5.1.296, *Son* 89.8 (Ard[2]). Cf. 126, 127, 155 and nn.

117 **aspects** aspècts; looks or glances (*OED n.* 1b, first citation); cf. 32 and n.

118 Cf. 3.2.41 and n.

119–24 In terms of rhetoric, cf. *TGV* 3.1.174–84.

119 **unurged** not urged (*OED adj.* 1, first citation)

120–4 Adriana describes her former ability to please Antipholus' senses (sound, sight, touch and taste). See also *VA* 427–50; *FQ*, 2.11.7–13; George Chapman's *Ovid's Banquet of Sense* (1595). Adriana's repetition of words (*That never*) at the beginning of successive phrases, with its climactic recapitulation in 124, is rhetorical *anaphora* (Cam[2]); it integrates the passage, makes its points parallel and sets its lines apart. The effect is strengthened by repetitions in the second halves of lines (*thine/thine*; *thy/thy*). For *anaphora*, cf. e.g. 141–4 and n.; 4.3.4–6 and n., 16–33 and n. At 124, Adriana employs a dignified hexameter to recapitulate her *That* clauses of 120–3, concluding with the intimate *I . . . to thee*. Pope marks the lines' elevated poetic quality, and he may have imitated 120 in his 'Epistle from Sappho to Phaon' (54) (Malone).

122 **well** certainly, indeed (used in a concessive sense) (*OED adv.* 8b)

123 **sweet-savoured** seasoned sweet (*OED* savour *v.* 5–8). Meat was sometimes baked with 'sweet suet' or basted with 'sweet . . . butter' (Harrison, 312). 'Sweet powder' (*OED* powder *n.*[1] C3), mixed

115] *verse Pope*   116 Ay, ay] *(I, I)*   117 thy] *some F2*

Unless I spake, or looked, or touched, or carved to
   thee.
How comes it now, my husband, O, how comes it,   125
That thou art then estranged from thyself?
'Thyself' I call it, being strange to me
That, undividable, incorporate,
Am better than thy dear self's better part.
[*Reaches for him.*]
Ah, do not tear away thyself from me!   130
For know, my love: as easy mayst thou fall

from aromatic spices and sometimes sugar, was used with pork and other dishes. Cf. 5.1.73.

124 to 'with a view to' (Abbott, 186), i.e. for

125–52 Adriana insists that husband and wife are literally one; cf. 2.1.94–8. Her view has scriptural basis: 'For this cause [i.e. marriage] shall a man leaue father and mother, and shallbe ioyned vnto his wife, and two shalbe made one flesshe' (Ephesians, 5.31; see also Genesis, 2.24, Matthew, 19.5–6). The Elizabethan marriage service refers to husband and wife being 'made one' (Shaheen, 109). Yet Adriana's mistaking of her husband undercuts her claims. Cf. Syracusan Antipholus to Luciana, 3.2.66 and n.

125 Adriana's repetition of a phrase constitutes rhetorical *diacope*; see 1.1.66–7 and n. Antipholus may show surprise at *my husband*. For another repetition, see 126–7 and n.

126 estranged estrangèd; echoing *strange* at 116

126–7 thyself? / **'Thyself'** rhetorical *epizeuxis*. Cf. 125 and n., 2.1.106–7 and n.

127–9 i.e. I call your being estranged from me the same as being estranged from yourself, since I am incorporated into you and indivisible from you, and that I-in-you is worth more than even the best, partial

aspect of you alone. See LN. Later, Syracusan Antipholus will woo Luciana with identical language, as if unconsciously remembered from Adriana; see 3.2.61 and n.

127 strange to 'a stranger to' (cf. 116); 'distant from'

129 better part perhaps 'best qualities' (Ard²) or soul (Ard¹); cf. 3.2.61 and n.; also 'My spirit is thine, the better part of me' (*Son* 74.8).

129 SD Adriana probably clutches after Antipholus, who pulls away, prompting Adriana's plea that he not *tear* (130) himself from her.

131–5 Adriana repeats Antipholus of Syracuse's drop-of-water image from 1.2.35–8. For Antipholus in 1.2, the image bespeaks his fear of self-negation and dissolution from mixing his identity with others (see 1.2.35–40 and n.). By contrast, Adriana embraces the marital incorporation of two selves into one (see 127–9n.). Images of watery dissolution will recur when Antipholus woos Luciana; see e.g. 3.2.45–52 and n.

131 fall let fall; in a secondary sense, 'fall as', since in Adriana's metaphor Antipholus is the drop and she (perhaps with unintended irony) the *breaking gulf* (i.e. the breaking coastal sea-waves: *OED* gulf *n.* 1) in 132; cf. *falling*, 1.2.37.

124 spake . . . touched] spake, look'd, touch'd *Steevens⁴*   to thee] *om. Pope*   127 'Thyself'] *Folg²*; Thy selfe *F*; Thy 'self' *Oxf¹*   128] *Theobald*; That vndiuidable Incorporate *F*; That, undividable, incorporate, *Kittredge*   129 SD] *this edn*   131 know,] *Rowe*; know *F*

A drop of water in the breaking gulf,
And take unmingled thence that drop again
Without addition or diminishing,
As take from me thyself, and not me, too.   135
How dearly would it touch thee to the quick
Shouldst thou but hear I were licentious?
And that this body, consecrate to thee,
By ruffian lust should be contaminate?
Wouldst thou not spit at me, and spurn at me,   140
And hurl the name of 'husband' in my face,
And tear the stained skin off my harlot brow,
And from my false hand cut the wedding ring,
And break it with a deep-divorcing vow?

136–52 Pursuing the implications of marital incorporation, Adriana argues that one partner's (Antipholus') breaking of the marriage vows makes the other partner (Adriana) equally guilty of adultery. Her speech underscores her earlier concern for her husband's reputation (Oxf[1]); see 2.1.108–12 and n.

136 **dearly** deeply, keenly (*OED adv.* 3c); Ard[1] glosses 'grievously'.
   touch ... quick proverbial (Dent, Q13). The *quick* is the core of one's being, the seat of feeling and emotion.

137 **licentious** sexually unrestrained by law or morality

138 **consecrate** consecrated

139 **ruffian lust** Personifications of lust (F has 'Ruffian Lust') as a lower-class criminal are not uncommon in the period; cf. *Luc* 693; *Son* 129.1–4; *FQ*, 3.1.17, 4.7.4–8.
   contaminate contaminated

140 **spurn** kick. Adriana applies to herself the word that Ephesian Dromio used to protest against her abusive treatment of him at 2.1.81–4 (see n.).

141–4 The repetition of *And* at the beginning of each line again instances *anaphora*

'when we make one word begin, and ... lead the dance to many verses' (Puttenham, 198). The successive *And*-plus-verb clauses, launched at 140, make Adriana sound, for a moment, possessed rhetorically while she talks of being 'possessed with an adulterate blot' (146). On *anaphora*, see also 120–4 and n.

142 Adriana imagines her forehead (*brow*) becoming stained from adultery and her husband ripping away the skin; cf. 'stain the brow', *1H4* 1.1.85. Later, Ephesian Antipholus will call Adriana a harlot (4.4.102 and n.; cf. 5.1.205) and threaten to disfigure her face (5.1.183 and n.). The *brow* – cloudy, frowning, bent, lifted, sad, gentle, angry, honest, gracious – recurs in Shakespeare as a place where disposition is revealed. See LN.
   stained dulled in beauty and morally defiled; stigmatized (*OED* stain *v.* 5a, b, c); cf. *MV* 1.3.139. The sense of *stain* recurs in *blot* (146) and *dis-stained* (152); cf. also 3.2.13 and n., on *tainted*.
   harlot unchaste

143 **false** deceitful, treacherous (Folg[2])

144 **it** the ring, grammatically; the marriage,

137 licentious?] licentious; *Rowe;* licentious! *Rann*   139 contaminate?] contaminate! *Rann*   141 'husband'] *Andrews subst.;* husband *F*   142 off] *(of)*

188

I know thou canst, and, therefore, see thou do it!   145
I am possessed with an adulterate blot;
My blood is mingled with the crime of lust:
For if we two be one, and thou play false,
I do digest the poison of thy flesh,
Being strumpeted by thy contagion.   150
Keep, then, fair league and truce with thy true bed:
I live dis-stained, thou undishonoured.

metonymically. Adriana's husband will obtain a ring from the Courtesan (see 4.3.70 and n.).

deep profoundly, intensely, earnestly (*OED adv.* 2); cf. 'deep contemplative' (*AYL* 2.7.31); see Blake, 3.3.3.1.

vow Here and at 145, Adriana may mean that Antipholus can divorce her simply by taking a vow, a classical Roman practice.

146 **I . . . with** Adriana may mean that she experiences Antipholus' infidelity as a moral blemish inducing physical effects (*OED* blot *n.*[1] 1, 2), with *possessed* suggesting 'endowed with' (*OED* possess *v.* 9a); cf. *TS* 3.2.50. More darkly, Adriana may perceive his infidelity as a possessing demon (see *OED* possess *v.* 4) (cf. the personification of lust at 139). Forms of 'possess' occur more frequently in *CE* than in any other Shakespearean play and take on varied meanings; see 183 and see also, with associated nn., 3.1.105–6; 3.2.165; 4.4.56, 93; 5.1.44, 246.

adulterate adult'rate; adulterous (*OED adj.* 2).

blot Cf. 142 and n., on *stained*.

147 **blood** Antipholus' alleged sin of adultery has tainted (*stained*, 142), i.e. morally and physically corrupted, Adriana's blood (see *OED* stain *v.* 4a, 5d), with sin having physiological consequences.

crime sin (*OED n.* 2); cf. *Oth* 5.2.26.

149 **poison** Lucrece describes her body as 'poison'd' and her blood as 'stain'd' by Tarquin's rape (*Luc* 1655–9).

150 **strumpeted . . . contagion** i.e. turned into a whore by your disease (of adultery); *OED*'s earliest citation for 'strumpet' as a verb; *contagion* can mean 'poison' (*OED n.* 3b) (cf. *Ham* 4.7.147, *Son.* 66.6), as well as 'disease' (*OED* 2). The imagery of 149–52 recalls the spectre of syphilis raised at 85–6.

151 **Keep . . . truce** To 'keep fair league' would be to 'keep honest agreement', with *league* meaning covenant (*OED n.*[2] 2), and *fair*, 'lawful' or 'proper' (Crystal & Crystal, *adj.* 10); both are military terms. Cf. 2.1.107.

Keep 'if you keep'

bed metonymy for marriage

152 *****dis-stained** unstained; clear of stain (Folg[2]) (cf. 142 and n., on *stained*). The usage is unconventional: the *OED* defines 'distain' as to defile, stain or dishonour (*OED v.* 2); 'distain' occurs in *Luc* with the sense of 'stain' (786), but here Shakespeare means the opposite. Theobald understood *dis-* in a 'privative sense, implying . . . negation, reversal of action', as in 'disjoin', 'displease' or 'dissuade' (*OED* dis- *prefix* 4). Such a nonce-use of *dis-* as negation occurs in 'dis-horn the spirit' (*MW* 4.4.64). John Palsgrave's *Lesclarcissement de la langue Francoyse* (1530) defines 'distayne' as 'chaunge the colour' (sig. 3E5ᵛ) (Folg[2]). Following Theobald, *dis-stained* is hyphenated to signify its usage.

undishonoured undishonourèd; *OED adj.*, first citation

149 thy] my *F2* 151–2] *lines transposed in Cam*[1] 152 dis-stained . . . undishonoured] *Theobald;* distain'd . . . vndishonoured *F;* distain'd, and . . . dishonoured *Rowe;* unstain'd . . . undishonoured *Hanmer (Theobald);* distain'd . . . one dishonoured *White;* undistain'd . . . undishonoured *Keightley*

ANTIPHOLUS OF SYRACUSE

Plead you to me, fair dame? I know you not:
In Ephesus I am but two hours old,
As strange unto your town as to your talk,   155
Who, every word by all my wit being scanned,
Wants wit in all, one word to understand.

LUCIANA

Fie, brother! How the world is changed with you:
When were you wont to use my sister thus?
She sent for you by Dromio home to dinner.   160

ANTIPHOLUS OF SYRACUSE   By Dromio?

DROMIO OF SYRACUSE   By me?

ADRIANA

By thee, and this thou didst return from him:
That he did buffet thee, and, in his blows,
Denied my house for his, me for his wife.   165

ANTIPHOLUS OF SYRACUSE [*to Dromio*]

Did you converse, sir, with this gentlewoman?
What is the course and drift of your compact?

DROMIO OF SYRACUSE

I, sir? I never saw her till this time.

---

153 **Plead . . . dame** Cf. *Men.*, 369.

154 **two hours old** another time marker

155–7 To match Adriana's manner, Antipholus speaks with heightened poeticism: parallelisms, alliteration (*t*, *w*), end-rhyme and (in 156–7) rhetorical *conduplicato* (repetition of a word, here *word*, in successive clauses).

155 **strange** responding to Adriana's *strange* (116) and *estranged* (126); see 116n.

156 **Who** The antecedent, *I* (154), occurs some distance away; see Abbott, 263. *Who* with *Wants* (157) has the grammatical force of third-person (Cam²).

scanned interpreted (*OED v.* 4); cf. *Ham* 3.3.75.

157 **Wants** See 55n.

158 **brother** i.e. brother-in-law

161–2 These lines break the pattern of verse and perhaps make room for physical reactions.

167 'What is the direction and meaning of your plot?' The terms *course* and *drift* constitute a repetition (*tautologia*) for effect, since the words can have approximately the same meaning (see *OED* course *n.* 19; drift *n.* 4b).

compact compàct; conspiracy (*OED n.* 1c)

161–2] *F4, Munro; verse Wells; printed on one line in F*   162 me?] *Rowe²;* me. *F;* me! *Dyce*   163 this] thus *F2*   166 SD] *Andrews subst.*

ANTIPHOLUS OF SYRACUSE
Villain, thou lie'st! For even her very words
Didst thou deliver to me on the mart.   170
DROMIO OF SYRACUSE
I never spake with her in all my life.
ANTIPHOLUS OF SYRACUSE
How can she thus, then, call us by our names? –
Unless it be by inspiration.
ADRIANA
How ill agrees it with your gravity
To counterfeit thus grossly with your slave,   175
Abetting him to thwart me in my mood.
Be it my wrong, you are from me exempt;
But wrong not that wrong with a more contempt.
Come, I will fasten [*taking his arm*] on this sleeve
    of thine:
Thou art an elm, my husband, I a vine,   180

---

169 **Villain** See 1.2.19n.
170 **mart** alluding to the site of 1.2 (see 1.2n.);
also the place of the present action (see
14n., on *here*), although conceptually the
action is moving closer to Adriana's house
(see Ard²)
173 **inspiration** knowledge gained through
supernatural agency (*OED n.* 3a); *-ion* is
two syllables.
175 **counterfeit** dissimulate (*OED v.* 6)
    grossly obviously (*OED adv.* 2), or
clumsily (*OED* 6b); cf. *MW* 2.2.142.
    slave Cf. 1.2.87 and n., on *slave.*
176 **mood** anger (*OED n.*¹ 2b); cf. *TGV* 4.1.49.
177–8 'Let it be an offence done to me that
you are estranged, but do not compound
that injustice with increased contempt.'
Adriana's phrase *my wrong* refers to the
injustice or harm that she has sustained
from Antipholus (*OED wrong n.*² 5a, b);
cf. 4.2.8 and n., on *spite*; *TS* 4.3.2. Her

exempt means 'cut off' or 'removed from
allegiance' (*OED adj.* 1c, d); cf. *AYL*
2.1.15, *1H6* 2.4.93; *more* is a comparative
intensifier: 'greater' (Blake, 3.2.3.4). The
repetition of *wrong* with different
meanings is rhetorical *antistasis*. The shift
here (177–208) into rhyme marks
Adriana's 'abandonment of anger' and
Antipholus' 'transition from hostility to
acceptance of a fantastic situation' (Ard²).
179 **sleeve** Luciana will later use *sleeve* as an
image of marital deception; see 3.2.23 and
n.
180 The comparison of man and wife to an elm
with a vine trained to grow around it was
proverbial ('The vine embraces the elm',
Dent, V61). The 'Homily on Matrimony'
alludes to Psalms, 128.3: '*Thy wife shall
be as a vine plentifully spreading about thy
house*' (*Homilies*, 540). Adriana will
contrast the fruitful vine to *Usurping*

---

169 lie'st! For] *Oxf¹;* liest, for *F*   172–3 names? – . . . inspiration.] *Ard²;* names? . . . inspiration. *F;*
names, . . . inspiration? *F4*   176 mood.] *(*moode;*);* mood? *F4;* mood! *Hanmer*   179 SD] *Folg² subst.;*
thine. *She clings to him.* / *Bevington*⁴

Whose weakness, married to thy stronger state,
Makes me with thy strength to communicate.
If aught possess thee from me, it is dross,
Usurping ivy, briar or idle moss,
Who, all for want of pruning, with intrusion   185
Infect thy sap, and live on thy confusion.

ANTIPHOLUS OF SYRACUSE [*aside*]
To me she speaks; she moves me for her theme.
What, was I married to her in my dream?
Or sleep I now and think I hear all this?
What error drives our eyes and ears amiss?   190
Until I know this sure uncertainty,

infectious *ivy* (184–6), i.e. Antipholus' presumed paramours. Adriana employs vivid but literary imagery. Although elms were common in Warwickshire, Shakespeare probably took the image of elm and trained vine from reading rather than observation (see Ellacombe, 88; Richens, 157). For classical antecedents and contemporary examples, see LN.

181 **Whose weakness** Cf. 'Lykewyse ye husbandes . . . geuyng honour vnto the wyfe, as vnto the weaker vessell' (1 Peter, 3.7; see Shaheen, 109).

182 **communicate** partake of (*OED v.* 6)

183 **possess** See 146n., on *I . . . with*; *possess* can also mean 'infect' (*OED v.* 2c). Shakespeare may be combining meanings: demonic possession and venereal disease; cf. 85–6 and n.
  from 'apart from' (Blake, 5.4.2)
  dross dregs, impure matter (*OED n.* 2)

184 **ivy . . . moss** parasitic plants, represented as destructive, troublesome and useless. On ivy, cf. *Tem* 1.2.86–7; on moss, *Tit* 2.3.95. On ivy and elm, cf. *MND* 4.1.43–4.
  briar 'A prickly, thorny bush or shrub' (*OED n.*[1])
  idle useless, barren (*OED adj.* 3a); cf. 214, *Oth* 1.3.140.

185 **with intrusion** by forced entry; cf.

3.1.103–4 and n., *Luc* 848.

186 **Infect** possibly alluding to syphilis; cf. 85–6 and n.
  confusion ruin, destruction (*OED n.* 1)

187 SD as the third-person *she* (187) and *her* (187, 188) indicate

187 [2]**she . . . theme** 'she takes me as the subject of her discourse'
  moves propounds or puts forward (*OED v.* 30); cf. *MA* 4.1.73. The word also carries the legal sense of 'plead' (*OED* 28).
  theme 'subject' (*OED n.* 1), as at 5.1.65

188–92 Cf. 5.1.352; *TN* 4.1.60–3 (Ard[2]).

188 implying that he has an uncanny recollection of her or that she is a dreamfigment. In *Men.*, Sosicles Menaechmus believes that Erotium is dreaming (395).

190 **error** first occurrence in the play of this key word; cf. 3.2.35; 5.1.388, 397. Here *error* refers to a prior state of mind that misleads the senses, a delusion (*OED n.* 3a), consistent with Antipholus' fear of Ephesian sorcery (see 1.2.97–102 and n.). See pp. 11–13.

191 **sure uncertainty** 'definite mystery', an oxymoron

191–2 **uncertainty . . . fallacy** an off-rhyme (after seven rhyming couplets), perhaps a 'fallacious' rhyme marking Antipholus' error-fraught decision

181 stronger] *F3;* stranger *F*   187 SD] *Capell subst.*

I'll entertain the offered fallacy.

LUCIANA

Dromio, go bid the servants spread for dinner.

DROMIO OF SYRACUSE [*aside*]

O, for my beads! I cross me [*crossing himself*] for
  a sinner.

This is the fairy land; O, spite of spites,   195

We talk with goblins, owls and sprites!

If we obey them not, this will ensue:

They'll suck our breath or pinch us black and blue.

---

192 **entertain . . . fallacy** i.e. treat the error as if it might be true (see *OED* entertain *v.* 14b). In *Men.*, Sosicles Menaechmus follows Erotium indoors for the purpose of material gain, 'booty' (441).
  *****the offered** F's 'the free'd' may reflect a 'compositor's misdivision of the contracted form "thofred" in the copy' (Cam¹).
  fallacy delusive notion, error; the condition of being deceived (*OED n.* 4, first citation); Shakespeare's only use
194 SD1 Dromio babbles to himself, as implied by his failure to respond to Luciana's command (193) and by her question, 'Why prat'st thou to thyself' (199). Both Syracusans are lost in wonder.
194 **beads** prayer beads, a rosary, implying that Dromio would repeat 'Hail Marys' and 'Our Fathers' to ward off evil spirits
  cross me cross myself, i.e. make the sign of the cross on my body for its evil-averting power; a reference to Catholic practice
195 **fairy land** Fairies were thought to possess not only a dark power but a passion and vitality exceeding those of quotidian life (see Lewis, 123–38). Protestant reformers associated fairies and the fairy realm with

Catholic superstition: 'what a world of hel-worke, deuil-worke, and Elue-worke had we walking amongst vs heere in England, what time that popish mist had befogged the eyes of our poore people' (Harsnett, sig. S3ᵛ); see also Woodcock, 9–29.
  spite of spites 'worst of all possible vexations'; *spite* denotes an outrage, harm or injury, produced by a malignant force (*OED n.* 1).
196 F's line, retained here, has been much emended by editors because of its shortness and its reference to *owls*; see t.n. and LN.
198 **breath** Demoniacs often experienced breathlessness (see Ewen, 96, 170, 191).
  pinch . . . blue proverbial (Dent, B160). Fairies pinched the lustful or the lazy; see e.g. *MW* 5.5.45–102. In *Tem*, Prospero charges his 'goblins' to make his enemies 'pinch-spotted' (4.1.258–60). For other examples, see Lyly, *Endymion*, 4.3.33–45 (Ard²); Jonson, *Alchemist*, 3.5.32, 36; Middleton, *The Witch*, 1.2.9–10.
  pinch This word will be made manifest in Doctor Pinch (4.4), who captures and binds ('pinches') Ephesian Antipholus and Dromio.

---

192 offered] *Capell;* free'd *F;* favour'd *Rowe³;* proffer'd *Collier² (Singer);* forced *Halliwell*   194 SD1] *Cowden Clarke*   SD2] *Bevington⁴ subst. (after* sinner.*)*   196 We . . . and] We talke with Goblins, Owles and Elves *F2;* We talk with goblins, owls, and elvish *Pope;* We talk with goblins, ouphs, and elvish *Theobald;* We talk with goblins, owles, elves, and *White;* For here we talk with goblins, elves, and *Keightley;* We talk with fairies, goblins, elves, and *Ard¹;* We talk with goblins, elves and *Ard²;* We talk with goblins, oafs, and *Oxf;* We talk with goblins, ouphs, and *Cam²ᵃ*   sprites!] *Staunton;* Sprights; *F*

LUCIANA

Why prat'st thou to thyself and answer'st not?
Dromio, thou *Dromio*, thou snail, thou slug,
    thou sot.   200

DROMIO OF SYRACUSE [*to Antipholus*]

I am transformed, master, am I not?

ANTIPHOLUS OF SYRACUSE

I think thou art in mind, and so am I.

DROMIO OF SYRACUSE

Nay, master, both in mind and in my shape.

ANTIPHOLUS OF SYRACUSE

Thou hast thine own form.

199 **prat'st** See 1.2.101n., on *prating*; cf.
2.1.80.

200 The line's first foot is trochaic, with
Dromio disyllabic; the second is iambic,
with *Dromio* again disyllabic for a
feminine ending (-*io*) before the epic
caesura, a standard variation (Wright,
Metrical, 165).
 Dromio, thou snail Luciana's second
Dromio turns the name into a representative
category (rhetorical *diaphora*) for an
unresponsive and idle servant, possibly
joking on the Greek etymology for Dromio's
name: *dromeos*, a runner (Oxf[1]; see List of
Roles, 5, 6n.). Plautus' *Asinaria* contains
a play on fast/slow (441), with Dromo as
the name of a slow-paying debtor. A model
for such etymological irony also occurs
in Lyly, *Campaspe*, 1.22–8. Luciana's
repetition of *thou*, rhetorical *diacope*,
creates a sense of vehemence.
 sot blockhead; drunkard (*OED n.*[1] 1, 2);
Ephesian Antipholus will use a similar
term against Ephesian Dromio at 3.1.10
(see n.).

201–8 On the danger of transformation in
Ephesus, see 1.2.97–102 and n.

201 **transformed** transformèd

201–2 **not . . .** [2]I a lapse in rhyme pattern

202 **art** i.e. are transformed

204 **ape** animal; counterfeit; fool. (1) Dromio
imagines himself literally an ape, probably
a Barbary ape, 'the tailless monkey
described in ancient Greek proverbs and
natural histories as tamable, trainable' and
substitutable for a human (Maisano, 67).
In performance, Dromio might pose and
gesture as an ape, such acting encouraged
by *shape* (203), which can denote a
species' visible appearance (*OED n.*[1] 5a)
(Maisano, 68). In Christopher Marlowe's
Doctor Faustus, Mephistophilis turns a
servant into an ape for attempting to
perform magic, and, like *CE*, Marlowe
rhymes *shape* and *ape* (1126–7). (2)
Dromio also draws on the meaning of 'to
play the ape' (*OED* ape *n.* 2b, 3), i.e. to
imitate or counterfeit reality. In that sense,
Dromio implies that he is transformed into
a kind of automaton, a magically manipulated counterfeit of himself. Shakespeare
invokes the notion of *ape* as counterfeit
elsewhere, e.g. *LLL* 5.2.325, *Cym* 2.2.31,
WT 5.2.99–100. (3) Finally, *ape* is a
synonym for 'fool' (*OED* 4), a character-
ization picked up in 205.

199 and answer'st not?] *om. F2*   200 [1]thou . . . snail] thou *Dromio*, snaile *F2;* thou drone, thou snail
Theobald; thou drumble, thou snail *Riv;* – thou, Dromio – thou snail *Folg*[2]   *Dromio*] F's italics retained
this edn   201 SD] *Oxf*   204] *verse as Steevens*[4]

DROMIO OF SYRACUSE   No, I am an ape.

LUCIANA

If thou art changed to aught, 'tis to an ass.   205

DROMIO OF SYRACUSE

'Tis true: she rides me, and I long for grass.
'Tis so, I am an ass, else it could never be
But I should know her as well as she knows me.

ADRIANA

Come, come, no longer will I be a fool,
To put the finger in the eye and weep,   210
Whilst man and master laughs my woes to scorn.
Come, sir, to dinner. – Dromio, keep the gate.
– Husband, I'll dine above with you today,

205 **ass** donkey; fool; see 207; 3.1.15–18, 47;
3.2.75; 4.4.28–9; and related nn. Both
Dromios will be likened to, and call
themselves, asses. On women as bridled
asses, see 2.1.13–14 and nn.

206–8 For a like sentiment from Ephesian
Dromio, see 3.1.15 and n., on *so . . .
appear*.

206 **'Tis true** Dromio now considers himself
changed into an ass. Shakespeare may
be recalling the transformation of
Nebuchadnezzar into an animal: 'thy
dwelling shalbe with the beastes of the
fielde: with grasse shalt thou be fed like
oxen' (Daniel, 4.25; not in Shaheen),
referred to in *AW* 4.5.20–1. Scot cites a
story of a young traveller transformed in
body, but not mind, into an ass by a witch
who beats him and makes him carry
burdens (54–5). In the background stands
the *Odyssey*'s witch Circe, who turns men
into beasts (Bk 10), invoked at 5.1.271
(see n.).

rides dominates, 'tyrannizes over' (Ard²),
'like a witch or nightmare' (Cam¹); cf. *TN*
3.4.290–1; with a play on *rides* as one
rides an ass.

I . . . grass Donkey-like, Dromio feels
hungry for grass. He is so fearful of
demonic transformation that he feels as if
he actually were possessed. In Elizabethan
England, mad individuals behaving as
animals were sometimes considered
'incarnations of the demonic realm'
(Almond, 35).

207 hexameter
I . . . ass Cf. 3.2.75, 4.4.30.

209 **Come, come** See p. 68.

210 a proverbial and derisive description of
crying (Dent, F229; *OED* eye *n.*¹ 2c); cf.
2.1.114 and n.

211 **laughs . . . scorn** i.e. mocks (*OED* laugh *v.*
3); a third-person plural verb might
sometimes end in *-s* (Hope, 2.1.8a).

212 **keep the gate** guard the door (to Adriana's
house); on *gate*, see *OED* door *n.*¹ 1; cf.
3.1.30 and n., on *door*; 5.1.156.

213 **above** upstairs (*OED adv.* 2), as *MW*
4.2.76; presumably denoting a private
chamber on the first floor of the house. The
word probably indicates the use of the
upper stage for Adriana in 3.1; see 3.1.60.1
and n.

210 ²the] thy *F2;* my *Collier*²

And shrive you of a thousand idle pranks.
– Sirrah, if any ask you for your master,   215
Say he dines forth, and let no creature enter.
– Come, sister. – Dromio, play the porter well.

ANTIPHOLUS OF SYRACUSE [*aside*]

Am I in earth, in heaven or in hell?
Sleeping or waking? Mad or well advised?
Known unto these, and to myself disguised?   220
I'll say as they say, and persever so,
And in this mist at all adventures go.

DROMIO OF SYRACUSE

Master, shall I be porter at the gate?

ADRIANA

Ay, and let none enter, lest I break your pate.

LUCIANA

Come, come, Antipholus, we dine too late.   225
                    [*Exeunt, with Dromio last.*]

---

214 **shrive you** (1) hear your confession and
administer absolution to you (*OED* shrive
v. 1); (2) question, examine (*OED* 7a); cf.
FQ, 4.12.26; (3) have sexual intercourse;
cf. 'shrives this woman to her smock', *1H6*
1.2.119; *3H6* 3.2.107. See Williams,
Glossary, 277.
idle foolish (*OED adj.* 2b); cf. 184n., on
idle.
216 **forth** away from home
217 **porter** doorkeeper
218–22 Cf. Sebastian at *TN* 4.1.60–3.
219 **well advised** prudent (*OED adj.* 1); in my
right mind (Wells)
221 **persever** persèver; continue staunchly,
persevere
222 **mist** doubt (*OED n.*[1] 6); confusion, hazi-
ness; proverbial (Tilley, M1017); cf. *vapours*
at 1.1.89 and n. Here, *mist* connotes the
aura of enchantment or 'mystification' cast

by the Ephesian women (see *OED n.*[1] 4b,
6) into which Antipholus enters wilfully (a
feature absent from *Men.*). The word also
carries extensive 16th-century associations
with conceptual error, Catholic superstition
and juggling deception; see LN. Such
connections suggest the exponential
dangers of entertaining fallacies.
at all adventures whatever the risk (*OED*
adventure *n.* 3c)
223–5 **gate . . . pate . . . late** a scene-closing
triple rhyme
224 **break your pate** See 1.2.65 and n.
225 SD *Dromio, as *porter at the gate* (see
212, 217, 223), would exit last, or he might
linger on stage, visible to the audience, as
the characters enter for 3.1. F lacks an exit
SD; it was either absent in the manuscript
or dropped because of crowded type at the
column's foot (see *Var.*).

---

218 SD] *Capell subst.*   224 Ay] *(I)*   225 too] *(to)*   SD *Exeunt*] *Rowe*[3]; *Exeunt into the Phoenix. Oxf; Exit* F
with Dromio last] *this edn; Dromio of Syracuse remains as porter, visible to the audience but not to those
approaching the door.* / *Bevington*[4]

3.1   *Enter* ANTIPHOLUS OF EPHESUS, *his man* DROMIO,
ANGELO *the goldsmith and* BALTHAZAR *the merchant.*

ANTIPHOLUS OF EPHESUS

Good Signor Angelo, you must excuse us all;
My wife is shrewish when I keep not hours.
Say that I lingered with you at your shop
To see the making of her carcanet,
And that tomorrow you will bring it home.   5
[*Indicates Dromio.*] But here's a villain that would
    face me down
He met me on the mart, and that I beat him
And charged him with a thousand marks in gold,
And that I did deny my wife and house.

3.1 The setting is before the Phoenix, the house of Antipholus of Ephesus and Adriana. On staging issues in the scene, see pp. 95–101.

1   **Signor** frequently used by Shakespeare with an Italian name or in an Italian setting (e.g. *TGV*, *TS*, *MV*); also at 19, 22; 4.1.36; 5.1.13. Cf. 5.1.423 and n., on *for the senior*. F's spelling, *signior*, is a variant of *Signor*, both pronounced as two syllables.
    Angelo perhaps pronounced 'Anj'lo' or treated as having a double feminine ending
    excuse us all i.e. excuse our lateness to Adriana, *all* meaning 'everything'

2–4 indicating to the audience that the speaker is the long-anticipated Ephesian Antipholus and recapitulating 2.1

2   **shrewish** given to scolding (*OED adj.* 2); cf. 4.1.51 and n., on *shrew*.
    when . . . hours 'when I am unpunctual' (Wells): Antipholus refers to his being late for dinner; *hours* makes another time reference.

4   **carcanet** ornamental collar or necklace, usually of gold, often set with pearls or

precious stones (see *OED n.* 1); cf. 'Like stones of worth . . . / Or captain jewels in the carcanet' (*Son* 52.7–8). It is the *chain* promised to Adriana (2.1.105 and n.; see 115 below), although *carcanet* evokes something richer than *chain*. In 1578, the Earl of Leicester gave Queen Elizabeth 'a carcanet of golde ennamuled nyne peces whereof are garnesshed with Sparkes of Diamondes and rubyes' (Lawson, 225). Shakespeare may have been influenced by *Solyman and Perseda* (1592), attributed to Thomas Kyd, where the loss of a bejeweled carcanet, or 'chain', exchanged as a lover's gift, helps to bring about tragedy (Vitkus, 121) and where a ring also functions as a lover's gift.

6   **face me down** 'insist saucily that' (see *OED* face *v.* Phrases P1a; see also *OED v.* 3); cf. 5.1.227 and n.; 5.1.245 and n., on *out-facing*.

8   **charged him with** 'accused him of having' (see *OED* charge *v.* 17)

9   **deny** 'refuse to admit the existence of' (*OED v.* 3b)

3.1] *(Actus Tertius. Scena Prima.);* ACT III. SCENE I. *Rowe*   0.2 BALTHAZAR] *F2; Balthaser F*   1+ SP] *(E. Anti., E.Ant., E.An., Anti., E. Ant., Ant.)*   1, 19, 22 Signor] *(signior)*   6 SD] *this edn*

[*to Dromio*] Thou drunkard, thou, what didst thou
    mean by this?   10
DROMIO OF EPHESUS
Say what you will, sir, but I know what I know;
That you beat me at the mart I have your hand to
    show.
If the skin were parchment and the blows you
    gave were ink,
Your own handwriting would tell you what I think.
ANTIPHOLUS OF EPHESUS
I think thou art an ass.
DROMIO OF EPHESUS   Marry, so it doth appear   15
By the wrongs I suffer and the blows I bear.
I should kick, being kicked; and, being at that pass,
You would keep from my heels and beware of an ass.

---

10 **drunkard** Luciana had called Syracusan
Dromio a *sot* (2.2.200 and n.).

11–85 Here the verse changes to couplets and
triplets, exaggerating the scene's disputes
and increasing the tempo. Although Antipholus and Balthazar address each other
largely in ceremonious hexameters, the
episode will become dominated by the
Dromios' tumbling verse, with many lines
of 12 or 14 syllables and typically four to
six stresses (cf. 2.2.47–8, and 45–8n).
These lines feature an irregular number
of unaccented syllables, with anapaestic
effect, inviting quick delivery. Such
tumbling verse, derived from medieval and
mid-century drama, was associated with
clowns and plebeian characters, and
employed by Shakespeare for raucous
comedy. Rapid-fire lines are shared among
speakers, individual voices homogenize
and characters become caught up in the
heat of the situation, creating a certain
aural anarchy. The reintroduction of blank
verse at 85 will mark a return to control and
civility (see O'Donnell, 403–9). Cf
3.2.71–7 and n., 5.1.420–5 and n.

11 **I . . . ²know** proverbial (Dent, K173). See
p. 68.

12 See 1.2.92 SD and n.
mart On the *mart* as the setting to 1.2, see
1.2.27n.
hand the marks of Antipholus' hand-blows
as his handwriting (*OED n.* 16) or signature
(*OED* 17).

13 **parchment** made from animal hide, thus
closer to human skin than paper; used for
official documents

15 **ass** Here and elsewhere both Dromios are
insulted with the same epithets; see 2.2.205
and n.
so . . . appear Cf. Syracusan Dromio's
embrace of *ass* at 2.2.206–8.

15–18 On Dromio's resentments, cf. 1.2.85–6
and n., 4.4.30–40 and n.

15–16 **appear . . . bear** a rhyme (Kökeritz,
404)

17 **at that pass** in that predicament (*OED* pass
n.³ 3); cf. Spenser, *FQ*, 6.3.14.

18 **beware . . . ass** Despite Dromio's implicit
anger, Antipholus does not respond.

10 SD] *Andrews subst.*   11+ SP] *(E.Dro., E.Drom., E. Dro.)*

ANTIPHOLUS OF EPHESUS

Y'are sad, Signor Balthazar. Pray God our cheer
May answer my good will and your good welcome
    here.   20

BALTHAZAR

I hold your dainties cheap, sir, and your welcome
    dear.

ANTIPHOLUS OF EPHESUS

O, Signor Balthazar, either at flesh or fish,
A table full of welcome makes scarce one dainty
    dish.

BALTHAZAR

Good meat, sir, is common; that every churl affords.

ANTIPHOLUS OF EPHESUS

And welcome more common, for that's nothing but
    words.   25

19–29 Here begins a courteous 'debate' (see 67) between host and guest about *cheer*, meaning both food (*OED n.*[1] 6a) and welcome (*OED* 5); the ideas are proverbial: 'Welcome is the best cheer' (Dent, W258). The conversation sounds conventional, even literary, and, in its elevated hexameters, a bit comic. Although the courtesy debate adds humour and facilitates dramatic irony (see 66–7), it also establishes decorum as a value. Humanists were interested in manners and hospitality. A similar debate occurs in Lyly's *Euphues* (2.161–2). Erasmus's colloquy 'A Feast of Many Courses' cites the already mentioned welcome proverb (40.805; see 802–8), and the hosts in Erasmus's feasting colloquies typically downplay their repast's delicacy. Such set themes provide matter for social discussion in Castiglione's *The Courtier* (1528) (Ard[2]).

19 **sad** grave or serious (chiefly applied to looks) (*OED adj.* 3a), establishing Balthazar's character and function

19, 22 **Signor** See 1 and n., on *Signor*.

19–20 **cheer . . . welcome** Cf. 66.

20 **my . . . welcome** The two phrases' syntactical similarity (equal length and equivalent structure) illustrates rhetorical *isocolon*, underscored by the repetition of *good* and the near-rhyme of *will* and *wel-*.

21 **cheap** of small account (*OED adj.* 5b)
   dear valuable, precious

22–3 In some productions, Adriana, Luciana and Syracusan Antipholus can be seen on the balcony dining as Antipholus speaks.

22 **either . . . fish** i.e. whether one eats meat or fish (with a possible reference to Catholic fasting (Oxf[1])); *at* means 'for' (Blake, 5.4.2) as a measure of value.

23 i.e. all the welcoming in the world cannot take the place of good food.

24 **common** an ordinary occurence (*OED adj.* 10a); perhaps playing on *commons* as provisions (*OED n.* 3a, b)
   churl peasant (*OED n.* 4)

21] *verse as Rowe*   21+ SP] *(Bal, Bal., Baltz., Balth.)*   24 common;] *Theobald; cõmon F*

199

BALTHAZAR
Small cheer and great welcome makes a merry feast.
ANTIPHOLUS OF EPHESUS
Ay, to a niggardly host and more sparing guest.
But though my cates be mean, take them in good
part:
Better cheer may you have, but not with better heart.
[*Attempts to open the door of his house.*]
But soft, my door is locked. [*to Dromio*] Go bid
them let us in.   30
DROMIO OF EPHESUS [*calling*]
Maud, Bridget, Marian, Cic'ly, Gillian, Ginn!
DROMIO OF SYRACUSE [*within, on the other side of the door*]
Mome, malt-horse, capon, coxcomb, idiot, patch!

26–7 **feast . . . guest** a rhyme (Kökeritz, 439)
27 **niggardly** stingy
  sparing frugal (*OED adj.* 1a, b)
28 **cates** food (*OED n.* 1); choice food,
  delicacies (*OED* 2); cf. *TS* 2.1.189.
  mean of poor quality
29 i.e. you may have better food elsewhere but
  not offered with more cordiality.
30 **door is locked** The ensuing dialogue will
  play on the sexual suggestiveness of open
  and closed gates, knocking at the door,
  entrance, denied entrance and the like; cf.
  120, 4.4.64 and n. (On *door* and 'gate' as
  slang for vagina, and on 'knock' as slang
  for coitus, see Williams, *Glossary*, 103,
  139, 179.) The scene recalls *Amph.*,
  341–462, 1018–34; see pp. 81–3.
  door interchangeable with *gate* (e.g.
  2.2.212); *door* has theatrical associations
  (Dessen & Thomson, 73–4, 99; see also
  OED gate *n.*[1] 1). For similar usages of *gate*,
  see e.g. *TS* 1.2.11; *TN* 1.5.126, 268.
31 These names, or forms of them, occur
  elsewhere in Shakespeare, *Maud* excepted

(although 'Maudlin[e]' appears at *AW*
5.3.68, *TNK* 3.5.25). Two are used for
servants: Cicely (*TS* Ind.2.89) and Gill (*TS*
4.1.50); and two for prostitutes: Bridget
(*MM* 3.2.79) and Jinny (*MW* 4.1.62). *Ginn*,
probably a variant of Jenny, may connote a
female 'Jack of all trades' (see *OED* gin *n.*[4]
2). The servants' number conveys a sense
of Ephesian Antipholus' wealth and status
(Wells).
32 SD *Syracusan Dromio responds from
  within the Phoenix, on the other side of the
  door upon which Antipholus has knocked,
  perhaps from behind a stage door (possibly
  with a grate or half-door); see pp. 97–9.
  The SD *within* for Dromio's speeches has
  been traditional since Rowe, suggesting
  a position offstage and inside the tiring-
  house (cf. 5.1.183 SD; see Dessen &
  Thomson, 253).
32 Syracusan Dromio's six abusive terms for
  fools mirror in their number of syllables
  and stress those of the corresponding
  women's names just uttered by his twin

---

27 Ay] *(1)*   29 SD] *Folg subst.; They approach the door of Antipholus of Ephesus' house. | Bevington*[4]
30, 31 SDs] *Oxf*   31 Cic'ly] *Riv; Cisley F;* Cicely *Theobald*   32+ SP] *(S.Dro., S. Dro.)*   32 SD *within*]
Rowe   on . . . door] *Bevington*[4] *subst.; the Phoenix Oxf*

Either get thee from the door or sit down at the hatch.
Dost thou conjure for wenches, that thou call'st for
　such store,
When one is one too many? Go, get thee from the
　door.   35

DROMIO OF EPHESUS

What patch is made our porter? – My master stays
　in the street.

DROMIO OF SYRACUSE [*within*]

Let him walk from whence he came, lest he catch
　cold on's feet.

brother. A *Mome*, in Shakespeare unique here, is a fool or dolt (*OED n.*[2]); *malt-horse*, a slow, heavy horse that grinds malt on a treadmill (*OED n.*; cf. *TS* 4.1.129); *capon*, a dullard and (as a castrated cock) also a eunuch (*OED n.* 1c, 2; cf. *Cym* 2.1.23); *coxcomb*, a person wearing a jester's cap, i.e. a simpleton (*OED* 3; cf. *MA* 4.2.69); *patch*, a fool or simpleton, alluding to the licensed fools' parti-coloured coat (Steevens) and deriving perhaps from the nickname for Cardinal Wolsey's jester (see *OED n.*[2] 1; cf. *MV* 2.5.46). Puck in *MND* calls the mechanicals 'A crew of patches' (3.2.9); see also Warner's translation of *Men.*, 37. Three of these terms, like *ass* (15), refer to animals.

33 **sit ... hatch** A *hatch* is a 'half-door' or 'gate ... with an open space above' or 'the lower half of a divided door' (*OED n.*[1]); it may signal a stage door divided horizontally with upper and lower halves on separate hinges, a meaning that occurs three other times in Shakespeare (*KJ* 1.1.171, 5.2.138; *KL* 3.6.73). Dromio's phrase probably recalls the proverb 'It is good to have a hatch before the door' (Tilley, H207), i.e. 'to close one's mouth and be silent' (see Ard[2]). The injunction thus sounds both literal and metaphorical: sit

down at the lower half of the door and be quiet (Oxf[1]). Understood differently, the *hatch* may be a 'grating or half-door in the upper part of the stage door' (Ard[2]) through which Syracusan Dromio speaks (see Gurr & Egan). A wooden or iron framework with 'bars' or 'gratings', in effect a grille, is one meaning of *gate* (*OED n.*[1] 6a; see 30n., on *door*); cf. 'gates of steel' (*Son* 65.8). Such language suggests that Shakespeare was writing this line with the public theatre rather than an indoor hall in mind.

34 Dromio imagines a catalogue of spirits' names from a conjuring book (with *conjure* alluding sexually; see Williams, *Glossary*, 80); cf. Hotspur on Glendower, *1H4* 3.1.154–6. For examples, see Scot, Bk 15 *passim*, especially chs 1–2.

34 **store** abundance (*OED n.* 4a)

35 **When ... many** especially if Ephesian Dromio is a *capon* (32)

36 Dromio addresses the first half-line to his companions, the second to Syracusan Dromio.

37 **catch ... feet** i.e. from standing in place while waiting at the door; proverbial (Dent, F579a). Cf. Lyly, *MB*, 5.3.98, where the phrase suggests being too stupid to come out of the cold.

ANTIPHOLUS OF EPHESUS

Who talks within there? Ho, open the door!

DROMIO OF SYRACUSE [*within*]

Right, sir, I'll tell you when, an you'll tell me
    wherefore.

ANTIPHOLUS OF EPHESUS

'Wherefore'? For my dinner: I have not dined today.   40

DROMIO OF SYRACUSE [*within*]

Nor today here you must not; come again when
    you may.

ANTIPHOLUS OF EPHESUS

What art thou that keep'st me out from the house
    I owe?

DROMIO OF SYRACUSE [*within*]

The porter for this time, sir, and my name is Dromio.

DROMIO OF EPHESUS

O villain, thou hast stolen both mine office and my
    name;

The one ne'er got me credit, the other mickle blame;   45

If thou hadst been Dromio today in my place,

Thou wouldst have changed thy place for a name,
    and thy name for an ass.

---

39 **I'll ... wherefore** alluding to the saying
'When? Can you tell?' (Dent, T88) (see
also 52) and suggesting rudely that
something will not come to pass. Cf. 52
and n., 2.2.44 and n.
    an if

41 **when you may** 'when you are invited'
(*Oxf*[1])

42 **owe** own

43 **Dromio** pronounced with three syllables
here for a playful rhyme with *I owe* (42);
typically two syllables

44 **office** position (in a public sense) (*OED n.*

2a). In *CE* offices are usurped, neglected or
contested; see 3.2.2 and n.; 5.1.99 and n.,
on *office*.

45 i.e. my name brought me no praise, and my
performance of duties brought me only
blame; *mickle* = much.

47 *F's line makes no clear sense. Generally,
Ephesian Dromio means that if the porter-
impostor had truly taken his place and
name, then he would have acquired the
appellation of *ass*, which Ephesian Dromio
has just been called (15). On the editorial
problem, see LN.

---

38 Ho] *(*hoa*)*   39 an] *(*and*)*   40 'Wherefore'] *this edn;* Wherefore *F*   41 not;] *Rowe subst.;* not *F*
46 been] bid *F2*   47] *Cam*[2a] *lines* name, / ass. /   place] *Oxf*[1] *(Gould);* face *F;* office *Ard*[2]*;* pate *Oxf* a
name] an aim *Cam*[1]   and] *this edn;* or *F*   an ass] a face *Collier*[2] *(Collier, Notes)*

Enter LUCE [*within the house*].

LUCE [*within*]

What a coil is there, Dromio! Who are those at
    the gate?

DROMIO OF EPHESUS

Let my master in, Luce.

LUCE [*within*]   Faith, no; he comes too late,
And so tell your master.

DROMIO OF EPHESUS   O Lord, I must laugh!   50
Have at you with a proverb: 'Shall I set in my staff?'

LUCE [*within*]

Have at you with another: that's 'When? Can you
    tell?'

DROMIO OF SYRACUSE [*within*]

If thy name be called 'Luce', Luce, thou hast
    answered him well.

ANTIPHOLUS OF EPHESUS [*to Luce*]

Do you hear, you minion? You'll let us in, I hope?

47.1 Luce 'enters' the scene but remains, like
Dromio, within the house (see 32 SDn.),
not visible to those outside. She probably
joins Dromio behind the door rather than
emerging on to the balcony. Luce is surely
the same character as Nell the kitchen
wench, described by Dromio in 3.2.78–152
(see 3.2.110n.).

48 **coil** noisy disturbance (*OED n.*[2] 1)

51, 52 **Have . . . with** 'I attack you with'

51 **'set . . . staff'** take up residence; hold fast
in an opinion or position (*OED* staff *n.*[1]
5d). The familiar proverbial form is 'To set
up one's staff' (Dent, S804). Dromio
threatens to hold his position by the door
and to cause further 'coil'. The preposition

in, the phallic connotations of *staff* (see e.g.
TGV 2.5.27) and the nature of Luce's reply
suggest an additional, bawdy meaning.

52 **'When . . . tell'** See 39n.

53 **'Luce'** possibly punning on 'loose' as
unchaste (see Williams, *Glossary*, 193–4);
'luce' can refer to a kind of fish, a pike
(*OED n.*[1] 1a); on 'fish' as a sexual term for
a woman, see Williams, *Glossary*, 126.
Dromio's comment that *Luce* has *answered
him well* suggests that she has made a
saucy answer to Ephesian Dromio's bawdy
request.

54, 59 **minion** See 2.1.86n.; Adriana's accusat-
ory *minions* there is now being turned
against her household.

47.1] *Oxf subst.; om. Rowe; Enter Luce. (within) / Collier*[2]*; *LUCE, *the kitchen-maid, comes out upon the
balcony Cam*[1] *(Dyce)* 48+ SP] Mai[d]. *Capell;* Nell *Oxf* 48 SD] *Rowe* 48 there, Dromio!] *Jorgensen;*
there *Dromio*? *F;* there! *Dromio / Capell* 49–51] *Rowe*[3]*; F lines* Luce. / Master. / Prouerbe, / staffe. /
49, 52, 53 SDs] *Dyce* 51 'Shall . . . staff?'] *Oxf (Theobald subst.);* Shall . . . staffe. *F* staff?] *Rowe;*
staffe. *F* 52 'When . . . tell?'] *Wells (Capell subst.);* when . . . tell? *F* 53 'Luce'] *Folg*[2]*; Luce F* 53–4] *Oxf
shows lacuna between 53 and 54* 54 SD] *Bevington*[4] 54] *prose Pope*[2] minion?] *Capell;* minion, *F*
hope] trow *Theobald* 54–5] *Oxf*[1] *shows lacuna between 54 and 55*

LUCE [*within*]

I thought to have asked you.

DROMIO OF SYRACUSE [*within*]   And you said, no.   55

DROMIO OF EPHESUS

So, come – help.   [*They beat the door.*]

Well struck! There was blow for blow.

ANTIPHOLUS OF EPHESUS

Thou baggage, let me in!

LUCE [*within*]   Can you tell for whose sake?

DROMIO OF EPHESUS

Master, knock the door hard.

LUCE [*within*]   Let him knock till it ache.

ANTIPHOLUS OF EPHESUS

You'll cry for this, minion, if I beat the door down.

[*Beats on the door.*]

LUCE [*within*]

What needs all that, and a pair of stocks in the town?   60

[*Exit.*]

55 The meaning of these retorts is unclear. Tilley considers the proverbial 'I had thought to have asked you' to be a 'mocking retort' (T225; also Dent, T225) and identifies other instances in Lyly, *MB* (2.3.73, 4.2.42). Given the line's opacity and the break in rhymed couplets at 54–5, many editors have concluded that at least one line is missing between 53 and 55. Malone conjectured that such a line may have contained a threat from Antipholus and ended with 'rope' (to rhyme with *hope*, 54) (Boswell–Malone).

56 **blow for blow** In return for their adversaries' rhetorical *blow*, Ephesian Dromio and Antipholus have now landed a physical *blow* against the door; hence the inserted SD (Ephesian Dromio refers to knocking on the door at 58).

57 **baggage** worthless woman, strumpet (*OED n.* 6)

tell say. This unclear line may be a variation on the riposte at 52.

58 **knock . . . ache** punning on *knock* as copulate (*OED v.* 2d; see 30n.) (Wells; see Williams, *Glossary*, 179; also *Dictionary*, 2.766); cf. 121. Luce's *it* makes a phallic allusion.

60 i.e. why tolerate all this shouting and pounding when the trouble-makers could be put in the stocks; *and* means 'since there is' (Wells).

60 SD2 Luce probably exits here, timed with the (perhaps simultaneous) entrance of Adriana. Some modern editors have Luce and Adriana leave together at 64, after Adriana's last speech, on the assumption that both are *above*, at the window. Yet if a character reasonably departs when he or she is out of lines and out of the action, then Luce might exit now, displaced by Adriana as the conflict changes tone.

55 SD1, 2] *Dyce*   55 you. And] *Keightley shows lacuna between* you. *and* And   56] *prose Pope*[2]   So, come – help.] *F4 subst.;* So come helpe, *F;* So; come, help! *Collier*   SD] *Bevington*[4]   struck] (strooke) *   57, 58 SDs] *Dyce*   59 SD] *Folg*[2] (*Bevington*[4] *subst.*)   60 SD1] *Dyce*   SD2] *this edn*

Enter ADRIANA[*, above, within the house*].

ADRIANA [*within*]

Who is that at the door that keeps all this noise?

DROMIO OF SYRACUSE [*within*]

By my troth, your town is troubled with unruly boys.

ANTIPHOLUS OF EPHESUS [*to Adriana*]

Are you there, wife? You might have come before.

ADRIANA [*within*]

Your wife, sir knave? Go, get you from the door.   [*Exit.*]

DROMIO OF EPHESUS

If you went in pain, master, this 'knave' would

go sore.   65

ANGELO [*to Antipholus*]

Here is neither cheer, sir, nor welcome; we would

fain have either.

BALTHAZAR

In debating which was best, we shall part with

neither.

DROMIO OF EPHESUS

They stand at the door, master; bid them welcome

hither.

60.1 Adriana speaks presumably from an upper-floor window or balcony; cf. 'Husband, I'll dine above with you today' (2.2.213 and n.). In Elizabethan SDs, *above* typically refers to the 'performance space over the main platform', often, fictionally, a 'window' (Dessen & Thomson, 1), or, theatrically, the stage balcony or balcony doorway. Adriana would be visible to the audience but not seen by the characters standing outside the Phoenix. See pp. 99–101.

61 **keeps** causes (*OED v.* 36)

62 **boys** knaves (*OED n.*[1] 2)

65 'If you were in pain, then this knave she

mentions would be in pain; i.e. she means you' (*Riv*); or perhaps, 'If you were already in pain, this "knave" insult would hurt even more'. Dromio enjoys exacerbating the injury.

66 Cf. 19–20.

fain gladly

66–8 **either . . . neither . . . hither** a triple rhyme (Kökeritz, 433)

67 **In** while (*OED prep.* 11b)

part depart

68 probably voiced naïvely but meant sarcastically; *They* refers to Balthazar and Angelo.

60.1] *Collier*[2]*, Cam*[1] *subst.; om. Rowe; Enter* ADRIANA *to Luce Ard*[2]   61+ SP] *(Adr., Adri.)*   61 SD] *Rowe*   62, 64 SDs] *Dyce*   63 SD] *Oxf*   64 SD1] *Dyce*   64 SD2] *Cam*[1] *subst.*   65 'knave'] *Theobald subst.;* knaue *F*   66+ SP] *(Angelo., Ang.)*   66 SD] *Oxf*

ANTIPHOLUS OF EPHESUS

There is something in the wind, that we cannot get in.

DROMIO OF EPHESUS

You would say so, master, if your garments were thin.   70
Your cake is warm within; you stand here in the cold.
It would make a man mad as a buck to be so bought
     and sold.

ANTIPHOLUS OF EPHESUS

Go fetch me something: I'll break ope the gate.

DROMIO OF SYRACUSE [*within*]

Break any breaking here, and I'll break your
     knave's pate.

DROMIO OF EPHESUS

A man may break a word with you, sir, and words
     are but wind;   75
Ay, and break it in your face, so he break it not
     behind.

69 **something . . . wind** i.e. something wrong; proverbial (Dent, S621)
    that such that
70 reinterpreting *wind* (69) literally (and bitterly): i.e. you would indeed comment on the cold wind if your clothing were thin (like mine).
71 *****cake** the still-warm dinner delicacies (*OED n.* 7a), or *dainties*, mentioned earlier (21–3); also Adriana (Ard²); cf. *TS* 1.1.108–9, *TC* 1.1.14–15. Williams glosses *cake* as 'a woman in her sexual capacity', noting this occurrence (*Glossary*, 61). Cf. the possible reference to Luce as a fish, 53 and n. F reads 'cake here', but F's two instances of 'here' suggest a compositorial error, especially since the first confuses the contrast between *within* and without.
72 **mad . . . buck** To be as 'wild as a buck' is to be angry (Dent, B692), but Dromio may also imply Antipholus' response to cuckolding; cf. *horn-mad* (2.1.56), and

buck as horned cuckold at *MW* 3.3.157–9.
    bought and sold tricked, betrayed; proverbial (Dent, B787)
73 **ope** open
74 **Break any breaking** a familiar Shakespearean formulation, often in the negative; e.g. 'Thank me no thankings, nor proud me no prouds' (*RJ* 3.5.152); cf. 77 and n.
    break . . . pate Cf. Adriana's similarly worded threats at 2.1.77, 2.2.224; see 1.2.65n.
75 **break a word** exchange words (see *OED* break *v.* 3)
    words . . . wind 'words uttered are made up only of breath'; proverbial (Dent, W833)
75–7 **wind . . . behind . . . hind** a triple rhyme (Kökeritz, 493)
76 **so** as long as; in order that. The word is playfully ambiguous.
    ²**break** i.e. break wind, pass gas; often accompanied by related stage business (Oxf¹)

71 cake] *Capell;* cake here *F;* cake there *White²* *(anon., per Cam)*   74, 77, 79 SDs] *Dyce*   75 you] *F2;* your *F*   76, 79 Ay] *(I)*

DROMIO OF SYRACUSE [*within*]

   It seems thou want'st breaking. Out upon thee, hind!

DROMIO OF EPHESUS

   Here's too much 'Out upon thee!' I pray thee let
      me in.

DROMIO OF SYRACUSE [*within*]

   Ay, when fowls have no feathers and fish have no fin.

ANTIPHOLUS OF EPHESUS

   Well, I'll break in: go borrow me a crow.   80

DROMIO OF EPHESUS

   A crow without feather? Master, mean you so?
   For a fish without a fin, there's a fowl without
      a feather.
   [*to Dromio of Syracuse*] If a crow help us in,
   sirrah, we'll pluck a crow together.

ANTIPHOLUS OF EPHESUS

   Go, get thee gone; fetch me an iron crow.

BALTHAZAR

   Have patience, sir. O, let it not be so!   85

---

77 'It seems that you need a beating. Curse
you, you peasant!' *Out upon* expresses
damning (*OED* out *int.* 2); *hind* means a
menial or a rustic (*OED n.*[2] 1, 3), often
used pejoratively (e.g. *1H4* 2.3.15).
Dromio quibbles on *hind* as 'deer', since
breaking, besides meaning 'beating'
(Crystal & Crystal, break *n.* 8; cf. 74,
1.2.79), can also mean the cutting up of a
deer (*OED* break *v.* 2b); *hind* may also
refer to the buttocks (*OED n.*[3]) as an object
of beating.

79 **when . . . fin** i.e. never. No related proverb
has been recorded (Ard[2]). In *Men.*,
Menaechmus replies angrily that the
inquisitive Doctor might as well ask him if
he eats 'birds with scales and fish with
feathers' ('*auis squamosas, piscis
pennatos*') (918).

80 **crow** crow-bar (*OED n.*[1] 5a)
81 **A crow . . . feather** confusing a *crow* as a
crow-bar with a *crow* as a 'fowl' (see 79)
and probably alluding satirically to Greene's
attack on Shakespeare, in *Greene's Groatsworth of Wit* (1592), as 'an upstart Crow,
beautified with our Feathers' (Greene,
12.144; see Appendix 1, p. 322; Godman,
58–60).
82 i.e. like a fish without a fin, the crowbar
will be a fowl without a feather (see *OED*
for *prep.* A27).
83 **pluck a crow** settle our disagreement
(*OED* crow *n.*[1] 3b), i.e. with fisticuffs;
proverbial (Dent, C855)
85 **Have patience** later repeated by Luciana to
Adriana at 4.2.16 (see n., on *patience*); on
calls for *patience*, see 1.2.86n.

---

78 'Out upon thee!'] *Theobald subst.;* out vpon thee, *F*   79 fin] fin. *Exit.* / *Bevington*[4]   81 feather?]
Collier; feather, *F*   so?] *F4;* so; *F*   82 a feather] *(*afether*)*   83 SD] *Oxf*   85 so!] so, *F;* thus. *Pope*

Herein you war against your reputation,
And draw within the compass of suspect
Th'unviolated honour of your wife.
Once, this: your long experience of her wisdom,
Her sober virtue, years and modesty   90
Plead on her part some cause to you unknown;
And doubt not, sir, but she will well excuse
Why at this time the doors are made against you.
Be ruled by me: depart in patience,
And let us to the Tiger all to dinner,   95
And about evening come yourself alone
To know the reason of this strange restraint.
If by strong hand you offer to break in
Now in the stirring passage of the day,
A vulgar comment will be made of it;   100
And that supposed by the common rout
Against your yet ungalled estimation,

86–8, 98–106 On reputation, see 2.1.108–12 and n.

87 **compass of suspect** range of suspicion (*OED* compass *n.*[1] 9). Balthazar launches a series of legalistic terms: *Plead . . . cause* (91), *restraint* (97), *intrusion* (103), *slander . . . succession* (105).

88 **Th'unviolated honour** imagining Antipholus' prospective damaging of his wife's reputation as a sexual assault (*OED* violate *n.* 2) and as a desecration (*OED* 3a)

89 **Once, this** 'In brief, let me put it this way'; *Once* means 'in short' (*OED adv.* 4); cf. *MA* 1.1.318 (Ard[1]).

89, 91 ***her** instead of F's 'your', to parallel Balthazar's discussion of 'your wife' (88), as emended by Rowe; on the typesetting here, see *Var*.

90 **years** maturity (Ard[2])

92 **excuse** 'remove the blame of' (*OED v.* 1b)

93 **made** shut; cf. *AYL* 4.1.161 (Ard[2]).

95 **let us** let us go (*OED* let *v.*[1] 14c, first citation)

the Tiger presumably an inn, although no such London inn (or brothel) has been discovered (Ard[2]). Shakespeare uses *Tiger* twice elsewhere, as a ship's name (*TN* 5.1.62, *Mac* 1.3.7). Cf. 1.2.9n., on *the Centaur*.

97 **restraint** 'keeping out' (Wells); act of stopping (*OED n.* 2a)

99 **stirring . . . day** i.e. busy passing-by of people at this time of day (see *OED* passage 1d, first citation). The time is about mid-afternoon.

100 **vulgar** coarse (*OED adj.* 13); also public (*OED adj.* 6)

101 **supposed** supposèd; believed

102 **ungalled estimation** ungallèd; uninjured reputation, with *-galled* closer to wounding or goring (as at *Ham* 3.2.272) than to rubbing or chafing (*OED* gall *v.*[1] 1, 2); *estimation* indicates repute, or sense of worth in the opinion of others (*OED n.* 2b); cf. e.g. *TGV* 2.4.56.

89 Once, this:] *Theobald subst.;* Once this *F*   her] *Rowe;* your *F*   91 her] *Rowe;* your *F*

That may with foul intrusion enter in
And dwell upon your grave when you are dead;
For slander lives upon succession,   105
Forever housed where it gets possession.

ANTIPHOLUS OF EPHESUS

You have prevailed. I will depart in quiet,
And in despite of wrath mean to be merry:
I know a wench of excellent discourse,

103–4 A scandalous reputation would enter Antipholus' grave (and body?) with the same *foul intrusion* he proposed against his own house. Adriana has earlier introduced *intrusion* as infection (see 2.2.185 and n.); here it also means thrusting oneself into a vacant estate or tenancy (*OED n.* 2a), anticipating *succession* at 105. Scandal and slander, like envy, were often associated with venomous serpents, and such an image may be implicit here. In *Cym*, slanderous serpents violate graves and dead bodies: 'the secrets of the grave / This viperous slander enters' (3.4.38–9). The association is biblical. In Genesis, the serpent beguiles Eve, and Satan will be linked to slander (see e.g. *MW* 5.5.155). Ecclesiastes, 10.1, relates that 'A sclaunderer is like a serpent that can not be charmed'; see also Psalms, 58.3–4, 140.3–4. Cf. Sclaunder at *FQ*, 4.8.23–6.

103 **That** i.e. the supposition (101), which may become belief

105–6 Slander outlives and takes *possession* of its human subject, perpetuating itself from generation to generation. (On *succession* as a legal term, see *OED n.* 5b.) Like a demon, slander occupies, 'possesses', a body's 'house' (*OED possess v.* 40). On *possession*, see 2.2.146n., on *I . . . with*. Christ tells of an unclean spirit resolved to repossess a man: 'I wyll returne into my house', says the spirit, and he and other spirits 'enter in, and dwell

there' (Matthew, 12.44–5; alluded to at *Tem* 1.2.459–60; see also Luke, 11.24–6).

105–6 **succession . . . possession** These two rhyming lines appear to be of unequal length. For 105 to be iambic pentameter, *succession* must be pronounced as four syllables, potentially throwing off its rhyme with *possession*. One solution, perhaps the best, is to accept 105 as a short line. However, if *Forever* is spoken as 'Fore'er', or *where it* as 'where't', the pronunciation of *possession* can follow either version of *succession*. Some editions mark *housed* as *housèd*, although F spells *hows'd*.

108 ***wrath** F's 'mirth' was emended to *wrath* by Theobald to create a contrast. Editors retaining F gloss 'in despite of mirth' as either 'despite the mockery or petty joke to which I have just been subjected' or, less plausibly, 'despite my normal disinclination to mirth'. Such readings diminish the implicit contrast and forfeit the drama of Antipholus' agreement to replace anger with patience. According to Cam¹, *wrath* written in secretary hand might have been easily misread as 'mirth'. **merry** See 3.2.183 and n.; cf. 1.2.21 and n., on *merry jests*.

109–10 The attributes listed are those that Adriana fears she lacks (Wells); see 2.1.88–92.

109 **discourse** See 2.1.90n., on *Are . . . dull*.

106 Forever] *(*For euer*)*; For e'er *Ard*   where it gets] where it once gets *F2;* where't gets *Steevens;* where once it gets *Oxf*   108 wrath] *Theobald;* mirth *F;* my wife *Keightley*

Pretty and witty, wild and yet, too, gentle.   110
There will we dine. This woman that I mean,
My wife – but I protest, without desert –
Hath oftentimes upbraided me withal.
To her will we to dinner. [*to Angelo*] Get you home
And fetch the chain; by this, I know, 'tis made.   115
Bring it, I pray you, to the Porpentine,
For there's the house. That chain will I bestow –
Be it for nothing but to spite my wife –
Upon mine hostess there. Good sir, make haste.
Since mine own doors refuse to entertain me,   120
I'll knock elsewhere to see if they'll disdain me.

ANGELO
I'll meet you at that place some hour hence.

---

110 **witty** See 2.1.90n., on *wit* (and *OED* witty *adj*. 7a, first citation as 'possessing wit'). **wild** perhaps 'lively' (Wells); or 'untamed', in contrast to *gentle*; *wild*'s connotations include 'licentious' or 'dissolute' (*OED adj*. 7b, citing *MW* 3.2.73). The meaning seems inexact.

111–13 Antipholus denies Adriana's suspicions, first voiced at 2.1.30, of his unfaithfulness with the Courtesan. In *Men.*, the resident Menaechmus regularly visits the concubine Erotium's house for both gastronomic and sexual pleasure. Likewise, the traveller Sosicles Menaechmus leaves Erotium's house saying, 'I had lunch, I had drinks, I lay with a prostitute' ('*prandi, potaui, scortum accubui*') (*Men.*, 476), or in Segal's memorable translation, 'I've wined, I've dined, I've concubined' (*Plautus*, Segal, 475)

113 **withal** therewith (*OED adv.* 2)

114–19 **Get . . . there** Cf. 4.1.23 and n.

115 **chain** Cf. 4 and n.
    this this time

116 **Porpentine** variant form of porcupine (also e.g. *2H6* 3.1.363, *Ham* 1.5.20); also at 3.2.172; 4.1.49; 5.1.222, 276. Cf.

1.2.9n., on *the Centaur*. The *Porpentine* was the name of a Bankside inn probably known to Shakespeare and his audience (Sisson, 1.93), which Cam[1a] calls a 'brothel'. See 4.3.45.1 and n.

117 **there's** gesturing towards the house's stage location (Oxf[1])
    house perhaps with the sense of 'brothel' (see Williams, *Glossary*, 165; also *Dictionary*, 2.694), the meaning it has at e.g. *MM* 1.2.95, 2.1.162–3; *Per* 4.6.77, 119

117–19 **That . . . there** perhaps indicating an intention to be maritally unfaithful, if even for the first time (Cam[2a]); the Courtesan later mentions Antipholus' promise of the chain (see 4.3.85 and n.). Antipholus may speak in an aside, unheard by Angelo (Wells), who will subsequently give the chain to the twin Antipholus (at 3.2.173) and tell him to take it home to his wife.

117 **bestow** For Antipholus' subsequent, darker use, cf. 4.1.16 and n., on *bestow*.

120 **doors** On 'door' as sexual slang, see 30n., on *door is locked*.

121 **knock** On *knock* as sexual slang, see 58n.

---

110 yet, too,] *Rowe[3] subst.*; yet too *F*   114 SD] *Capell subst., Cam*

ANTIPHOLUS OF EPHESUS

Do so; this jest shall cost me some expense.
*Exeunt [Antipholus and Dromio of Ephesus, Angelo
and Balthazar. Exit separately Dromio of Syracuse].*

[**3.2**]   *Enter* [LUCIANA] *with* ANTIPHOLUS OF SYRACUSE.

LUCIANA

And may it be that you have quite forgot
A husband's office? Shall, Antipholus,
Even in the spring of love, thy love-springs rot?
Shall love, in building, grow so ruinous?

123 **expense** as in money, effort or time (cf. *H8* 3.2.108); perhaps also 'ejaculation' (cf. *Son* 129.1)

3.2 The setting is either inside or just outside the Phoenix, the house of Antipholus of Ephesus and Adriana.

0.1 *****LUCIANA** All editors follow (1) F2 in emending F's '*Iuliana*' to *Luciana*; and (2) Rowe in correcting F's first SP, '*Iulia.*', to *Luciana* (1); see List of Roles, 8n.

1–52 These two speeches employ iambic pentameter lines of alternating rhyme (ABABCDCD, etc.), typical of Elizabethan love sonnets. Their felicitous rhymes, placed in line- and clause-ending positions, drive home the sentiments: e.g. *forgot/rot*; *Antipholus/ruinous*. Luciana's participation in the form may imply her susceptibility to Antipholus' protestations. Alternating rhyme also occurs at 4.2.1–4 (see 1–6n.), 25–8, 62–5.

1–4 The action starts in mid-conversation, as if the wooing had begun while 3.1 was in progress. Luciana challenges Antipholus with a series of questions, rhetorical *erotesis*, that pursue the issue of proper husband–wife relations launched in 2.1 (but see 5–28n. below); also at 15–16.

2 **office** duty (as a husband) (*OED n.* 3a)*;* see 3.1.44 and n.; 5.1.99 and n., on *office*.

2–3 **Shall . . . rot** Young shoots of love (*OED* spring *n.*[1] 9a) may eventually decay, but such *rot*, Luciana implies, seems unseasonable here. The reversal of *love* and *spring(s)* in word order creates rhetorical chiasmus. Cf. 'Love's tender spring' (*VA* 656); also *Luc* 950 (Ard[2]).

3 **spring** springtime, as if Adriana had married only recently; see also 5.1.137–8 and n.; cf. *TGV* 1.3.84–5.

4 *****building** increasing or growing structurally (see *OED* build *v.* 3); Theobald turned F's 'buildings' into the gerund *building*. Adriana earlier imagined herself as *ruins* (see 2.1.95–6 and n.). On love and building, see e.g. 'ruin'd love when it is built anew' (*Son* 119.11); *TC* 4.2.103.

*****ruinous** Capell's emendation of F's 'ruinate' allows a rhyme with *Antipholus*. That Shakespeare uses 'ruinate' elsewhere only as an infinitive or active indicative (e.g. *Luc* 944) suggests a compositorial error here. Cf. 'Lest growing ruinous, the building fall' (*TGV* 5.4.9) (Steevens[2]).

123 so;] so. *Exit Angelo Oxf*   SD *Antipholus . . . Syracuse.*] *this edn; Dromio of Syracuse within the Phoenix, and the others into the Porcupine Oxf*   **3.2**] *Pope (SCENE II.)*   0.1 *Enter*] *Enter, from the house / Dyce²*   LUCIANA] *F2; Iuliana, F*   SYRACUSE] *Rowe; Siracusia F*   1–52] *alternating indentation as Pope*   1 SP] *Rowe (Luc.); Iulia. F*   2 Antipholus] *Antipholis, Hate, Theobald*   4 building] *Theobald; buildings F*   ruinous] *Capell (Theobald); ruinate F*

If you did wed my sister for her wealth,   5
  Then for her wealth's sake use her with more
    kindness.
Or if you like elsewhere, do it by stealth:
  Muffle your false love with some show of
    blindness;
Let not my sister read it in your eye;
  Be not thy tongue thy own shame's orator;   10
Look sweet, speak fair, become disloyalty;
  Apparel vice like virtue's harbinger;
Bear a fair presence, though your heart be tainted;
  Teach sin the carriage of a holy saint;
Be secret-false: what need she be acquainted?   15
  What simple thief brags of his own attaint?

5–28 Luciana sounds oddly politic and devious, given her earlier conservative views about marriage (see e.g. 2.1.7–25 and n.). Wells speculates that Shakespeare is adapting from Marlowe's translation of Ovid's *Amores*, where a lover asks his beloved not to reveal her infidelities to him (see Marlowe, 2.315–16).

6 **use** treat (Crystal & Crystal, *v.* 2)

8–9 The sense of *Muffle* shifts (Ard²): Antipholus should (1) conceal (*OED v.* 1) his *false* ('illegitimate', i.e. adulterous (Crystal & Crystal *adj.* 6)) *love* from Adriana; then (2) blindfold (*OED v.* 2) himself, so that she cannot see it in his eyes, making him, in effect, a blind Cupid; cf. 'love, whose view is muffled still' (*RJ* 1.1.171).

9, 11 **eye . . . disloyalty** a rhyme (Kökeritz, 436)

10 i.e. do not let your own tongue proclaim your shameful deeds.

10, 19 **shame's, Shame** See 2.1.112n.

11 **fair** courteously or with kindness (*OED adv.* 2a)
  become disloyalty i.e. make disloyalty becoming, pleasing (see *OED* become *v.*

9c); cf. *TS* 2.1.258–9. Shakespeare puns similarly at *AC* 1.1.49.

12 **harbinger** forerunner (*OED n.* 3). Luciana's injunction is to dress vice to look like virtue; proverbial (Tilley, V44) (Ard²); cf. *R3* 2.2.28. In Tudor morality plays, Vice-characters typically disguise themselves as Virtues.

13 Luciana proposes doing what the proverb 'Fair face, foul heart' (Dent, F3) (Ard²) warns against.
  tainted recalling the language of moral stain at 2.2.142 (see n., on *stained*); cf. 16 and n., on *attaint*.

14 **carriage** bearing, deportment (*OED n.* 14a, first citation)

15–16 **what . . . attaint** rhetorical *erotesis*; see 1–4n.

15 **acquainted** informed (*OED v.* 4c, first citation)

16 **simple** foolish
  ***attaint** dishonour (*OED n.* 6); figuratively, stain (see 13n., on *tainted*); also with the legal sense of criminal false witness (see *OED* 4); cf. *KL* 5.3.83–4. Rowe's emendation preserves the rhyme (see t.n.).

15 secret-false] *(*secret false*)*   16 attaint] *Rowe;* attaine *F*

'Tis double wrong to truant with your bed
   And let her read it in thy looks at board.
Shame hath a bastard fame, well managèd;
   Ill deeds is doubled with an evil word.   20
Alas, poor women! Make us but believe,
   Being compact of credit, that you love us;
Though others have the arm, show us the sleeve:
   We in your motion turn, and you may move us.
Then, gentle brother, get you in again;   25
   Comfort my sister, cheer her, call her 'wife'.
'Tis holy sport to be a little vain
   When the sweet breath of flattery conquers strife.

17 **truant with** stray from (especially school).
Luciana assumes Antipholus' infidelity.

18 **at board** at table, i.e. at meals

18, 20 **board . . . word** a rhyme (Kökeritz, 413)

19–20 i.e. disgrace (*Shame*) when hidden (*managed*) can allow for a counterfeit (*bastard*) reputation (see *OED* bastard *adj.* 4; and 'bastard hope' *MV* 3.5.7, 13), whereas exposing wrong actions (*Ill deeds*) only doubles their harm; *evil word* refers to a husband confessing infidelity, with *evil* as a transferred epithet. On reputation, see 2.1.108–12 and n. Folg² cites the proverb 'To do evil and then brag of it is a double wrong' (cf. Tilley, T140). *Ill deeds* takes *is* (20): a plural subject can take a singular verb when the subject has a collectively singular sense (Abbott, 333; Hope, 2.1.8a); cf. 4.4.78 and n., on *bones bears*; 93.

19 **managed** managèd

21 **us** Luciana's sentiments turn personal.

22 **compact of credit** composed, made up (*OED* compact *adj.*¹ 2) of trust (*OED* credit *n.* 1); cf. *MND* 5.1.8.

23 i.e. though another woman has your affection, at least show us the appearance of love; continuing Luciana's false-apparel language. Adriana had earlier fastened on Antipholus' sleeve; see 2.2.179 (Ard²). Cf. wearing one's heart upon one's sleeve (see e.g. *Oth* 1.1.64), but here the heart would be false. In *arm*, Williams suspects a phallic innuendo (*Glossary*, 30, citing *TGV* 5.4.57, *AC* 5.2.82).

24 **We . . . turn** 'We turn according to your movements'. In Ptolemaic astronomy, the Prime Mover imparts movement to the concentric celestial spheres and to the planets within them; cf. *MND* 1.1.193, *MV* 5.1.61.

move including the sense of 'affect with emotion' (*OED v.* 25b). Luciana's *you*, like *us* and *We*, hints that she herself is being moved. The second clause in the line repeats the idea of the first (rhetorical *tautologia*), perhaps to intensify effect.

26 **Comfort . . . cheer . . . call** rhetorical *commoratio*, an idea repeated in different words; cf. 152 and n., on *Go, hie . . . post*; 158 and n.; 4.3.69 and n., on *leave . . . gone*. The repetition creates emphasis.

27 **vain** deceptive (Crystal & Crystal, *n.* 1); also 'empty' (*OED adj.* 2), as in 'empty words' (Ard²); see also 185.

28 **flattery** probably pronounced 'flatt'ry'

20 is] are *F2* 21 women!] *Theobald*²*; women, F* but] *Theobald; not F* 21–2 believe, / Being . . . credit,] *Rowe*; beleeue / (Being . . . credit) *F* 26 wife] *F2;* wise *F*

ANTIPHOLUS OF SYRACUSE

Sweet mistress – what your name is else, I know not,
   Nor by what wonder you do hit of mine –   30
Less in your knowledge and your grace you show not
   Than our earth's wonder, more than earth divine.
Teach me, dear creature, how to think and speak;
   Lay open to my earthy, gross conceit –
Smothered in errors, feeble, shallow, weak –   35
   The folded meaning of your words' deceit.
Against my soul's pure truth why labour you
   To make it wander in an unknown field?
Are you a god? Would you create me new?
   Transform me, then, and to your power I'll yield.   40
But if that I am I, then well I know,

29 **else** otherwise
30 **wonder** miracle (*OED n.* 2a)
   hit of light upon (*OED* hit *v.* 12); *of* sometimes means 'on' (Abbott, 175).
31 'in your knowledge and your grace you manifest yourself to be not less'
32 **our earth's wonder** perhaps Queen Elizabeth (Douce, 226). *CE* is presumed to have been performed before Elizabeth's Court on 27 December 1594; see pp. 103–4.
   more . . . divine 'more divine than is earth'
34 **earthy, gross conceit** earth-bound, dull (*OED* gross *adj.* 13a) understanding (*OED* conceit *n.* 2); on *conceit*, cf. 4.2.64–5 and n., *MV* 3.4.2–3. The neo-Platonic opposition between fallible, earthly human understanding and the divine *soul's pure truth* (37) occurs elsewhere in Shakespeare: e.g. *MV* 5.1.63–5 (Ard[2]).
35 **Smothered** suppressed, covered up (*OED v.* 3a, first citation)
   errors Antipholus' second reference to error; see 2.2.190 and n. Here *errors* means mistakes of perception and judgement based on humankind's inherent limitations (Ard[2]).

36 **folded** concealed, i.e. enfolded, enveloped (*OED v.*[1] 8a); cf. *Luc* 675.
37 **my . . . truth** 'my inner knowledge of the uncorrupted truth' (about whom he loves)
38 **it** i.e. my soul
   wander referring indirectly to *errors* (35), since Latin *errare* means to wander; on *wander* and its recurrence, see 1.2.31 and n.
   unknown with perhaps a denial of carnal knowledge (i.e. of Adriana). Shakespeare sometimes uses 'know' euphemistically for sexual relations; e.g. *AW* 5.3.287 (see Williams, *Glossary*, 179–80); Malcolm claims himself 'yet / Unknown to woman' (*Mac* 4.3.125–6).
39–40 Antipholus now invites the transformation he previously feared; see 1.2.97–102 and n.
39 **Would you** do you wish to
   create me new drawing power from the Pauline vision, emphasized by Protestants, that one can be created anew, reborn, into Christ; see, e.g. Romans, 6.4; Ephesians, 4.22–4.
41 **I am I** Cf. *I am thee* (66); 'Am I Dromio? . . . Am I myself?' (72–3); 'I am not Adriana' (2.2.118).

29+ SP] (*S. Anti., Ant., Anti.*)   34 earthy, gross] *Riv;* earthie grosse *F;* earthy-gross *Cam (Walker, Critical)*

Your weeping sister is no wife of mine,
Nor to her bed no homage do I owe.
Far more, far more, to you do I decline.
O, train me not, sweet mermaid, with thy note,   45
To drown me in thy sister's flood of tears:
Sing, siren, for thyself, and I will dote.
Spread o'er the silver waves thy golden hairs,
And as a bed I'll take thee, and there lie,

---

42 **weeping** On Adriana's crying, see 2.1.114
and n.

43 **homage** See 2.1.103 and n.; there Adriana
uses *homage* bitterly.

44 **Far ... ²more** rhetorical *palilogia*, repetition for emotional intensity
decline 'incline' (*OED v.* 4), but with more
forcefulness (Ard¹); cf. *declining*, 139 and
n.; *de-* perhaps implies his turning away
from Adriana (Ard²).

45–52 The conjoining here of love and water
(*mermaid*, *drown*, *flood*, *waves*, *drowned*,
sink) calls up the play's extensive water
imagery, beginning in the shipwreck story
in 1.1 and continuing in the drop-of-water
simile (1.2.35–40, 2.2.131–5). That
imagery associates the loss of individual
identity and the search for a completing
other with liquefaction; here, such dissolution of identity facilitates love. Antipholus
avoids being drowned in Adriana's tears
but wishes to be consumed in Luciana's
waters. Cf. 169 and n.

45 **train** 'entice ... into a mistake', 'deceive',
'lure' (*OED v.*¹ 4); 'entrap' (*OED v.*² 1)
not ... note an off-rhyme; each *n-* word
concludes a three-syllable phrase.
mermaid meaning both the beautiful, fish-
tailed woman of popular belief and the
dangerous siren (see 47) of classical tradition, the latter generally being represented
as winged, with a woman's upper body and
bird's legs (see Homer, *Od.*, 12.165–200,
Ovid, *Met.*, 5.551–63). Golding translates

Ovid's 'Sirenes' (*Met.*, 5.555) as
'Meremaides' (5.689); see also Spenser,
FQ, 2.12.30–2. Both mermaids and sirens
sang with surpassing sweetness (cf. *Luc*
1411, *VA* 777), which lured men to drown-
ing. Shakespeare elsewhere associates
mermaids with sirens (e.g. *3H6* 3.2.186, *VA*
777). Steevens quotes Philemon Holland's
translation of Pliny's *The History of the
World* (1601): '*Mermaids in Homer were
witches, and their songs enchauntments*'
(Table to the Second Tome). Antipholus
apprehends Luciana as, alternately, a
goddess (39) or a destructive temptress
(45–6).
note song (*OED n.*² 6)

46 **flood of tears** Cf. 2.1.114 and n.

46, 48 **tears ... hairs** a rhyme (Kökeritz, 486)

47 **siren** See 45n., on *mermaid*.

48 **golden hairs** Mermaids had flowing
blonde hair. In Golding's translation of
Met., the mermaids/sirens have 'yellow
feathers' (5.694) ('*flavescere pennis*',
Ovid, *Met.*, 5.560). See also 188 and n.

49 ***bed** F2 corrected F's 'bud' to *bed*; see
50n.; cf. *bed* at 17, 43.
take suggesting 'possess sexually' (see
Williams, *Glossary*, 301), as at *RJ* 4.5.10
thee sometimes emended to *them* (Capell)
to refer to Luciana's *hairs* (48), a gain in
decorousness but a loss of Elizabethan
sexual frankness. The coital consumma-
tion of *die* (51) makes most sense with
thee.

44 decline] incline *Collier²* (*Collier, Notes*)   46 sister's] *F2* (sisters*)*; sister *F*   49 bed] *F2*; bud *F*; bride
Dyce   thee] them *Capell*

And in that glorious supposition think　　　　50
He gains by death that hath such means to die.
Let love, being light, be drowned if she sink!

LUCIANA
What, are you mad, that you do reason so?

ANTIPHOLUS OF SYRACUSE
Not mad, but mated; how I do not know.

LUCIANA
It is a fault that springeth from your eye.　　　　55

ANTIPHOLUS OF SYRACUSE
For gazing on your beams, fair sun, being by.

50 **supposition** fancy (*OED n.* 3b), quibbling on the Latin *suppositio*, 'placing underneath', since, in Antipholus' fantasy, Luciana would be underneath him. The image reinforces the sexual quibble on *die* (51) and strengthens the case for F2's *bed* (49). The word may also bring to mind Gascoigne's *Supposes* (1566), whose action is structured by false suppositions; see p. 91.

51 **die** experience mortal death, or sexual orgasm (*OED v.*[1] 7d); *die* is sexual slang common in Shakespeare (see Williams, *Glossary*, 98). Portia promises her tears as 'the stream / And wat'ry death-bed' for Bassanio (*MV* 3.2.46–7).

52 True love will not sink because of its buoyant airiness (cf. 'love's light wings', *RJ* 2.2.66); if it sinks, it does not deserve to survive (cf. 'Love is a spirit all compact of fire, / Not gross to sink, but light, and will aspire', *VA* 149–50). Antipholus' *light* (*luce* in Italian) is associated with 'Luciana' (see 56 and List of Roles, 8n.). But *light* can also mean frivolous, or unchaste (*OED adj.*[1] 14a, b), making *light* love liable to sink for its earthiness. Roberts sees an allusion to the practice of women suspected for witches 'being swum': if the woman floated, she was guilty of witchcraft; if she sank, she was innocent (although liable to drown). For Antipholus, if love floats, it

would be proved sorcery, associated with lasciviousness (Roberts, 'Circe', 197–8). Antipholus' feelings about Luciana appear conflicted.
  drowned drownèd
  she i.e. love
53–60 stichomythia: see 2.1.10–41n. The intensifying verbal contest will culminate in the shared tripartite line at 60.
53–4 See 4.1.93 and n., on *madman*.
54 **mated** a triple pun: (1) overcome (*OED mate v.*[1] 1); (2) amazed (*OED mated adj.*[1] 1; cf. *Mac* 5.1.78); and (3) matched, married (*OED adj.*[3] 1; cf. 5.1.282).
55 See 56n., on *fair sun*.
  fault defect
56 **For** from
  gazing intent, even rapt, staring (*OED gaze v.* 1a); used similarly at 57; see 1.1.88n., on *gazing*. In Shakespeare, *gazing* often feeds love; e.g. *TGV* 2.1.43.
  fair sun another play on 'Luciana' as light (see 52n.). The sunlight brightness of the mistress's eyes is a sonnet convention: 'a bright light burned unmeasured in her eyes / . . . a spirit all celestial, a living sun / was what I saw' (Petrarch, 90.3–13). In the poetic commonplace, the mistress's eyes incite love (sight being the most intense of the senses); see e.g. Helena on Hermia's eyes, *MND* 1.1.183, 230; 2.2.91–2. The image grew so clichéd that Shakespeare

52 she] he Rowe　53+ SP] (*Luc.*)

216

LUCIANA

Gaze where you should, and that will clear your sight.

ANTIPHOLUS OF SYRACUSE

As good to wink, sweet love, as look on night.

LUCIANA

Why call you me 'love'? Call my sister so.

ANTIPHOLUS OF SYRACUSE

Thy sister's sister.

LUCIANA   That's my sister.

ANTIPHOLUS OF SYRACUSE   No;   60

It is thyself, mine own self's better part,

Mine eye's clear eye, my dear heart's dearer heart,

My food, my fortune and my sweet hope's aim,

My sole earth's heaven, and my heaven's claim.

LUCIANA

All this my sister is, or else should be.   65

ANTIPHOLUS OF SYRACUSE

Call thyself 'sister', sweet, for I am thee.

---

mocked it: 'My mistress' eyes are nothing like the sun' (*Son* 130.1); cf. 102–49 and n. **by** nearby

57 **gaze** See 56n., and 1.1.88n., on *gazing*.

58 **wink** close my eyes (*OED v.*[1] 1a). Antipholus means that closing his eyes and missing Luciana's sunlight are the same as looking into the night.

 night meaning perhaps Adriana, in opposition to Luciana as *sun* (56) (Oxf[1])

60 **That's** The antecedent is *love* (59).

61 **better part** i.e. soul; cf. 2.2.129 and n. Antipholus employs (here and at 64) language picked up from Adriana in 2.2 (see 2.2.127–9n.); he is still caught up in the heightened suggestiveness, or 'enchantment', created in that scene.

62 Cf. 'The clear eye's moiety and the dear heart's part' (*Son* 46.12) (Ard[2]).

63 **aim** object, target

64 **my heaven's claim** 'my claim to heaven', i.e. my salvation; see 79 and n., on *claims*.

66 **for . . . thee** Although F's *I am thee* has sometimes been emended, it squares with Antipholus' previous declarations and imitates Adriana's similar claim of identity with her husband (cf. 2.2.125–52 and n.). Antipholus may mean that, because he is united with Luciana, she should call herself the sister-wife referred to in 65. The line is hardly clear. Cf. 41 and n.

66–7 **thee. / Thee** rhetorical *anadiplosis*, repetition of a word from the end of a previous line in the beginning of the next. In the second part of 66 and in 67, *thee* appears three times: as a predicate nominative, a direct object and an indirect object.

---

57 where] *Rowe*[3]*; when *F*   59 'love'] *Theobald subst., Wells;* loue *F*   60–1] *Pope; F lines* sister. / sister. / part: /   66 thyself 'sister', sweet,] *Folg*[2]*; thy selfe sister sweet, *F;* thy self, sister sweet; *F4;* thy self Sister, Sweet; *Rowe*[3]   am] mean *Rowe*[3]*; aim *Capell;* claim *(Cuningham)*

217

Thee will I love, and with thee lead my life;
Thou hast no husband yet, nor I no wife:
Give me thy hand.   [*Offers to take her hand.*]
LUCIANA   O, soft, sir, hold you still;   69
I'll fetch my sister to get her good will.   *Exit.*

Enter DROMIO [OF SYRACUSE, *running*].

ANTIPHOLUS OF SYRACUSE
Why, how now, Dromio, where run'st thou so fast?
DROMIO OF SYRACUSE   Do you know me, sir? Am I
Dromio? Am I your man? Am I myself?
ANTIPHOLUS OF SYRACUSE
Thou art Dromio, thou art my man, thou art thyself.
DROMIO OF SYRACUSE   I am an ass, I am a woman's   75
man, and besides myself.

68 **nor I no** The double negative heightens
emphasis (Blake, 6.2.3.1); see also *no* at
4.2.7.
69 SD *Antipholus attempts physically to take
Luciana's hand, as his 'Give me thy hand'
(a binding offer of marriage) and Luciana's
reaction in the second part of the line
indicate.
70 **good will** favourable regard (*OED* goodwill *n.* 2); approval (Cam²); perhaps
hinting unconsciously that she is weaken-
ing towards Antipholus' advances (Wells)
71–7 These lines of alternating verse and prose
provide a transition from the lyricism of
the Antipholus–Luciana interlude to the
bawdy prose satire of the Antipholus–
Dromio exchange about Nell the kitchen
wench. Dromio's comic vision infiltrates
and usurps the episode in style and tone.
Although F sets all the lines as verse, the
present edition treats Dromio's speeches as
prose because they seem too varied in
number of syllables, too rhythmically
irregular and too devoid of alliteration for

tumbling verse (see 3.1.11–85n.). The
speeches through to 93 employ rhyming or
repeated end-words, mixing the sense of
prose and poetry; their monosyllabic,
short-phrased, urgent bursts of imagery
displace Antipholus' love-fantasy in favour
of Dromio's fantasticality.
73 **Am I myself** Cf. 41 and n.
74 perhaps with *Thou art* and ¹*thou art* elided
75–149 Dromio's experience mirrors parodic-
ally that of Antipholus. Both Syracusans
are claimed by women; undergo challenges
to their identity; wonder if they are transformed. Nonetheless, Antipholus enters
pursuing Luciana, while Dromio arrives
fleeing Nell, so that the scene divides and
caricatures male responses to women. To
Antipholus, Luciana is a romance goddess,
yet potentially a dangerous siren. To
Dromio, Nell is a nightmare version of the
possessive, domineering woman, whose
gigantism reflects her capacity to devour
him. Nell functions as a comic inversion of
Luciana and a displaced representation

69 SD] *this edn*   70.1 OF SYRACUSE] *Rowe; Siracusia* F   *running*] *Collier²*   72+ SP] *(S. Dro., Dro.)*
72–3] *Rowe³; verse* F   75–6] *Rowe³; verse* F

ANTIPHOLUS OF SYRACUSE

What woman's man? And how besides thyself?

DROMIO OF SYRACUSE   Marry, sir, besides myself I am
due to a woman: one that claims me, one that haunts
me, one that will have me.   80

ANTIPHOLUS OF SYRACUSE   What claim lays she to thee?

DROMIO OF SYRACUSE   Marry, sir, such claim as you
would lay to your horse; and she would have me as a
beast – not that, I being a beast, she would have me,
but that she, being a very beastly creature, lays claim   85
to me.

ANTIPHOLUS OF SYRACUSE   What is she?

DROMIO OF SYRACUSE   A very reverend body: ay, such
a one as a man may not speak of without he say,
'sir-reverence'. I have but lean luck in the match, and   90
yet is she a wondrous fat marriage.

of Adriana. Antipholus and Dromio fear
being 'possessed' in multiple ways; see e.g.
haunts (79).

75   **ass** See 2.2.205n.

76   **besides myself** out of my wits (*besides* =
beside) (*OED* beside *prep.* 5a); see 4.1.93
and n.; cf. e.g. *1H4* 3.1.177.

78   **besides myself** 'in addition to belonging to
myself'

79   **claims** Cf. *claim* at 64; either asserts a right
to (marry) (*OED* claim *v.* 3), or asserts
possession of (by marriage) (*OED* 2a); cf.
4.1.110, 4.4.156 and n.
      haunts pursues (see *OED* haunt *v.* 4); also
'molests [me]' as a supernatural being'
(*OED* 5b)

80, 84   **have** suggesting sexual possession
(Wells); cf. lust in *Son* 129.10 as 'Had,
having, and in quest to have, extreme'. See
Williams, *Glossary*, 153.

81, 85   **lays** possibly punning on 'lay' as 'have
sexual intercourse with' (see Williams,
Glossary, 183)

84–6   **not . . . me** Dromio's need to differ-
entiate between two meanings suggests
that 'have me as a beast' might provoke
ribald audience laughter and then require
clarification. Ard[1] sees a pun on *a beast* and
'abased' (citing W.J. Craig); for other
examples, see *2H4* 2.1.37–8, *Tim* 4.3.325.

88   **reverend** worthy of great respect (*OED*
adj. 1a), applied ironically to Nell's *body*.
Cf. 5.1.5, 124 and n., 134.

89   **without** unless (*OED conj.* 2)

90   **sir-reverence** 'with all respect' (*OED n.*
1b), a contracted version of the deferential
'saving your reverence', or 'save-
reverence' (Boswell–Malone), with Nell
masculinized in *sir*. The contraction
sometimes occurs as an apologetic formula
in relation to excrement (*OED* 2); cf. *RJ*
1.4.41–2 (Ard[2]).
      lean poor, meagre (*OED adj.* 2), playing
against *fat* (91)

91   **fat** obese; also abundant (*OED adj.* 10)

82 such] such a *Theobald*[2]   88 reverend] *(reuerent)*   ay] *(I)*   90 'sir-reverence'] *Dyce*[2]; sir reuerence *F;*
sir-reverence *Capell*

ANTIPHOLUS OF SYRACUSE　How dost thou mean, a 'fat marriage'?

DROMIO OF SYRACUSE　Marry, sir, she's the kitchen wench, and all grease; and I know not what use to　95 put her to but to make a lamp of her, and run from her by her own light. I warrant her rags and the tallow in them will burn a Poland winter. If she lives till doomsday, she'll burn a week longer than the whole world.　100

ANTIPHOLUS OF SYRACUSE　What complexion is she of?

DROMIO OF SYRACUSE　Swart like my shoe, but her face nothing like so clean kept. For why? She sweats; a man may go overshoes in the grime of it.

ANTIPHOLUS OF SYRACUSE　That's a fault that water will　105 mend.

94–5 **kitchen wench** Cf. 'kitchen-maid', 4.4.75 and n.

95 **grease** animal fat for cooking; body fat (*OED n.* 1a); perspiration (Crystal & Crystal, *n.*) (cf. *MW* 3.5.113–14); also punning on 'grace' (Cam¹) and pronounced the same (Kökeritz, 110)

96 **lamp** in contrast to Luciana as *sun* (56)

97 **rags** ragged clothes (Folg²)
tallow animal fat (used for making candles)

98 **a Poland winter** i.e. for a very long time, as in the long, dark span of a northern European winter

98–100 **If . . . world** At doomsday the world will be consumed by fire; cf. 2 Peter, 3.12, 7 (Shaheen, 110). Dromio's *doomsday* subtly recalls Egeon's *doom* at 1.1.2; see also 154.

99 **week** possibly punning on the homonymic 'wick' (Ard¹; Kökeritz, 153; although Cercignani questions, 150)

101 **complexion** Antipholus probably means temperament (*OED n.* 1) (cf. *TN* 2.5.26), but Dromio (102) understands skin colour (*OED n.* 4a).

102–49 Dromio's virtuosic catalogue of Nell's properties parodies Antipholus' rhapsodizing of Luciana and the blazoning typical of Elizabethan Petrarchan love sonnets (see 56n., on *fair sun*; cf. Petrarch, *Canzoniere*, 157; Sidney, *A&S*, 9; Spenser, *FQ*, 2.3.22–6). In response to Antipholus' catechism-like questions, Dromio anatomizes the woman into descriptive properties, but does so in a burlesque, anti-Petrarchan spirit (cf. Donne, 'Elegy 14: The Comparison'). This set-piece is typically a highpoint in theatrical productions. For comic proto-types, see e.g. Launce's itemizing in *TGV* 3.1.274–370 (Cam¹); Licio's inventory of Celia in Lyly's *Midas*, 1.2.30–85 (Ard²).

102 **Swart** black or dark brown (*OED adj.* 1a, b); cf. *Son* 28.11; sometimes used for blackamoors and fairies: 'No goblin or swart Faëry of the mine' (Milton, *Comus*, 436) (Steevens⁴)

104 **overshoes** shoe-deep (cf. *TGV* 1.1.24); the image is proverbial (Dent, S380).
grime soot, coal-dust deposited on the skin (*OED n.*), from working in the smoky kitchen

106 **mend** amend, put right; also at 2.2.110

92–3 'fat marriage'] *Folg²* (*Dyce subst.*);　fat marriage *F*　　103 sweats;] *Knight;* sweats *F*

DROMIO OF SYRACUSE   No, sir, 'tis in grain; Noah's flood could not do it.

ANTIPHOLUS OF SYRACUSE   What's her name?

DROMIO OF SYRACUSE   Nell, sir; but her name and three   110
quarters – that's an ell and three quarters – will not measure her from hip to hip.

ANTIPHOLUS OF SYRACUSE   Then she bears some breadth?

DROMIO OF SYRACUSE   No longer from head to foot   115
than from hip to hip: she is spherical, like a globe. I could find out countries in her.

---

107 **in grain** dyed fast, indelible (*OED* grain *n.*[1] 10c); cf. *TN* 1.5.237–8; see 5.1.311 and n.

107–8 **Noah's . . . it** *Noah's flood* was the biblical anticipation of baptism; thus, Dromio alludes to the water of baptism that mends the fault of original sin (cf. *Mac* 2.2.64). God flooded the earth to cleanse it of sinful man, with only Noah, the lone righteous man, and his family allowed to live; see Genesis, 6.9–9.17. Dromio perpetuates the play's water and sea imagery.

110 **Nell** *Nell* the 'kitchen wench' (94–5) is probably the same character as Luce, introduced at 3.1.47.1 (see n.), later recalled as the railing 'kitchen-maid' (4.4.75) and alluded to as the 'fat friend' (5.1.414). Concerning the inconsistency in names, Dromio may use *Nell* generically, as he later does 'Dowsabel' (4.1.110), or perhaps Shakespeare simply renamed her, not wanting to repeat *Luce* as too close to *Luciana* and wishing to pun on *Nell*.

110–11 *****name . . . ell** The kitchen wench is 'a Nell', that is, 'aN ell'. An *ell* was a length of 45 inches (*OED n.*[1] 1a); thus, *Nell*, from *hip to hip* (112), measures more than her name, an *ell*, by at least an additional three-quarters (altogether, over six feet). This reading derives from Theobald's emendation of F's 'name is' to *name and*.

Nell's sphericalness may be inspired by the name of *Men.*'s cook, Cylindrus (Oxf[1]).

116–44 **spherical . . . low** Correlations between body and geography amused Elizabethans. Among numerous Shakespearean examples, Falstaff in *MW* celebrates Mistress Page as 'a region in Guiana, all gold and bounty' (1.3.69). Cf. Donne's love poems, such as 'Elegy 2: To His Mistress Going to Bed' ('Oh my America, my new found land', swoons the lover before his naked mistress (27)).

116 **globe** perhaps prompted by a recent public interest in cartographic globes. The first English ones, made by Emery Molyneux, appeared in 1592, although Germany had manufactured them since the early 1500s. Molyneux 'Englished' his globe by showing the circumnavigational routes of Sir Francis Drake and Thomas Cavendish, by displaying an English coat of arms on North America and by marking English discoveries (see Cohen, 46–57). See Appendix 1, p. 319, and 4.1.111 and n.

117 **find out countries** perhaps as in a grammar school exercise; at Westminster School, in 1630, for example, seventh-form students ' "practised to describe and find out cities and countries in the mappes" ' (Baldwin, *Small Latine*, 1.360).

110–11 and . . . ²quarters –] *Theobald subst. (Thirlby, per Theobald);* is three quarters, that's an Ell . . . quarters, *F*

ANTIPHOLUS OF SYRACUSE   In what part of her body
stands Ireland?

DROMIO OF SYRACUSE   Marry, sir, in her buttocks; I   120
found it out by the bogs.

ANTIPHOLUS OF SYRACUSE   Where Scotland?

DROMIO OF SYRACUSE   I found it by the barrenness, hard
in the palm of her hand.

ANTIPHOLUS OF SYRACUSE   Where France?   125

DROMIO OF SYRACUSE   In her forehead, armed and
reverted, making war against her hair.

ANTIPHOLUS OF SYRACUSE   Where England?

DROMIO OF SYRACUSE   I looked for the chalky cliffs,
but I could find no whiteness in them. But I guess it   130

---

121 **bogs** wet, spongy ground, typical in Ireland. '[N]o doubt' *bogs* here means anus (Williams, *Glossary*, 47); it reflects an Elizabethan linking of Irish 'savagery' and 'anality' (Hadfield, 54). Also *bogs* probably puns on 'bog' as 'boggard', meaning a privy (*OED* bog *n.*⁴, although 'bog' is not recorded as a short form until 1789).

123–4 with *barrenness* as a 'conventional English slur' on Scotland's 'alleged unfruitfulness and poverty' (Oxf¹); *hard* means 'exactly' (Ard¹) but also refers to the calluses on a kitchen-maid's hands (Cam¹). Nell's dry hand signals infertility, in contrast to the proverb 'A moist hand argues fruitfulness' (Tilley, H86) (Ard¹). Cf. 4.2.19 and n., on *sere*; *MA* 2.1.118, *TN* 1.3.73.

126–7 Dromio makes two jokes: one involving Nell's scabs and lost hair from syphilis (the French disease, as recorded by Johnson); the other invoking French religious wars over succession (Theobald) (see 127n., on *hair*). Syphilis functions here as a metaphor for civil war. For allusions to venereal disease, see 2.2.85–6n.

126 **forehead** with the connotation of audacity, impudence (*OED n.* 2b), referring to the succession war in France; see 127n., on *hair*. On *forehead*, see 2.2.142n.

armed furnished with weaponry; also perhaps 'covered with encrusted eruptions' of pustules from venereal disease (Johnson); on such disease imagery, see 2.2.85–6n.

127 **reverted** revolted, rebelled (Crystal & Crystal, *adj.*); returned to its original possessors (*OED v.* 3), those being Catholics in the case of the French succession wars (see next note); also 'turned the wrong way', 'reversed' (*OED* reverted *adj.* 2, first citation).

*hair F2's emendation of F's 'heire' to *hair* maintains Dromio's metaphor, with a pun on 'heir' ('heire' is a spelling variant of both *hair* and 'heir'), referring to the war of succession in France involving the then-Protestant Henri of Navarre as the heir to the Catholic King Henri III (Theobald); see Appendix 1, p. 317.

129 **chalky cliffs** i.e. Nell's teeth (Cam¹), alluding to the white cliffs of Dover

---

124 her] *Rowe; the F*   127 reverted] revolted *White*   hair] *F2;* heire *F*

stood in her chin, by the salt rheum that ran between
France and it.

ANTIPHOLUS OF SYRACUSE   Where Spain?
DROMIO OF SYRACUSE   Faith, I saw it not, but I felt it hot
in her breath.   135
ANTIPHOLUS OF SYRACUSE   Where America, the Indies?
DROMIO OF SYRACUSE   O, sir, upon her nose, all o'er
embellished with rubies, carbuncles, sapphires,
declining their rich aspect to the hot breath of Spain,
who sent whole armadas of carracks to be ballast at   140
her nose.

131 **by** judging by (Norton)
  salt rheum mucus discharged from the
  nose (*OED* salt rheum *n.* 1, first citation),
  or perhaps perspiration (given Nell's
  fatness), or even watering of the eyes
  (Oxf[1]) (cf. *Oth* 3.4.51); *rheum* stands for
  the English Channel.
134–5 **hot . . . breath** probably referring to
  hot Spanish winds (the humid year-round
  Sirocco from the south or the dry summer
  Terral from the north); perhaps breath
  heated by spicy Spanish food (hotness was
  associated with the Spanish disposition;
  see e.g. Heywood, *Stuckeley*, 13.93);
  perhaps the fiery threats of Catholic Spain
  against England (Malone).
136 **America** Shakespeare's only reference to
  America, known for its wealth and for the
  syphilis that spread to Europe (Williams,
  Glossary, 27)
  Indies the western hemispheric lands
  discovered by Europeans in the 15th and
  16th centuries, thought to be part of India
  (*OED n. pl.* 1). *Indies* came to represent
  figuratively a place yielding great wealth
  (*OED* 2); cf. *MW* 1.3.71–2.
138–41 **rubies . . . nose** employing two images:
  (1) Nell's nose, grossly spotted with
  pimples, pustules and boils, curving down
  towards her mouth (see 139n.); (2)
  America's new world yielding valuable

shiploads of luminous red and blue gems
to Spanish conquerors. Gillies sees a mock
reference to Marlowe's treatment of maps
as 'images of desire' (60).
138 **rubies** rare and valuable precious stones
  varying in colour from deep crimson to
  pale red (*OED n.*[1] 1a); red facial pimples
  (*OED* 4)
  carbuncles large precious red stones
  (*OED n.* 1); inflammatory red skin lesions,
  boils, pustules (*OED* 3)
139 **declining** bending down (implying a
  hooked nose (Wells)); perhaps bending
  from the weight of the nose's riches, i.e.
  pustules (Oxf[1]). Cf. 44 and n., on *decline*.
140 *****armadas of carracks** fleets of galleons.
  The application to Nell's physiognomy is
  unclear, although the general sense may be
  that something offensive in Nell's breath
  (bad odour?) finds it way to her nose. The
  term *armadas* recalls Philip II's war fleet
  sent against England in 1588 (see also
  LLL's Spaniard Don Armado; *KJ* 3.4.2);
  carracks were large ships of burden, fitted
  for war but also used for trading by the
  Portuguese and Spanish in the East Indies,
  i.e. galleons (*OED n.*); also at *Oth* 1.2.50.
  ballast i.e. ballasted (*ppl.*), 'loaded' (*OED
  v.* 4, first citation); perhaps the bad breath
  'loaded' into Nell's nose

140 armadas] *(*Armadoes*)*   carracks] *(*Carrects*)*

ANTIPHOLUS OF SYRACUSE   Where stood Belgia, the
Netherlands?

DROMIO OF SYRACUSE   O, sir, I did not look so low. To
conclude, this drudge or diviner laid claim to me,   145
called me 'Dromio', swore I was assured to her, told
me what privy marks I had about me – as the mark of
my shoulder, the mole in my neck, the great wart on
my left arm – that I, amazed, ran from her as a witch.
And I think if my breast had not been made of faith,
⌐and my heart of steel,   150
She had transformed me to a curtal dog, and made
me turn i'th' wheel.

ANTIPHOLUS OF SYRACUSE
Go, hie thee presently, post to the road;
An if the wind blow any way from shore,

142 **Belgia** the Low Countries; cf. *3H6* 4.8.1.
144 **low** The Low Countries as the genital region also occurs in *2H4* 2.2.21–2 (Williams, *Glossary*, 195).
145 **diviner** practitioner of divination, here sorceress; cf. Luciana as a goddess or siren.
146 **assured** betrothed
146–9 **told . . . witch** As in other works, the inexplicable possession of intimate personal knowledge can lead to a (here humorous) accusation of witchcraft; cf. Middleton, *The Witch*, 1.2.201–2.
147 **privy** private, personal
147–9 **marks . . . arm** Birthmarks are common identifying signs in romance; cf. *TN* 5.1.242.
147–8 **of . . . in** = on . . . on
149 **as** as if she were
150–1 These lines occur as prose in F, but their scansion as loose fourteeners and their end-rhyme (*steel/wheel*) argue for verse, marking a transition from bawdy comic prose to normalizing blank verse (from 152).
150 **breast . . . steel** alluding to the armour of the Christian knight, especially 'the brest plate of righteousnesse' and 'the shielde

of fayth', donned in the struggle 'agaynst worldy gouernours of the darknesse of this worlde' (Ephesians, 6.14, 16, 12) (Ard[2]), passages sometimes cited to prove faith's efficacy against witches and the devil; see e.g. Gifford (sig. C2[v]). The images 'heart of steel' and 'true as steel' are proverbial (Dent, H310.1; Tilley, S840) (Oxf[1]). Cf. 4.2.34 and n.
151 **curtal dog** dog with a docked (curtailed) tail, thus not capable of running well (Ard[1]); also suggesting emasculation
    turn i'th' wheel i.e. go round like a dog inside a treadmill turning a roasting spit in a kitchen (Hudson); proverbial (Tilley, M87) (Ard[2])
152 **Go, hie . . . post** On such repetition of verbs, see 26 and n.
    hie See 1.2.90n.
    presently immediately (*OED adv.* 1a); also at 5.1.31
    post hurry, as does a post-rider (*OED v.* 2a, 1); cf. 1.2.63 and n.
    road place where ships ride safely at anchor, roadstead (*OED n.* 3a)
153 **An if** *An* intensifies *if* (Abbott, 103); also at 4.1.43, 4.3.76.

146 'Dromio'] *this edn; Dromio F*   150–1] *Knight; prose F*   150 faith] flint *Hanmer*   153 An] *(And)*

I will not harbour in this town tonight.
If any bark put forth, come to the mart,   155
Where I will walk till thou return to me.
If everyone knows us, and we know none,
'Tis time, I think, to trudge, pack and be gone.

DROMIO OF SYRACUSE

As from a bear a man would run for life,   159
So fly I from her that would be my wife.   *Exit.*

ANTIPHOLUS OF SYRACUSE

There's none but witches do inhabit here,
And therefore 'tis high time that I were hence.
She that doth call me 'husband', even my soul
Doth for a wife abhor. But her fair sister,
Possessed with such a gentle, sovereign grace,   165
Of such enchanting presence and discourse,
Hath almost made me traitor to myself.
But lest myself be guilty to self-wrong,
I'll stop mine ears against the mermaid's song.

Enter ANGELO *with the chain.*

ANGELO

Master Antipholus –

ANTIPHOLUS OF SYRACUSE   Ay, that's my name.   170

154 **harbour** lodge (*OED v.* 1a)

155 **bark** See 1.1.116n.

158 **trudge ... gone** three different ways of saying 'leave'; *trudge* means 'depart' (*OED v.* 1c); cf. 26 and n.; 4.3.69. *OED* cites *New Custom* (1573): 'Hence out of my sight, away, packing, trudge' (1.2).

159 On this action, see also *KL* 3.4.9 and, famously, *WT* 3.3.58 SD.

161 **witches** applicable to both sexes (Ard[1]); see 1.2.100 and n. Antipholus' notion later takes concrete form; see 4.3.49 and n.

165 **Possessed** Cf. 2.2.146 and n.

166 **enchanting** capturing Antipholus'

competing images of Luciana as beatific goddess and destructive siren (Ard[2])

discourse See 2.1.90n., on *Are ... dull.*

168 **to** of; perhaps compositorial eye-skip from *to myself* (167)

169 See 45–52 and n. Sailors who listened to the sirens' song cast themselves overboard; Odysseus stopped his sailors' ears with wax, but he listened safely by having himself tied to the mast (*Od.*, 12.165–80). The image was conventional: 'To these mermaids and their bates of error / I stop mine ears' (Psalms, 6.165–6, trans. Wyatt).

170+ SP1] *(Ang.)*   170 Antipholus –] *Theobald subst.; Antipholus.* F   Ay,] *(I)*

ANGELO

    I know it well, sir. Lo, here's the chain.

    I thought to have ta'en you at the Porpentine;

    The chain, unfinished, made me stay thus long.

    [*Presents the chain.*]

ANTIPHOLUS OF SYRACUSE

    What is your will that I shall do with this?

ANGELO

    What please yourself, sir: I have made it for you.   175

ANTIPHOLUS OF SYRACUSE

    Made it for me, sir? I bespoke it not.

ANGELO

    Not once, nor twice, but twenty times you have.

    Go home with it, and please your wife withal,

    And soon at supper-time I'll visit you,

    And then receive my money for the chain.   180

ANTIPHOLUS OF SYRACUSE

    I pray you, sir, receive the money now,

    For fear you ne'er see chain nor money more.

ANGELO

    You are a merry man, sir; fare you well.   *Exit.*

ANTIPHOLUS OF SYRACUSE

    What I should think of this I cannot tell;

---

171 perhaps with a one-beat pause after *sir*

172 **ta'en** taken; i.e. overtaken; spelled *tane* in F. This consonant suppression occurs also at 5.1.387.

the Porpentine See 3.1.116 and n.

175 **What please yourself** whatever may please you (see Abbott, 254)

178 Angelo may be subtly urging marital reconciliation.

179 **soon at supper-time** *soon at* means 'at about'; cf. 'Soon at five o'clock' (1.2.26 and n., on *Soon at*); a common Elizabethan supper-time was five o'clock. The phrase

provides another time marker and anticipates the climactic convergence of characters.

182 The line prepares for Angelo's discomfiture in 4.1 (Ard²).

183–90 Heroic couplets complete the scene.

183 **merry** Angelo apparently recalls that Antipholus declared, after the lock-out, that he would be *merry* regardless of the circumstances (3.1.108). He repeats the term to Antipholus at 4.1.27 (see n., on *merry*). See also 1.2.21 and n., on *merry jests.*

---

171 here's] here is *Pope*   172 ta'en] *(tane)*   173 SD] *Bevington⁴*   175] *Cam; prose F*   176] *Pope²; prose F*   sir?] *Collier;* sir, *F;* sir! *Rowe*

But this I think: there's no man is so vain   185
That would refuse so fair an offered chain.
I see a man here needs not live by shifts,
When in the streets he meets such golden gifts.
I'll to the mart, and there for Dromio stay;   189
If any ship put out, then straight, away!   *Exit.*

4.1   *Enter* [Second] Merchant, [ANGELO *the*] *goldsmith
and an* Officer.

2 MERCHANT [*to Angelo*]
You know since Pentecost the sum is due,
And since I have not much importuned you;
Nor now I had not, but that I am bound
To Persia, and want guilders for my voyage.

---

185 **vain** foolish; cf. 27n.
186 **so . . . chain** a chain offered so courteously (*OED* fair *adv.* 2a)
187 **shifts** fraudulent schemes, subterfuges (*OED n.* 4a), as if Antipholus might practise them
188 **golden** Cf. 48 and n., associating the mysterious 'gift' of the chain with Luciana's aura of magic.
189 **I'll to** 'I'll go to'; the context supplies the active infinitive (*OED* will *v.*[1] 19a).
190 **straight** See 1.1.86n.
4.1 The scene takes place on the mart (as indicated at 5.1.262), although exactitude seems unnecessary.
0.1 **Second** See List of Roles, 15n. The Second Merchant wishes to collect a debt from Angelo before departing for Persia; he and Antipholus are unacquainted (see *stranger* at 36; 5.1.4); also at 5.1.0.1.
0.2 **Officer** See List of Roles, 16n.
1 **Pentecost** The 50th day (seventh Sunday) after Easter, celebrating the descent of the Holy Spirit upon Christ's disciples (Acts,

2.1–41); i.e. Whitsun. In 1 Corinthians, Paul remarks that he will tarry until Pentecost in Ephesus (16.8). Pentecost was associated with the payment of financial debt, and 'Pentecostal' sometimes meant a fixed payment by a parish to the bishop at Pentecost, or a payment by parishioners to their priest (*OED n.* 1; see Ollard, 454).
2 **since** since then
  importuned impòrtuned
3 Verse lines in the scene often favour monosyllabic words, apt for rapid-fire delivery.
  bound See 1.1.81n.
4 **Persia** roughly, modern Iran. In Shakespeare's day, Persia was identified not only with heroic military action (see Marlowe's *1 Tamburlaine*; also *MV* 2.1.25) but with luxury goods. Elizabethans traded with Persia for silks, carpets, shawls, pearls and precious stones (see e.g. Marlowe's *Jew of Malta*, 1.1.88).
  guilders See 1.1.8n., on *guilders*.

---

185 think:] *Wells;* thinke, *F*   190 straight,] *Ard²;* straight *F*   away!] *Kittredge;* away. *F*   **4.1**] *(Actus Quartus. Scoena Prima.);* ACT IV. SCENE I. *Rowe*   0.1 Second Merchant] *Dyce;* a Merchant *F;* SECOND MERCHANT OF EPHESUS *Riv*   1+ SP] *Dyce subst.; Mar. F; Mer. F2*   1 SD] *Oxf*

Therefore make present satisfaction,   5
Or I'll attach you by this officer.

ANGELO

Even just the sum that I do owe to you
Is growing to me by Antipholus,
And in the instant that I met with you
He had of me a chain; at five o'clock   10
I shall receive the money for the same.
Pleaseth you walk with me down to his house,
I will discharge my bond, and thank you, too.

> *Enter* ANTIPHOLUS [OF] EPHES[US, *wearing the*
> *Courtesan's ring, and*] DROMIO [OF EPHESUS]
> *from the Courtesan's.*

5   **present** immediate
     satisfaction payment in full of the debt
     (*OED n.* 1a); with *-ion* pronounced
     disyllabically; also at 5.1.253. The word
     launches a series of legalistic terms and
     phrases in the scene.
6   **attach** arrest (on the authority of a writ of
     attachment); also at 73
     officer here, a bailiff, i.e. an official under
     a sheriff who executes writs and processes
     and makes arrests (*OED* bailiff 2); a private
     suitor could employ his services for a fee.
     The Officer is later called a *sergeant* (see
     4.2.55, 60n.; *sergeant* also occurs at 4.3.31,
     40; see 4.3.31n.).
7   **Even** possibly 'to be sure' (*OED adv.* 8b);
     or possibly referring to the present
     moment, i.e. 'only now' (see Abbott, 38;
     also *OED* 9b); probably pronounced 'e'en'
8   **growing** accruing (*OED* grow *v.* 5b; see
     also *OED* accrue *v.* 2, 3); cf. 4.4.122, 135.
10   **chain** the first of 13 occurrences of *chain*
     in this scene, making it an aural marker; in
     subsequent scenes, the chain will also
     function as a visual marker (see O'Donnell,
     414–16).

     five o'clock the hour appointed for Egeon's
     execution and for the meeting of other

parties; see 1.2.26 and n., on *five o'clock*;
1.1.100n., on *five*.
12   **Pleaseth you** 'if it may please you to'; i.e.
     polite address. *Pleaseth* is third-person
     singular subjunctive (see Blake, 4.3.2.1.e).
13   **bond** legal obligation of financial debt
     (*OED n.* 9a); *bond* is related to *bound* (see
     1.1.81n.) and occurs in different forms and
     senses at 4.4.126; 5.1.250, 339 (*bonds*);
     5.1.141, 288, 289 (*bondman*; see 5.1.288–
     91n.).
13.1–2 *wearing . . . ring* The Courtesan's ring
     now identifies Ephesian Antipholus, just as
     the chain will distinguish his twin brother;
     see also 4.4.0.1. Both signal misappro-
     priation, and each will be returned
     ultimately to its rightful owner. In the latter
     part of the play, the ring is introduced as an
     important prop and a source of dispute;
     references to it occur at 4.3.70, 78, 84, 96;
     4.4.0.1, 139, 140; 5.1.144, 185.1, 277, 278,
     391, 392 SD. In Shakespeare, rings often
     have vaginal connotations (see Williams,
     Glossary, 260).
13.3 *from the Courtesan's* i.e. from her house,
     the Porpentine (see 3.1.116) a 'fictional'
     SD; cf. *from the bay* (84.1 and n.) and *to
     the priory* (5.1.37.1 and n.).

7+ SP] *Rowe (Ang.); Gold. F*   8 growing] owing *Pope*   13.1 OF EPHESUS] *Rowe subst.; Ephes. F*
13.1–2 *wearing . . . and*] *this edn*   13.2 OF EPHESUS] *Rowe subst.*

OFFICER

That labour may you save: see where he comes.

ANTIPHOLUS OF EPHESUS [*to Dromio*]

While I go to the goldsmith's house, go thou 15
And buy a rope's end. That will I bestow
Among my wife and her confederates
For locking me out of my doors by day. –
But soft, I see the goldsmith. – Get thee gone,
Buy thou a rope and bring it home to me. 20

DROMIO OF EPHESUS

I buy a thousand pound a year, I buy a rope.   *Exit.*

ANTIPHOLUS OF EPHESUS [*to Angelo*]

A man is well holp up that trusts to you:

15–18 ²**go . . . day** Antipholus plans to beat his wife (see 2.1.15 and n.). Wife-beating was repudiated by Elizabethan proponents of companionate marriage; for a man to beat his wife and to treat her 'like a slave' was to incur the 'greatest shame that can be', according to the 'Homily on the State of Matrimony' (*Homilies*, 545, 544); notwithstanding, Elizabethan husbands had a common-law right to beat their wives (Dolan, 33).

16 **rope's end** short section of rope used for flogging (*OED* rope's end); also at 98. The item is introduced at 4.4.7.1 and named at 4.4.16; see also 4.4.44 and n. 'Rope' was also a slang word for penis (Levinson, 2.3.136n.; Levin, 'Rope'), giving Antipholus' aggression a sexual edge; *rope's end* may allude to the phalluses and slapsticks of the *commedia dell'arte* tradition. The phrase occurs in Warner's translation of *Men.* (34).

will I I will; *will* (as opposed to 'shall') emphasizes volition.

bestow distribute (Crystal & Crystal, *v.* 7) (cf. *JC* 1.3.151); confer as a gift (*OED v.* 6a), here used ironically. Previously, Anti-

pholus had angrily declared his intention to *bestow* (3.1.117) the chain, meant for his wife, upon the Courtesan; now he intends to *bestow* a rope upon Adriana.

17 **confederates** accomplices for unlawful purposes (*OED n.* 2). 'Confederacy' appears in cony-catching pamphlets associated with trickery and juggling, e.g. Rid, *Art of Juggling* (1612), sig. C1ᵛ (see Caputo, 318). Forms of the word recur with magical-trickster connotations at 4.4.103, 5.1.237.

19 **But soft** See 2.2.115n., on *But soft*.

21 i.e. sometimes I am sent to buy valuable items (i.e. *a thousand pound*s' worth), now I am sent for something trivial (*a rope*); on *thousand*, cf. 1.1.21 and n., on *a thousand marks*. In addition, by buying a rope, Dromio will perhaps be securing a thousand 'poundings' of Adriana or himself from Antipholus (Jorgensen), although this reading forfeits a contrast of clauses. Despite its opacity, this exit line typically gets a laugh in the theatre. It scans metrically as a hexameter.

22 **holp up** helped; archaic past tense (*OED* help *v.*)

14+ SP] *(Offi., Offic.)*   15+ SP] *(Ant., Eph.Ant., Anti., An.)*   15 SD] *Oxf*   16 end. That] end, that *F* 17 her] *Rowe;* their *F;* these *Collier² (Collier, Notes)*   21 SP] *Malone subst. (Dro. E.); Dro. F* year, . . . rope.] year! . . . rope? *Collier³;* year: . . . rope. *Cam*   SD] *(Exit Dromio)*   22 SD] *Oxf*

I promised your presence and the chain,
But neither chain nor goldsmith came to me.
Belike you thought our love would last too long   25
If it were chained together, and therefore came not.

ANGELO
Saving your merry humour, [*offering a paper*]
        here's the note
How much your chain weighs to the utmost carat,
The fineness of the gold and chargeful fashion,
Which doth amount to three odd ducats more   30
Than I stand debted to this gentleman.
I pray you see him presently discharged,
For he is bound to sea, and stays but for it.

ANTIPHOLUS OF EPHESUS
I am not furnished with the present money;
Besides, I have some business in the town.   35
Good signor, take the stranger to my house,
And with you take the chain, and bid my wife

---

23 **promised** promisèd; i.e. to the Courtesan.
Antipholus had asked the goldsmith to
bring the chain to him at the Porpentine
and declared that he would *bestow* it on the
Courtesan (see 3.1.114–19; 'he promised
me a chain', 4.3.85).

25–6 **our ... it** 'our mutual loves of one for
the other would last too long if they'. By
love Antipholus presumably means friendship, but his image conveys a hint of sexual
aggressiveness; cf. 48 and n.

26 **chained together** The chain links characters together metaphorically, although
not always in the spirit of *love*.

27 **Saving** 'with due respect for'
merry repeated by Angelo from 3.2.183
(see n.); also at 90 below; cf. 1.2.21 and n.,
on *merry jests*.
humour See 1.2.21n.

29 **chargeful fashion** costly workmanship

(*OED* chargeful *adj.* 1; fashion *n.* 1); cf.
5.1.18 and n., on *charge*.

30 **ducats** gold (or silver) coins, originating in
13th-century Venice and copied by other
Renaissance European countries, so that
values varied; loosely, money. A thousand
ducats is 'substantial' (Fischer, 69); *ducats*
recurs (see 4.3.84, 97 and n.; 4.4.13), and
the word figures prominently in *MV*.

32 **presently** immediately
discharged paid (*OED v.* 10)

33 **bound** See 1.1.81n.
it i.e. receiving payment; 'it' can refer
generally to the previous context (Blake,
3.3.2.1.e).

34 **present money** ready money (*OED*
present *adj.* 5); cf. *MV* 3.2.273.

36 **signor** See 3.1.1 and n., on *Signor*.
stranger i.e. the Second Merchant, with
the implication that he is a foreigner (*OED*
n. 1); see 4.1.0.1n.

---

23 I promised] you promisèd *Dyce²*   27 SD] *Folg²* subst.   28 carat] (charect)   36 signor] (Signior)

Disburse the sum on the receipt thereof.
Perchance I will be there as soon as you.

ANGELO

Then you will bring the chain to her yourself?   40

ANTIPHOLUS OF EPHESUS

No, bear it with you, lest I come not time enough.

ANGELO

Well, sir, I will. Have you the chain about you?

ANTIPHOLUS OF EPHESUS

An if I have not, sir, I hope you have,
Or else you may return without your money.

ANGELO

Nay, come, I pray you, sir, give me the chain;   45
Both wind and tide stays for this gentleman,
And I, to blame, have held him here too long.

ANTIPHOLUS OF EPHESUS

Good Lord! You use this dalliance to excuse
Your breach of promise to the Porpentine.
I should have chid you for not bringing it,   50
But, like a shrew, you first begin to brawl.

---

41 12 syllables; the context argues for treatment as verse.
    time enough in time
43 **An if** See 3.2.153n.
46 an odd reversal of 'Time and tide stays for no man' (Dent, T323). The intended sense may be that wind and tide 'await', or are ready for, the merchant (OED stay $v.^1$, 14b).
    stays The *s*-inflection of *stays* indicates either a plural ending in the present indicative (Blake, 6.1.1) or a plural subject taking a singular verb; see 3.2.19–20n.
47 ***to** The F compositor may have mistakenly set 'too' from seeing *too* at the end of the line. Alternatively, F's 'too blame' might mean 'too blameworthy' (as Wells); cf. 'too willful-blame', *1H4* 3.1.175.
48 **dalliance** light talk (*OED n.* 1); idle delay (*OED* 4). The word carries a sexual con-

notation consistent with Antipholus' other expressions (*OED* 2); see 25–6n., 59n.
49 **breach of promise** The phrase was often used specifically in relation to marriage contracts (*OED* breach *n.* 3b); see 48n.
    to i.e. to come to
    the Porpentine See 3.1.116n.
51 Cf. 'I do the wrong, and first begin to brawl' (*R3* 1.3.323); dubiously proverbial (see Dent, C579).
    shrew railing or scolding woman; cf. *shrewish* at 3.1.2. Antipholus now transfers the term to the goldsmith, continuing the tone of 25–6, 48–9. Antipholus uses *shrew* emasculatingly here, although, regarding a man, it could mean wretch or villain (*OED n.*² 1d).
    begin probably present tense, but possibly past, with the implied modal *did*: 'you did first begin'

40–2] *Pope; prose F*   40 yourself?] *Theobald;* your selfe. *F*   42 will.] *F4 subst.;* will? *F*   43 An] *(And),*
Capell   47 I, to blame,] *Theobald;* I too blame *F;* I to blame *F3*

231

2 MERCHANT [*to Angelo*]
The hour steals on; I pray you, sir, dispatch.

ANGELO [*to Antipholus*]
You hear how he importunes me. – The chain!

ANTIPHOLUS OF EPHESUS
Why, give it to my wife, and fetch your money.

ANGELO
Come, come, you know I gave it you even now.   55
Either send the chain, or send me by some token.

ANTIPHOLUS OF EPHESUS
Fie! Now you run this humour out of breath.
Come, where's the chain? I pray you, let me see it.

2 MERCHANT
My business cannot brook this dalliance.
[*to Antipholus*] Good sir, say whe'er you'll answer
    me or no.   60
If not, I'll leave him to the officer.

ANTIPHOLUS OF EPHESUS
I answer you? What should I answer you?

ANGELO
The money that you owe me for the chain.

---

brawl wrangle, squabble; 'we say men do brawl, when between them is altercation in words' (Elyot, 95).

52 **steals on** comes on unobserved (*OED* steal *v.*[1] 11a)

53 **me. – The chain!** Angelo loses his patience; rhetorical *aposiopesis*; see 1.1.94 and n., on *came – . . . more*.

55 with perhaps either 'gav't' (Walker, *Versification*, 145) or 'e'en'; *gave it* also occurs at 65.

56 **Either** perhaps one syllable, as *whe'er* (60) (Abbott, 466); cf. *JC* 4.1.23, *R3* 1.2.64.
[2]**send . . . token** i.e. send me for the chain by means of some authenticating sign; cf. e.g. *R3* 4.2.79; *by* means either 'by means of' (*OED prep.* 30a) or 'with' (*OED* 3).

The line implies a chiasmus: 'either send the chain to me or send me to the chain'.

57 **run . . . breath** 'jest too far' (Ard[2]), from the proverbial 'He runs himself out of breath' (Dent, B641)
humour Antipholus repeats Angelo's *humour* (27): each character believes that the other is joking. See 1.2.21n.

59 **dalliance** waste of time in trifling delay; see 48 and n.; also perhaps 'play' (*OED* 3). Words are being appropriated and repeated accusatorially. At 48 *dalliance* scans as two syllables, but at 59 it scans as three, perhaps with new emphasis and connotation.

60 **whe'er** whether

60, 62 **answer** recompense (*OED v.* 7)

61 **him** i.e. Angelo

52, 53 SDs] *Oxf*   53 me. – The] *Dyce subst.;* me, the *F*   60 SD] *this edn*   whe'er] *(whe'r)*

ANTIPHOLUS OF EPHESUS

I owe you none till I receive the chain.

ANGELO

You know I gave it you half an hour since.   65

ANTIPHOLUS OF EPHESUS

You gave me none. You wrong me much to say so.

ANGELO

You wrong me more, sir, in denying it.

Consider how it stands upon my credit.

2 MERCHANT

Well, officer, arrest him at my suit.

OFFICER [*to Angelo*]   I do,

And charge you in the Duke's name to obey me.   70

ANGELO

This touches me in reputation.

[*to Antipholus*] Either consent to pay this sum for me,

Or I attach you by this officer.

ANTIPHOLUS OF EPHESUS

Consent to pay thee that I never had?

Arrest me, foolish fellow, if thou dar'st.   75

ANGELO [*Gives money to Officer.*]

Here is thy fee: arrest him, officer.

– I would not spare my brother in this case

If he should scorn me so apparently.

---

65 **gave it** See 55n.

hour probably pronounced disyllabically

66 **You . . . none** Angelo will later treat this denial as an oath; see 5.1.11 and n., on *forswore*.

68 **stands upon** affects (*OED* stand *v.* to stand upon 17)

credit reputation for financial trustworthiness; see 71.

69–70 In F, *I do* begins 70; Hanmer first set it as the completion of 69, with the line-

ending position underscoring its force as a speech-act.

70 **charge . . . me** formulaic language of arrest; cf. e.g. Fennor, sig. B1ᵛ.

71 **reputation** with *-ion* as two syllables; see 68n., on *credit*. On reputation, see 2.1.108–12 and n.

73 **attach** See 6n., on *attach*.

74 **that** for what

77–8 probably spoken to the Second Merchant or the audience

78 **apparently** manifestly; openly (*OED adv.* 1)

69–70] *Hanmer subst.; F lines* suite. / me. / ; *Hanmer lines* suit. / do, / me. /   69 SD] *Oxf*   72 SD] *Capell subst.*   76 SD] *Capell subst.*

The Comedy of Errors

OFFICER [*to Antipholus*]
I do arrest you, sir; you hear the suit.

ANTIPHOLUS OF EPHESUS
I do obey thee till I give thee bail.   80
[*to Angelo*] But, sirrah, you shall buy this sport
    as dear
As all the metal in your shop will answer.

ANGELO
Sir, sir, I shall have law in Ephesus,
To your notorious shame, I doubt it not.

Enter DROMIO [OF SYRACUSE] *from the bay.*

DROMIO OF SYRACUSE
Master, there's a bark of Epidamium   85
That stays but till her owner comes aboard;
And then, sir, she bears away. Our fraughtage, sir,
I have conveyed aboard, and I have bought
The oil, the balsamum and *aqua-vitae*.

81 **sirrah** meant contemptuously, and completing the descent in Antipholus' terms of address to Angelo: *Good signor* (36), *you* (37), *sir* (43), *thee* and *thou* (74, 75), *fellow* (75), *sirrah* (Ard²)

81–2 **you . . . answer** i.e. 'This joke is going to cost you all the gold you have'; *metal* refers to precious metal, esp. gold (*OED n.* 1e).

83 **law** Similarly, Adriana and Ephesian Antipholus will ask the Duke for *Justice* (5.1.133, 190, 197) against each other; cf. *MV* 4.1.142.

84 **shame** See 2.1.112 and n.

84.1 *from the bay* In *Men.*, the left side of the stage leads to the harbour; cf. 13.3 and n. Dromio might carry several bottles with him (see 88–9), instead of the expected *rope's end* (16), prompting Antipholus' charge of drunkenness (96).

85–92 Dromio's first trochaic line disrupts the preceding iambic squabble, and his sub-

sequent alliteration, internal rhyme, off-rhyme, balanced lines and repetitions introduce lyricism into the scene. The speech's style and content enhance the humour of Antipholus' *How now? A madman?* (93).

85, 99 **bark** See 1.1.116n.

85 **Epidamium** with -*ium* pronounced as one syllable

87 with the first *sir* as an extra-metrical vocative
    bears away sails away (*OED* bear *v.*¹ 37a); 'to bear away' means nautically 'to alter course away from the wind' (*Shakespeare's England*, 1.162).
    fraughtage freightage (*OED n.* 2, first citation); from 'fraught' (*OED v.*), to load or store; the now-archaic spelling enhances assonance. Also at *TC* Prol.3; cf. *waftage* (95).

89 **oil . . . *aqua-vitae*** oil: possibly olive oil;

79, 81 SDs] *Oxf*   84.1 OF SYRACUSE] *Theobald²; Sira. F*   85+ SP] *(Dro., S.Dro., S. Dromio.)*   85, 94 Epidamium] *Epidamnium / Rowe; Epidamnum / Pope;* Epidamnus *Oxf¹*   87 And . . . she] Then sir she *F2;* And then she *Capell;* And then, sir, *Stevens⁴*   fraughtage] freightage *Oxf*

The ship is in her trim; the merry wind 90
Blows fair from land: they stay for naught at all
But for their owner, master, and yourself.

ANTIPHOLUS OF EPHESUS

How now? A madman? Why, thou peevish sheep,
What ship of Epidamium stays for me?

DROMIO OF SYRACUSE

A ship you sent me to, to hire waftage. 95

ANTIPHOLUS OF EPHESUS

Thou drunken slave, I sent thee for a rope,
And told thee to what purpose and what end.

DROMIO OF SYRACUSE

You sent me for a rope's end as soon!
You sent me to the bay, sir, for a bark.

ANTIPHOLUS OF EPHESUS

I will debate this matter at more leisure, 100

---

balsamum: the aromatic, resinous vegetable juice from the balsam tree, thought to possess soothing, healing or restorative properties; '*aqua-vitae*' ('water of life'): strong distilled liquor such as brandy. These goods were typical of Mediterranean trade. The *balsamum* and '*aqua-vitae*' are probably restoratives, perhaps much needed by the beleaguered Syracusans.

90 **in her trim** rigged and ready to sail
merry Cf. 27 and n., on *merry*.

92 **master** presumably Antipholus rather than the ship's master

93 **madman** Reacting from their private worlds, characters are increasingly seeing others as mad, or feeling themselves as mad (Ard²); see e.g. 3.2.53–4, 76.
peevish foolish (*OED adj.* 2); perverse (*OED* 1); cf. 4.4.115. The reversal of consonantal order in *peevish sheep* offers an aural 'crossing' similar to rhetorical *antimetabole*. Antipholus' poeticism perhaps mocks Dromio's.

93–4 **sheep ... ship** a pun. Cf. 'he is shipp'd already, / And I have play'd the sheep in losing him' (*TGV* 1.1.72–3); also *LLL* 2.1.219–20 (see also Cercignani, 150; Kökeritz, 145).

95 **hire** commonly disyllabic (Cercignani, 25; Walker, *Versification*, 136)
waftage passage; conveyance by water (*OED n.* 2a). Its echo of *fraughtage* (87) and its sense of breeze give Dromio a last gasp of poeticism.

96 **drunken** See 84.1n.

96, 107 **slave** See 1.2.87 and n., on *slave*.

98 **rope's end** i.e. so that Dromio could be flogged; see 16 and n., on *rope's end*. Antipholus' redundant *and what end* (97) sets up Dromio's *rope's end* (repeating Antipholus' phrase from 16). Later, Ephesian Dromio will proffer a *rope's end* to Ephesian Antipholus (see 4.4.16 and n.). Some editors make *rope's* disyllabic to fill out the line, which can be made humorous in performance; others introduce 'sir'.

95 hire] *(hier)* 98 me for] me, sir, for *Steevens⁴* rope's] *(ropes)*; ropè's *Keightley (Malone)* end] end, sir, *Ard²*

And teach your ears to list me with more heed.
To Adriana, villain, hie thee straight:
[*offering Dromio a key*] Give her this key, and tell
  her, in the desk
That's covered o'er with Turkish tapestry,
There is a purse of ducats: let her send it.   105
Tell her I am arrested in the street
And that shall bail me. Hie thee, slave. Be gone!
– On, officer, to prison, till it come.
                              Exeunt [all but Dromio of Syracuse.]
DROMIO OF SYRACUSE
'To Adriana': that is where we dined,
Where Dowsabel did claim me for her husband;   110
She is too big, I hope, for me to compass.
Thither I must, although against my will,
For servants must their masters' minds fulfil.
                              Exit [with the key.]

101 **teach your ears** i.e. by boxing them
  list listen to (*OED v.*² 2), also at *MW* 5.5.42
102–5 Cf. 4.2.29 and n., on *Here*.
102 **straight** See 1.1.86n.
104 **Turkish tapestry** The details of this scene
  – a merchant bound for Persia, Dutch coins
  for Ephesian debts, a Turkish tapestry –
  evoke a cosmopolitan exoticism. 'Turkey
  work' – tapestries, chairs, stools, cushions
  and the like – was much prized by
  Elizabethans. A Turkish tapestry covers a
  table in Hans Holbein's famous painting
  The Ambassadors (1533) in the National
  Gallery, London.
105 **purse of ducats** Cf. 4.2.61.1 and n., 4.4.97
  and n.
108 This action gains resonance if the arresting
  Officer corresponds to the 'Jailer' who led
  Antipholus' father away for debt at
  1.1.155–6; see List of Roles, 16n.
110 **Dowsabel** sweetheart (*OED n.*), i.e. Nell;
  perhaps from the French *douce et belle*

('sweet and pretty') (Halliwell) or the
Italian *dulcibella*. See 3.2.110 and n., on
Nell. *Dowsabel* is associated with pastoral
poetry: a beautiful country maiden named
Dowsabell appears in Michael Drayton's
Idea, The Shepherd's Garland (1593)
(1.130) (Steevens²).
  claim See 3.2.79 and n., on *claims*.
111 **compass** encircle with arms (*OED v.*¹ 8);
  gain (*OED* 11b); cf. *TGV* 2.4.214.
  Dromio's inability to embrace Nell
  demonstrates his unsuitability for her.
  Associated with cartography and
  navigation, *compass* recalls the image of
  Nell as a globe (3.2.116).
112–13 Messenio in *Men.* likewise utters such
  sentiments (see e.g. 444). He hopes that his
  punctilious obedience will forestall
  beatings and win him freedom (see e.g.
  Men., 966–89). On *servants*, cf. 1.1.127n.,
  on *attendant*.

103 SD] *Capell subst.*   108 SD *all . . . Syracuse*] *Capell subst.*   109 'To Adriana':] *this edn;* To *Adriana,*
F; To *Adriana? Rowe³;* To *Adriana! Pope*   113 SD *with the key*] *this edn*

236

[4.2]   *Enter* ADRIANA *and* LUCIANA.

ADRIANA
Ah, Luciana, did he tempt thee so?
Mightst thou perceive austerely in his eye
That he did plead in earnest? Yea or no?
Looked he or red or pale, or sad or merrily?
What observation mad'st thou in this case   5
Of his heart's meteors tilting in his face?

LUCIANA
First he denied you had in him no right.

ADRIANA
He meant he did me none; the more my spite.

LUCIANA
Then swore he that he was a stranger here.

ADRIANA
And true he swore, though yet forsworn he were.   10

4.2 As in 2.1, the setting is within or just outside the Phoenix.
1–6 The rhyme scheme resembles the sestet of a sonnet (cf. esp. *RJ* Prol.1–14, 1.5.93–106, 2.Chor.1–14). Adriana's quatrain recalls Luciana's opening speech at 3.2 (see 3.2.1–52n.); see also 25–8, 62–5 below.
1 **tempt** lure sexually (Williams, *Glossary*, 304; see also *OED v.* 4a)
2 **austerely** seriously (Crystal & Crystal, *adv.*); strictly (*OED adv.*); Adriana double-checks Luciana's claim.
2, 4 **eye . . . merrily** a rhyme (Kökeritz, 436); also at *LLL* 5.2.475–7, 480–1
4 ¹**or . . .** ²**or** See 1.1.136n., on *Or . . . or*.
red or pale *red* from blushing, *pale* from fear
³**or . . . merrily** *sad* means serious; cf. 'Look how we can, or sad or merrily' (*1H4* 5.2.12). The sense of *merrily* seems adjectival; cf. 'he looks so merrily' (*MW*

2.1.191). Perhaps pronounced 'merr'ly', as at *AW* 2.2.61, *WT* 4.3.124.
5 **case** particular situation (*OED n.*¹ 6a); elsewhere *case* can refer to a facial mask; cf. *1H4* 2.2.53. See 42 and n.
6 **heart's . . . face** His heart's passions vie with each other by alternating *red or pale* (4) in his facial colours, with the extravagant *meteors tilting* suggesting courtly chivalric combat; cf. 'meteors' at *1H4* 1.1.10.
7 Luciana does not answer Adriana's questions. On *right*, cf. 2.1.40.
no any; see 3.2.68n.
8 **he . . . none** i.e. 'He claimed towards me no rights of a husband.'
spite injury (*OED n.* 1a); cf. *wrong* at 2.2.177, and 177–8n.
10 i.e. he has sworn truly in that he has been a stranger to his home, but he has perjured himself by his absence in performing his conjugal duties.

4.2] Capell (*SCENE* II.) (*Theobald subst.*)   1–4] *alternating indentation as Capell*   1+ SP] *(Adr., Adria., Adri.)*   2 austerely] assuredly *Hudson*² (*Heath*); a surety *Cam*¹ᵃ (*Kellner*)   5–6 case, / Of . . . face?] *F4*; case? / Oh, . . . face. *F*   7+ SP] *(Luc.)*

237

LUCIANA

    Then pleaded I for you.

ADRIANA   And what said he?

LUCIANA

    That love I begged for you, he begged of me.

ADRIANA

    With what persuasion did he tempt thy love?

LUCIANA

    With words that in an honest suit might move.

    First he did praise my beauty, then my speech.   15

ADRIANA

    Didst speak him fair?

LUCIANA   Have patience, I beseech.

ADRIANA

    I cannot, nor I will not, hold me still;

    My tongue, though not my heart, shall have his will.

    He is deformed, crooked, old and sere,

    Ill-faced, worse bodied, shapeless everywhere;   20

    Vicious, ungentle, foolish, blunt, unkind,

    Stigmatical in making, worse in mind.

---

14 hinting that Antipholus' wooing had moved her; cf. 4.4.51 and n.

16 This shared line reverses the order of speakers from 11: there Adriana's half-line betrays her urgency; here Luciana interjects to calm her, effecting a kind of chiasmus.
speak him fair speak kindly or courteously to him (*OED* fair *adv.* 2a); cf. 4.4.153–4.
patience Luciana again preaches *patience* to Adriana; see 1.2.86 and n. Balthazar has used the same phrase towards Ephesian Antipholus; see 3.1.85 and n.

18 perhaps playing on the proverb 'What the heart thinks the tongue speaks' (Dent, H334) (Ard²)
his its, i.e. the tongue's (see Blake, 3.2.3.3)

19–22 Adriana 're-invents' Ephesian Antipholus; perceptions of identity are becoming unstable; see pp. 22–3. Cf. *R3* 1.3.227–32.

19 **deformed** deformèd; cf. 1.2.100, 5.1.299.
sere dry, withered (*OED adj.*[1] 1a), perhaps with sexual connotation (on 'dry' see 3.2.123–4n.); cf. *Mac* 5.3.23; rhyming with *everywhere* (20) (Kökeritz, 479)

20 **shapeless** ugly, unshapely (*OED adj.* 2); cf. *LLL* 5.2.303.

21 **Vicious** 'addicted to vice or immorality' (*OED adj.* 2a)
ungentle discourteous, unmannerly (*OED adj.* 2a)
blunt unfeeling; stupid (*OED adj.* 4b, 1); cf. *3H6* 5.1.86.
unkind lacking in natural feeling

22 **Stigmatical in making** deformed or blemished at conception as a mark of infamy (*OED* stigmatic *adj.* 1–2). Antipholus is *Stigmatical* 'as a token of his vicious disposition' (Johnson). Cf. Greene: those who are 'ill fauored and deformed

LUCIANA

Who would be jealous, then, of such a one?
No evil lost is wailed when it is gone.

ADRIANA

Ah, but I think him better than I say,   25
    And yet would herein others' eyes were worse.
Far from her nest the lapwing cries away;
    My heart prays for him, though my tongue do
        curse.

Enter DROMIO [OF SYRACUSE, *running, with the key*].

DROMIO OF SYRACUSE [*Offers the key.*]

Here, go – the desk, the purse! Sweet now,
    make haste!

LUCIANA

How hast thou lost thy breath?

DROMIO OF SYRACUSE   By running fast.   30

ADRIANA

Where is thy master, Dromio? Is he well?

eyther in face or body: such I holde as a principle to be counted stigmaticall, as noted by nature to be of a bad constitution' (*Orpharion* (*c.* 1589), 12.67). Cf. 'Foul stigmatic' (*2H6* 5.1.215), 'foul misshapen stigmatic' (*3H6* 2.2.136), both phrases applied to Richard, who is also called 'elvish-mark'd' (*R3* 1.3.227). With its sense of being marked or branded, *Stigmatical* implies supernatural agency.

23–4 **one . . . gone** a rhyme (Kökeritz, 468)

25–8 See 1–6n., 3.2.1–52n.

25 On Adriana's hopeful imagination, see 65 and 64–5n.

26 **would** wish (Abbott, 329)
    others' eyes i.e. the eyes of other women

27 proverbial (Dent, L68). The lapwing makes a false cry to distract predators, as would

Adriana. The proverb was current in works by Greene, Lyly and Nashe.

28.1 ***running . . . key*** See 1.2.43n. Stage Dromios typically enter out of breath and staggering from *running fast* (30).

29 **Here** Dromio proffers the key, presumably to Adriana (see 4.1.102–5) although Luciana responds first (30). Adriana will tell Luciana to *Go fetch* the purse (47), as if she were passing her the key (objects move among characters in *CE*); cf. 62 and n.
    Sweet perhaps an adverb: make haste 'sweetly', i.e. agreeably (*OED adv.* 3b), as at *RJ* 2.2.187. If an epithet, *Sweet* implies supplication (see *OED adj.* 8b) (Halliwell). For *Sweet now*, see also *Tem* 4.1.124.

29–30 **haste . . . fast** a rhyme (Kökeritz, 448)

25–8] *alternating indentation as Capell*   28.1 DROMIO OF SYRACUSE] *Theobald; S. Dromio F   running*] *Collier² with the key*] *Bevington⁴*   29+ SP] *(Dro., S.Dro.)*   29 SD] *this edn   Sweet*] swift *(Collier, Notes);* sweat *Cam¹*

DROMIO OF SYRACUSE

No, he's in Tartar limbo, worse than hell:
A devil in an everlasting garment hath him,
One whose hard heart is buttoned up with steel;
A fiend, a fairy, pitiless and rough;   35
A wolf, nay, worse, a fellow all in buff;

32–40 perhaps echoing Greene's characteriza-
tion of a bibulous, greedy and pitiless
sergeant who arrests debtors. Greene's
sergeant wears a '*buffe* leather ierkin', has
'worne his mace smooth, with onely
clapping it on [a man's] *shoulder*' in order
to bring him 'to *Limbo*', 'to the *counter*'.
He is 'eager . . . as a *dog*' and ravenous like
'a butchers *cur*', with 'his *hart* robd of al
remorse & *pity*'. He 'was framd by the
Diuell, of the rotten carion of a *woolfe*, and
his soule of an vsurers damned ghost
turned out of *hell* into his body' (*A Quip
for an Upstart Courtier* (1592), 11.249,
253–4, emphasis added). See Appendix 1,
pp. 321–2. On false arrests and bilkings of
victims, see also Hutton, *The Black Dog of
Newgate* (1596). Dromio imagines the
Officer in terms of Ephesian demonism.
His lines, mostly in couplets, mix
pentameter and hexameter.

32 **Tartar limbo** harsh confinement or prison.
Tartar refers to Tartarus (*OED* Tartar *n.*⁴),
the infernal pit of Greek and Roman
mythology (see *Aen.*, 6.548–627) and the
deepest part of the classical underworld; an
Elizabethan slang term for hell; cf. 'To the
gates of Tartar' (*TN* 2.5.205; see also *H5*
2.2.123). In Elizabethan argot, *limbo*
referred to prison (*OED n.*¹ 2a) and
sometimes to the place where condemned
prisoners were kept before execution
(Judges, 506). Luke Hutton recounts a
dream-vision of being arrested and cast 'in
Lymbo' (Newgate prison) by a black dog
(sig. B3ʳ⁻ᵛ). See LN.

33–4 A line may be missing, since the end-

words *him*/*steel* disrupt the pattern of
rhyming couplets.

33 **devil** For the recurrence of *devil* with *fiend*
(35), see 4.3.51, and 67 and n.
   everlasting a sturdy, protective material,
also called 'durance', characteristically
worn by sergeants and catchpoles (i.e. tax-
gatherers) (*OED n.* 3a); see *suits of
durance*, 4.3.26. The Officer's coat is
presumably made of *buff* leather (36).
Portrayed as a *devil*, the Officer appropriately wears something *everlasting*.

34 **buttoned . . . steel** more realistic imagery:
Fennor refers to 'peuterbuttond, shoulder-
clapping Catch-poles' (sig. B1ᵛ); *steel* may
function as a metonymy for the hardness
(like armour) of the Officer's leather coat
and, by extension, of the Officer himself;
see *heart of steel* (3.2.150); cf. 'As hard as
steel' (Dent, S839). Hutton's Black Dog of
Newgate has a 'hart of hardest Steele' (sig.
B3ᵛ); see 32–40n. Cf. 3.2.150 and n.

35 **A fiend . . . fairy** Fairies in popular
tradition were demonic and dangerous,
despite the mere prankishness attributed to
Robin Goodfellow (see *MND*). In some
accounts, fairies had the power to possess
and even abduct people (Latham, 163; see
Lewis, 122–38). Falstaff fears destruction
from fairies (*MW* 5.5.47–8). See also 55n.

36 **wolf** See 32–40n.
   buff a stout leather typically made of
oxhide (or *calf's skin*, 4.3.18), oiled, with a
fuzzy surface, and dull whitish-yellow in
colour; worn as protection by sergeants and
catchpoles (see *OED n.*² 2b); also at 45.
Soldiers also wore *buff*; see 4.3.28n.

33 him] him fell *Collier*²*; opp.* him . . . *Keightley;* him by the heel *Ard*¹ *(Spedding, per Ard*¹*)*   34 One]
*(*On*)*   35 fairy] fury *Pope*² *(Theobald)*

A backfriend, a shoulder-clapper, one that
   countermands
The passages of alleys, creeks and narrow lands;
A hound that runs counter, and yet draws dry-foot
   well,

37–40 hexameters

37 **backfriend** secret enemy, false friend (*OED n.* 1), here a 'friend' who, like a bailiff, approaches one from behind
shoulder-clapper The Officer 'claps' (seizes or 'strikes': *OED* clap *v.*[1] 6) his victim from behind on the 'shoulder' (*OED* shoulder *n.* C3, only citation) (see 32–40n.). Greene describes a sergeant as wearing down his 'mace' (his staff of office) from shoulder-clapping, i.e. tapping the mace on the victim's shoulder (see *OED* mace *n.*[1] 1, 2); cf. 4.3.27 and n. Shoulder-clapping was a signature action of the bailiff: Fennor refers to 'that long suspected blow vpon their [i.e. debtors'] shoulders' (sig. A3[v]; see also 34n.).
countermands gives command against (*OED v.* 6, first citation); thus, *countermands / The passages* means 'prohibits from using the passageways'. The Officer prevents his quarry from escaping into the labyrinthine byways of the city and, instead, commands him to the 'counter'. 'Counter' (or 'compter') was a term for a debtors' prison (or dungeon); there were several in and around London, including Southwark (*OED n.*[3] 7), Wood Street and the Poultry; see also 39n., on *runs . . . well*.

38 **creeks** narrow or winding passageways penetrating the interiors of places and passing out of sight, as in a labyrinth (*OED n.*[1] 5)
narrow lands a puzzling phrase. Fc's 'lands' is a correction of 'lans'. In the best explanation to date, Steggle argues that 'narrow lands' invokes the image of an

isthmus, a narrow passageway. He further notes that an area known as Alsatia (including Ram Alley) in the Inns of Court district enjoyed legal status as a sanctuary from arrest for debt (see also Sugden, 14, 426), a status also claimed for the area around Gray's Inn. Dromio's allusion, then, may be to the sergeant attempting to prevent debtors from escaping into such sanctuary passageways (the gloss is partially anticipated by Ard[1]).

39 **hound** The association of sergeants and bailiffs with dogs (particularly bloodhounds) was common: e.g. 'a brace of Bandogs . . . came snarling behind me, and fastened on my shoulder' (Fennor, sig. B1[v]); see also 32–40n. Later, the sergeant becomes a horse; see 4.3.25 and n., on *sob*.
runs . . . well Two contradictory meanings seem to be in play. The *hound* (i.e. hunting dog) *runs counter* in that it follows the scent mistakenly, in the direction opposite to that taken by the prey (*OED* counter *adv.* 1), with a quibble on *counter* as the jail towards which the Officer hastens his victim (see 37n., on *countermands*). However (*and yet*), the hound (or Officer) also tracks game (*OED* draw *v.* 74a) well by the mere scent of the foot (*OED* dry-foot *adv.* 2, first citation) (see also *Shakespeare's England*, 2.336). On the primary level, the second image of effectiveness appears to cancel out the first of errancy, unless the hound, by pursuing its quarry in the wrong direction, picks up the right trail. On the secondary level, the Officer both runs victims to the Counter prison and tracks others relentlessly.

38 lands] *Fc;* lans *Fu;* launds *Oxf;* lanes *(Grey)*

One that before the Judgement carries poor souls
    to hell.   40

ADRIANA

Why, man, what is the matter?

DROMIO OF SYRACUSE

I do not know the matter; he is 'rested on the case.

ADRIANA

What, is he arrested? Tell me at whose suit?

DROMIO OF SYRACUSE

I know not at whose suit he is arrested well;

---

40 **One** i.e. the Officer, as at 34. Since *One* incorporates *hound* (39), the line may allude to urban legend, such as of the 'Black Dog of Newgate', a phantom beast that terrified prisoners and harried condemned men to the gallows (see Hutton). Hutton likened the Black Dog to Cerberus, the many-headed dog in Greek mythology that guards the gates of Hades (sig. B3ʳ).
Judgement both legalistic and theological. In Hutton, 'Iudgment' refers to the condemnation of Newgate prisoners to death (sig. C3ᵛ). *Judgement* recalls the medieval morality-play tradition, e.g. in *Everyman*, where Death comes as an arresting officer ('every man I reste', 116) requiring a 'rekeninge' (106). The morality-play devil sometimes *carries* his victim offstage to hell. Richard Willis, a contemporary of Shakespeare, recalls seeing as a boy a morality play in which an officer with a mace acted as a nightmarish figure of divine judgement (see Bishop, 69–70).
hell another cant term for prison, especially debtors' prison (*OED n.* 5); also the theological place of final torment; cf. *Tartar limbo* (32). *OED* (*n.* 4) cites Fuller's *Worthies of England* (1662): 'There is a place partly under, partly by the *Exchequer Court* commonly called *Hell*; . . . formerly this place was appointed a prison for the Kings debtors, who never were freed thence, untill they had paid their uttermost due demanded of them' (2.236).

Fuller also alludes to the proverb 'There is no redemption from Hell' (see Tilley, R60). Dromio plays upon the proverb in his request for Antipholus' *redemption* (46).

41, 42 **matter** Dromio misunderstands Adriana's question, 'what's wrong' (41), for 'what's the legal issue' (42).

42, 45 **'rested** arrested; ''rest' is an apheptic form of 'arrest' (*OED* rest *v.²*); also at 4.4.3. That form morphs into Dromio's pun at 4.3.25.

42 **on the case** on an action in law for damage between individuals (*OED* case *n.¹* P8). Dromio may also pun on *case* as suit of clothes (*OED n.²* 7a) (Malone); the Officer arrests Antipholus by laying hand on his clothing. That conjunction of legal case and apparel may be reiterated by Dromio in the next scene; see 4.3.13–14 and n. As a legal phrase, *on the case* refers to a form of common-law suit between private parties, developed, by analogy with trespass, to facilitate legal actions that lacked any prescribed ways to proceed; such litigations became known in abbreviated form as 'actions on the case' (*Shakespeare's England*, 1.390). Dromio's *on the case* echoes Adriana's *in this case* (5).

43 **What . . . arrested?** Adriana is baffled by Dromio's fantastical, quibble-drenched talk (32–40).

44 **well** modifying *know*; placed for the rhyme with 45, *well/tell*

41] *verse as Munro*   42, 45 'rested] *(rested)*   44–6] *Capell; prose F*

> But is in a suit of buff which 'rested him, that can
> I tell.   45
> Will you send him, mistress, redemption – the
> money in his desk?

ADRIANA
> Go fetch it, sister.   *Exit Luciana [with the key].*
> – This I wonder at,
> That he unknown to me should be in debt.
> Tell me, was he arrested on a band?

DROMIO OF SYRACUSE
> Not on a band, but on a stronger thing: 50
> A chain, a chain – do you not hear it ring?

ADRIANA
> What, the chain?

45–6 Dromio shifts into tumbling verse.

45 **is** he is (see Blake, 6.3.1); the context implies the subject.
buff See 36n., on *buff*; see also 4.3.23 and n.
which who

46 **mistress, redemption** with *redemption* in apposition to *money*, since Dromio is playing upon, and reversing, the proverb 'There is no redemption from Hell' (see 40n., on *hell*). F4 emended to 'Mistress Redemption', as if Dromio were so addressing Adriana, making for a contrast to *Mistress Satan* at 4.3.50.

47 SD *Exit Luciana* In F, this SD occupies a separate line after a full stop at *at* (47). Here the SD is relocated to immediately after Adriana's 'Go, fetch it, sister', leaving Adriana to address her expression of 'wonder' to herself or to Dromio and making her *This* (47) refer to the relative clause begun by *That* (48; an F2 emendation for F's 'Thus').

49 **band** i.e. bond (*OED n.*[1] 10), a written obligation of debt; also a common neck ornament worn by gentlemen; also at 4.3.31, 33. Thus, *band* introduces the

secondary image of a fabric neck-cloth (Steevens) or ruff (Crystal & Crystal, band *n.* 6) and sets up Dromio's asseveration (at 50) that a *chain* is stronger than a mere *band*. Here and subsequently, Dromio's agitation shows itself in quibbles.

50–1 [2]**on . . .** [1]**chain** perhaps punning on 'for a chain' and 'attached by a chain' (e.g. handcuffs)

51 Dromio's repetition of *chain* makes the word chime like a bell or clock, thus confusing Adriana with his question. When Dromio says *chain*, a bell (the priory bell, for example (Cam[2])) might be sounded off-stage. Adriana may mishear *chain* for 'chime' (although Kökeritz records no rhyme of these two words). The clock-like chiming of *chain* ties it to the motif of time, as it had earlier been tied to the motif of debt (as in 4.1) (O'Donnell, 416). Ringing, *ring* and *chain* will be again associated at 4.3.78 (see n.). Although Dromio was not present when the debt for the *chain* was mentioned, the audience assumes his knowledge.

52 Combined, these two speeches constitute a 13-syllable verse line parallel to, and

46 him, mistress, redemption] *Theobald*[2]*;* him Mistris redemption *F;* him Mistris Redemption *F4*   redemption –] *Wells;* redemption, *F*   47 SD] *Cam subst.; opp.* at. *F*   with the key] *this edn*   at,] *Rowe;* at. *F*   48 That] *F2;* Thus *F*   51 chain –] *Dyce*[2] *subst.;* chaine, *F*   51, 54 hear] *(here)*

DROMIO OF SYRACUSE   No, no, the bell; 'tis time that
    I were gone:
    It was two ere I left him, and now the clock strikes
    one.
ADRIANA
    The hours come back! That did I never hear.
DROMIO OF SYRACUSE
    O, yes, if any hour meet a sergeant, 'a turns back
    for very fear.   55
ADRIANA
    As if time were in debt? How fondly dost thou
    reason!

rhyming with, 53. From here to 61, the lines vary in form (tumbling verse, hexameter, pentameter), perhaps underlining their speakers' agitation.

53 **one** Though F reads *one*, Dromio means 'on' (i.e. onward). 'On' and 'one' were Elizabethan near-homonyms, both probably sounded as *un* (Kökeritz, 132; Cercignani, 41; see e.g. *TGV* 2.1.1–2); F spells *One* as 'On' at 34 (see t.n. and *OED* on *prep*.). Thus, Adriana hears *one* confusedly and wonders whether the clock is striking backwards (54), one o'clock, since Dromio had said that it was *two* o'clock when he left Antipholus. For a similar pun, see 'Their arms are set, like clocks, still to strike on' (*1H6* 1.2.42). The large clock in Theodore Komisarjevsky's production (1938) turned itself an hour back at this point, heightening the playworld's fantasticality.

54 **hours** F4 inserted an apostrophe, 'hour's' (i.e. 'hour is'), making Adriana's reference concrete and drawing attention to F's more generalizing statement, which may allude obliquely to the sense of recurrence in farce (see pp. 59–60).

    That primarily, the sound of the clock

striking one; secondarily, the idea of time running in reverse

55 i.e. a sergeant is so terrifying that he could frighten time, or the clock (*hour*), into moving backwards. That would especially be so if the sergeant is a *devil* (33) or *fairy* (35). Additionally, *hour* probably involves a pun on 'ower' (debtor) or 'whore'; see also *hour* at 61. See LN, and cf. 2.2.29 and n., on *hours*.

55, 60 **sergeant** judicial officer charged with the arrest of offenders (*OED n*. 4a; see also 7b); cf. 4.3.31 and n. Cf. 4.1.6n., on *officer*.

55 **'a** he, i.e. the *hour*

56 Although one can be in debt to time or to nature (cf. the proverb 'To pay one's debt to nature', Dent, D168), it is nonsensical, Adriana claims, to imagine time itself being in debt. In 55, Dromio seems to have reversed a principle of nature; he had previously reversed an eschatological one in denying redemption from hell (46). Adriana has momentarily entertained the image of time running in reverse (54). A sense of topsy-turvydom, of inversion of normal laws and principles, is infecting Ephesus.

    fondly foolishly

54 hours] *(*houres*)*; hour's *F4*   55 'a] it *Pope*; he *Capell*   56 debt? . . . reason!] *this edn*; debt: . . . reason? *F*

DROMIO OF SYRACUSE

Time is a very bankrupt, and owes more than he's
    worth to season.
Nay, he's a thief, too: have you not heard men say
That Time comes stealing on by night and day?
If 'a be in debt and theft, and a sergeant in the way,   60
Hath he not reason to turn back an hour in a day?

Enter LUCIANA [*with the purse*].

ADRIANA [*Offers the purse.*]
    Go, Dromio, there's the money. Bear it straight

---

57 The line is puzzling; Slights glosses,
'Time . . . is bankrupt because it is indebted
to season (i.e. the occasions appointed by
people for certain purposes) for more
worth or value than it intrinsically has'
(24); i.e. *season* confers value greater than
that possessed by mere time (cf. 1.2.68 and
n., on *out of season*; 2.2.47 and n.; also
2.2.67n. and the wit-debate about time in
2.2). For Dromio, the significant occasion
is Antipholus' arrest, an event with more
significance or value than that possessed by
undifferentiated time; thus, the value
presumed by *Time* is actually owed to
occasion. But this, like other glosses for the
line, strains to make sense. Dromio's rapid-
fire patter and mental leaps appear
meaningful but are difficult to comprehend.
bankrupt F's spelling, 'bankerout', may
have been pronounced as three syllables
(not discussed by Kökeritz); 'bankerout'
derives from French *banqueroute*.

58–61 **say . . . day . . . way . . . day** a quadruple
rhyme, concluding the scene's intermittent
couplets

58–9 Time is a *thief* because it moves forward
stealthily as well as inexorably (*by night
and day*). Dromio may be alluding to the
proverb 'Time steals' (Dent, T334.1); cf.

'Take Time when time comes lest time
steal away' (Tilley, T313) (Ard²).

60–1 Time will turn itself back (by *an hour*) to
avoid being apprehended by a sergeant for
theft and debt. Dromio offers a superficially
rational proposition fashioned out of pun
and metaphor. No wonder Adriana does not
answer him.

60 **'a** he (i.e. Time)
    in . . . theft in debt and guilty of theft

61 **hour** See 55n.

61.1 ***with the purse** A purse is a common
property on the Renaissance stage (Dessen
& Thomson, 173); Ephesian Antipholus
had asked for a *purse of ducats* (4.1.105)
and will later complain that Adriana has
denied him the *bag of gold* (4.4.97).
Accordingly, the *'Nursery' Prompt-book*
employs a purse (rather than loose *money*,
62) as the suitable property here (Evans,
3.1.20).

62–5 See 1–6n., 3.2.1–52n.

62 **there's the money** Luciana might hand the
purse either to Dromio directly or to
Adriana, who gives it to Dromio. The latter
possibility underscores Adriana's authority
and follows in reverse the movement of the
key (see 29n., on *Here*).

62–5 **straight . . . injury** The scene ends, as it

---

57 bankrupt] (*bankerout*)   60 'a] *Staunton;* I *F;* Time *Rowe;* he *Malone*   61.1 *with the purse*]
Dyce   62–5] *alternating indentation as Capell*   62 SP] *Luc. F3*   SD] *this edn*

And bring thy master home immediately.
                          [*Exit Dromio with the purse.*]
Come, sister, I am pressed down with conceit: 64
Conceit, my comfort and my injury.   [*Exeunt.*]

[**4.3**]   *Enter* ANTIPHOLUS [OF SYRACUSE, *with the chain*].

ANTIPHOLUS OF SYRACUSE
There's not a man I meet but doth salute me
As if I were their well-acquainted friend,
And everyone doth call me by my name.
Some tender money to me; some invite me;
Some other give me thanks for kindnesses;   5
Some offer me commodities to buy.
Even now a tailor called me in his shop,
And showed me silks that he had bought for me,

began, with a quatrain of alternating end-rhymes; on *straight*/*conceit*, see Kökeritz, 198; on *straight*, see 1.1.86n.

64–5 **I . . . injury** Adriana feels burdened (*pressed down*) by the imaginative part of her mind. She takes *comfort* from her ability to imagine hopefully (cf. 25), while she feels *injury* from her suspicions and doubts about Antipholus, established at the scene's opening. By *conceit* she means both fanciful conception, i.e. imagining, and imagination as an attribute or faculty (*OED n.* 7a, b); a common term in Shakespeare; cf. 3.2.34 and n. That Adriana now lives in her *conceit* suggests how much events are being transformed by the characters' imaginations.

4.3 The location is presumably the mart, although, again, exactitude is not essential.

0.1 **with the chain* Antipholus might wear the chain, carry it or otherwise display it, signifying his good fortune. It will become evidence for the Courtesan in deducing

Antipholus' madness (85–8); also at 5.1.8.1 (see n.).

1–11 Antipholus echoes the musings of *Men.*'s traveller Menaechmus, to whom a series of 'strange things' ('*mira*') have been happening 'in strange ways' ('*miris modis*', 1039); see *Men.*, 1039–48. (The Latin *mirus* includes the senses of 'astonishing' and 'wondrous'.)

4–6 **Some** rhetorical *anaphora*; see 2.2.120–4 and n.

4   **tender** offer under formal and legal terms (*OED v.*[1] 1a). The word hints at Ephesian geniality, and behind it the mercantile, contractual Ephesian world that has ensnared his twin.

5   **other** others. Indefinite pronouns could be used as singular or plural (Blake, 3.3.2.7).

7   **Even** perhaps pronounced 'e'en'

8   **silks** eastern luxury commodity, evocative of Elizabethan London. English imports of Mediterranean raw silk increased dramatically during the last third of the 16th

63 SD *Exit Dromio*] *Cam*[1] *subst.   with the purse*] *this edn   *65 SD] *Rowe; Exit. F*   **4.3**] *Capell (SCENE III.) (Theobald subst.)   *0.1 OF SYRACUSE] *Rowe; Siracusian F   with the chain*] *this edn; wearing the chain / Collier*[2]   1+ SP] *F2 subst.; not in F*

And therewithal took measure of my body.
Sure, these are but imaginary wiles,   10
And Lapland sorcerers inhabit here.

Enter DROMIO [*OF* SYRACUSE, *with the purse*].

DROMIO OF SYRACUSE   Master, [*presenting the purse*]
here's the gold you sent me for. – What, have you got
the picture of old Adam new-apparelled?
ANTIPHOLUS OF SYRACUSE
What gold is this? What Adam dost thou mean?   15
DROMIO OF SYRACUSE   Not that Adam that kept the
paradise, but that Adam that keeps the prison: he that

century. London (especially Cheapside)
was becoming notable for its dyeing,
finishing and retailing of silk cloth (Jack,
106–7; Clay, 2.20, 39; Peck, 225).

10   **imaginary wiles** deceitful tricks of the
imagination, illusions

11   **Lapland sorcerers** Lapland was famous
for witches (see *OED n*. b). 'For practise of
witchcraft and sorcery', the Lapps 'passe
all nations in the world' (Fletcher, sig. L5ʳ).

13   **here's the gold** The converse of 1.2.54,
where Antipholus demanded to know the
whereabouts of his gold and the other
Dromio expressed bafflement, as Antipholus does here (15).

13–14   **What . . . new-apparelled** a perplex-
ing line. Dromio is surprised at Antipholus'
freedom from the Officer. He jokes by
applying *old Adam*, a proverbial image of
fallen man, to the officer of the law (Dent,
A29) (Cam²ᵃ). But *new-apparelled* makes
for difficulty. (1) If it alludes to *suit*
(4.2.43–5) in both its sartorial and legal
senses, then Dromio may be asking
whether Antipholus has found a *new*
victim/legal case ('suit') for the Officer, i.e.
got rid of him (Singer) (on 'case', see
4.2.42n.); cf. 26n. (2) Instead of the victim,
new-apparelled may describe the pursuer:

'Do you have with you the Officer, who
appears clothed like Adam after the Fall?',
referring to biblical Adam's *picture* or
image in his post-Edenic clothing, and
perhaps to a real picture (Douce). When
casting Adam out of Eden, God dressed
him in 'garmentes of skinnes' (Genesis,
3.21), recalled to Dromio by the Officer's
coat of *calf's skin* (18) and *buff* (4.2.36 and
n., on *buff*). On old and new Adam in the
New Testament, see 14 LN.

16–33   **Adam . . . that** Dromio's repetitions of
proper noun or pronoun + relative pronoun
– *Adam that* (16, 17), *he that* (17, 19, 22–3,
26, 32), *the man . . . that* (23–4), *he . . .
that* (25), *one that* (33) – give an incantatory rhythm to his speeches and constitute
rhetorical *anaphora*; see also 2.2.121–4
and n.

16–17   **kept the paradise** 'And the Lord God
toke the man, and put hym in the garden of
Eden, that he myght worke it, and kepe it'
(Genesis, 2.15); *paradise* may also be an
allusion to a London inn or even room or
chamber (Wells) (see *OED n*. 4b), although
no such locale has been found.

17–18   **he . . . Prodigal** The Officer's *calf's
skin* coat reminds Dromio of the fatted calf
killed to celebrate the return home of the

11.1 OF SYRACUSE] *Rowe; Sir. F   with the purse*] *Bevington⁴; running Cam¹; with the money Oxf*   12+ SP]
(S.Dro., S. Dro.)   12 SD] *Capell subst.*   15+ SP] *(Ant.)*   15] *verse as Theobald²*

goes in the calf's skin that was killed for the Prodigal;
he that came behind you, sir, like an evil angel, and
bid you forsake your liberty.   20
ANTIPHOLUS OF SYRACUSE   I understand thee not.
DROMIO OF SYRACUSE   No? Why, 'tis a plain case: he
that went like a bass viol in a case of leather; the
man, sir, that when gentlemen are tired gives them a
sob and rests them; he, sir, that takes pity on decayed   25
men and gives them suits of durance; he that sets up

Prodigal Son, who had squandered his
inheritance (Luke, 15.23). Here the
'prodigal', i.e. spendthrift, is being arrested
by an officer wearing a coat associated
with prodigality. The prodigal story was
a recurrent metaphor related to debt (see
e.g. *MV* 1.1.128–30); Fennor mentions
it adorning a wall in a debtors' prison
(sig. B3ʳ). Further associations may be in
play. In *KJ*, 'calve's-skin' is treated as
the clothing of the traditional fool (*KJ*
3.1.129). *Var. KJ* also notes calf's skin's
association with dastardly and cowardice
(3.1.59n.). See 4.2.36 and n., on *buff*.

19 **evil angel** referring to the bad angel
represented in morality drama, who
whispers temptations from behind into the
Mankind-figure's ear (see e.g. *Doctor
Faustus*, 2.1, 2.2, 5.2); cf. 42 and n., on
angels; for other Shakespearean examples,
cf. e.g. *MV* 2.2.1–32, *Son* 144. On guardian
angels, see Matthew, 18.10; Acts, 12.7, 15
(Shaheen, 113).

20 **bid . . . liberty** perhaps an ironic reference
to the disciple Peter's miraculous escape
from prison, in which 'the Angel of the
Lorde' stirs Peter awake, makes 'his
chaynes' fall 'from his handes' and leads
him away (Acts, 12.7; see Shaheen, 113);
cf. 42 and n., on *deliver*. The image of an
evil angel depriving one of *liberty* may also
allude, again ironically, to 2 Corinthians,
3.17: 'where the spirite of the Lorde is
there is libertie' (Ard²). For references to

liberty, see 2.1.7 and n., on *liberty*; on
'liberties', see 1.2.102 and n.

21 Antipholus now falls in with Dromio's
comic prose.

23 **bass . . . leather** The *bass viol* was a
rotund-looking, deep-sounding stringed
musical instrument transportable in a
leather case (see *OED n.*, first citation).
Fennor describes an attendant in debtors'
prison as 'grumbling vp staires' 'like a base
violl' (sig. B3ᵛ, noted by Halliwell).
Dromio moves punningly from *case* (22)
as 'legal proceeding' to *case* as 'outer
clothing'; cf. 4.2.45. Dromio's *case of
leather* echoes his twin's *case me in leather*
(2.1.84).

25 **sob** rest given to a horse after exertion so
that it may recover its wind (*OED n.*¹ 1c). It
leads to the pun on *rests* and *rest* in 25 and
27. Now a horse, the sergeant had
previously been imagined as a hound
(4.2.39).

rests The Officer gives gentlemen a respite
by 'arresting' them; see 33–4 and n.,
4.2.42, 45 and n., on *'rested*.

decayed declined in health, prosperity,
fortune, etc. (*OED adj.* 1)

26 **suits of durance** *suits* repeats the double-
meaning of *case* as legal proceeding and
item of outerwear; see also 13–14n.
Dromio's *durance* works a triple pun: (1) a
'stout durable cloth' (*OED n.* 3); (2)
endurance against fatigue (for *decayed*
men needing a *rest*) (*OED* 4); and (3)

his rest to do more exploits with his mace than a
morris-pike.

ANTIPHOLUS OF SYRACUSE   What, thou mean'st an
officer?   30

DROMIO OF SYRACUSE   Ay, sir, the sergeant of the band:
he that brings any man to answer it that breaks his
band; one that thinks a man always going to bed and
says, 'God give you good rest'.

ANTIPHOLUS OF SYRACUSE   Well, sir, there rest in your   35
foolery. Is there any ships puts forth tonight? May
we be gone?

---

imprisonment (*OED* 5), for which one
would need sturdy clothing. Rann sees a
suit of durance as a 'stone doublet', i.e.
prison. Cf. 'devil in an everlasting garment'
(4.2.33, and see n., on *everlasting*).

26–7 **sets . . . rest** 'sets his resolve' (see *OED*
rest *n.*³ P2f), punning on *rests* at 25; see *RJ*
5.3.110, *MV* 2.2.103. The phrase
anticipates the *morris-pike* image (28):
infantrymen typically fixed their pikes in
the ground as support against attack from
mounted knights (Edelman, 253; see *OED*
*n.*¹ 9a). The phrase also means 'to venture
all' in the game of Primero (*OED n.*³ 5).

27 **mace** staff or club, often with a spiked
metal head, borne as a sign of office or
authority. The sergeant's *exploits* were to
tap the shoulders of his arrestees with his
mace (see *OED n.*¹ 1, 2), as compared to a
soldier's *exploits* with a *morris-pike*.
Fennor calls sergeants 'Mace-mongers'
(sig. A4ʳ). See also 4.2.37n., on *shoulder-
clapper*.

28 **morris-pike** pike, or long lance, sup-
posedly of Moorish origin (*OED*), pre-
eminently an infantry weapon in the 16th
century (see Edelman, 252–5). In the early
1590s, thousands of English soldiers –
among them many 'pike-men' from
London – were fighting for Protestants in

the Low Countries (Knight, *Buffs*, 1.33–
40). Soldiers also wore buff clothing (*OED
n.*² 2b) (Ard²); on *buff*, see 4.2.36 and n.

31 **sergeant . . . band** a 16th-century title for
a high-ranking military officer (*OED*
sergeant *n.* 8; Digges, sigs L3ᵛ–4ʳ (pp.
86–7); Edelman, 308); on *sergeant*, cf.
4.2.55, 60 and n., on *sergeant*. Cf. 4.1.6n.,
on *officer*.

31, 33 **band** punning on *band* as (1) an
instrument for restraining the limbs, a
fetter (*OED n.*¹ 1a); (2) a 'bond' or written
obligation (here for debt) (*OED n.*¹ 10; see
4.2.49 and n., 4.4.126 and n.); and possibly
(3) a neck-band or ruff (*OED n.*² 4), in that
a man who *breaks* or removes *his band*
might be understood as *going to bed* (33)
(Ayscough).

32 **answer it** i.e. before the law

33–4 **one . . . rest** Because the sergeant
wishes his victims good *rest* (arrest and
detention as a form of respite) he must be
'one that thinks a man always going to
bed'; see 25n., on *rests*.

36 **Is . . . puts** In Elizabethan 'is there'
formulations, with the subject 'future
and . . . unsettled', the singular verb can
precede a plural subject (see Abbott, 335;
Hope 2.1.8a); see also 3.2.19–20n.

---

28 morris-pike] *(*Moris Pike*), Theobald;* Moorish pike *Oxf*   31 Ay] *(*I*)*   34 'God . . . rest'] *Cam¹;*
God . . . rest *F*   35–7] *Capell; F lines as verse* foolerie: / gone? / *; Steevens² lines* there / gone? /

DROMIO OF SYRACUSE Why, sir, I brought you word an
hour since that the bark *Expedition* put forth tonight,
and then were you hindered by the sergeant to tarry   40
for the hoy *Delay*. [*Offers the purse.*] Here are the
angels that you sent for to deliver you.

ANTIPHOLUS OF SYRACUSE
The fellow is distract, and so am I,
And here we wander in illusions –
Some blessed power deliver us from hence!   45

---

39 **bark** See 1.1.116n.

39, 41 **Expedition . . . Delay** Dromio treats
his master's changing circumstances
allegorically as named ships. *Expedition* =
haste.

40 **sergeant** See 4.2.55, 60n. Cf. 4.1.6n., on
officer.

41 **hoy** ' "a small vessel, usually rigged as a
sloop, and employed in carrying passengers
and goods, particularly in short distances
on the sea-coast" ' (*OED n.*[1], quoting
Smyth, *Sailor's Word-book*, 1867)

42 **angels** (1) English gold coins, first minted
in 1465, with one side depicting the
archangel Michael piercing the dragon and
the other a ship with a mast (*OED n.* 6),
each worth about half a pound (see Fig. 9,
p. 44). The coin has miraculous and
redemptive associations; a patient touched
for the disease of 'the king's evil' (scrofula)
was presented with an angel coin; (2)
divine ministering spirits ('good angels'),
here for deliverance from prison; as
opposed to *an evil angel* (19).

deliver with meanings both fiduciary and
religious (e.g. 'deliver us from evil'; see
45n.). As at 20, Dromio refers to Peter's
miraculous escape from prison: 'the Lorde
hath sent his Angel, and hath deliuered me'
(Acts, 12.11; see Shaheen, 113). The idea
of delivering angels prepares for the
Courtesan's appearance (45.1).

43 **fellow** The third-person usage implies that

Antipholus speaks in an aside or to the
audience.

distract i.e. distracted: deranged in mind,
mad; perplexed, with thoughts drawn in
different directions (*OED adj.* 3, 4)

44 **wander** recapitulating the idea of error;
cf. 'wander in an unknown field' (3.2.38
and n., on *wander*). On *wander* and its
recurrence, see 1.2.31 and n.

illusions deceptions of the imagination
caused by demonic spirits. This scene
heightens the sense of Ephesus as a
haven of sorcery, where one needs
divine assistance (Cam[2a]); see 10–11. The
word 'illusion' occurs similarly at *MND*
3.2.98, *Mac* 3.5.28 and – closer to 'ghost'
– at *Ham* 1.1.127. Antipholus' *illusions*
may recall Peter's thought, upon his
angel-led escape from prison, that 'he had
seene a vision' (Acts, 12.9; see Shaheen,
114).

45 This invocation is prompted by Dromio's
references to *an evil angel* (19) and to
angels that can *deliver you* (42); it is
answered in the figure of the Courtesan,
who to Antipholus is the *devil* (51) and *a
fiend* (67). The world responds uncannily
to Antipholus' fears. One brother seeks
angels to deliver him from evil, the other
needs monetary angels to deliver him from
arrest.

blessed blessèd

power probably pronounced as one
syllable

41 hoy] *(Hoy),* Pope   *Delay*] Fc; delay *Fu*   SD] *Capell subst.*   43 distract] distracted *Gentleman*

Enter a Courtesan.

COURTESAN

Well met, well met, Master Antipholus.
I see, sir, you have found the goldsmith now:
Is that the chain you promised me today?

ANTIPHOLUS OF SYRACUSE

Satan, avoid! I charge thee, tempt me not!

DROMIO OF SYRACUSE   Master, is this Mistress Satan?   50

ANTIPHOLUS OF SYRACUSE   It is the devil.

DROMIO OF SYRACUSE   Nay, she is worse, she is the
    devil's dam, and here she comes in the habit of a
    light wench, and thereof comes that the wenches say,
    'God damn me' – that's as much to say, 'God make   55

45.1 The *Courtesan*, a figure above a common prostitute, enters from the Porpentine (see 3.1.116 and n.). She may wear distinctive clothing in flame colours or red, since her *habit* is associated with fire (53–9; see 49n.

46 In *Men.*, the prostitute Erotium mistakes the traveller Menaechmus for his brother, her client (see 357–82).

49 **Satan, avoid** *avoid* means 'be gone'; cf. 67 and n., on *Avoid then, fiend*; 69 and n., on *conjure*. Antipholus is increasingly convinced that Ephesian women are dangerous witches (see 3.2.161). His words recall Jesus's 'Auoyde Sathan' (Matthew, 4.10). That phrase from the Bishops' Bible was revised in 1572 to 'Geat thee hence behind me, Satan', while the Geneva Bible retained 'Auoide Satan'. The *BCP* also uses 'Auoyd Satan' in its Gospel reading on the first Sunday after Lent (quoted from Shaheen, 114). The Courtesan's presumably suggestive apparel and her manner inspire fear of sexual temptation, a standard stratagem of Satan. Lust in the Renaissance is sometimes imagined as demonism; cf. Joan de Pucelle as a 'vile fiend and shameless courtezan' (*1H6* 3.2.45).

50 **Mistress Satan** Cf. 4.2.46 and n.

52–3 **Nay . . . dam** On the typesetting of this line in F, see LN.

53 **devil's dam** devil's mother, proverbial, sometimes applied opprobriously to women (see *OED* dam *n.*[2] 2b; Dent, D225); i.e. the fountainhead of devilry. Since Dromio's *devil's dam* responds to Antipholus' *devil* (51), the characters may be enacting the proverb 'Bring you the Devil and I'll bring out his dam' (Tilley, D223).

habit clothing, costume

54 **light wench** wanton or unchaste woman (*OED* light *adj.*[1] 14; see Williams, *Glossary*, 188); Shakespeare frequently uses *light* in the sense of sexually promiscuous; see e.g. *MV* 5.1.130, *2H4* 2.4.295.

comes it comes

55 **damn** Because F's *dam* is both a variant spelling of *damn* and a separate word, it introduces a triple pun: (1) 'God turn me into a wanton woman' (see 53 and n., on *devil's dam*); (2) 'God stop me up' (*OED* dam *v.*[1] 2), with a bawdy implication (*dam* in the sense of 'stop up' occurs also at *2H6* 4.1.73); and (3) 'God condemn me' for sin.

as much as much as

45.1 Courtesan] *(Curtizan)*   46+ SP] *(Cur.)*   50 Mistress] *(Mistris); mistress Pope*   52–3 Nay . . . dam] *Pope; verse F*   55–6 'God damn me' – that's . . . 'God . . . wench'.] *Capell subst.;* God dam me, That's . . . God . . . wench: *F*

me a light wench'. It is written they appear to men
like angels of light; light is an effect of fire, and fire
will burn: *ergo*, light wenches will burn. Come not
near her.

COURTESAN
Your man and you are marvellous merry, sir.   60
Will you go with me? We'll mend our dinner here.

DROMIO OF SYRACUSE   Master, if you do, expect spoon-
meat, or bespeak a long spoon.

ANTIPHOLUS OF SYRACUSE   Why, Dromio?

DROMIO OF SYRACUSE   Marry, he must have a long spoon   65
that must eat with the devil.

---

56 **It is written** formulaic biblical language
(see Shaheen, 114)

57 ¹**light** perhaps referring to the Courtesan's
flame-coloured or red clothing; see 45.1n.;
54n., on *light wench*. Dromio alludes to the
proverb 'The Devil can transform himself
into an angel of light' (Dent, D231) and
to the scriptural passage 'Satan himselfe
is transfourmed into an angel of lyght'
(2 Corinthians, 11.14; see Shaheen, 114).
Devils were legendarily bright (Weyer,
13). A 'wench' damned by God (see *light
wenches*, 58) could become a demon with
the power to effect this illusion.

58 *ergo* therefore; a Latin word used to
conclude the kind of scholastic argument
imitated by Dromio
light . . . burn i.e. *light wenches* – agents
of the fiery devil; also carriers of venereal
disease – will *burn* others and inwardly
themselves, as with gonorrhoea. For other
allusions to venereal disease, see 2.2.85–
6n. Some medical experts, applying
humoural theory, regarded venereal disease
as an effect of lust, produced by too
much heat in the body. The word *burn*
can evoke sexual disease elsewhere, e.g.
TGV 2.5.51–3 (see also Williams, *Glossary*, 59–60). Eschatologically, the destiny
of *light wenches* and their dupes is to *burn*
eternally in hell.

60 **marvellous** probably pronounced as two
syllables: 'marv'lous'
merry See 1.2.21n., on *merry jests*.

61 The Courtesan is the second woman, after
Adriana (2.2.212–13), to invite Antipholus
to *dinner*. Such repetition itself might
encourage Antipholus to consider the city
enchanted and the woman a *fiend* (67).
If *go* takes the line's first stress, then
the preceding two syllables constitute a
'double onset'.
go perhaps with a play on 'copulate' (see
Williams, *Glossary*, 143)
mend improve by additions, supplement
(*OED v.* 11a, b). Since the Courtesan has
already dined with Ephesian Antipholus
(70), she may be proposing additional
delicacies – or recreation.
here probably gesturing towards the
Porpentine

62–3 **spoon-meat** soft or liquid food taken
with a spoon, given to infants or the infirm
(*OED n.*). Dromio may be commenting on
Antipholus' childishness or folly (Oxf¹) or
just setting up a joke.

63 **or** 'in other words'; perhaps prompted by
Antipholus' difficulty in understanding
Dromio (see 64)
bespeak arrange for, order (*OED v.* 5a)

65–6 proverbial (Dent, S771); a *long spoon*
because to come too near the devil is

---

61 me? . . . here.] *Steevens;* me, . . . here? *F*

ANTIPHOLUS OF SYRACUSE [*to Courtesan*]
Avoid then, fiend! What tell'st thou me of supping?
Thou art, as you are all, a sorceress;
I conjure thee to leave me and be gone.

COURTESAN
Give me the ring of mine you had at dinner,   70
Or for my diamond the chain you promised,
And I'll be gone, sir, and not trouble you.

DROMIO OF SYRACUSE   Some devils ask but the parings
of one's nail, a rush, a hair, a drop of blood, a pin,
a nut, a cherry-stone; but she, more covetous, would   75

---

dangerous (e.g. burning); hence, the devil's dinner companion must only *expect spoon-meat* (62–3).

67 **Avoid then, fiend** See 49n. For F's *then* some editors have adopted F4's emendation, 'thou'; notwithstanding, *then* implies that Antipholus' resistance has been strengthened by Dromio's warning. Antipholus' *fiend* and *devil* (51) occur in conjunction at 4.2.33, 35.
   What why

68 **you** presumably the women of Ephesus

69 **conjure** This formal charge is the culmination of Antipholus' *Satan, avoid* (49) and *Avoid then, fiend* (67), and is often performed with a ritualistic gesture. The word marks the first of two conjurations or exorcisms, this one aimed at an external *fiend*, the second (by Doctor Pinch), aimed at the internal demon presumably possessing Ephesian Antipholus (4.4.55–8). Cf. 1.2.51n.
   leave . . . gone rhetorical *commoratio*; see 3.2.26n. Cf. 3.2.158 and n.

70 **ring** See 4.1.13.1n. Adriana had invoked her own ring as an endangered symbol of marriage at 2.2.144 (see n.).

72 **gone . . . you** more *commoratio*, as at 69

73–7 Some editors turn this prose speech in F

into verse, but awkwardly so and with some loss of its emotional urgency. Shakespeare's prose often contains word groups that scan as iambic pentameter (Wright, *Metrical*, 110–13).

73–6 **parings . . . chain** The devil facilitates his spells with the possession of some small item from his victim. Dromio's list (rhetorically a *congeries*) suggests the totemic power attributed to objects (see Bruster, 63–9). The working of magic effects through objects associated with a person is a form of sympathetic magic; see 5.1.397 and n.

73–4 **parings . . . nail** Cf. *1H6* 3.1.102.

74 **rush** leaf of green rush, with which floors were often strewn (see *OED n.*[1] 1)
   drop of blood Devils like blood. Faustus spills his blood to sign his contract with Mephistopheles (Marlowe, *Doctor Faustus*, 2.1). A 1590 witchcraft trial reports a devil asking for a sample of his intended victim's blood (see Rosen, 187).

75 **cherry-stone** pit of a cherry; typifying a thing of trifling value (*OED n.* 1). Sir Toby warns that a serious man should not 'play at cherry-pit with Sathan' (*TN* 3.4.116), referring to 'a child's game of throwing cherry-stones into a hole' (Lothian & Craik).

---

67 SD] *Wells*   then] thou *F4*   73–7] *Capell lines* nail, / pin, / covetous, / chain: – / it her, / it. /

> have a chain. Master, be wise: an if you give it her,
> the devil will shake her chain and fright us with it.

COURTESAN

> I pray you, sir, my ring, or else the chain;
> I hope you do not mean to cheat me so.

ANTIPHOLUS OF SYRACUSE

> Avaunt, thou witch! – Come, Dromio, let us go.　　　　80

DROMIO OF SYRACUSE

> 'Fly pride', says the peacock; mistress, that you
>　　know.

[Exeunt Antipholus and Dromio of Syracuse.]

COURTESAN

> Now, out of doubt, Antipholus is mad,
> Else would he never so demean himself.
> A ring he hath of mine worth forty ducats,
> And for the same he promised me a chain;　　　　85
> Both one and other he denies me now.
> The reason that I gather he is mad,

76　**an if** 'if', intensified
77　**devil . . . it** a traditional image. In Matthew, 8.29, a demoniac's breaking of his chains prompts Christ's exorcism. In Revelation, 20.1–3, an angel with 'a great chaine' binds the devil in a 'bottomlesse pit' for 'a thousande yeres' (see Shaheen, 115).
78　**ring . . . chain** repeating the aural play on *ring* and *chain* at 4.2.51 (O'Donnell, 417); the sounds there have become objects here; on the ring, see 4.1.13.1n.
79–81　**so . . . go . . . know** Antipholus and Dromio will exit on a triple rhyme.
80　**Avaunt** 'Be off!'; a formulaic command, 'to give the avaunt', exercised against a witch (see *OED* avaunt *n.*[2]; *v.*[2] 3). The Catholic Rheims Bible uses 'Auant Satan' instead of 'Auoyde Sathan' in Matthew, 4.10 (see Shaheen, 115).
81　alluding to the proverb 'As proud as a peacock'; the peacock's gaudy plumage emblematized pride (Dent, P157). Dromio

comments on the irony of a prideful wanton accusing another person of impropriety, i.e. cheating (79); *pride* may also signify sexual desire; see *Luc* 437–8, *Son* 144.8; *OED n.*[1] 11; Williams, *Glossary*, 246. Cf. 4.4.43 and n.
83　**demean** probably meaning 'conduct' (*OED v.*[1] 1a), although *demean* as 'lowering one's character' was an emerging meaning, first recorded in 1601 (*OED v.*[2] 1); cf. 5.1.88 and n.
84, 96　**ring** See 4.1.13.1–2n.
84, 97　**ducats** see 4.1.30n. The Courtesan says that her ring is worth 40 ducats; the Officer will tell Adriana that for the chain her husband owes 200 ducats (4.4.135).
85　**for the same** i.e. for the ring. Ephesian Antipholus had declared his intention to 'bestow' the chain upon the Courtesan (see 3.1.117–19 and n.; see also 4.1.23 and n.). The trade appears much to the Courtesan's advantage.

76 an] *(and)*　81] *Theobald; prose F*　81 'Fly pride'] *Dyce subst.;* Flie pride *F*　81 SD] *F2 subst.; Exit. F*

Besides this present instance of his rage,
Is a mad tale he told today at dinner
Of his own doors being shut against his entrance.   90
Belike his wife, acquainted with his fits,
On purpose shut the doors against his way.
My way is now to hie home to his house
And tell his wife that, being lunatic,
He rushed into my house and took perforce   95
My ring away. This course I fittest choose,
For forty ducats is too much to lose.   [*Exit.*]

[4.4] *Enter* ANTIPHOLUS [OF EPHESUS, *wearing the ring,*]
          with a jailer[, *the* Officer].

ANTIPHOLUS OF EPHESUS
Fear me not, man, I will not break away;
I'll give thee, ere I leave thee, so much money
To warrant thee as I am 'rested for.
My wife is in a wayward mood today

88 **rage** madness, insanity; a fit of mania (*OED n.* 1), echoed in *fits* (91); cf. 4.4.138; 5.1.48, 75, 144.

90 **being** perhaps pronounced as one syllable (Kökeritz, 384)

91 **Belike** probably

93 **way** most advisable course of action (*OED n.*[1] 12b)
     hie See 1.2.90n., on *hie*.

95–6 **He . . . away** The Courtesan intends to deceive Adriana (see 4.4.138–9 and n.), lending some justice to Adriana's suspicion of her (4.4.142).

95 **perforce** by force (*OED adv.* A1)

96 **away** completing the Courtesan's rhetorical play on *way* in 92 and 93
     fittest The Courtesan contrasts her prudent (*fittest*) choice with Antipholus' madness (*fits*) (91).

96–7 **choose . . . lose** The scene ends on a couplet.

4.4 The location remains presumably the mart.

0.1 ***wearing the ring** See 4.1.13.1 and n.

0.2 ***a . . . Officer** The *jailer* here is the arresting Officer from 4.3, as F's SPs make clear; *jailer* signals a shifting conception of the Officer's function.

3 **warrant thee as** 'guarantee to you the amount that' (see *OED v.* 8). The money will stand surety for the alleged debt, so that Antipholus can be released without the Officer assuming liability. Cf. *warrant* at 10; see 1.1.139 and n., on *warrant*.
     'rested See 4.2.42, 45n.

4 **wayward** unreasonable; perverse (*OED adj.* 1); see *TGV* 1.2.57, *LLL* 3.1.179.

97 SD] *F2* **4.4**] *Capell (SCENE* IV.*) (Theobald subst.)* 0.1 OF EPHESUS] *Rowe; Ephes. F   wearing the ring*] *this edn* 0.2 *the* Officer] *Folg*[2] *(Capell subst.)* 1+ SP] *(An., Anti., Ant.)* 3 'rested] *(rested),
Theobald*[2]

And will not lightly trust the messenger;   5
That I should be attached in Ephesus,
I tell you 'twill sound harshly in her ears. –

Enter DROMIO [OF EPHESUS] *with a rope's end.*

Here comes my man; I think he brings the money.
[*to Dromio*] How now, sir? Have you that I sent
    you for?
DROMIO OF EPHESUS [*Offers the rope.*]
Here's that, I warrant you, will pay them all.   10
ANTIPHOLUS OF EPHESUS
But where's the money?
DROMIO OF EPHESUS
Why, sir, I gave the money for the rope.
ANTIPHOLUS OF EPHESUS
Five hundred ducats, villain, for a rope?
DROMIO OF EPHESUS
I'll serve you, sir, five hundred at the rate.
ANTIPHOLUS OF EPHESUS
To what end did I bid thee hie thee home?   15

5–7 Modern editors sometimes eliminate F's comma after *messenger*, making *That . . . Ephesus* into the message to his wife. Yet, as Oxf[1] perceives, F's punctuation 'leave[s] the sense ambiguous'. Antipholus' reflection (6), with its subjunctive *should*, seems half spoken to himself, as if the possibility rings as harshly in his own ears as the fact will sound in Adriana's.
5 **lightly trust** easily believe (*OED* lightly *adv.* 2)
6 **attached** arrested
7.1 *rope's end* i.e. piece of rope long enough to serve as a lash; cf. 4.1.16 and n., on *rope's end.*
9, 10 **that** that which (the relative pronoun is omitted; see Blake, 3.3.2.6f)

10 **warrant** echoing Antipholus (3)
   pay discharge a debt; flog, punish by beating (*OED v.*[1] 12c). Dromio means the latter; Antipholus understands the former.
11 In F, the form, either prose or verse, is unclear. As short verse (here), the line invites a verbal pause at the end for theatrical action or reaction. As prose, it breaks the tone of Antipholus' previous verse speeches.
13 **ducats** See 4.1.30n.
14 **serve** provide, supply (*OED v.*[1] 38)
   five hundred of ropes; on the recurrence of *five*, see 1.1.100n., on *five.*
   rate price (*OED n.*[1] 3)

5 messenger;] *F4; Messenger, F; messenger Ard²*   7 SD OF EPHESUS] *Rowe; Eph. F*   9 SD] *Capell subst.*   10+ SP] *(E.Dro., E. Dro., Dro.)*   10 SD] *Bevington⁴ subst.*   11] *verse as Wells*

DROMIO OF EPHESUS

To a rope's end, sir, and to that end am I returned.

ANTIPHOLUS OF EPHESUS

And 'to that end', sir, I will welcome you.

[*Beats Dromio with the rope's end.*]

OFFICER   Good sir, be patient.

DROMIO OF EPHESUS   Nay, 'tis for me to be patient:

I am in adversity!   20

OFFICER   Good now, hold thy tongue.

DROMIO OF EPHESUS   Nay, rather persuade him to hold

his hands.

ANTIPHOLUS OF EPHESUS   Thou whoreson, senseless

villain! [*Beats him.*]   25

DROMIO OF EPHESUS   I would I were senseless, sir, that

I might not feel your blows.

ANTIPHOLUS OF EPHESUS   Thou art sensible in nothing

but blows, and so is an ass.

---

16 The line scans as hexameter with a first-foot 'double onset'.

rope's end See 4.1.16 and n., on *rope's end*.

returned perhaps cueing Antipholus to take the rope, since he is about to *welcome* (17) Dromio by 'turning' the rope against him

18 **be patient** the same advice that Luciana gave to Antipholus' wife at 2.1.9 (see n.), with a similar reception; cf. 5.1.174 and n., on *patience.* Turning towards farce, the scene now moves into prose.

19–20 **patient . . . adversity** alluding to Psalms, 94.13: 'That thou mayest geue hym patience in tyme of aduersitie' (see Shaheen, 115); also proverbial (Dent, A42.1)

21 **Good now** an interjection or entreaty (*OED*); cf. *WT* 5.1.19.

22–3 sometimes set as verse, but tonally similar to Dromio's prose at 19–20

24, 26 **senseless** Antipholus means 'without rational sense'; Dromio means 'without physical sense or feeling', his pun giving him the verbal upper hand even as Antipholus may be beating him. Cf. 2.2.35–9, and *AW* 2.1.124, *TS* 1.2.36.

25 SD more beating, as Dromio's response (26–7) suggests

28–9 Antipholus takes back the meaning of 'sense': Dromio, like an *ass*, can only be brought to reason by being forced to feel pain (see *OED sensible adj.* A11, 14). The remark perpetuates the play's animal imagery, especially the Dromios' association with asses (see 2.2.205 and n.). Cf. Sidney's *Old Arcadia*, describing Dameta as 'not so sensible in anything as in blows' (234).

16] *Reed; prose F*   17 'to that end'] *this edn;* to that end *F*   17 SD *Beats Dromio*] *Pope subst.*   with the rope's end] *this edn*   19–20] *verse Rann*   21] *verse Steevens*   25 SD] *Collier⁴*

DROMIO OF EPHESUS   I am an ass, indeed: you may   30
    prove it by my long ears. – I have served him from
    the hour of my nativity to this instant and have
    nothing at his hands for my service but blows. When
    I am cold, he heats me with beating; when I am
    warm, he cools me with beating. I am waked with it   35
    when I sleep, raised with it when I sit, driven out of
    doors with it when I go from home, welcomed home
    with it when I return. Nay, I bear it on my shoulders
    as a beggar wont her brat, and I think when he hath
    lamed me, I shall beg with it from door to door.   40

30–40 A set-piece showcasing wit, energy and
rhetorical skill, Dromio's speech deploys
nouns and verbs in paralleling and contrasting relationships (such as *hour/instant*),
culminating in the virtuoso series *waked/
raised/driven/welcomed* (35–7) and
reprised in *door to door* (40). The repetitions of *beating* (34, 35) and *with it* (35–8)
at the ends of clauses exemplify rhetorical
antistrophe. (For other examples of rhetorical repetition-with-variation, see 1.1.57n.)
Actors often mime the child on the beggar's
back, whose weight lames Dromio. Since
beatings identify the stages of Dromio's
day and his life, they also provide a
variation on the theme of time. Audiences
can find Dromio's sense of injustice
sympathetic and disturbing (see Turner,
181). See also 1.2.85–6 and n. Antipholus
makes no verbal response, just as he had
similarly failed to do at 3.1.15–18 (see n.).
30 **I . . . ass** also spoken by Syracusan Dromio
at 2.2.207, 3.2.75
30–1 **ass . . . ears** proverbial (see Dent, A355);
ears probably puns on 'years' (i.e. ''ears')
(Cam); thus, Dromio is an *ass* for having
served Antipholus so long. Or perhaps his
ears are long from their being pulled by his
master (Cam).
31 **ears. – I** Dromio redirects his address from
Antipholus to the audience (or the Officer),

as indicated by his shift from *you* (30) to
him (31); cf. 78 and n., on *did; –*.
32 **hour . . . nativity** recalled at 5.1.404 in
'calendars of their nativity'; see 5.1.404,
406n.
39 **wont** 'is accustomed to do with'
40 **beg with it** Beating was a frequent punishment for begging (Ard[2], citing *Shakespeare's England*, 2.489–91); *with* = 'as a
result of' (*OED prep.* 39a); cf. *TGV* 1.1.69.
40.2 *schoolmaster* Pinch's profession remains
ambiguous, partly from his function in the
play and partly from the stereotype he
embodies. (1) Although in the dialogue he
is never called a '*schoolmaster*', the
probability of that profession is urged by
Adriana's reference to him as *Master
Doctor* (123). It takes a learned man to
know the proper language of exorcism and
conjuration (as at *Ham* 1.1.42); a scholar
was expected to be able to 'cast out diuels'
(Vaughan, sig. Y8ᵛ). Pinch is called a
conjuror at 5.1.177, 243. (2) Alternatively,
Pinch may be a physician, since he behaves
as one: he arrives to cure a madman, takes
Antipholus' pulse (53) and refers to
humoural medical theory (82). A '*Medicus*'
functions similarly in *Men.* (889–956), and
medical quacks appear in early English
drama (e.g. the medieval Croxton *Play of
the Sacrament*) and Italian *commedia*

31 ears] 'ears *Hudson[2] (Cam)*

Enter ADRIANA, LUCIANA, Courtesan *and*
a schoolmaster called PINCH.

ANTIPHOLUS OF EPHESUS
Come, go along; my wife is coming yonder.
DROMIO OF EPHESUS   Mistress, *respice finem*, 'respect
your end'; or rather, to prophesy like the parrot,
'beware the rope's end'.

dell'arte. (3) In the more distant background hover other related types: the Elizabethan village 'cunning men' who dispensed magical remedies for bewitchment (see Thomas, *Religion*, e.g. 178, 185, 233); the sorcerers of biblical Ephesus (Acts, 19.13–19); and Catholic exorcists parodied by Protestants for superstition (see e.g. Nashe, *Terrors of the Night* (1594), 1.363–7). On Pinch's name, see List of Roles, 18n.

41 **Come, go** 'Come on, let's go'. The imperative *Come* functions as an invitation or encouragement (*OED v.* 34a); also at 5.1.114.

42 *respice finem* 'look to the end,' or *respect your end* (42–3). Dromio instructs Adriana to look at the *rope's end* in Antipholus' hand, implying that a beating will be her *end* or destiny; also 'look to your posterior'. Additionally, Dromio is setting up a popular quibble, *respice funem*, 'beware the rope'; see 44 and n. A familiar medieval Latin maxim (see Baldwin, '*Finem*'), the saying was also proverbial in English (Dent, E125) and arises frequently in morality plays and other writings.

43 *to . . . parrot Dromio prophesies by speaking omnisciently (*OED* prophesy *v.* 1a) rather than predictively (*OED* 1b). To 'speak like a parrot' was proverbial for talking nonsense (Wilson, 760; see Dent, P60). Early editors maintained that Elizabethan parrots were sometimes jokingly taught to say 'the rope' to strangers –

indicating hanging as their fate (Theobald, citing Warburton). Samuel Butler's *Hudibras* (1663), 1.1.54–62, refers to the practice. Dromio prophesies like the parrot; similarly, his twin brother has enjoined the Courtesan by quoting the peacock (see 4.3.81 and n.). Singer emended F's 'the prophesie' to *to prophesy*, as here, and editors have typically followed. The parrot image may allude to Nashe's *An Almond for a Parrot* (1590), a pamphlet (in the Martin Marprelate religious controversy) dedicated to the comic actor Will Kemp, who probably performed in *CE* as one of the Dromios (see p. 103; Appendix 3, p. 353). In *Almond*, Nashe exposed, attacked and called for the death of John Penry as the pseudonymous Puritan Marprelate; Penry was tried and hanged in May 1593. Dromio, *like the parrot*, warns Adriana of hanging or beating.

44 '**beware . . . end**' alluding to the Latin *respice funem* ('look to the rope' – that is, 'watch out that you are not hanged', or, here, 'flogged') and playing on Dromio's initial maxim, *respice finem* (42; see n.). As at 4.1.16 (see n., on *rope's end*), *rope* probably constitutes a phallic allusion. The proverbial phrase 'A rope for Parrot' can suggest a pun on both hanging and sexual congress (Dent, R172.1). Shakespeare may also be alluding to Nashe's *Strange News* (1592), which satirizes the academic Gabriel Harvey (cf. Appendix 1, p. 320) being 'bidde *Respice funem*,

40.1–2] *opp. 41 Collier*   40.2 PINCH] Pinch, *and Assistants* / *Capell*   41] *verse as Johnson*   42–3 'respect your end'] *Wells*; respect your end *F*   43 to prophesy] *Singer²*; the prophesie *F*; prophesie *Rowe*; I'll prophesy *(Rann)*   44 'beware . . . end'] *Capell subst.*; beware . . . end *F*

ANTIPHOLUS OF EPHESUS   Wilt thou still talk?   45
     Beats Dromio.
COURTESAN [*to Adriana*]
     How say you now? Is not your husband mad?
ADRIANA
     His incivility confirms no less.
     – Good Doctor Pinch, you are a conjuror:
     Establish him in his true sense again,
     And I will please you what you will demand.   50
LUCIANA
     Alas, how fiery and how sharp he looks!
COURTESAN
     Mark how he trembles in his ecstasy.
PINCH
     Give me your hand, and let me feel your pulse.
ANTIPHOLUS OF EPHESUS
     There is my hand, and let it feel your ear.
     [*Offers to strike Pinch.*]

looke backe to his Fathers house' (1.268). Harvey's father was a rope-maker; thus, says Nashe, 'Thou dost liue by the gallows' (1.270) (see Tobin, 'Touch', 48–51; 'Pinch', 23); cf. 62n., on *saffron*; 86–7n.

45 **still** See 2.1.11n., on *still*.
47 **incivility** rudeness (*OED n.* 2). In the Elizabethan world, *incivility*, a breach of decorum, can be seen as madness; a comparable inference occurs regarding Malvolio, *TN* 3.4.8–9.
48 **Doctor** See 40.2n.
49 **sense** Adriana unconsciously picks up the word that had been the root of prior punning between Dromio and Antipholus (24–9). Here *sense* means normal mental faculties (*OED n.* 10a); exorcizing the demon will restore sanity.
50 **please** requite, pay (*OED v.* 5b)
     what whatever
51 Luciana's scrutiny here, and at 109, 130,

betrays emotional sympathy, as if her wooing by 'Antipholus' in 3.2 had made a favourable impression (see also 4.2.14 and n.); see 131n. If Luciana is falling in love with Syracusan Antipholus, she will do so, in part, for the sufferings of his brother.

fiery fiercely irritable (*OED adj.* 3d); also suggesting red with anger. Sosicles Menaechmus' complexion turns green and his pale eyes burn under like circumstances (see *Men.*, 828–30).

sharp angry (*OED adj.* 5b); cf. *2H6* 3.1.156.
52 **trembles** a sign of demonic possession; see 56, 93, 108.
     ecstasy frenzy, with the sense of being 'beside oneself' or entranced (*OED n.* 1, 2); cf. 'restless ecstasy', *Mac* 3.2.22.
54 SD **offers** Farce virtually demands that the attempted blow connects, but Pinch makes no reference to being struck.

46 SD] *Oxf*   54 SD] *Capell subst.*

PINCH

I charge thee, Satan, housed within this man,   55
To yield possession to my holy prayers,
And to thy state of darkness hie thee straight;
I conjure thee by all the saints in heaven.

ANTIPHOLUS OF EPHESUS

Peace, doting wizard, peace; I am not mad.

ADRIANA

O, that thou wert not, poor distressed soul.   60

ANTIPHOLUS OF EPHESUS

You minion, you, are these your customers?
Did this companion with the saffron face
Revel and feast it at my house today,

55–8 the second of the play's two conjuration or exorcism passages; see 4.3.67–9, 80, and 4.3.69n., on *conjure*. The speech may recall the Ephesian Jews' ineffectual attempt at exorcism in Acts, 19.13, although Shaheen finds it closer to other biblical exorcisms, e.g. Mark, 9.25 (116). The episode may satirize Catholic or even Puritan exorcism (see Landau, 194). Pinch's supernatural approach will contrast to the Abbess's more medical one; cf. 5.1.102–7 and n. Also, cf. 1.2.51 and n.

56 **possession** i.e. inhabitation; see 2.2.146n.

57 **hie** See 1.2.90n., on *hie*.
   straight See 1.1.86n.

58 **by . . . heaven** One might conjure by invoking sacred beings for their miraculous power (see *OED v.*[1] 5a); Pinch's invocation would be accompanied by appropriate gestures. Antipholus finds the ritual absurd (61).

59 **doting** foolish (*OED adj.* 1)
   wizard man skilled in occult arts (*OED n.* 2a)

60 **distressed** distressèd

61–107 In *Amph.*, Amphitryon and his wife, Alcumena, argue similarly (660–860). The husband and his slave wonder whether Alcumena is deceitful, mad, enchanted or in a Bacchic frenzy (703); Amphitryon even speculates whether he himself is 'bewitched' (844).

61 **minion** See 2.1.86n.
   customers as if Adriana were a prostitute, although it was Antipholus who visited the Courtesan (Ard[2]). Elsewhere *customer* means not the client but the prostitute; see *Oth* 4.1.119, *AW* 5.3.286.

62 **companion** i.e. Doctor Pinch; used contemptuously, as at *MW* 3.1.120, *1H4* 3.2.68
   saffron orange-yellow (see *OED adj.*, and *n.* 3), probably a sign of age (cf. 'yellow' at *2H4* 1.2.181) or of sickliness, as from an excess of yellow bile causing jaundice (see Walkington, sigs H4[r], H7[r] (pp. 52b, 55b)). Actors also used saffron as a cosmetic dye (see Drew-Bear, 21, 101–2). Originating from Greece or Asia Minor, saffron was cultivated extensively (though not exclusively) in Saffron Walden and valued as a spice, a cooking and baking dye (*AW* 4.5.2–4, *WT* 4.3.45–6) and an all-purpose medicine (Page & Round, 2.359–66). The word may allude to Gabriel Harvey, who was from Saffron Walden (see 44n.). Tobin sees Pinch as a satirical representation of Harvey ('Pinch', 25).

63 **it** colloquial direct object with no reference to anything previously mentioned (Abbott, 226)

Whilst upon me the guilty doors were shut,
And I denied to enter in my house? 65

ADRIANA

O husband, God doth know you dined at home,
Where would you had remained until this time,
Free from these slanders and this open shame.

ANTIPHOLUS OF EPHESUS

'Dined at home'? [*to Dromio*] Thou, villain, what
sayst thou?

DROMIO OF EPHESUS

Sir, sooth to say, you did not dine at home. 70

ANTIPHOLUS OF EPHESUS

Were not my doors locked up, and I shut out?

DROMIO OF EPHESUS

Perdie, your doors were locked, and you shut out.

ANTIPHOLUS OF EPHESUS

And did not she herself revile me there?

DROMIO OF EPHESUS

Sans fable, she herself reviled you there.

ANTIPHOLUS OF EPHESUS

Did not her kitchen-maid rail, taunt and scorn me? 75

DROMIO OF EPHESUS

Certes she did; the kitchen vestal scorned you.

---

64 **guilty doors** with *guilty* as a transferred epithet (rhetorical *hypallage*); *doors* may function sexually as it did in 3.1; see 3.1.30n., on *door is locked*.

68 **these . . . shame** Adriana views her husband's slanders of her as a shame to him. On *shame*, see 2.1.112 and n.; *shame* occurs again at 81, *shameful* at 106.

69–80 rhetorical stichomythia (except in 78–9); see 2.1.10–41n. Dromio's witty initial asseverations and his reiterations provide a sense of rhythmic and verbal repetition that mark off the passage. The

exchange recalls academic debate or legal inquiry.

72 *Perdie* 'By God', a variant of the Anglicized French *pardie*, from *par dieu*. This oath and Dromio's subsequent ones seem intended 'to mock as well humour Antipholus' (Wells).

74 *Sans fable* without doubt (French *fable*)

75 **kitchen-maid** demonstrating that Luce the taunting servant in 3.1 and Nell the *kitchen wench* (3.2.94–5) are the same character; see also 3.2.110 and n.

76 *Certes* certainly

69] *verse as Theobald* 'Dined at home'] *Folg²;* Din'd at home *F* SD] *Capell subst.* sayst] *Rowe;* sayest *F*

ANTIPHOLUS OF EPHESUS
And did not I in rage depart from thence?

DROMIO OF EPHESUS
In verity, you did; – my bones bears witness,
That since have felt the vigour of his rage.

ADRIANA [*to Pinch*]
Is't good to soothe him in these contraries?   80

PINCH
It is no shame: the fellow finds his vein
And, yielding to him, humours well his frenzy.

ANTIPHOLUS OF EPHESUS [*to Adriana*]
Thou hast suborned the goldsmith to arrest me.

ADRIANA
Alas, I sent you money to redeem you,
By Dromio here, who came in haste for it.   85

DROMIO OF EPHESUS
Money by me? – Heart and good will you might,

---

vestal ironic reference to Luce's virginity and kitchen employment, since *vestal* derives from the virgins who tended the sacred fire of Vesta, the Roman goddess of hearth, home and family

78 **did; –** my] Dromio's shift in pronouns from *you* (78) to *his* (79) indicates a shift in address from Antipholus to other characters or to the audience, as with his earlier monologue about beatings (30–40); his lines here recall that speech (see 31n., on *ears. – I*). Dromio has been parroting Antipholus' charges (72–9), with a slyly different tone.
bones bears See 3.2.19–20n.

80 **soothe** humour (*OED v.* 4). F's 'sooth' means *soothe*, since 'sooth' (*n.* truth) did not occur as a verb.
contraries 'inaccurate claims' (Oxf¹)

81–2 Pinch's belief that Dromio is merely humouring Antipholus will change into his belief, at 93, that the servant is as possessed as the master.

81 **It . . . shame** i.e. it is no disgrace inflicted on Antipholus; on *shame*, see 2.1.112n.
fellow . . . his i.e. Dromio . . . Antipholus'
vein mood or frame of mind, like the *merry vein* of raillery at 2.2.20 (see n.). The word may recall Pinch's attempt to feel Antipholus' pulse at 53.

82 **humours** On 'humour', see 1.2.21n.

83 **suborned** i.e. induced to commit a misdeed by bribery or other corrupt means (*OED v.* 1a)

84 **redeem** See 1.1.8n, on *redeem*.

86–7 **Heart . . . money** 'You might have received sympathy and good will from me but not a bit of money.' Two proverbs converge (Oxf¹): 'With heart and good will' (Dent, H338.1; cf. *MND* 3.2.164) and 'Not a rag of money' (Dent, R6.1); *rag* is a cant term for 'farthing', i.e. a minuscule amount of money (*OED* rag *n.²* 6c). These conjoined proverbs echo Nashe's satirizing of Harvey's brother in *Strange News* for

---

78 did; – my] *Capell*; did, my *F*   79 his] your *Rowe³*   80 SD] *Oxf subst.*   soothe] *(sooth); smooth F2*   81 It] *aside to Adriana* It *Oxf*   shame] harm *(McKerrow, per Oxf)*   83 SD] *Oxf*

But surely, master, not a rag of money.

ANTIPHOLUS OF EPHESUS

Went'st not thou to her for a purse of ducats?

ADRIANA

He came to me, and I delivered it.

LUCIANA

And I am witness with her that she did.   90

DROMIO OF EPHESUS

God and the rope-maker bear me witness

That I was sent for nothing but a rope.

PINCH

Mistress, both man and master is possessed:

I know it by their pale and deadly looks.

They must be bound and laid in some dark room.   95

ANTIPHOLUS OF EPHESUS

[*to Adriana*] Say wherefore didst thou lock me forth
     today?

[*to Dromio*] And why dost thou deny the bag of
     gold?

ADRIANA

I did not, gentle husband, lock thee forth.

DROMIO OF EPHESUS

And, gentle master, I received no gold,

But I confess, sir, that we were locked out.   100

---

dying without leaving anything to his siblings: 'heart and good will, but neuer a ragge of money' (1.301); cf. 44n.; 62n., on *saffron*.

93 **is** See 3.2.19–20n.
   possessed inhabited by a demon; mad (*OED adj.* 2a); see 2.2.146n., on *I . . . with*.
94 **deadly** death-like (*OED adj.* 7)
95 **bound . . . room** as madmen were commonly treated; a similar fate befalls Malvolio (see *TN* 3.4.135–6); see also Reed, *Bedlam*, 11; cf. 5.1.247–9.

bound See 1.1.81n. Pinch's resort to hempen bonds offers an instance of 'materialization', the prior language of *band* and *bond* now calling forth, as it were, the physical binding of Antipholus and Dromio; cf. 126n. The *rope's end* (44) has multiplied into lengths of rope.

96, 98 **forth** See 1.2.37 and n., on *find . . . forth*.
97 **bag of gold** Cf. 4.1.105 and n., 4.2.61.1 and n.

96 SD] *Oxf*   today?] *Capell;* to day, *F*   97 SD] *Oxf (Capell subst.)*

ADRIANA

Dissembling villain, thou speak'st false in both.

ANTIPHOLUS OF EPHESUS

Dissembling harlot, thou art false in all,
And art confederate with a damned pack
To make a loathsome, abject scorn of me;
But with these nails I'll pluck out those false eyes   105
That would behold in me this shameful sport.
    [*Threatens Adriana.*]

ADRIANA

O, bind him, bind him! Let him not come near me!

PINCH

More company!

Enter three or four and offer to bind him. He strives.

The fiend is strong within him.

LUCIANA

Ay me, poor man, how pale and wan he looks.

---

102 **harlot** unchaste woman; prostitute (*OED n.* 5c); 'harlots' occurs at 5.1.205 (see n.); cf. 2.2.142 and n.

103 **confederate** united in league (*OED adj.* A); cf. 4.1.17 and n.
    damned damnèd
    pack i.e. gang of conspirators (see *OED n.*[1] 4a); cf. 5.1.219 and n., on *packed with*; *TN* 5.1.378.

104 **scorn** mockery (*OED n.* 1a)

105 In *Men.*, the traveller Menaechmus, feigning madness, threatens to 'burn out that woman's [i.e. his brother's wife's] eyes with flaming torches' (841); cf. 5.1.183 and n., *KL* 3.6.15–16.

106 **shameful** See 2.1.112n.

108 SD *This entrance SD occurs after 106 in F, but its unclear relationship to the

dialogue has caused editors to locate it variously. It may have been written in the margins of the MS from which the compositors worked. The present position is warranted because only Pinch cries *More company!*; the attendants are under his authority; and his statement in the second part of 108 responds to Antipholus' striving.
    strives struggles (*OED v.* 3e)

108 **fiend . . . him** Unusual strength was a sign of demonic possession (see Almond, 27): Antipholus has begun to act as if he really were possessed; cf. 127 and n., on *mad me*.

109 On Luciana's increasing sympathy for Antipholus, see 51n.

---

105 those] *Rowe*; these *F*   106 SD] *Capell subst.*   108 SD] *this edn; after 106 F; after 109 Dyce; after 108 Cam*[1]*; after 107 Ard*[2]

ANTIPHOLUS OF EPHESUS

What, will you murder me? – Thou, jailer, thou,   110
I am thy prisoner: wilt thou suffer them
To make a rescue?

OFFICER   Masters, let him go:
He is my prisoner, and you shall not have him.

PINCH

Go bind this man, for he is frantic too.
[*They offer to bind Dromio.*]

ADRIANA [*to Officer*]

What wilt thou do, thou peevish officer?   115
Hast thou delight to see a wretched man
Do outrage and displeasure to himself?

OFFICER

He is my prisoner; if I let him go,
The debt he owes will be required of me.

ADRIANA

I will discharge thee ere I go from thee;   120
Bear me forthwith unto his creditor,
And, knowing how the debt grows, I will pay it.
– Good Master Doctor, see him safe conveyed
Home to my house. O, most unhappy day!

ANTIPHOLUS OF EPHESUS

O, most unhappy strumpet!   125

111–13 Most editors, following F's prose speeches into blank verse, as here. Although an iambic pentameter phrase may occur within a prose speech, when sequential prose speeches scan neatly, they are likely to be verse (see Wright, *Metrical*, 108–13).

112 **make a rescue** forcibly take someone out of legal custody (*OED* rescue *n*. 2); cf. *Cor* 3.1.275.

114 Dromio is probably struggling with Pinch's men to save Antipholus.

115 **peevish** foolish; mad (*OED adj.* 2a, b); see 4.1.93 and n., on *peevish*.

117 **displeasure** injury, harm (*OED n*. 3); also at 5.1.142

118–19 **if...me** 'In Elizabethan times the jailer could be held responsible for the prisoner's debts' (Wells).

120 **discharge** pay

121 **Bear** take (*OED v*.¹ 1e)
    forthwith immediately

122 **grows** arises; see 4.1.8 and n.

125 Some editions print this brief speech as prose, but the line (124) that Antipholus parodies is verse.
    unhappy mischief-causing, evil (*OED adj.* 5a)

111–13] *Pope; prose F*   114 this] *his Wells (Tannenbaum)*   SD] *Cam*   115 SD] *Folg²*   125] *verse this edn*

DROMIO OF EPHESUS

Master, I am here entered in bond for you.

ANTIPHOLUS OF EPHESUS

Out on thee, villain! Wherefore dost thou mad me?

DROMIO OF EPHESUS   Will you be bound for nothing? Be
mad, good master: cry 'The devil!'

LUCIANA

God help, poor souls! How idly do they talk.   130

ADRIANA

[*to Pinch*] Go bear him hence.   [*Exeunt Pinch and his
                    men with Antipholus and Dromio of Ephesus.*]
                                        – Sister, go you with me.

[*to Officer*] Say now, whose suit is he arrested at?

OFFICER

One Angelo, a goldsmith; do you know him?

ADRIANA

I know the man. What is the sum he owes?

---

126 **bond** (1) physical bondage; (2) a contract for debt (recalling *creditor* and *debt* at 121, 122, *bond* in 4.1.13 (see n.)); cf. 4.3.31–3 and 31, 33n. See also 95n., on *bound*.

127 **Out on** curses upon (*OED* out *int*. 2)
    mad me 'enrage me' (*OED v*. 2), but suggesting that Antipholus is turning into the madman that his antagonists imagine; see also 108n.

128–9 sometimes divided into verse, as with 111–13. Here and at 126, Dromio's speech wavers between prose and verse.

128 **bound** See 1.1.81n.

128–9 **Be . . . devil** Dromio encourages Antipholus, if he is to be bound as a madman, to act as a madman (see 127n., on *mad me*). To *cry 'The devil!'* is to express impatience, irritation or vexation (*OED* devil *n*. 20a). In *Men.*, Sosicles Menaechmus, accused by his wife of being insane, decides to simulate insanity and to

call out the names of gods who are speaking to him ('*quid mi meliust . . . ego med assimulem insanire . . . euhoe Bacche, Bromie . . .*', 831–5). Cf. e.g. Edgar in *KL* 3.4. See also mad Orlando in Greene's play *Orlando Furioso* (1592), 13.845–52, and half-mad Hieronymo in Kyd's *Spanish Tragedy*. Dromio understands theatrical conventions.

130 **idly** deliriously (*OED adv*. 1b)

131 SD2 **F locates the exit SD after 132, but Pinch and his men would probably begin to remove Antipholus and Dromio (into the Phoenix) immediately upon Adriana's order, 'Go bear him hence'.

131 **Sister . . . me** Adriana's instruction suggests that Luciana has started to follow the bound Antipholus offstage, acting on the sympathetic feelings that she expressed earlier; see 51 and n.

126] *verse as Steevens*[4]   129 'The devil!'] *Dyce*[2]*; the diuell F*   130 help, poor] *Theobald;* help poor *F*
idly] *(idlely)*   131 SD1] *Folg*[2]   131 SD2] *Folg*[2] *subst.; Exeunt. Manet Offic. Adri. Luci. Courtizan F, after 132; after 131 Theobald*   132 SD] *Capell subst.*

OFFICER

Two hundred ducats.

ADRIANA   Say, how grows it due?   135

OFFICER

Due for a chain your husband had of him.

ADRIANA

He did bespeak a chain for me, but had it not.

COURTESAN

Whenas your husband all in rage today

Came to my house and took away my ring –

The ring I saw upon his finger now –   140

Straight after did I meet him with a chain.

ADRIANA

It may be so, but I did never see it.

– Come, jailer, bring me where the goldsmith is;

I long to know the truth hereof at large.

Enter ANTIPHOLUS [OF SYRACUSE,
wearing the chain,] *with his rapier drawn,
and* DROMIO [OF SYRACUSE].

LUCIANA

God, for thy mercy! They are loose again.   145

---

135 **Two hundred ducats** Cf. 4.3.84 and
4.3.84, 97n.
  grows See 122n., 4.1.8 and n.
137 **bespeak** order (as with merchandise)
(*OED v.* 5a)
  had it perhaps 'had't' (Walker, *Versification*, 77)
138–9 The Courtesan lies about how she came
into possession of the ring, as she had
promised; see 4.3.95–6 and n.
138 **Whenas** when (*OED adv.* 1)
  rage See 4.3.88 and n.

139, 140 **ring** See 4.1.13.1–2n.
141 **Straight** See 1.1.86n.
142 Adriana is rightly suspicious; see 138–9
and n.
144 **at large** in full (Crystal & Crystal, 1)
144.2 **with . . . drawn** The SD in F designates a
drawn sword for Antipholus but none for
Dromio, although various editors (and
theatrical directors), following Dyce, have
both Syracusans entering with swords in
hand, reflecting Adriana's exclamation at
146; see also 5.1.151.

144.1 OF SYRACUSE] *Theobald²; Sirac.* F 144.2 *wearing the chain*] *Oxf* 144.3 OF SYRACUSE]
Theobald²; Sirac. F; *of Syracuse with their rapiers drawn.* / *Dyce*

ADRIANA

And come with naked swords! Let's call more help
To have them bound again.

OFFICER　　　　　　　　　　　　Away, they'll kill us!

Exeunt [all but Antipholus and Dromio of Syracuse],
as fast as may be, frighted.

ANTIPHOLUS OF SYRACUSE

I see these witches are afraid of swords.

DROMIO OF SYRACUSE

She that would be your wife now ran from you.

ANTIPHOLUS OF SYRACUSE

Come to the Centaur; fetch our stuff from thence:　　150
I long that we were safe and sound aboard.

DROMIO OF SYRACUSE　　Faith, stay here this night; they
will surely do us no harm. You saw they speak us
fair, give us gold: methinks they are such a gentle
nation that, but for the mountain of mad flesh that　155

146–7 Modern editions, as here, often combine F's three irregular lines ('swords, / againe. / vs. / ') into two pentameters, implying immediately continuous reactions.

Let's ... again Adriana's speech is followed in F by the SD '*Runne all out.*' (omitted here), then by the Officer's line (*Away ... us!*) and after that by yet another SD (retained here) for the characters to exit. On F's embarrassment of SD riches, see Appendix 2, pp. 333–7, 341–3. This edition follows the standard practice of admitting only one exit direction, here after *us!* at the end of 147. If the exit were to begin after *again*, the Officer might be the last character off; if it starts after *us!*, he may lead the charge. In the spirit of theatrical frenzy, Cam[2a] retains both F's SDs by amending the first to '*Run all out [and re-enter with others]*', thus enabling a

second chase at 148 (SD *Exeunt . . .*). That ingenious solution, however, seems more Keystone Cops than Elizabethan. A distant possibility is that the first direction, '*Runne all out.*', was meant to apply to the women and to distinguish their exit from the Officer's.

147 **bound** See 1.1.81n.

148, 157 **witches ... witch** See 1.2.100 and n.

149 **would be** pretended to be (Abbott, 329)

151 **safe and sound** proverbial (Dent S21.1)

153 **saw ... speak** An irregular sequence of verb tenses (here past shifting to present) is not uncommon (see Abbott, 370). Past events were sometimes narrated in the present tense, creating the impression that the speaker could barely distance himself from them (Hope, 2.0a).

153–4 **speak us fair** See 4.2.16n., on *speak him fair.*

146–7] *Hanmer; F lines* swords, / againe. / vs. / 147 again.] *Pope;* again. *Runne all out. F* SD *all . . . Syracuse*] *Pope subst.; omnes F*　148+ SP] *(S.Ant., Ant.)*　149+ SP] *(S.Dro., Dro.)*

claims marriage of me, I could find in my heart to
stay here still and turn witch.

ANTIPHOLUS OF SYRACUSE

I will not stay tonight for all the town;
Therefore, away, to get our stuff aboard.   *Exeunt.*

5.1   *Enter the* [Second] Merchant *and* [ANGELO]
the goldsmith.

ANGELO

I am sorry, sir, that I have hindered you,
But I protest he had the chain of me,
Though most dishonestly he doth deny it.

2 MERCHANT

How is the man esteemed here in the city?

ANGELO

Of very reverend reputation, sir,   5
Of credit infinite, highly beloved,
Second to none that lives here in the city;
His word might bear my wealth at any time.

---

156 **claims . . . me** See 3.2.78–83 and
3.2.79n., on *claims*. Whether Nell *claims*
the promise of marriage or marriage itself
is unclear.

156–7 **I . . . still** Dromio is now willing to stay
in Ephesus: 'The tide begins to turn'
(Wells).

157 **still** See 2.1.11n., on *still*.

5.1 The location remains the mart, as in 4.3–4.

0.1 ***Second** See 4.1.0.1 and n.

1 **hindered** i.e. obstructed (*OED v.* 2) by
failing to pay the debt (see 4.1.1–6);
perhaps also injured or damaged (*OED* 1a)
monetarily. Angelo's arrest for debt at the
suit of the Second Merchant (see
4.1.69–70) has apparently been resolved.

2 **protest** declare, affirm

3 **dishonestly** fraudulently (*OED adv.* 3, first
citation)
deny i.e. deny having; *deny* is reiterated at
16, 22, 23, 25, 378, 380; see 378, 380n.

4 suggesting the Merchant's unfamiliarity
with Ephesus; see 4.1.0.1n.

5 **reverend** See 3.2.88n.; also at 124 (see n.),
134.
reputation See 2.1.108–12 and n.

6 **credit** (1) reputation for solvency (*OED n.*
11); (2) trustworthiness (*OED* 2b);
financial probity and personal honour
merge. See p. 19.

7 **here . . . city** repeated from 4; perhaps a
compositorial error but also the first of the
scene's several repeated phrases and words

8 **His . . . wealth** i.e. I would loan my wealth

5.1] *(Actus Quintus. Scoena Prima.);* ACT V. SCENE I. *Rowe* 0.1 Second] *Dyce* ANGELO] *Rowe*
1+ SP] *Rowe; Gold., Goldsmith. F* 4+ SP] *Dyce subst.; Mar. F* 5 reverend] *(reuerent)*

Enter ANTIPHOLUS [OF SYRACUSE, *wearing the chain,*]
and DROMIO [OF SYRACUSE] *again.*

2 MERCHANT

Speak softly; yonder, as I think, he walks.

ANGELO

'Tis so, and that self chain about his neck   10
Which he forswore most monstrously to have.
Good sir, draw near to me; I'll speak to him:
– Signor Antipholus, I wonder much
That you would put me to this shame and trouble,
And not without some scandal to yourself,   15
With circumstance and oaths so to deny
This chain which now you wear so openly.
Beside the charge, the shame, imprisonment,
You have done wrong to this my honest friend,
Who, but for staying on our controversy,   20
Had hoisted sail and put to sea today.
This chain you had of me; can you deny it?

---

to him on his assurance; *bear* suggests that
an airless *word* can carry heavy *wealth*.
The verb *bear* recurs variously at 35, 41,
89, 143 and 158.

8.1–2 *See 2.1.42.1 LN.

8.1 ***wearing the chain** as observed at 10; see
4.3.0.1 and n.

8.2 *again* suggesting that Shakespeare
conceived 5.1 as continuous with 4.4. The
Syracusans may enter carrying pouches or
stuff (4.4.150, 159).

10 **self** same, very; *self* functions as a
demonstrative adjective used to specify
and emphasize the noun referred to (Blake,
3.3.4.5; Abbott, 20).

11 **forswore** swore falsely (*OED v.* 4a);
denied by oath (*OED* 2), although Ephesian
Antipholus had not precisely 'sworn': see
4.1.66 and n.; see also at 24, 25 (*forswear*).

monstrously unnaturally (*OED adv.* 1),
recalling Adriana's denunciations of her
husband (e.g. 4.2.19–22) and the likening
of characters to animals (e.g. 3.1.15–18):
oath-breaking makes men monsters.

12 **to me** i.e. as Angelo approaches Antipholus

13 **Signor** See 3.1.1n., on *Signor*.

14, 18 **shame** See 2.1.112n.

16 **circumstance** detailed narration, i.e.
excuses (*OED n.* 6); cf. *MV* 1.1.154.
oaths See 11n., on *forswore*.
deny i.e. deny having; see 3n., on *deny*.

18 **Beside** besides
charge expense, cost (*OED n.*[1] 10a); cf.
'chargeful' at 4.1.29 and n.; perhaps
inconvenience (echoing *trouble*, 14)
(Ard[2]).

20 **on** because of (*OED prep.* 9); cf. *TNK*
4.1.50.

8.1–2] *after 9 F*   8.1 OF SYRACUSE] *Rowe   wearing the chain*] *Oxf*   8.2 OF SYRACUSE] *Rowe*   12 ¹to]
with Collier²   13 Signor] *(Signior)*

ANTIPHOLUS OF SYRACUSE

I think I had; I never did deny it.

2 MERCHANT

Yes, that you did, sir, and forswore it, too.

ANTIPHOLUS OF SYRACUSE

Who heard me to deny it or forswear it?　25

2 MERCHANT

These ears of mine, thou knowst, did hear thee.
Fie on thee, wretch! 'Tis pity that thou liv'st
To walk where any honest men resort.

ANTIPHOLUS OF SYRACUSE

Thou art a villain to impeach me thus!
I'll prove mine honour and mine honesty　30
Against thee presently, if thou dar'st stand.

2 MERCHANT

I dare, and do defy thee for a villain!　*They draw.*

Enter ADRIANA, LUCIANA,
Courtesan *and others* [*with ropes*].

ADRIANA

Hold, hurt him not, for God's sake; he is mad!
Some get within him, take his sword away.
Bind Dromio too, and bear them to my house.　35

24, 25 **forswore, forswear** See 11n., on
forswore.
27–31 The Second Merchant takes honesty in
business dealings as a life-and-death
matter. Antipholus treats his reputation
with a like seriousness.
29 **impeach** accuse (*OED v.* 4a)
31 **presently** See 3.2.152 and n.
stand fight, 'take up an offensive or defens-
ive position against an enemy' (*OED v.* 10)
32–7 The drawing of swords marks the
crescendo of violence towards which the
play has been building with the beatings of

the Dromios and the threats by Ephesian
Antipholus against Adriana (Ard²). Fit-
tingly, the priory is here first mentioned
(37), with its hint of a providential solution.
32 **defy thee for** challenge you to combat as
(*OED* defy *v.*¹ 2a; for *prep.* 19a)
32 SD At 263, the Second Merchant suggests
that he drew first.
32.2 **with ropes* as 35 indicates
34 **within him** inside his guard (*OED* within
prep. 8b), i.e. inside the reach of his sword
35 **bear** Adriana uses *bear* similarly at 41,
158; cf. 187 and n.; see 8n.

23+ SP] *(Ant., S.Ant., S. Ant.)*　32.2 SD *with ropes*] *this edn*　33 God's] *F3 (*Gods); God *F*

DROMIO OF SYRACUSE

Run, master, run; for God's sake, take a house!
This is some priory; in, or we are spoiled!

Exeunt [Antipholus and Dromio of Syracuse]
to the priory.

Enter [Emilia, *the*] Lady ABBESS.

ABBESS

Be quiet, people. Wherefore throng you hither?

ADRIANA

To fetch my poor distracted husband hence;
Let us come in, that we may bind him fast   40
And bear him home for his recovery.

ANGELO

I knew he was not in his perfect wits.

2 MERCHANT

I am sorry now that I did draw on him.

ABBESS

How long hath this possession held the man?

ADRIANA

This week he hath been heavy, sour, sad,   45

36   **take** enter for refuge (*OED v.* 25a); see also *took*, 94.

37   **priory** nunnery governed by a prioress; offshoot of an abbey (*OED n.* 1a), occurring in Shakespeare only here and in 37 SD; afterwards the text uses *abbey* (see 122n., on *abbey*). Egeon's execution is scheduled to take place in the 'melancholy vale . . . Behind the ditches of the abbey' (120, 122), i.e. on the low waste ground beyond the abbey wall; see 120–2n.; cf. *TGV* 5.1.9. In pre-Shakespearean England abbeys and priories had been numerous until Catholic foundations were suppressed by Henry VIII in the 1530s.

spoiled destroyed (*OED v.*[1] 10a)

37.1   The Abbess enters from *the priory* (37 SD) into which Antipholus and Dromio

have escaped. F often uses 'fictive' SDs, but inconsistently: later an attendant exits *to the Abbess* (282 SD), i.e. to a person rather than to a building. Cf. 4.1.13.3 and n.

39   **distracted** crazed, mad (*OED adj.* 5, first citation)

41   **bear** See 35n.

44   **possession** madness; domination or control by a demon; see 2.2.146n., on *I . . . with*. Here as elsewhere, these two agencies are treated as the same.

45   **heavy** despondent, weighed down mentally (*OED adj.*[1] 27a)
      sour morose; discontented (*OED adj.* 6a); pronounced as two syllables, as in F's spelling, 'sower'
      sad grave

36+ SP] *(S.Dro., S. Dromio., S.Drom.)*   37 SD *Antipholus . . . Syracuse*] *Capell subst.*   37.1 Emilia, *the*] *Ard*[2]   39 SP] *(Ab., Abbesse., Abb.)*   45 sour, sad] *(sower sad)*

273

And much different from the man he was;
But till this afternoon his passion
Ne'er broke into extremity of rage.

ABBESS

Hath he not lost much wealth by wrack of sea?
Buried some dear friend? Hath not else his eye   50
Strayed his affection in unlawful love? –
A sin prevailing much in youthful men,
Who give their eyes the liberty of gazing.
Which of these sorrows is he subject to?

ADRIANA

To none of these, except it be the last,   55
Namely, some love that drew him oft from home.

ABBESS

You should for that have reprehended him.

ADRIANA

Why, so I did.

ABBESS   Ay, but not rough enough.

ADRIANA

As roughly as my modesty would let me.

---

46 If *different* is pronounced 'diff'rent', the
line lacks a stressed syllable; not so if it
is given three syllables, as at e.g. *MND*
1.1.135, *RJ* 2.3.14. Cam²ᵃ reads the line
trochaically, as lending to Adriana a sense
of 'puzzlement' and 'wonder'. F2 makes
up the syllable by emending to 'much
much', a change that can be compared with
MV 3.2.61, and a solution often followed.

47 **passion** affliction, bodily disorder (*OED n.*
4a); overpowering or strong emotion (*OED*
6a); pronounced as three syllables

48 **rage** See 4.3.88n.

49 **wrack of sea** shipwreck. The question
presciently evokes Egeon's narration in
1.1. It also suggests that Ephesian Antipholus may be a merchant trader. Cf.
Antonio's melancholy, *MV* 1.1.1–45.

50 **eye** Cf. 2.1.102.

51 **Strayed** led astray (*OED v.²* 4c)

53 **liberty** See 340; 2.1.7n., on *liberty*; on
liberties, see 1.2.102 and n.
gazing See 1.1.88n., on *gazing*; also
3.2.56n., on *gazing*.

57 **reprehended** rebuked, reprimanded (*OED
v.* 1a)

58–61 A mini-drama plays out through
versification, with Adriana and the Abbess
vying for argumentative supremacy by
completing each other's verse line or by
taking up a whole line (consequently, 61 is
best understood as a short verse line). Cf.
Adriana and Luciana, 2.1.10–41 and n.

58 **rough** harshly (*OED adv.*); also at 88. In
EM English, adjectives often function as
adverbs (Abbott, 1).

---

46 much] much much *F2; too much Hudson² (Jervis, per Dyce²)*   48 broke] *Oxf¹;* brake *F*   58, 61 Ay] *(I)*

ABBESS
Haply, in private.
ADRIANA　　　　　　　And in assemblies, too.　　　60
ABBESS
Ay, but not enough.
ADRIANA
It was the copy of our conference:
In bed he slept not for my urging it;
At board he fed not for my urging it;
Alone, it was the subject of my theme;　　　65
In company I often glanced at it;
Still did I tell him it was vile and bad.
ABBESS
And thereof came it that the man was mad:
The venom clamours of a jealous woman
Poisons more deadly than a mad dog's tooth.　　　70

60　**Haply** by chance; perhaps (*OED adv.*); also at 284; on *hap*- words, see 1.1.37n.
　　assemblies social gatherings (*OED n.* 7)
62–86　These descriptions reflect ironically on Adriana's earlier romantic catalogue; see 2.2.120–4 and n.
62　**copy** subject-matter, theme (*OED n.* 11b); deriving from the Latin phrase *copia verborum*, the word suggests here 'abundance of language' (*OED* 1c).
　　conference serious conversation (*OED n.* 4a), a common Shakespearean usage; see e.g. *TS* 2.1.251, *MA* 2.3.221. Adriana's elevated Latinate diction (*copy, conference*) reasserts her dignity.
63, 64　**urging it** 'pressing it upon [his] attention' (*OED n.* 1a). Repeating a closing phrase is rhetorical *antistrophe*.
65　**theme** academic exercise (e.g. a school essay; see *OED n.* 3). In Shakespeare, *theme* can mean a 'subject treated by action' (*OED* 1b), as at *Tit* 5.2.80.
66　***glanced at*** Pope's addition of *at* fills out F's line metrically and makes *glanced* into

an intransitive verb; *glanced at* means referred to (*OED v.*[1] 3); cf. *MND* 2.1.75, *JC* 1.2.320.
67　**Still** See 2.1.11n., on *still*. Adriana brings her argument about persistence to a rhetorical climax: *In bed*, *At board*, *Alone*, *In company*, *Still*.
68, 72　**And thereof** The repeated sentence-openings, rhetorical *anaphora*, reinforce the argument; also *Thereof* (75); likewise with *Thou sayst*, 73, 77.
68　**mad** The Abbess tops Adriana by means of her rhyme, leading to her triumphant counter-argument.
69　The four front-stressed disyllabic words give the pronouncement weight.
70　**Poisons** a verb, whose subject is *clamours* (69); singular because *clamours* is collectively singular in sense; see 3.2.19–20n.
　　mad dog's tooth capable of transmitting rabies (which induces mania). The accusation of madness is now turned back on Adriana herself.

66 glanced at] *Pope subst.;* glanced *F*　67 vile] *(*vilde*)*　69–70 clamours . . . Poisons] clamours . . . Poison *Pope;* clamour . . . Poisons *Capell*　69 woman] *Pope;* woman, *F*

275

It seems his sleeps were hindered by thy railing,
And thereof comes it that his head is light.
Thou sayst his meat was sauced with thy
    upbraidings:
Unquiet meals make ill digestions;
Thereof the raging fire of fever bred,   75
And what's a fever but a fit of madness?
Thou sayst his sports were hindered by thy brawls:
Sweet recreation barred, what doth ensue
But moody and dull melancholy,
Kinsman to grim and comfortless despair,   80
And at her heels a huge infectious troop
Of pale distemperatures and foes to life?
In food, in sport and life-preserving rest
To be disturbed would mad or man or beast;
The consequence is, then, thy jealous fits   85

72 **light** giddy, 'wandering in mind' (*OED adj.*[1] 22)

73, 77 **Thou sayst** See 68, 72n.

73 possibly alluding to the proverb 'Sweet meat must have sour sauce' (Dent, M839, but not recorded for *CE*)
    sauced seasoned (*OED v.* 1), but with a sense of making bitter (*OED* 1c); cf. *sweet-savoured* at 2.2.123 and n.

75 **raging** echoing *rage* at 48

77 ***sayst** See t.n.

77, 83 **sports**, **sport** pastimes

78–82 Personifications of activities and qualities such as *recreation*, *melancholy* and *despair* were common in Elizabethan literature. For Despair personified, see e.g. Spenser, *FQ*, 1.9.29. In Tudor thinking, lack of recreation could lead to despondency.

79 The iambic tetrameter may invite the performer to pause. Editors have sometimes added words, with little increase in sense.

80–1 **Kinsman . . . her** The *melancholy* (79) disposition was the one most susceptible to

madness (e.g. *despair*, 80) in humoural theory (on Antipholus' presumed madness and despair, see 139–40). Grammatically, *her* presumably refers to *despair*. Melancholy is female in emblematic depictions, e.g. Albrecht Dürer's famous engraving 'Melencolia 1' (1514), although male in Spenser's *FQ*. Ard[1] (following Ritson) sees *her* referring to *Kinsman* used 'generically', i.e. without gender. *Kinsman* is cited here by *OED* as its first figurative use.

81 **infectious** infected (*OED adj.* 2); cf. *Oth* 4.1.21.

82 **distemperatures** disordered conditions of the humours; ailments (*OED n.* 2). Cf. e.g. *MND* 2.1.106, *RJ* 2.3.40.

84 **or . . . or** See 1.1.136n., on *Or . . . or*.

85–6 **fits . . . wits** The rhyme and oppositional meanings drive home the Abbess's point; *fits* identifies Adriana's own 'attacks' of jealousy, or, more extremely, her own 'paroxysm[s] of lunacy' (*OED* fit n.[2] 3a, b); see 139 and 'fits' at 4.3.91, and cf. *TA* 4.1.17.

77 sayst] *Rowe;* sayest F   79 moody and dull] muddy and dull *F2;* moody, moping, and dull *Hanmer*
80 Kinsman] A'kin *Hanmer;* kins- / woman *79–80 in Capell*   81 her] their *Rann (Heath);* his *Collier*[3] *(Walker, Critical)*

Hath scared thy husband from the use of wits.

LUCIANA

She never reprehended him but mildly,
When he demeaned himself rough, rude and wildly.
[*to Adriana*] Why bear you these rebukes and
　answer not?

ADRIANA

She did betray me to my own reproof.　　　　　　90
– Good people, enter and lay hold on him.

ABBESS

No, not a creature enters in my house.

ADRIANA

Then let your servants bring my husband forth.

ABBESS

Neither. He took this place for sanctuary,
And it shall privilege him from your hands　　　　　95
Till I have brought him to his wits again
Or lose my labour in assaying it.

ADRIANA

I will attend my husband, be his nurse,

86　Cf. *MND* 1.2.79–80.
87–8 This defence (strengthened by its couplet) is surprising, since Luciana had previously criticized Adriana for *impatience* (see 2.1.9, 85 and nn.); see also 102 and n.; 174 and n., on *patience*; on the patience motif, see 1.2.86n.
88　**demeaned** conducted, but with the sense of treating badly (*OED* demean $v.^1$ 1a, 4a); see 4.3.83n.; cf. e.g. *2H6* 1.1.188, 1.3.103; *3H6* 1.4.7.
　　rough . . . wildly On *rough*, see 58n. In a linked series of EM adjectives functioning as adverbs, the final one sometimes takes *-ly* (Blake, 5.1.2.2). Luciana's *wildly* means roughly, savagely (*OED adv.* 3b, first citation).
90　'She has exposed me to my own self-censure'; *betray* means give up or expose to punishment (*OED v.* 1b, first citation) (see also *MW* 3.3.195); *reproof* means

censure, rebuke (*OED n.* 1a). Adriana speaks either to Luciana or to herself. Her speech marks a self-awareness beyond that of the other characters.
94　**Neither** reinforcing the Abbess' previous *No* (92) (*OED adv.* 3b, first citation as intensifier); see also 302 and n.
　　took See 36n.
　　sanctuary In Shakespeare's England, a fugitive from secular justice or debt could take refuge (*sanctuary*) in a church or other holy place and be immune from arrest (see *OED n.*[1] 6a). This vestigial medieval practice was abolished by Parliament in the 17th century.
95　**privilege** give immunity to (as from civil law) (*OED v.* 2)
98–9 perhaps recalling the marriage vows in *BCP*: 'to haue and to holde, . . . in sickenesse, and in health' (sig. O6^r; see Shaheen, 117)

89 SD] *Johnson subst.*

277

> Diet his sickness, for it is my office,
> And will have no attorney but myself; 100
> And therefore let me have him home with me.

ABBESS

> Be patient, for I will not let him stir
> Till I have used the approved means I have,
> With wholesome syrups, drugs and holy prayers,
> To make of him a formal man again. 105
> It is a branch and parcel of mine oath,
> A charitable duty of my order;
> Therefore depart, and leave him here with me.

ADRIANA

> I will not hence and leave my husband here;
> And ill it doth beseem your holiness 110
> To separate the husband and the wife.

ABBESS

> Be quiet and depart: thou shalt not have him.   [*Exit.*]

99 **Diet** treat through healthful food (*OED v.* 2a)
office duty (as a wife); see 3.1.44 and n. Adriana fulfils her *office* although her husband has forgotten his (see 3.2.2 and n.).
100 **attorney** substitute, agent (*OED n.*[1] 1)
101 **have** bring (*OED v.* 16a)
102–7 The Abbess 'claims genuine healing skills, a practical extension of her religious vocation', in contrast to Doctor Pinch's 'sham occult powers' (Oxf[1]); see 4.4.55–8 and n. In *RJ*, Friar Lawrence extols the medicinal virtue and 'powerful grace that lies / In plants, herbs, stones, and their true qualities' (2.3.15–16).
102 **Be patient** suggesting that Adriana has spoken heatedly in 98–101 (cf. 87–8n.; see also 174 and n., on *patience*); the Abbess repeats Luciana's phrase from 2.1.9 (see n.); on patience, see 1.2.86 and n.
103 **approved** proven, tried (*OED adj.* 1a); perhaps pronounced 'th'approvèd'
105 **formal** normal in intellect, sane (*OED adj.*

4c, only citation). Cf. 'this is evident to any formal capacity', *TN* 2.5.117 (Ard[1]); also *AC* 2.5.41.
106 **branch and parcel** 'part and parcel'; *branch* = part (*OED n.* 2a); the synonyms increase emphasis.
oath i.e. as a nun
106–7 **mine . . . my** See 1.1.33n.
107 **order** i.e. the religious society of nuns to which she belongs (see *OED n.* 5a)
109 **will not** with 'go' implied (Abbott, 41)
110–11 In *BCP*, one reason that a couple is 'ioyned' in marriage is for their 'mutuall societie, helpe and comforte' (sig. O5ᵛ). 'Those whome God hath ioyned together, let no man putte a sunder' (sig. O6ᵛ): thus, for a member of a religious order to *separate* (111) husband and wife would be ill-fitting.
110 **your holiness** used either to indicate spiritual quality (*OED* holiness *n.* 1) or as an address to a high ecclesiastical official (*OED* 2), perhaps here ironically

112 SD] Hanmer

LUCIANA [*to Adriana*]
Complain unto the Duke of this indignity.

ADRIANA
Come, go; I will fall prostrate at his feet,
And never rise until my tears and prayers   115
Have won his grace to come in person hither
And take perforce my husband from the Abbess.

2 MERCHANT
By this, I think, the dial points at five;
Anon, I'm sure, the Duke himself in person
Comes this way to the melancholy vale,   120
The place of death and sorry execution,
Behind the ditches of the abbey here.

ANGELO
Upon what cause?

2 MERCHANT
To see a reverend Syracusan merchant,

114 **Come, go** see 4.4.41n.
115 **tears** another association of Adriana with crying; see 2.1.114 and n.
116 **his grace** i.e. the Duke; a title of respect for one of noble rank (*OED* grace *n.* 8a); cf. *your holiness* (110); *grace* recurs at 136.
117 Perhaps after this line Adriana and Luciana step upstage.
118–28 This exchange reintroduces the Egeon family subplot (for the first time since 1.1–2), as the story-lines of long-term romance and one-day farcical misprisions now begin to merge.
118 **By this** 'By this time'; perhaps cueing 'the ringing of the priory bell' (Cam²)
     dial . . . five The time towards which the lines of action have been climactically heading; see 1.2.26n., on *five o'clock*. On the convergence of story-lines, see 1.1.27n., on *evening sun*, and 1.1.100n., on *five*.

119 **Anon** soon, shortly; also at 148
120–2 **melancholy . . . here** The inspiration may be 'Holywell Priory, near where Shakespeare lived and worked' (Ard¹, xli). See 37n., on *priory*, and Appendix 1, p. 319.
121 **death** A few editors retain F's 'depth' because it accords with *vale* (120) and because *death* and *execution* seem pleonastic, although the repetition adds rhetorical gravity to the sentiment.
     sorry sorrowful
122 **ditches** trenches probably used for drainage
     abbey religious establishment under an abbot or abbess (*OED* *n.* 1b), i.e. a nunnery; earlier called a *priory*: see 37 and n., on *priory*.
124 **reverend** See 3.2.88n.; also at 5. The word's occurrence here and again at 134 enhances the spiritual aura of the last act.

113 SD] *Oxf*   117 Abbess.] Abbesse. *Exeunt.* / *Enter Merchant and Goldsmith. F2*   118, 124 SP]
ANGELO *Oxf¹*   118 points] point's *Oxf (McKerrow, per Oxf)*   121 death] *F3;* depth *F*   123, 128 SP]
SECOND MERCHANT *Oxf¹*   124 reverend] *(reuerent)*   Syracusan] *Pope; Siracusian F*

Who put unluckily into this bay   125
Against the laws and statutes of this town,
Beheaded publicly for his offence.

Enter [Solinus,] *the* DUKE *of Ephesus, and* [EGEON,]
the Merchant of Syracuse[,] *barehead*[*ed and bound*],
with the Headsman and other Officers.

ANGELO
See where they come; we will behold his death.
LUCIANA
Kneel to the Duke before he pass the abbey.
DUKE
Yet once again proclaim it publicly,   130
If any friend will pay the sum for him,
He shall not die, so much we tender him.
ADRIANA [*kneeling*]
Justice, most sacred Duke, against the Abbess!
DUKE
She is a virtuous and a reverend lady;
It cannot be that she hath done thee wrong.   135

125 **put** nautical term for driving a vessel in a certain direction (*OED v.* 5b)
126 **statutes** sovereign decrees, as distinct from parliamentary *laws*
127 **offence** perhaps ironical, given *unluckily* (125)
127.1–3 *Relocated here from their position in F after 129; see 2.1.42.1 LN.
127.2 **bareheaded** conventional for beheading (the SD thus implies that in 1.1 Egeon wore a hat)
and bound See 294 and n., 1.1.81n.
127.3 *Headsman* thus carrying an axe or broadsword
129 **pass** i.e. passes; the subjunctive, with an implied auxiliary: 'before he should pass the abbey'

130–2 Cf. 1.1.150–4. The Duke reveals implicitly his sympathy for Egeon, anticipating his sparing of Egeon's life at 390.
130 **proclaim** The Duke presumably addresses one of his officers (although, effectively, he makes the proclamation himself), whose responding action might be halted by Adriana's intervention.
132 **tender** hold dear (*OED v.*[2] 3a)
133 Ephesian Antipholus will employ the same form at 190, 197; see also 4.1.83 and n. Such mirroring language follows the pattern of repetition-with-variation.
134 **reverend** See 124n.

127.1–3 SD] *this edn; after 129 F*   127.1 Solinus,] *Ard*[2]   EGEON] *Capell (Rowe subst.)*   127.2 *bareheaded*] *F2 subst.; bare head F*   *and bound*] *Bevington*[4]   133 SD] *Oxf*[1]

ADRIANA

May it please your grace, Antipholus, my husband,
Who I made lord of me and all I had
At your important letters – this ill day,
A most outrageous fit of madness took him,
That desp'rately he hurried through the street,   140
With him his bondman, all as mad as he,
Doing displeasure to the citizens
By rushing in their houses, bearing thence
Rings, jewels, anything his rage did like.
Once did I get him bound and sent him home,   145
Whilst to take order for the wrongs I went,
That here and there his fury had committed.
Anon, I wot not by what strong escape,
He broke from those that had the guard of him,
And with his mad attendant and himself,   150

---

136 **May it** perhaps contracted: 'May't'
   your grace See 116 and n.
137–8 Cf. 198 for a slightly different version
   of the marriage arrangements; according to
   each, however, the Duke took a hand in the
   nuptials, as he confirms at 161–4. See also
   3.2.3 and n.
137 **Who** whom; common in Shakespeare (see
   Abbott, 274)
138 **important** importunate, urgent (*OED adj.*
   3); cf. *MA* 2.1.71, *Ham* 3.4.108.
   ill unlucky, unpropitious (*OED adj.* 5)
139–40 Cf. 80–1 and n.
139 **fit** See 'fits', 85, and 85–6n.
140–4 Adriana has accepted the fabricated
   story from the Courtesan that Antipholus
   broke into her house and snatched away
   her ring (4.3.93–6). She even enlarges
   upon the falsehood with the report of
   Antipholus' committing public outrage.
140 **That** so that; 'so' before 'that' is frequently
   omitted in Shakespeare (Abbott, 283).
   desp'rately with reckless violence (Ard²),

with a hint of 'despair' (*OED adv.* 1); cf.
80 and 80–1n.
141 **bondman** slave (*OED n.* 2); cf. 'To make
   a bondmaid and a slave of me' (*TS* 2.1.2);
   see 288–91 and n.; cf. 4.1.13n.
142 **displeasure** See 4.4.117n.
144 **Rings** The Courtesan's ring has multiplied
   into *Rings* in general. On the ring, see
   4.1.13.1n.
   rage Antipholus' presumed madness
   personified, as with *fury* at 147; on *rage*,
   see 4.3.88n.
146 **take order for** make arrangements for
   settling (Ard²) (see *OED order n.* 14a)
148 **Anon** See 119n.
   wot know; first-person present indicative
   of 'wit' (see *OED v.* 1)
   strong performed with muscular strength
   (*OED adj.* 1d)
150 **with . . . himself** Because 'with himself'
   sounds redundant, the text is sometimes
   emended. But Adriana's locution reflects
   the spontaneity of rushed, emotional speech,
   as does her grammar elsewhere in these lines.

---

150 with] here *Capell;* then *Hudson² (Ritson, per Steevens⁴)*   and] mad *Hanmer*

Each one with ireful passion, with drawn swords,
Met us again and, madly bent on us,
Chased us away; till, raising of more aid,
We came again to bind them. Then they fled
Into this abbey, whither we pursued them, 155
And here the Abbess shuts the gates on us,
And will not suffer us to fetch him out,
Nor send him forth, that we may bear him hence.
Therefore, most gracious Duke, with thy command,
Let him be brought forth and borne hence for help. 160
DUKE [*Raises Adriana.*]
Long since, thy husband served me in my wars,
And I to thee engaged a prince's word,
When thou didst make him master of thy bed,
To do him all the grace and good I could.
– Go, some of you, knock at the abbey gate 165
And bid the Lady Abbess come to me;
I will determine this before I stir.

Enter a Messenger.

[MESSENGER]
O, mistress, mistress, shift and save yourself!

---

151 **drawn swords** See 4.4.144.2 and n.
152 **bent on** headed towards (*OED* bent *adj.* 4), perhaps also connoting 'determined' (*OED* 3). The word *bent* functions as a participial adjective, i.e. 'being madly bent on us'; the phrase creates a moment of suspension before the climactic *Chased us away* (153).
153 **of** typically used after a participle (Abbott, 178)
156 **gates** doors; see 2.2.212 and n.
157 **suffer** allow (*OED v.* 13a)
158 **bear** See 35n.
161 SD If Adriana kneels at 133 (see 129), then the Duke might reasonably raise her here.
161 **wars** perhaps including that with Syracuse; see 1.1.11–12; cf. 192.

163 emphasizing Adriana's choosing of her marriage partner; cf. 198 and n.; also 3.2.3 and n.
165 **Go ... you** Neither F nor subsequent editions inserts a SD pursuant to this command, presumably because the entrance of the Messenger forestalls any action. At 281, the Duke again orders the Abbess called forth.
167 The Duke suspends the execution march to resolve the domestic dispute: private 'errors' now conclusively invade, disrupt and alter Ephesus's public proceedings.
168 **shift** depart (*OED v.* 22a), escape (Wells); cf. *Luc* 1104.

161 SD] *Oxf* 168 SP] *F2 (Mess.); not in F*

My master and his man are both broke loose,
Beaten the maids a-row and bound the doctor,   170
Whose beard they have singed off with brands
   of fire,
And ever as it blazed, they threw on him
Great pails of puddled mire to quench the hair.
My master preaches patience to him, and the while
His man with scissors nicks him like a fool;   175
And sure, unless you send some present help,
Between them they will kill the conjuror.

ADRIANA

Peace, fool; thy master and his man are here,
And that is false thou dost report to us.

MESSENGER

Mistress, upon my life, I tell you true;   180
I have not breathed almost since I did see it.
He cries for you and vows, if he can take you,

---

169 **are** In the perfect tense, the auxiliary verb *are* was used with intransitive verbs (Blake 3.3.7.1); it stands in for *have* with *Beaten* and *bound* in 170; cf. 388.
170–3 For possible allusions, see LN.
170 **a-row** in a row (Abbott, 24)
171 **brands** torches, probably of wood from a fireplace (*OED n.* 2); see 183 and n.
173 **puddled mire** filthy, muddy water; urine (*OED* puddle *n.* 1a, b); household sewage. Although *OED* records 'puddle' as urine first in 1649, Shakespeare employs it elsewhere, e.g. *AC* 1.4.62; see also *2H6* 4.1.71.
174 An alexandrine (unless some syllables are elided, as in Ard²); cf. 208 and n. Compositor B's abbreviation of master as *Mʳ* (he spells it out fully at 178) suggests that he was making room for the line's unusual length (Oxf¹).

patience Impatient Antipholus (e.g. 4.4.18–19) sarcastically preaches patience (Ard²); cf. 87–8 and n., 102; on patience and impatience, see 1.2.86n.
175 **nicks . . . fool** suggesting with *nicks* a patchy, indiscriminate clipping that leaves notches (*OED v.²* 1a). Such nicking might create the effect of the fool's coxcomb (Folg²). Simon Robson's *The Choice of Change* (1585) refers to monks being '*shaven* and *notched* on the head, like *fooles*' (sig. K1ᵛ) (Boswell–Malone, quoted from *Var.*). Alternatively, *nicks* might suggest that Pinch's hair, in places, was left as close-cropped as that of a court jester or professional fool (Steevens²).
176 **present** instant, immediate (*OED adj.* 9a)
177 **conjuror** See 243, 4.4.40.2n.
178, 188 **here** probably spoken with a gesture towards the abbey; also at 258, 264, 272, 279

---

171 singed] *(*sindg'd*)*   174 to him] *om. Capell*   and the] *the Hanmer; om. Steevens⁴ (Heath)*
175 scissors] *(*Cizers*)*   180 SP] *(*Mess.*)*

283

To scorch your face and to disfigure you.
 Cry within
Hark, hark! I hear him, mistress; fly, be gone!

DUKE

Come, stand by me. Fear nothing. – Guard with
  halberds!   185

Enter ANTIPHOLUS [OF EPHESUS, *wearing the ring,*]
        and DROMIO OF EPHESUS.

ADRIANA

Ay me, it is my husband! Witness you
That he is borne about invisible:
Even now we housed him in the abbey here,
And now he's there, past thought of human reason.

---

183 **scorch** burn, recalling 'singed off with
brands of fire' (171); see also e.g. *MW*
1.3.67. The word may pun on *scorch* as
'slash' (*OED v.*³) (cf. *Mac* 3.2.13), fulfilling Adriana's fearful imaginings at
2.2.142. Antipholus is conceived as a
demon loosed from hell ('a dark and
dankish vault', 248) and advancing with
hell-fire. Syracusan Antipholus had earlier
questioned whether he was 'in heaven or
in hell' (2.2.218); his brother now emerges
figuratively from the latter. Ephesian
Antipholus had looked *fiery* at 4.4.51. Hell
references abound in *CE*: e.g. prison as
hell (4.2.40); the Officer as a *devil* and
fiend (4.2.33, 35); the Courtesan as *devil*
(4.3.51). In Plautus' *Men.*, the itinerant
Menaechmus threatens to burn out his
brother's wife's eyes with torches (see
4.4.105n.).
183 SD On *within*, see 3.1.32 SD and n.
185 **Guard with halberds!** The Duke's
soldiers probably gather defensively

around him. A halberd resembles a spear
with a battle-axe head (*OED n.* 1).
185.1–2 *This entrance SD occurs in F after
189. Yet Adriana's speech, 186–9 ('it is
my husband! Witness you . . . there'),
suggests that Ephesian Antipholus stands
before her eyes. A pause by Antipholus
upon entering would heighten tension.
Collier³ places the entrance after 188. See
2.1.42.1 LN. On the '*ring*', see 4.1.13.1n.
186–9 Adriana is now fully absorbed into the
experience of Ephesus as the place of
magic that the Syracusans had feared (see
e.g. 1.2.97–102) (Ard²).
187 **borne about** carried around (as if by
demons); Adriana, who had wanted to
bear Antipholus hence (35, 41, 158), now
sees him *borne*.
188 **housed** pursued him into the house (*OED
v.*¹ 1c); also at 272.
189, 197 **there** taking on a deictic function like
that of *here* (cf. 178, and 178, 188n.; 276;
413)

---

183 scorch] scotch *Hanmer*   185.1–2] *Cam¹ subst.; after 189 F; after 188 Collier³*   185.1 OF EPHESUS]
F3 subst.   wearing the ring] *this edn*   185.2 DROMIO OF EPHESUS] *E. Dromio of Ephesus F*

ANTIPHOLUS OF EPHESUS

Justice, most gracious Duke! O, grant me justice,   190
Even for the service that long since I did thee,
When I bestrid thee in the wars and took
Deep scars to save thy life; even for the blood
That then I lost for thee, now grant me justice!

EGEON [*aside*]

Unless the fear of death doth make me dote,   195
I see my son Antipholus and Dromio.

ANTIPHOLUS OF EPHESUS

Justice, sweet prince, against that woman there:
She whom thou gav'st to me to be my wife,
That hath abused and dishonoured me,
Even in the strength and height of injury;   200
Beyond imagination is the wrong
That she this day hath shameless thrown on me.

DUKE

Discover how, and thou shalt find me just.

ANTIPHOLUS OF EPHESUS

This day, great Duke, she shut the doors upon me

190 Cf. 133, 197; also 4.1.83 and n.
192 **bestrid . . . wars** i.e. stood over you when you were down in battle; cf. *1H4* 5.1.121–2.
    wars Cf. 161.
195–6 In F, Egeon's SP starts as *Mar.Fat.*, for 'Merchant Father', but then turns exclusively into forms of *Father* (*Fa.*; *Fath.*; *Father.*; *Fat.*), as if Shakespeare were now thinking of him less in his mercantile and more in his paternal role (see List or Roles, 1n.; and Appendix 2, p. 338). Since no one responds to Egeon's claim and since Antipholus simply continues his plea, the father may speak in an aside (although why he would do so is unclear). These lines are prose in F;

perhaps because F's SP, *Mar.Fat.*, pushed out 195, the compositor lacked room to fit in *dote* (Ard²).
195 **dote** be deranged (*OED v.*[1] 1); also at 329
197 Cf. 133, 190; on *there*, see 189, 197n.
198 emphasizing the Duke's authority over whom Adriana married; cf. 163.
199 **abused** abusèd
200 **in . . . height** 'to the greatest degree possible'
202 **shameless** shamelessly. Shakespeare freely uses adjectives as adverbs (Abbott, 1).
    thrown Following *abused* (199), *strength and height* (200) and *Beyond imagination* (201), *thrown* completes a hyperbolic attribution of malicious power to Adriana.
203 **Discover** reveal (*OED v.* 3a)

190+ SP] (*E.Ant., E.Anti., Ant., E. Ant., E.An.*) 190 justice,] justice, *Kneeling.* / *Collier*[4] 195+ SP] *Capell (Rowe subst.); Mar.Fat., Fa., Fath., Father., Fat.* F SD] *Boswell–Malone* 195–6] *Rowe*[3]; *prose* F

285

While she with harlots feasted in my house. 205

DUKE

A grievous fault. – Say, woman, didst thou so?

ADRIANA

No, my good lord. Myself, he and my sister
Today did dine together; so befall my soul
As this is false he burdens me withal.

LUCIANA

Ne'er may I look on day nor sleep on night 210
But she tells to your highness simple truth.

ANGELO

O perjured woman! They are both forsworn:
In this the madman justly chargeth them.

ANTIPHOLUS OF EPHESUS

My liege, I am advised what I say,
Neither disturbed with the effect of wine, 215
Nor heady-rash, provoked with raging ire,
Albeit my wrongs might make one wiser mad.
This woman locked me out this day from dinner;

---

205 **harlots** men of loose morals, fornicators (*OED n.* 1), a unisex insult although frequently applied to women; cf. *R3* 3.4.71, *RJ* 2.4.42. Adriana had imagined having a *harlot brow* (2.2.142 and n.), and Antipholus had previously called her a *harlot* (4.4.102).
feasted perhaps connoting 'banqueted sexually' (Williams, *Glossary*, 122). Antipholus accuses Adriana of the kind of offence that she suspected of him, e.g. at 2.1.30.

208 the second alexandrine in the scene (see 174 and n.), perhaps adding weight to Adriana's asseveration

208–9 **so ... false** 'May the fate of my soul depend on the falsehood of these accusations.' The *so* clause states the result, the *As* clause the condition (cf. *R3* 2.2.10).

209 **this ... withal** Adriana's formulation will be repeated by Antipholus at 269; *withal* = with.

210 **on** at (see Blake, 5.4.2)

211 **But she tells** 'if she does not tell'

212–13 Some editions make Angelo's lines an aside, since he does not pursue his assertion until 255, yet the speech seems too vehement and interjectory for an aside. Angelo has no reason here to withhold his claim, and Antipholus immediately responds to the accusation of madness (214–17); but see 219–20n.

214 **advised** advisèd; heedful of (Folg²); cf. e.g. *MV* 1.1.142.

216 **heady-rash** impetuously rash (*OED* heady *adj*. 1; first citation of compound); the phrase is redundant and used for rhetorical effect.

212 O] *Aside* O *Ard²*

286

That goldsmith there, were he not packed with her,
Could witness it, for he was with me then,   220
Who parted with me to go fetch a chain,
Promising to bring it to the Porpentine,
Where Balthazar and I did dine together.
Our dinner done, and he not coming thither,
I went to seek him. In the street I met him,   225
And in his company that gentleman.

    [*Indicates Second Merchant.*]

There did this perjured goldsmith swear me down
That I this day of him received the chain,
Which, God he knows, I saw not. For the which
He did arrest me with an officer.   230
I did obey, and sent my peasant home
For certain ducats; he with none returned.
Then fairly I bespoke the officer
To go in person with me to my house.
By th' way, we met   235
My wife, her sister and a rabble more
Of vile confederates; along with them

219–20 Antipholus charged previously that Adriana suborned Angelo to have him arrested (4.4.83), as if Angelo were a conspirator, an idea now lodged in Antipholus' mind. He appears oblivious to Angelo's corroborating claim at 212–13.

219 **there** See 189, 197n.
   packed with in league with (*OED* pack *v.*[2] 1b); see 4.4.103 and n., on *pack*.

221 **parted with** departed from (*OED* part *v.* 1b)

222 **Promising** perhaps pronounced 'prom'sing' (Walker, *Versification*, 66)

227 **swear me down** 'swear emphatically, as if to silence me by his vehemence' (Oxf[1]). Cf. *face me down*, 3.1.6; 245 and n., on *out-facing*.

230 **with** through the agency of (*OED prep.* 37a)

231 **peasant** See 2.1.80 and n.

233 **bespoke** asked (*OED* bespeak *v.* 5c, first citation)

235–6 constituting one line in F, but so atypically long (heptameter) that editors have conjectured that some words were dropped so that the original two lines could be compressed to save space in typesetting. Treating *By . . . met* as a single line makes sense on the grounds that the play elsewhere employs short lines, e.g. 61. The typesetting in F, 'By'th'way', suggests contraction and iambic metre; cf. *KL* 4.1.43.

237 **confederates** See 4.1.17 and n.

226 SD] *Bevington*[4] *subst.* 235–7] *Malone; F lines* more / them / *; Capell lines* [To which he yielded:] by the way we met / more / them / *; Steevens lines* and / confederates; / them / 235 By] *Rowe;* By' *F*

They brought one Pinch, a hungry, lean-faced villain,
A mere anatomy, a mountebank,
A threadbare juggler and a fortune-teller,   240
A needy, hollow-eyed, sharp-looking wretch,
A living dead man. This pernicious slave,
Forsooth, took on him as a conjuror,
And gazing in mine eyes, feeling my pulse
And with no-face, as 'twere, out-facing me,   245
Cries out, I was 'possessed'. Then all together
They fell upon me, bound me, bore me thence,
And in a dark and dankish vault at home
There left me and my man, both bound together,
Till, gnawing with my teeth my bonds in sunder,   250
I gained my freedom, and immediately
Ran hither to your grace, whom I beseech

238–42 This description's sordidness and excess evokes Pinch's uncanny grip on Antipholus' imagination. Syracusan Antipholus' fear of demonic possession seems registered now in the Ephesian brother. The repetition of the same idea in many figures is rhetorical *exergasia.* Pinch's depiction may be an exaggerated description of his actor, John Sinkler. Sinkler, strikingly thin and pale, probably played similar roles in Shakespeare, such as Starveling in *MND,* Slender and a beadle in *2H4* and the Apothecary in *RJ* (see *RJ* 5.1.37–54), along with parts in *3H6* and *TS,* and related ones in other non-Shakespearean plays (Gurr, *Company,* 241). See p. 103, and Appendix 3, pp. 52–3.

239 **anatomy** walking skeleton (*OED n.* 6a, first citation)
    mountebank See 1.2.101 and n., on *mountebanks.*

240 **juggler** See 1.2.98 and n. Antipholus' terms (*mountebank,* 239; *juggler, fortune-teller,* 240; *conjuror,* 243; cf. also *wizard,* 4.4.59) recall his brother's apprehensive

speech about tricksters and sorcerers in Ephesus, 1.2.97–102. See also 4.4.40.2n.

241 **sharp-looking** hungry-looking (*OED* sharp *adj.* 4f); narrow-faced, emaciated (*OED* 10e, f; *OED* C3 notes this as the compound's first citation)

242 **pernicious** wicked (*OED adj.* 2b); perhaps also evil, harmful (*OED* 2a)
    slave See 1.2.87 and n., on *slave.*

243 **took . . . as** assumed the part of (*OED* take *v.* 16a)
    conjuror See 177, 4.4.40.2n.

244 **gazing** also at 53; see 1.1.88n., on *gazing.*

245 **no-face** because so *lean-faced* (238)
    out-facing maintaining with boldness or impudence (*OED v.* 3c); cf. *face me down,* 3.1.6 and n.; also 227 and n.

246 **'possessed'** See 2.2.146n., on *I . . . with.*

247–9 recalling 4.4.95 (see n., on *bound . . . room*)

247 **bore** Cf. 2.1.72 and n.

249, 250 **bound, bonds** See 4.1.13n.

250 **in sunder** asunder, apart (*OED* sunder *adv.*)

251–2 **immediately . . . grace** Antipholus omits his beating of the maids and tormenting of Pinch; see 170–7.

246 'possessed'] *this edn;* possest F   all together] *Rowe;* altogether *F*

To give me ample satisfaction
For these deep shames and great indignities.

ANGELO

My lord, in truth, thus far I witness with him: 255
That he dined not at home, but was locked out.

DUKE

But had he such a chain of thee, or no?

ANGELO

He had, my lord, and when he ran in here
These people saw the chain about his neck.

2 MERCHANT [*to Antipholus*]

Besides, I will be sworn these ears of mine   260
Heard you confess you had the chain of him,
After you first forswore it on the mart,
And thereupon I drew my sword on you;
And then you fled into this abbey here,
From whence, I think, you are come by miracle.   265

ANTIPHOLUS OF EPHESUS

[*to Second Merchant*] I never came within these
     abbey walls,
Nor ever didst thou draw thy sword on me;
[*to Angelo*] I never saw the chain, so help me heaven,
[*to Adriana*] And this is false you burden me withal.

DUKE

Why, what an intricate impeach is this!   270

253 **satisfaction** redress; see 4.1.5n., on *satisfaction*.
254 **shames** Cf. 2.1.112 and n.
258, 264 **here** See 178, 188n.
262 **mart** See 4.1n.
263 See 32 SD and n.; the Second Merchant implies that he drew first.
265 **you are** perhaps pronounced 'y'are' (Pope)
266–9 Antipholus responds to his accusers successively, first to the Second Merchant, addressed disdainfully as *thou* (267). With

his second *I never*, he turns to Angelo, his antagonist regarding the chain; his 'I never saw the chain' (268) repudiates Angelo's 'These people saw the chain' (259). Finally, he confronts Adriana, repeating (269) her reply to him at 209, perhaps as sarcasm, perhaps as unconscious linguistic transfer or 'sympathy' (see 397n., on *sympathized*).
269 **withal** See 209n.
270 **impeach** accusation; calling into question (*OED n.* 3)

260 SD] *Wells subst.*   266, 268, 269, 273 SDs] *this edn*

289

I think you all have drunk of Circe's cup:
[*to Second Merchant*] If here you housed him, here
    he would have been;
[*to Adriana*] If he were mad, he would not plead so
    coldly;
[*to Luciana*] You say he dined at home; the
    goldsmith here
Denies that saying. [*to Dromio*] Sirrah, what
    say you?   275

DROMIO OF EPHESUS [*Points to the Courtesan.*]
Sir, he dined with her there, at the Porpentine.

COURTESAN
He did, and from my finger snatched that ring.

ANTIPHOLUS OF EPHESUS
'Tis true, my liege, this ring I had of her.

DUKE [*to Courtesan*]
Saw'st thou him enter at the abbey here?

COURTESAN
As sure, my liege, as I do see your grace.   280

271–5 Imitating Antipholus (266–9) and demonstrating the *intricate impeach* (270), the Duke addresses different participants in turn. He responds first to the Second Merchant (272), the character who most recently had mentioned Antipholus' disappearance into the abbey. At 273, he reproves Adriana, who in particular had asserted Antipholus' madness (e.g. at 141). Next he challenges Luciana (274–5), the corroborator (at 210–11) of Adriana's claim (207–8) that Antipholus had *dined at home*. He completes the circuit with Dromio, *Sirrah* (275).

271 **drunk … cup** making them as irrational as animals (recalling the theme of bestial metamorphosis (e.g. 2.2.201–8; see 2.2.206n.,

on *'Tis true*; see also 24–5, 42)). Homer's enchantress *Circe* (*Od.*, 10) drugs Odysseus' men and turns their bodies into swine. The Duke implies, however, that *CE*'s characters are altered in mind and not in body. In the Renaissance, Circean enchantment commonly stood for 'the loss of reason', with *Circe* as the archetype of the witch (Roberts, 'Circe', 199). Cf. *1H6* 5.3.35.

272, 279 **here** See 178, 188n.

272 **housed** See 188 and n.

273 **coldly** calmly (*OED adv.* 2a); rationally (Crystal & Crystal, *adv.* 1)

276 **there** Dromio probably refers deictically to Adriana; see 189, 197n.

277, 278 **ring** See 4.1.13.1n.

272 SD] *this edn (Andrews subst.)*   274, 275 SDs] *this edn (Capell subst.)*   276 SD] *Oxf subst.*   her there,] her, there, *Collier*   277+ SP] *(Cur., Curt.)*   279 SD] *Oxf*

DUKE

Why, this is strange: – Go call the Abbess hither.
– I think you are all mated, or stark mad.

Exit one to the Abbess.

EGEON

Most mighty Duke, vouchsafe me speak a word;
Haply I see a friend will save my life
And pay the sum that may deliver me.   285

DUKE

Speak freely, Syracusan, what thou wilt.

EGEON [*to Antipholus*]

Is not your name, sir, called Antipholus?
And is not that your bondman Dromio?

DROMIO OF EPHESUS

Within this hour I was his bondman, sir,
But he, I thank him, gnawed in two my cords: 290
Now am I Dromio, and his man, unbound.

EGEON

I am sure you both of you remember me.

DROMIO OF EPHESUS

Ourselves we do remember, sir, by you,
For lately we were bound as you are now.

281 **Go . . . hither** the Duke's second command to call for the Abbess; see 165–6, and 165n.

282 **mated** bewildered, amazed (*OED adj.*[1] 1); cf. 3.2.54 and n.

   stark mad Cf. 2.1.57 and n. The distinction between *mated* and *stark mad* is presumably that between a temporary and a semi-permanent condition.

284 **Haply** See 60n.; evoking the *hap*-words of 1.1; see 1.1.37n.

   friend kinsman, relative (*OED n.* 3), recalling *friends* at 1.1.152; cf. *TGV* 3.1.106, *AYL* 1.3.62.

288–91 **bondman . . . unbound** Although a *bondman* is a slave (*OED n.* 2; see 141 and

n.), Dromio puns on his being recently tied up (bound) and now loosed. This passage may recall Plautus' *Men.* (1146–8), where the slave Messenio is released from slavery by Sosicles Menaechmus as recompense for unravelling the play's confusions (cf. 294, 305). On *bound*, see 1.1.81 and n.; on *bond*, see 4.1.13n.

288 **Dromio** pronounced here as three syllables

292 **I am** perhaps pronounced 'I'm'

294 referring to Dromio and Antipholus' rope-binding by Pinch and his men (see 4.4.107–14), but also alluding to the play's larger knot of errors; Egeon entered *bound* at 127.1–2. On knots of errors, see pp. 10, 12–3, 28, 85.

286 Syracusan] *F2; Siracusian F*   287 SD] *Oxf*   292 sure you] sure *F2*

You are not Pinch's patient, are you, sir?   295
EGEON [*to Antipholus*]
Why look you strange on me? You know me well.
ANTIPHOLUS OF EPHESUS
I never saw you in my life till now.
EGEON
O, grief hath changed me since you saw me last,
And careful hours with Time's deformed hand
Have written strange defeatures in my face.   300
But tell me yet, dost thou not know my voice?
ANTIPHOLUS OF EPHESUS
Neither.
EGEON   Dromio, nor thou?
DROMIO OF EPHESUS
No, trust me, sir, nor I.
EGEON   I am sure thou dost!
DROMIO OF EPHESUS   Ay, sir, but I am sure I do not, and
whatsoever a man denies, you are now bound to   305
believe him.

---

295 **Pinch's patient** perhaps a theatrical
in-joke if Egeon and Pinch were played by
the same actor; see Appendix 3, pp. 352–3.
For another possible allusion to Pinch, see
337 and n., on *ghost*.
296 **look you strange** See 2.2.116n.
299 **careful** full of care
Time's deformed hand deformèd (at
4.2.19; see n.); *Time's hand* is both
deformed in itself and deforming of others;
the word *deformed* probably signifies old
age. See LN. Syracusan Antipholus had
feared the power of witches to 'deform the
body' (1.2.100). On Father Time, see
2.2.72 and n.
300 **strange** alien; not of one's own family
(*OED adj.* 1a, 3)

defeatures disfigurements, here with the
sense of ruins; cf. 2.1.97 and n., on
defeatures. The *defeatures* are wrinkle-
lines   metaphorically   *written*   by
Time's . . . hand.
302–3 Steevens first treated these lines as
shared. The lines printed here as 302
constitute a six-syllable verse line, and
those printed as 303 constitute an iambic
pentameter line (with *I am* elided, 'I'm').
302 **Neither** i.e. neither face nor voice; an
emphatic 'no'; see 94n., on *Neither*.
305 **bound** a pun: both trussed and obliged (cf.
294), the latter suggesting that a restrained
prisoner is in no position to exact a
different answer. On *bound*, see 1.1.81n.

---

296 SD] *Folg² subst.*   299 Time's] *Malone*; times *F*   302–3] *verse as Steevens⁴; Dyce lines* thou? /
I. / dost. /   304–5] *Hanmer lines* whatsoever / him. / (I sir *om.); Capell lines* sir, / whatsoever / him. /
304 Ay, sir,] (I sir); I, Sir? *Pope*

EGEON

Not know my voice! – O Time's extremity,
Hast thou so cracked and splitted my poor tongue
In seven short years that here my only son
Knows not my feeble key of untuned cares?   310
Though now this grained face of mine be hid
In sap-consuming winter's drizzled snow,
And all the conduits of my blood froze up,
Yet hath my night of life some memory,
My wasting lamps some fading glimmer left,   315
My dull deaf ears a little use to hear;
All these old witnesses – I cannot err –
Tell me thou art my son Antipholus.

307–18 Egeon's vivid detailing of the *defeatures* that he has suffered from age prepares the audience for the rebirth that he will experience through reunion with his family (Oxf[1]).

307 **extremity** extreme severity, rigour (*OED n.* 6)

308 **splitted** recurring here from the shipwreck story of 1.1; see 1.1.103n., on *splitted*. As before, *splitted* divides the line metrically.

309 **seven** Egeon claimed to have searched after his son for *Five summers* (1.1.132). Perhaps *seven* encompasses two years after Antipholus' departure but before Egeon's (see 320) (Oxf[1]); see also 400n., on *Thirty-three years*. In Shakespeare, *seven* often stands for an indefinite length of time (Dent, Y25).

310 i.e. does not know my voice, made weak and discordant from my woes. With its alliterations and assonances, the line is harmonic despite Egeon's claim. His *key* refers to a system of musical notes comprising a scale; *untuned* means 'not melodious' (*OED adj.* 1a); cf. *Luc* 1214, *R2* 1.3.134. The application of *untuned* to Egeon's *cares* (the agent) rather than his voice (the object) creates another

transferred epithet or rhetorical *hypallage* (see 5.1.299 LN). The line-ending *cares* recalls Egeon's language in 1.1: *woes* (1.1.2, 27), *griefs* (32) and various forms of *care* (see 1.1.42n., on *care*); see also 299 above.

311 **grained** grainèd; furrowed or lined like the markings of wood (*OED adj.*[1] 4), i.e. wrinkled; cf. *Cor* 4.5.108. See 3.2.107 and n.

312 'in my white beard and hair, like the snow of winter, the season that dries up the vital sap of plants'; *drizzled* means falling in a fine, spray-like manner (*OED v.* derivatives, first citation).

313 **conduits** channels
    froze frozen; Elizabethans sometimes dropped the *-en* inflection, using the preterite as the past participle (Abbott, 343); cf. *arose* at 388.

315 **wasting lamps** i.e. dimming eyes (*OED lamp n.*[1] 2b, first citation); cf. *1H6* 2.5.8.
    glimmer feeble light (*OED n.*[1] 1, first citation)

317 **I cannot err** This insistence on the integrity of personal observation via the senses marks the end of the outward spiralling of error.

307 Time's] *Staunton;* times *F*

ANTIPHOLUS OF EPHESUS

I never saw my father in my life.

EGEON

But seven years since, in Syracusa, boy,   320
Thou knowst we parted. But perhaps, my son,
Thou sham'st to acknowledge me in misery.

ANTIPHOLUS OF EPHESUS

The Duke and all that know me in the city
Can witness with me that it is not so.
I ne'er saw Syracusa in my life.   325

DUKE

I tell thee, Syracusan, twenty years
Have I been patron to Antipholus,
During which time he ne'er saw Syracusa.
I see thy age and dangers make thee dote.

Enter [Emilia,] *the* ABBESS,
with ANTIPHOLUS [OF SYRACUSE, *wearing the chain,*]
and DROMIO [OF SYRACUSE].

ABBESS

Most mighty Duke, behold a man much wronged.   330
    All gather to see them.

ADRIANA

I see two husbands, or mine eyes deceive me.

---

320 **But** only
    seven years See 309n.
    boy suggesting some impatience (Cam[1]),
    rectified with *my son* (321)
322 an unflattering suggestion, but the pressure
    of shame has been felt throughout *CE*; on
    shame, see 2.1.112n.
    to acknowledge perhaps pronounced
    't'acknowledge'
324 **witness** The witnessing activity of social
    life is brought against the *witnesses* (317)

of the senses.
329 **dote** See 195 and n.; the Duke confirms
    Egeon's fear.
330 SD The Abbess and the Syracusans some-
    times enter unnoticed, so that the surprised
    crowd turns at the Abbess's pronouncement
    and gathers to surround the new threesome.
    The twins are now finally and wondrously
    on stage together. In productions, Egeon is
    sometimes left standing alone.

326 Syracusan] *F2; Siracusian F*   329.1 Emilia] *Ard[2]*   329.2 OF SYRACUSE] *Theobald[3]; Siracusa F*
wearing the chain] *Oxf*   329.3 OF SYRACUSE] *Theobald[3]; Sir. F*

DUKE

One of these men is genius to the other;
And so of these, which is the natural man
And which the spirit? Who deciphers them?

DROMIO OF SYRACUSE

I, sir, am Dromio; command him away.   335

DROMIO OF EPHESUS

I, sir, am Dromio; pray, let me stay.

ANTIPHOLUS OF SYRACUSE

Egeon, art thou not? Or else his ghost.

DROMIO OF SYRACUSE

O my old master! – Who hath bound him here?

ABBESS

Whoever bound him, I will loose his bonds,
And gain a husband by his liberty.   340
    [*Unbinds him.*]
– Speak, old Egeon, if thou be'st the man
That hadst a wife once called Emilia

---

332 **genius** in pagan belief, the 'attendant spirit allotted to every person at his birth, to govern his fortunes and determine his character' and accompany him throughout life (*OED n.* 1a). The Duke takes the *genius* as an exact likeness, a double, capable of becoming visible. F italicizes '*genius*', apparently as a foreign term. It occurs similarly at e.g. *JC* 2.1.66 (see 63–9), *TN* 3.4.129. In Spenser's *FQ*, '*Genius*' is described as an invisible, intuitive 'Selfe' (2.12.47). Warner's translation of *Men.* reads, 'Your ghoast . . . Your Image' (36).

334 **deciphers** discovers (*OED v.* 4), i.e. distinguishes (Wells); cf. *1H6* 4.1.184, *Tit* 4.2.8.

335–6 The mirrored syntax and rhyme emphasize the Dromios' likeness.

337 **Egeon** The reintroduction of the merchant father's name here (see 1.1.140), repeated at 341 and 344, continues his humanizing; see 195–6n.

ghost Egeon looks like a revenant or perhaps a *living dead man*, the term applied to Pinch (242); see 295n.

338, 339 **bound** See 1.1.81n.

339 **bonds** i.e. the ropes that bind him, but also with metaphoric narrative implications (see 340 SDn.). See 4.1.13n., on *bond*, and 1.1.81n., on *bound*.

340 **liberty** See 53; 2.1.7n., on *liberty*; on *liberties*, see 1.2.102 and n.

340 SD The knot of errors is becoming undone (see 294n.).

341–5 The repetition of *Speak/speak* lends an incantatory quality, while the reiterated names call Egeon and the Abbess into being as individuals in the family romance.

---

332 genius] *(genius)*   340 SD] *this edn*   342, 345, 352 Emilia] *Capell; Æmilia F*

That bore thee at a burden two fair sons.
O, if thou be'st the same Egeon, speak,
And speak unto the same Emilia.   345

DUKE

Why, here begins his morning story right:
These two Antipholus', these two so like,
And these two Dromios, one in semblance –
Besides his urging of her wrack at sea –
These are the parents to these children,   350
Which accidentally are met together.

EGEON

If I dream not, thou art Emilia;
If thou art she, tell me, where is that son
That floated with thee on the fatal raft?

ABBESS

By men of Epidamium he and I   355
And the twin Dromio all were taken up;

---

343 **at a burden** at a single birth (Cam[2]); see 1.1.55 and n.; cf. 402 and n., on *burden*. The scene's language is reconnecting to the play's beginning.
fair Cf. *goodly* at 1.1.50.
344–5 **speak,** / **And speak** rhetorical *anadiplosis*
346–51 See LN.
347–8 **These two . . . these two** more phrasal repetition, here rhetorical *conduplicatio*
347 **Antipholus'** i.e. Antipholuses
348, 350 Both lines appear to be tetrameter, unless perhaps *semblance* (348) is read as trisyllabic, i.e. 'sèmbelànce' (Malone), and *children* (350), as 'chìlderèn', after ME childeren (*OED* child *n.*) (White, following Walker, *Versification*, 7). On the extra syllable at medial *r*, see Abbott, 477.
348 **semblance** outward appearance (*OED n.* 4a); the word also carries the sense of apparition (*OED* 4b).

349 ***his urging** *his* for F's probably erroneous 'her', perhaps caused by the compositor's eye looking ahead towards *her* later in the line and then reading it back into the earlier part of the line. While *his urging* recalls the first scene, F's 'her urging' posits a prior conversation that never occurs in the play.
352 **dream not** Cf. 376; also 2.2.188–92 (and see n.), where Syracusan Antipholus enters into the Ephesian dream.
354 **fatal** decreed by fate (*OED adj.* 1)
355–9 A new version of the shipwreck's aftermath. According to Egeon earlier, Emilia and her set of boys were simply 'taken up / By fishermen of Corinth, as we thought' (1.1.110–11). The Abbess's story introduces the information necessary to explain her separation from the boys under her charge (for which Egeon's *as we thought* had left some wiggle-room).

---

343 sons.] *Rann (*sons!*); sonnes? F* 346–51] *after 361 Capell* 346 Why] *aside* Why *Munro* 347 Antipholus'] *Ard[2]; Antipholus F* 349 his] *Collier[2] (Mason); her F* her] their *Hanmer* 355, 359 Epidamium] *Epidamnium / Rowe; Epidamnum / Pope; Epidamnus Oxf[1]*

But, by and by, rude fishermen of Corinth
By force took Dromio and my son from them,
And me they left with those of Epidamium.
What then became of them I cannot tell; 360
I, to this fortune that you see me in.

DUKE [*to Antipholus of Syracuse*]
Antipholus, thou cam'st from Corinth first.

ANTIPHOLUS OF SYRACUSE
No, sir, not I; I came from Syracuse.

DUKE
Stay, stand apart; I know not which is which.

ANTIPHOLUS OF EPHESUS
I came from Corinth, my most gracious lord – 365

DROMIO OF EPHESUS
And I with him.

ANTIPHOLUS OF EPHESUS
– Brought to this town by that most famous warrior,
Duke Menaphon, your most renowned uncle.

ADRIANA
Which of you two did dine with me today?

ANTIPHOLUS OF SYRACUSE
I, gentle mistress.

ADRIANA   And are not you my husband? 370

ANTIPHOLUS OF EPHESUS
No, I say nay to that.

ANTIPHOLUS OF SYRACUSE
And so do I, yet did she call me so;
And this fair gentlewoman, her sister here,

---

357 **rude** uncivilized, barbarous (*OED adj.* 4a), or possibly worse, violent, harsh (*OED* 2); see 1.1.112 and n., on *seized on.*

361 **fortune** besides fate or chance, also condition in life (*OED n.* 5)

368 **Menaphon** an arbitrary name, perhaps recalled from Greene's *Menaphon* (1589),

a pastoral romance involving shipwreck, conflicted love and themes of misrecognition, fortune and time; or possibly from Marlowe's *Tamburlaine* (*c.* 1587).
renowned renownèd

370 **And ... husband** In performance, Adriana's surprise often induces laughter.

362 SD] *Cam¹ subst.*

297

Did call me brother. [*to Luciana*] What I told you
　　then
I hope I shall have leisure to make good,　　　　　　375
If this be not a dream I see and hear.

ANGELO

That is the chain, sir, which you had of me.

ANTIPHOLUS OF SYRACUSE

I think it be, sir; I deny it not.

ANTIPHOLUS OF EPHESUS [*to Angelo*]

And you, sir, for this chain arrested me.

ANGELO

I think I did, sir; I deny it not.　　　　　　　　　380

ADRIANA [*to Antipholus of Ephesus*]

I sent you money, sir, to be your bail,
By Dromio, but I think he brought it not.

DROMIO OF EPHESUS

No, none by me.

ANTIPHOLUS OF SYRACUSE [*Shows the purse to Adriana.*]

This purse of ducats I received from you,
And Dromio my man did bring them me.　　　　　　385
– I see we still did meet each other's man,
And I was ta'en for him, and he for me,
And thereupon these errors are arose.

---

374 **What . . . then** referring to 3.2.29–69

376 Antipholus conditionally invokes the witness of sight and sound, as if just coming out of the dream he entered in 2.2 (see e.g. 2.2.188–9); see 352n. above. Cf. *TGV* 5.4.26, *MND* 4.1.192–4 (Ard²).

377–81 **sir** The medial repetition (rhetorical *mesodiplosis*) restores decorum to frayed relationships.

377–9 **That . . . this** The change in pronouns hints that the chain may be handed from Syracusan Antipholus to Angelo to

Ephesian Antipholus (Dawson, 141). Who finally departs with it is left unclear.

378 **be** may be (Wells); see Abbott, 298.

378, 380 **deny** The repetition of *deny* here evokes and closes the circle of earlier accusations and denials about the chain; see 3n., on *deny*.

386 **still** See 2.1.11n., on *still*.

387 **ta'en** See 3.2.172 and n., on *ta'en*.

388 **errors** another closing of the circle; see 2.2.190 and n.
　　are See 169n.
　　arose arisen; see 313n., on *froze*.

---

374 SD] *Capell subst.*　　379 SD] *Folg² subst.*　　381 SD] *Wells*　　384 SD] *Capell subst.*　　387 ta'en] *(tane)*

ANTIPHOLUS OF EPHESUS [*to the Duke*]
These ducats pawn I for my father here.

DUKE
It shall not need: thy father hath his life.   390

COURTESAN [*to Antipholus of Ephesus*]
Sir, I must have that diamond from you.

ANTIPHOLUS OF EPHESUS [*Gives the ring.*]
There, take it, and much thanks for my good cheer.

ABBESS
Renowned Duke, vouchsafe to take the pains
To go with us into the abbey here
And hear at large discoursed all our fortunes;   395
– And all that are assembled in this place,
That by this sympathized one-day's error

---

389 This offer of ransom money from one son fulfils the dramatic possibility begun at 1.2.8 (see n.) with the mention of the purse of money belonging to the other son; expectations are fulfilled although not exactly in the way that might have been predicted.

390 The Duke's pardon reveals him to be not strictly bound by Ephesian laws, despite his earlier claim to the contrary; see 1.1.4, 5–10 and n., 142–5 and n. Instead, the laws of romance fiction now apply. Although the Abbess earlier released Egeon's bonds (339–40), his liberty is not established until the Duke frees him, which he does after the money is offered.

391 **that diamond** her ring. On the ring, see 4.1.13.1n.

392 SD *ring* See 4.1.13.1n.

392 **much . . . cheer** 'a termination of a relationship, a salacious reminiscence, or a genuine expression of gratitude' (Maguire, 369)

393 **Renowned** renownèd; the first in a series of past tense verbs with noticeably syllabified endings (*-èd*; see 395n., on *discoursed*; 397n.; 402n., on *delivered*), plus an elongated *-ion* (see 399n.), whose

effect is to poeticize and elevate the language and the action

395 **at large** at liberty, without restraint (*OED* large Phrases 5a)
discoursed discoursèd; see 393n.

397 **sympathized** sympathizèd; see 393n. 'Compounded of corresponding parts' (*OED adj.* a, citing only this line); shared by all (Wells); cf. *LLL* 3.1.51. But such definitions miss the word's strong connotations of mysterious agency. The *OED* defines 'sympathy' as 'affinity between certain things' that allows them to be 'similarly or correspondingly affected by the same influence' (*OED n.* 1a). That and related definitions (see *OED* 2, 3a) emphasize a 'mystical affinity leading to a correspondence of experience' (van Elk, 'Genre', 70); cf. *Luc* 1112–13. 'Sympathy' in Elizabethan texts has a strong connection with magic and denotes a capacity to work long-distance magical effects on a person by performing actions on an object associated with that person, as alluded to by Syracusan Dromio at 4.3.73–6 (see n.). Sympathetic magic, with its sense of correspondences, recalls the way that

---

389 SD] *Folg²; offering money / Bevington⁴*   391 SD] *Folg²*   392 SD] *Capell subst.*

Have suffered wrong, go, keep us company,
And we shall make full satisfaction.
– Thirty-three years have I but gone in travail　　　400
Of you, my sons, and till this present hour
My heavy burden ne'er delivered.
– The Duke, my husband and my children both,
And you, the calendars of their nativity,
Go to a gossips' feast, and go with me;　　　405

feelings expressed by one character become manifested in the experiences of an associated character. See pp. 13–14, 30, 64.

error Cf. 2.2.190 and n.

399 **satisfaction** with *-ion* pronounced as two syllables; see 393n. As the play draws to a close, *satisfaction*, or compensation (see *OED n.* 1a) for *wrong* (398), will come in the form of narrative.

400 **Thirty-three years** The elapsed years previously mentioned, *eighteen* (1.1.125) and *seven* (see 309 and n.), add up to only 25 (Theobald). Shakespearean plays often lack arithmetic exactitude. Because of the scene's Christian resonances (e.g. *nativity*, 404, 406), *thirty-three years* may recall Christ's lifespan (see Kinney, 'Kinds', 32), yet such specificity of reference squares awkwardly with what is otherwise a quality of suggestiveness.

travail labour, as in childbirth (*OED n.*[1] 4); F's 'trauaile' is rendered here as *travail*, but see 1.2.15n., on *travel*. Both senses, *travail* and 'travel', may be in play.

402 **burden** an image of childbirth; see 343 and n., on *at a burden*; 400 and n., on *travail*.

*ne'er** Dyce's *ne'er*, instead of F's 'are', has been almost universally accepted. F's 'are' is incompatible with the futurity of *till* (401) and disagrees with *burden*. Dyce's simple emendation also keeps the

idea of deliverance in suspense until the Abbess's final lines.

delivered deliverèd; see 393n.

404 **calendars** i.e. the Dromios. Cf. *almanac* at 1.2.41 (see n.).

404, 406 **nativity . . . nativity** F's repetition of *nativity* has seemed to many a compositorial error, reducing the impact of each occurrence. Editors sometimes emend the second *nativity* to 'festivity' or 'felicity'. Another suggestion is to change the first *nativity* to 'maturity' on the hypothesis that *nativity* was inadvertently transposed from 406 into 404, although 'maturity' problematically shifts focus away from birth. F's repetition of *nativity* makes sense, since the first instance refers to the actual birth, the second to the metaphorical rebirth of the Abbess's children (see 343 and n.). The dual instances of *nativity* could have been differentiated in sound, with *-vity* at 404 foreshortened to *-v'ty* (Walker, *Versification*, 201), maintaining the pentameter, but then accorded its full and climactic syllabification at 406, *-ivity*; repetition-with-variation is a characteristic strategy of *CE* (for related examples, see 1.1.57n.). Cf. Richard's exercising of the line-ending word 'crown' four times in quick succession (*3H6* 3.2.168–79).

405 **gossips' feast** a celebration of the birth and christening of a child, to which *gossips* (or

398 wrong, go] *Rowe;* wrong. Goe *F*　400 Thirty-three] Twenty five *Theobald;* twenty three *Capell* travail] *(*trauaile*),* travell *F2*　401–2 and till . . . burden ne'er delivered] *Hudson (Dyce, Remarks);* and till . . . burthen are deliuer'd *F;* nor, 'till . . . are delivered *Theobald;* and, 'till . . . burthen not delivered *Capell;* until . . . burden not delivered *Boswell–Malone (Boaden, per Boswell–Malone);* and at . . . burdens are delivered *Collier*[2] *(Collier, Notes)*　404 nativity] maturity *(Clayton)*　405 go] gaude *Warburton;* joy *Rann (Heath);* come *Keightley*

After so long grief, such nativity!

DUKE

With all my heart I'll gossip at this feast.

> *Exeunt omnes[, except] the two Dromios*
> *and two [Antipholus] brothers.*

DROMIO OF SYRACUSE [*to Antipholus of Ephesus*]

Master, shall I fetch your stuff from shipboard?

ANTIPHOLUS OF EPHESUS

Dromio, what stuff of mine hast thou embarked?

DROMIO OF SYRACUSE

Your goods that lay at host, sir, in the Centaur.   410

ANTIPHOLUS OF SYRACUSE [*to Antipholus of Ephesus*]

He speaks to me; – I am your master, Dromio.

Come, go with us; we'll look to that anon.

Embrace thy brother there; rejoice with him.

> [*Exeunt the Antipholus brothers.*]

DROMIO OF SYRACUSE

There is a fat friend at your master's house,

That kitchened me for you today at dinner;   415

She now shall be my sister, not my wife.

DROMIO OF EPHESUS

Methinks you are my glass and not my brother:

godparents (*OED n.* 1a)), relatives and family friends were invited; cf. 419. The *gossips' feast* honoured both the fact of a birth and the spiritual affinity of a familial community (see Phillips, 156–7). *CE*'s metaphoric *gossips' feast* thus mends and replaces the 'failed dinners' of Adriana and the Courtesan (Candido, 236). Cf. *gossip's bowl* at *MND* 2.1.47, *RJ* 3.5.174.

go This second *go* maintains the pattern of repeated language. The Abbess's second clause, *go with me*, clarifies the vaguer first clause.

408 a perfectly trochaic pentameter line,

perhaps meant to alter the mood, after the sentiment-laden iambic verse

410 **at host** at the inn (*OED n.*[3] b); see 1.2.9 and n., on *the Centaur.*

413 **there** See 189, 197n.

413 SD In some productions, the two exit arm in arm, anticipating (and contrasting with) the Dromios' more intimate *hand in hand* at 426.

414 **fat friend** See 3.2.110n.

415 **kitchened** entertained in the kitchen (*OED v.* 1a, citing only this usage as a transitive verb)

417 **glass** mirror (*OED n.*[1] 8a)

406 nativity] felicity *Hanmer*; festivity *Singer*[2] *(Johnson)*   407 SD] *Cam*[2]; *Exeunt omnes. Manet the two Dromio's and two Brothers.* F   *Antipholus*] *Rowe subst.*   408, 411 SDs] *Folg*[2]   413 SD] *Theobald subst.; Exit F; Exeunt the two* ANTIPHILUS'S, ADR. *and* LUC. / *Capell*

I see by you I am a sweet-faced youth.
Will you walk in to see their gossiping?

DROMIO OF SYRACUSE   Not I, sir; you are my elder.   420

DROMIO OF EPHESUS   That's a question; how shall we try it?

DROMIO OF SYRACUSE   We'll draw cuts for the senior; till then, lead thou first.

DROMIO OF EPHESUS

Nay then, thus: [*embracing him*] we came into the
world like brother and brother;   425
And now let's go hand in hand, not one before
another.   *Exeunt.*

FINIS

418 **sweet-faced** good-looking; also at *MND* 1.2.86, referring (indirectly) to Bottom

419 **gossiping** See 405n., on *gossips' feast*.

420–5 **Not … thus** Pope ingeniously saw a way to scan F's four lines (*Not … thus*) as three lines of shared iambic pentameter (see t.n.). His first two combinations (*Not … question* / *how … senior*) work well, the third (*till … thus*) more awkwardly, since that shared line contains only eight syllables. Despite Pope's clever but speculative solution, the present edition leaves 420–4 as in F, treating them as rhythmic prose that changes the tempo and tone from iambic pentameter. At 425, Ephesian Dromio's *thus* cues the action of embracing (Rowe), with the Dromios thereby fulfilling the exit request of Syracusan Antipholus at 413. Ard[1] rightly offers 425 as one line, rather than as F's two lines ('thus: / brother: / '), because the resulting couplet (*brother/another*) argues that 425 and 426 comprise two parallel lines of tumbling verse (see 3.1.11–85n.). Thus, the Dromios

in this last sequence (a kind of epilogue) offer a witty reprise of the play's basic aural rhythms: iambic pentameter (417–19), prose (420–4) and tumbling verse (425–6).

420 **Not I, sir** Syracusan Dromio refuses to exit ahead of his brother, deferring to him as the *elder*, who would go first.

423 **draw cuts** cast lots by drawing sticks or straws of unequal length (*OED* cut n.[1] 1a) **for the senior** i.e. to discover by fortune who is the elder; F's 'Signior' implies a pun on seniority by rank as well as age. See 3.1.1n., on *Signor*.

425 SD fulfilling the general injunction of Antipholus of Syracuse at 412

426 This boldly egalitarian statement addresses a line of conflict and action that has commenced with the Antipholuses' beatings of their servants and with Luciana's speech defending male mastery (2.1.15–25). The Dromios achieve, at least with each other, the kind of equality whose lack they have complained of throughout the play.

420–4] *Kittredge; Pope lines* elder. / question: / it? / senior: / first. / ; *Capell lines* elder. / question; / it [brother]? / draw / first. / ; *Steevens⁴ lines* elder. / it? / first. / thus: / ; *prose F*   423 senior] *Rowe³;* Signior *F;* Signiority *F3*   425–6] *Ard¹; F lines* thus: / ²brother: / another. /   425 SD] *Rowe subst.*

LONGER NOTES

1.1.41 Epidamium This edition prefers F's spelling, 'Epidamium', over
Pope's 'Epidamnum' (Latin accusative; 'Epidamnus' in the nominative).
No classical city spelled 'Epidamium' existed, although 'Epidamnus' did
(see below), while Ephesus, Syracuse, Epidaurus and Corinth, all
mentioned in the play, are real place-names. Pope's 'Epidamnum' keeps
alive Plautus' punning witticism from *Men.* that no one can stay in
Epidamnus without being damned ('*propterea huic urbi nomen Epidamno
inditum est, | quia nemo ferme huc sine damno deuortitur*' (263–4)).
Proponents of Pope's emendation point out that the accusative form,
'Epidamnum', is the declension that appears in *Men.*'s *Argumentum* and
Prologus more often (five times) than any other form. A few twentieth-
century editions – Baldwin, *Riv*, Folg[2] – have retained F's 'Epidamium'.
The place-name occurs seven times in F, and was typeset by two different
compositors, C and B: such consistency makes it unlikely that F's spelling
was an inadvertent printing-house error. The proponents of 'Epidamnum'
(or of 'Epidamnium') must also account for their avoidance of the
nominative form, 'Epidamnus', which does occur in Plautus' text.
Advocates of 'Epidamnum' sometimes hypothesize the influence of
William Warner's then-unpublished translation of *Men.* (1595), which
employs 'Epidamnum', but such argumentative grounds are marshy.
Altogether, the case for emendation has too much to explain. Shakespeare
may have written *Epidamium* as the misremembered form of the real city-
name, Epidamnus, or of a variant in Plautus – or he simply may have
invented it. At any rate, *Epidamium* seems to be intended.

 Epidamnus was called Dyrrachium under the Romans, became Durazzo
in the late Middle Ages and the Renaissance, and is now the Albanian city
of Durrës. Roman Dyrrachium was a military and naval base; Pompey fought
a battle against Julius Caesar there in 48 BC, and the city was a stopping-
point on routes into Macedonia and to Constantinople. As Durazzo, the
city was held by the Venetians from 1392 until 1501 when they surrendered
it to the Turks, who ruled in Shakespeare's time (see Davis & Frankforter,
154–5; Sugden, 180; *OCD*, 'Dyrrhachium'; Seltzer 543–4).

1.1.93 Epidaurus The text imagines Epidaurus to be on the eastern shore
of the Adriatic. It was displaced in the Middle Ages by nearby Ragusa,
now Dubrovnik (north of Epidamnus) in modern Croatia (part of ancient
Illyria). Adriatic Epidaurus had an eastern twin, the Aegean Epidaurus,
near Corinth on the Peloponnesian peninsula, with which it could have

been confused. The Aegean Epidaurus (south-east of Epidamnus) was an ancient Greek city famous for its theatre and as the legendary birthplace of Aesculapius, the god of medicine. Julius Solinus Polyhistor, to whom *CE* may allude, mentions Aesculapius' temple and occult dreams of the sick (see Solinus, sig. I4ʳ), but also, in the margin, identifies this Epidaurus mistakenly with Ragusa and Dubrovnik. Both Epidauruses appear on Abraham Ortelius's *Theatrum Orbis Terrarum* (1584), and Thomas Cooper describes Aegean Epidaurus in his *Thesaurus* (1565). The rescue from shipwreck makes most sense if the Adriatic Epidaurus is imagined.

1.2.102 ***such – like liberties** This phrase poses a long-standing interpretative problem, because *liberties*'s subject of comparison is difficult to identify. When the phrase is taken as 'such-like liberties' (introducing a hyphen into F's 'such like'), *liberties* has been understood as 'Unrestrained action, conduct, or expression . . . beyond what is . . . recognized as proper' (*OED* liberty *n.*[1] 5a). Thus, *liberties* might be interpreted as referring to the actions – deceptions, deformations – performed by Antipholus' gallery of rogues. Grammatically, however, *liberties* should refer to the preceding nouns, from *jugglers* to *mountebanks*, but these are not comprehended by *liberties*. On those grounds Hanmer (followed by Oxf[1]) emends to 'libertines'. The change contributes grammatical clarity but creates a redundancy in the phrase 'libertines of sin' (because libertines might be considered inherently sinful), collapses differences (as between *sorcerers* and *cheaters*) and lacks a Shakespearean ring ('libertines' occurs only once elsewhere, at *MA* 2.1.139). The emendation also forfeits the textual resonance of *liberties*, since in the next scene Adriana and Luciana argue over male and female *liberty* (2.1.7, 10); indeed *liberties* and *liberty* occur seven times in the play. Compositor D set *libertie(s)* four times elsewhere, which might be reason to trust his accuracy here.

The present version entails its own difficulties. It requires the listener to reach back five lines in memory, and then to recollect the first of two nouns in a phrase, *town . . . cozenage*. It also has the disadvantage of being anomalous, since Shakespeare typically uses *such* + *like* as a compound word, e.g. 'such-like toys' (see *TGV* 4.1.50, *R3* 1.1.60, *VA* 844, *Ham* 5.2.43, *TC* 1.2.254–5, *Tim* 3.2.22, *Tem* 3.3.59). On the other hand, Shakespeare sometimes employs *such* to identify particulars that lead to a general comparison, *like*: for example, '*such* advice . . . / *Such* temperate order . . . / . . . Who hath read or heard / Of any kindred action *like* to this?' (*KJ* 3.4.11–14 (emphasis added); see also *KJ* 4.3.108–10, *TC* 3.2.35–8, *KL* 2.2.72–4). No reading answers all objections.

2.1.15–25 In Genesis, 1.26–8, God gives man 'rule of the fisshe of the sea, & of the foule of the ayre, and of cattell', creates man both male and female and instructs man to 'replenishe the earth, and subdue it' (for the Bishops' Bible's 'cattell', the Geneva Bible reads 'beastes'). Psalm 8 reiterates man's 'dominion' over 'the beastes of the fielde: the foules of the ayre, and the fishe of the sea' (5–8). Luciana's term *pre-eminence* suggests that Shakespeare may have recalled Ecclesiastes, 3.19, which likens the condition of men and beasts in that they both die, 'so that in this a man hath no preeminence aboue a beast' (for 'preeminence', the Geneva Bible uses 'excellencie'). Shaheen notes verbal similarities (*indued*, *pre-eminence*) between Luciana's speech and a passage from Calvin's *Institution of Christian Religion*, as translated by Thomas Norton (1587): man is 'endued with reason . . . the nature of man hath preeminence among al kind of liuing creatures'. Shaheen adds, however, that such language was part of the Elizabethan 'standard religious vocabulary' (106). Luciana is putting the biblical passages to 'special use in applying them to the relations of husband and wife' (Ard²). For the submission of females to males in marriage, the most famous biblical passage was St Paul's exhortation in Ephesians, 5.22–3: 'Wyues, submit your selues vnto your owne husbandes, as vnto the Lorde: For the husbande is the head of the wyfe, euen as Christe is the head of the Church.' Paul's position is cited specifically in the Elizabethan 'Homily on the State of Matrimony': '*Let women be subject to their husbands, as to the Lord*' (*Homilies*, 539). Luciana's emphasis on *liberty* (10, 15) may reflect the marriage homily, which insists that in matrimony women 'relinquish the liberty of their own rule' (*Homilies*, 540). Further biblical passages paralleling Luciana's contention that men are *masters* and *lords* over women (24) include Genesis, 3.16; 1 Corinthians, 11.3; 1 Peter, 3.1; Titus, 2.5 (Shaheen, 107; see also Baldwin, *Genetics*, 166–9).

2.1.42.1   *In F, Dromio enters after 43, so that Luciana announces him (at 43) in advance of his entrance SD. By contrast, in the previous scene, Dromio's entrance SD (at 1.2.40) comes just before Antipholus' announcement (41). The Folio *Errors* has some 11 occasions when an *Enter* direction is coupled with a dialogue announcement, the SD preceding the announcement five times and following six. In these latter instances, SDs have been relocated editorially to anticipate their announcements (2.1.42.1; 2.2.6 SD, 114.1; 5.1.8.1–2, 127.1–3, 185.1–2; see also 4.4.108 SD). Variations in the placement of entrance SDs in *CE* and elsewhere may arise from their having been written in the margins of the manuscript copy-text, forcing the compositor to decide their precise placement for print. Even relocated entrance SDs reflect editing conventions more than exact theatrical practice. An Elizabethan actor may have taken two to four dialogue lines to move from a door in the *frons scaena* to a downstage position (Gurr & Ichikawa, 84). Thus, in 2.1, Dromio might have entered the stage as early as 40 or 41 (*fool-begged* in 41 makes an attractive entrance cue for him) to be available for address at 44. Entrance SDs might be understood, then, not as moments when an actor takes precisely his first step on to the stage but as moments by which a character must be available to participate in the action and dialogue.

2.1.57–8 *These two lines are set as three in F (ending 'villaine? / Cuckold mad, / stark mad: / '), which editors since Pope and Hanmer have typically combined into two lines, but with two possible configurations, ending 'villain? / stark mad: / ' (after Pope) or 'cuckold-mad. / 'stark mad: / ' (as verse, after Collier). In Pope's configuration, followed here, Adriana's 57 can be understood as prose, while Dromio's 58 returns to verse. In Collier's version, 57 and part of 58 make up a line of blank verse, and the remainder of 58 is left as a short verse line. If Adriana's speech (57) shifts the tone to prose, Dromio's two F lines (the two parts of 58) allow, as a single line of blank verse (with *he is* contracted), the re-establishment of some rhetorical order.

2.1.108–12 *The lines, as they appear in F, have confounded readers and editors. They start paradoxically and become manifestly nonsensical and corrupt: 'yet the gold bides still / That others touch, and often touching will, / Where gold and no man that hath a name, / By falshood and corruption doth it shame'. Cam[1] supposed that lines had been lost between 'Where gold' and 'and no man' (111). The present reading combines emendations from Theobald (F's 'yet' to *and*, 109), Hanmer (F's 'the' to *though*, 109), Theobald again (F's 'and' to *yet*, 110; F's 'Where' to *Wear*, 111) with a recent conjecture by Weiss (F's 'no' to *any* at 111), plus dashes as employed by Weiss at 109, 111. These changes render the three clauses roughly parallel in argument: the jewel will lose beauty, the gold will wear and the name will be shamed. Weiss's conjecture has three advantages: (1) it makes only one fairly simple change at 111 and requires no change at 112; (2) it regularizes the metre of 111 by adding a syllable; and (3) it avoids a confusingly negative statement in 111–12.

As editorial contortions demonstrate, the meaning in F's passage must be inferred. Adriana's recollection of the piece of jewellery, the *chain* (105) – perhaps standing as a guilt-payment from Ephesian Antipholus for his suspected infidelity, and thus even standing for Adriana – triggers her elliptical reflection on the fate of an enamelled ornament (*jewel*, 108). In this train of thought, the *jewel* represents Adriana's beauty (cf. 88), as Gollancz (per Ard[1]), Ard[2] and Wells advocate. Indeed, Shakespeare often associates *jewel* with women or makes it a metaphor for female qualities such as beauty or chastity (e.g. *AW* 4.2.45–6, *Cym* 1.4.153), so that for Adriana the dulling or wearing away of an ornament's lustre evokes the idea of loss of *beauty* (109). That idea will have its correlative in her determination to erode her own *beauty* with tears (113–14). Shakespeare also sometimes uses *jewel* as a metaphor for reputation (as in *Oth* 3.3.155–6); the multivalence of this image may facilitate the movement of Adriana's thought towards reputation at the end of the passage.

The image of a *jewel* prompts the associated image of *gold*, more durable than enamel. (The suggestion, by Ard² and others, that the *gold* in question lies underneath the enamel seems overly complicated.) A further contrast arises (based on Theobald's emendation of F's 'Where' to *Wear*): occasional touching of *gold* versus too-frequent *touching* (110). That contrast emerges from the emendations of F's 'yet the' to *and though* (109) and F's 'and' to *yet* (110). Malone notes *Damon and Pythias*'s 'Gold in time doo wear away, and other precious things do fade', and Ard² cites the proverb 'Gold by continual wearing wasteth' ('Gold with often handling is worn to nothing', Dent, I92). Still, the awkwardness in the present reading of *and . . . gold* (109–11) should be acknowledged, for the *gold* at first does not wear and then does, making it initially unlike and subsequently like the *jewel* and the *name*. That eventuality, however, may be the point: everything touched, literally or metaphorically, becomes blemished in the end, no matter how resistant.

With the image of worn *gold*, the implicit referent shifts; Adriana's *beauty* is now replaced by Antipholus' golden reputation as the thing dulled. The succeeding idea, as emended, about a man's tarnished *name* (111), becomes roughly parallel to that about gold: even good reputation can be worn away by misdeeds. Similar ideas are expressed elsewhere in the play (e.g. 'Herein you war against your reputation'; 'A vulgar comment will be made of it; / And that supposed . . . / Against your yet ungalled estimation', 3.1.86, 100–2). Indeed, Adriana's next speech, 2.2.116–52, takes as its moral the *contagion* (150) of corrupt behaviour. If the image of worn *gold* fits her husband better than it does her, then Adriana's thoughts have moved associatively from her *ruined* (2.1.96) *beauty* to his ruinous behaviour, a rhetorical connection already made in 88–98, where she accuses Antipholus of being 'the ground / Of my defeatures'. While Adriana imagines herself as the enamelled *jewel*, her analogical thinking leads her to connect ornamental *gold* with good reputation ('even as pure as Gold' (Theobald)), and the diminishing of *gold* with her husband's self-sullying of his reputation, a train of thought that maintains a link between her condition and his behaviour.

Some of the passage's difficulties come about through the doubleness of particular words. Lines 109–11, for example, contain a sequence of verbs that can have not only ambiguous but contradictory senses. Thus, *touch* (110) can mean both feel with the hand (*OED v.* 1) and 'test the fineness of', or assay, 'by rubbing it on a touchstone' (*OED* 8); *bides* (109) can mean both withstands (*OED v.* 7) and submits (*OED* 8); *Wear* (111) to suffer decay through use (*OED v.*¹ 14a) but also, when used intransitively, to withstand that decay (*OED* 15). These ambiguities may express Adriana's conflicted attitudes about herself, her husband and her sense of their inextricable relationship. In performance, any clear meaning in these complicated

307

lines is difficult to communicate, and many productions cut all or most of them. When the passage is retained, most Adriana-actors emphasize the aphoristic phrases, such as 'yet often-touching will / Wear gold', and try for a sense of closure by raising their voices on the speech's final couplet.

In a perceptive and ingenious interpretation different from the present one, Gary Taylor proposes only three emendations: 'I see the jewel best enamellèd / Will loose [her] beauty. Yet the gold bides still / That others touch; and often touching will / [Wear] gold, and [yet] no man that hath a name / By falsehood and corruption doth it shame' (Taylor, 'Crux'). Taylor's solution seems to read 'I see . . . beauty' as referring metaphorically to a woman as retaining her beauty by being touched. It also entails the argument that in 'and [yet] . . . shame', Adriana protests against the sexual double standard, in that a man (as opposed to a woman) will retain his good name, however false and corrupt his behaviour. That reading contravenes views about reputation maintained elsewhere in *CE* as well as Adriana's customary position (see 2.2.125–52) that husband and wife are so interconnected that the transgression of one is a stain on the other. More than gender equality, Adriana wants her husband back.

2.2.127–9 Antipholus' physical reaction to Adriana's *estranged from thyself* (126) may prompt her repetition and amplification of *thyself*. Her relative pronoun *That* (128) refers to *me* (127). Likewise, *undividable* and *incorporate* (128) describe her ('me, who is indivisible from and incorporated into you'). Shakespeare uses *undividable* uniquely here (but cf. 'undivided' at e.g. *Son* 36.2); *incorporate* means 'united in one body' (*OED ppl. adj.* 1); cf. *VA* 539–40. He returns to this theme of incorporation often, e.g. *MND* 3.2.208–11, *RJ* 2.6.37, *JC* 2.1.273. Ephesians, 5.21 touches on the idea of mutually constituted selfhood: 'He that loueth his wyfe, loueth hym selfe.' The biblical statement that a man 'shalbe ioyned with his wife: and they shall become one fleshe' (Genesis, 2.24; repeated in Ephesians, 5.31) was quoted in an alternative marriage homily in the Elizabethan *BCP*.

2.2.142 The forehead, whose prominences constitute the *brow* (*OED* brow *n.*[1] 4a), can display beauty but can also betray boldness or lust; it is the place where cuckold's horns appear. The forehead or *brow* makes evident the hidden truths of one's character. Berowne refers to the 'forehead' as exposing the perjury that he has committed against his friends by falling in love (*LLL* 4.3.123), and Adam speaks of wooing with 'unbashful forehead' (*AYL* 2.3.50). Editors of *CE* often cite Laertes' image of a mother branded as a harlot between her brows (*Ham* 4.5.119–21), and Hamlet describes how lust 'takes off the rose / From the fair forehead of an innocent love / And sets a blister there' (3.4.42–4). The image of the self-revealing *brow* or forehead is proverbial ('In the forehead and in the eye the lecture of the heart (mind) doth lie' (Tilley F590)). As Sidney puts it, 'verity be written in their foreheads' (*Apology*, 83). The idea is classical and humanist in origin: '*Ex fronte perspicere*' ('to see on the face of it' (Erasmus, *Adages*, 191)).

2.2.180 As well as biblical, the metaphor has classical antecedents. Ovid employs it in *Met*., where a lover urges marriage: 'But if (quoth hee) this Elme without the vyne did single stand, / It should have nothing (saving leaues) to bee desyred: and / Ageine if that the vyne which ronnes upon the Elme had nat / The tree too leane unto, it should vppon the ground ly flat' (Golding, 14.758–61) (Steevens). Writers contemporary with Shakespeare were fond of the vine–elm metaphor for love relationships. It occurs, for example, in Lyly (*MB*, 1.3.137), Kyd (*ST*, 2.4.45) (Shaheen), and Spenser (*FQ*, 1.1.8). An eclogue in Sidney's *Arcadia* likens bridegroom and bride to 'the elm and vine' (692), and Samuel Daniel's 'Complaint of Rosamond' (1592) imagines a love-embrace as 'the Vine married vnto the Elm' (1.839).

2.2.196 Editors have emended this line because (1) it appears to be missing a metrical foot; and (2) *owls* appears inconsistent with the more anthropomorphic *goblins* and *sprites* (i.e. spirits). Efforts to fill out the metre have often made recourse to 'elves', but such intervention seems unwarranted. The play contains other short lines, often creating dramatic effect, such as 1.1.156, where a short line signals a change in tone and action; 1.2.16, where the line may make room for physical action; and 5.1.371, where comic effect seems intended. Here the tetrameter has a fitting jingle, and its shortness may be the occasion for physical action. Concerning *owls*, Theobald thought it 'Nonsense' for Dromio to suggest that 'Owls [could] suck their Breath, and pinch them black and blue'. But, as Warburton contended, in popular lore some owls were believed to suck the breath and blood of children (the classical *striges*, or screech owls, in Ovid's *Fasti*, 6.131–43, feed on children's blood). The fifth Hag in Ben Jonson's *Masque of Queens* describes sucking a child's breath (171–3), and Jonson makes clear in his notes that he is alluding to the *striges* (see Roberts, 'Owl'). Owls could be part of *fairy land* (195): in John Baret, *An Alveary, or Quadruple Dictionary* (1580), one meaning for screech owl is 'a witch that chaungeth the fauor of children: an hagge or fairie' (quoted in Halliwell). Shakespeare invokes owls frequently elsewhere but typically treats them as augurs of evil fortune and death; see e.g. *3H6* 2.6.56–9, 5.6.44; *MND* 5.1.376–8; *JC* 1.3.26–8. On this difficult line, Whitworth comments wisely that 'Dromio's feverish imagination coins monsters pell-mell' (Oxf[1]).

2.2.222 **mist** Although *mist* occurs only once in *CE*, it comes freighted with a volatile set of early modern associations regarding the obscuring of truth – (1) historical, (2) conceptual, (3) moral, (4) urban and (5) religious. (1) Sidney famously admires Chaucer's ability to see clearly in his earlier, 'misty time' (*Apology*, 110); *mist* is often associated with a dimness produced by time (*OED n.*[1] 2b). (2) The image also occurs frequently for conceptual errors. In *The Steel Glass* (1576), Gascoigne speaks of 'such errour springs, / Such grosse conceits, such mistes of darke mistake' (sig. C1[r]). Sidney applies it to the philosopher's abstruse arguments (see *Apology*, 90); and Francis Bacon suggests with *mist* a 'facility of credit and accepting or admitting things weakly authorized or warranted', especially ideas based more on superstition than on evidence (142). (3) Morally, *mist* is often associated with conceptual errors that are wilful, culpable, even dangerous (*OED* 5a). At the House of Pride in *FQ*, 'mist' signifies moral confusion (1.4.36); a similar mist surrounds Guyon and the Palmer as their boat moves towards the Bower of Bliss (2.12.34–5). Marlowe's Tamburlaine tells the Virgins that their 'fearful minds are thick and misty' when they fail to recognize Death sitting on his sword (*1 Tamburlaine*, 5.1.110). (4) In urban England, *mist* was particularly linked to the falsehood inherent in 'juggling', a term connoting criminal deception and foolery, among other things (on *jugglers*, see 1.2.98n.). Henry Chettle's *Kind-heart's Dream* (1593) inveighs against London tricksters, swindlers and 'jugglers' who have learned 'the mysterie of casting mysts' (sig. F3[r]) (cf. Gosson, 2). (5) Mists and juggling extend to magic, demonism and religious error. In Acts, Paul brings confusion to a magician and false prophet by imposing 'a myste, and a darcknesse' on him (13.11), in symbolic imitation of his falsehood. Protestant reformers such as John Frith associate 'juggling mists' with Papist obfuscation and with an 'ignorance' that was sometimes 'wilful' (3.86); to Frith, the Catholic apologist Sir Thomas More 'caste[s] a mist before your eyes, that you might wander out of the right way' (3.267). Chettle compares 'jugglers' in the religious sphere to 'Schismatikes, Heretikes, and suchlike' – i.e. Catholics – who 'make Scripture a cloake for their detested errors' (sig. G1[r]). Likewise, Samuel Harsnett refers to a time when 'popish mist had befogged the eyes of our poore people' (sig. S3[v]). In the Tudor imagination, then, *mist* opens upon the charged topics of historical distance, erroneous conceptions, chicanery, magic and religious superstition. Shakespeare could have hardly chosen a more loaded term for the terrain on to which Antipholus voluntarily enters.

3.1.47 Editors have emended F's 'face' to 'office', 'pate' or 'place'. A change to 'office' would arguably entail emending the preceding *thy* to 'thine'. Oxf[1]'s 'place', adopted here, employs the word of the preceding line. Further, changing F's 'or' to *and* clarifies Ephesian Dromio's logic of substitution: in his place simply the name *Dromio*, and in that name's place, *ass* (with *place* (46) and *ass* effecting a concluding end-rhyme; see Cercignani, 176). The repetition of *name* from the end of one clause to the beginning of the next is rhetorical *anadiplosis*. However read, the line's *reductio ad absurdum* (or *ad asinum*) has a rude humour consistent with the scene's spirit (see 75–6), so that precise logic may be less important than effect.

4.2.32 **Tartar limbo** 'Tartarus' or *Tartar* refers to prison; in Homer, it was a region far below Hades (Sugden, 502), and the prison of the Titans, with 'gates . . . of iron' (*Il.*, 8.14). Socrates, in *Gorgias*, calls Tartarus 'a prison of vengeance and torture' (Plato, 303, par. 523). Confinement in classical Tartarus was worse than in Christian hell (Shaheen, 111). Ethnically, *Tartar* also designates a native of Central Asia, especially a feared Mongol or Turk warrior; thus, figuratively, *Tartar* indicates roughness, violence or intractability (*OED n.*[2] 1, 3). Tartars were famous for cruelty and savagery (Sugden, 502), connotations perhaps applied satirically to the Officer. Shakespeare may also be alluding to the physiognomy of the Officer-actor; in *MND* he refers to ethnic Tartars as 'tawny', that is, of a brownish-orange hue suggestive of mixed blood (3.2.263; see also 101). Fennor speaks of sergeants in a similar vein: 'The other of these Pagans had a phisnomy much resembling the Sarazens head without Newgate' (sig. B2[r]). In Elizabethan cant, *limbo* meant hell or prison; for Catholics it was also the abode of unbaptized infants and just souls born before Christ; cf. *Tit* 3.1.149.

4.2.55 Dromio's *hour* may pun on 'ower', i.e. debtor (Wells conj.) (*OED* ower *n.* 2) or on 'whore'. Since a sergeant makes arrests for debt, an 'ower' would obviously shun him (as in 55). Dromio uses *owes* at 57. A pun on 'ower' clarifies the meaning of *'a* as 'he' later in the line. Although neither Kökeritz nor Cercignani discusses 'ower', the former notes that *hour* rhymes with 'bower', 'flower' and 'power', making *hour* disyllabic here and at 61 (though not at 54); a variant spelling of *hour* is *hower*, which occurs elsewhere in F (e.g. *MND* TLN 1030, *MA* TLN 2499) and in Shakespeare's quartos. This reading's limitation is that Shakespeare nowhere uses 'ower', even though he uses 'owe' and 'owes'; *CE*, however, contains a number of unique word-occurrences. 'Ower' was a contemporary word, occurring in Jonson (see *OED* ower *n.* 2). Most critics have seen a pun on *hour*/whore (see Kökeritz, 117–18; Cercignani, 74): a whore, when seeing a sergeant, would turn around and walk the other way for fear of being arrested.

4.3.14 **the picture . . . new-apparelled** The opposition implied between an *old* and a *new* Adam recalls Paul's exhortation in Ephesians '[t]o lay downe . . . the olde man . . . And to put on that newe man' (4.22–4), which finds a parallel in the baptismal service prayer: 'Mercyfull god, graunte that the olde Adam in these chyldren maye bee so buryed, that the newe man may be raysed up in them' (*BCP*, sig. N5[v]; see Shaheen, 112). For Paul, the old man, or old Adam, is bound to the Jewish law, while the new man, or new Adam, is liberated by God's grace. Thus, *new-apparelled* may evoke the idea of transformation or redemption. It also alludes to the theme of time, for historical time begins with Adam's expulsion from the Garden of Eden: 'Since leathern Adam till this youngest hour' (*E3* 2.2.116).

4.3.52–3 Nay . . . dam In F (TLN 1234), this part of Dromio's speech appears set as verse, but the speech as a whole is prose like the rest of Dromio's speeches in the scene. Two explanations are possible. (1) Some compositors occasionally ended lines at punctuation marks near the margin, instead of setting type all the way to the rule, as Werstine ('Line division') has shown; that practice may have occurred here. (2) Perhaps more likely, this line marks the end of compositor D's setting of this column, with the text continued by compositor C (see Appendix 2, p. 331); the difference in compositorial styles may account for the way this line differs in appearance from the remainder of the speech.

5.1.170–3 The allusion best known by Elizabethans would probably be to the tyrant Dionysius of Syracuse, who, for fear of having his throat cut, was 'wont to *singe* his *beard* himself with coal and *firebrands*' (Richard Edwards, 'Prudence: The History of Damocles and Dionysius', in *The Paradise of Dainty Devices* (1576); see Edwards, *Works*, 210; emphasis added). The detail is repeated in Edwards's play *Damon and Pythias* (*DP*, 12.38); it derives from Plutarch, *Life of Dion* (noted in Boswell–Malone) and is reported in Cicero's *Tusculan Disputations* (5.20) – although the circumstances of Dionysius' shaving differ from Pinch's. The *puddled mire* (173) and the shaved beard may allude to Marlowe's *Edward II*, in which the King's murderers wash his face in 'puddle water' and shave his beard, the King having already been forced to stand in 'mire and puddle' (Brooks, 'Marlowe', 79; see *Edward II*, 5.3.30, 5.5.59).

5.1.299 Time's deformed hand According to Ard², Shakespeare has in mind 'the withered hand of Father Time, as commonly personified and depicted', and that gloss has been followed by subsequent modern editions. Although Shakespeare refers elsewhere to Time's 'cruel hand' (*Son* 60.14), his 'injurious hand' (*Son* 63.2), his 'fell hand' (*Son* 64.1) and his 'fairer' (i.e. non-scythe-holding) hand (*Tim* 5.1.123), nowhere does he invoke Time's *deformed* or withered *hand*. Likewise, Renaissance paintings of Time and Elizabethan emblem-book images of Time do not show a *deformed hand* (although Time may occasionally be depicted as skeletal) (see Fig. 5). Thus, *pace* Ard², Shakespeare here does not seem to be drawing upon a common or traditional image of Father Time. A different approach is to treat *deformed* as a transferred epithet (rhetorically sometimes called *hypallage*). In the present case, the modifier (*deformed*) that is properly applied to an object (*face*) when acted upon by the agent (*hand*) is transferred to that agent, so that Father Time's *hand* now becomes the thing *deformed* (when it is properly the thing 'deforming'). A transferred epithet makes the effect part of the agency. The image of the *deformed* *hand* thus brings Time and Egeon into resemblance, especially so if, when Egeon speaks 299–300, he also gestures with his own aged hand towards his face. On Father Time, see also 2.2.72 and n., on *Father Time*. On Renaissance representations of Time, see Panofsky, 69–93, and Macey, esp. 40–66.

5.1.346–51 Capell moved the Duke's speech to follow the next two speeches of Egeon and the Abbess, 352–61. Doing so allows the Abbess's call for Egeon to *speak* (345) to be answered immediately by his 'If I dream not, thou art Emilia' (352), while Egeon's concluding allusion to the shipwreck (354) would prompt the Duke's exclamation, 'Why, here begins his morning story right' (346). Capell's relineation attracted numerous editors, until the original order in F was restored by Cam[1]. F's arrangement makes sense as it is, since the father might plausibly stand in awed silence – a pause filled by the Duke – before he can acknowledge a reality beyond his expectations or hopes. The Duke's interjection also allows for dramatic intensity to build before the reunion of husband and wife. In F's ordering, the Duke's lines might verbalize the hopeful speculation going on in the Merchant's mind that leads him finally to embrace Emilia as his own.

APPENDIX 1

Date of composition

The Comedy of Errors was composed within the five-year period 1589–94.[1] The 1594 *terminus ad quem* (the latest possible composition date) reflects the virtual certainty that *Errors* was performed on 28 December 1594 for the Christmas revels at Gray's Inn (see pp. 103–10). The play was in existence and known to the public when Francis Meres referred to it in *Palladis Tamia: Wit's Treasury* (Stationers' Register, 7 September 1598):

> As *Plautus* and *Seneca* are accounted the best for Comedy and Tragedy among the Latines: so *Shakespeare* among ye English is the most excellent in both kinds for the stage; for Comedy, witnes his *Ge[n] tleme[n] of Verona*, his *Errors*, his *Loue labors lost*, his *Loue labours wonne*, his *Midsummers night dreame*, & his *Merchant of Venice*: for Tragedy, his *Richard the 2. Richard the 3. Henry the 4. King Iohn, Titus Andronicus*, and his *Romeo and Juliet*.

> (Meres, 282)

Meres, with BA and MA degrees from Cambridge University, arrived in London in the early 1590s and became active in literary circles; he probably knew the plays cited from having seen them in person.[2]

Because its first recorded performance was at Gray's Inn, *The Comedy of Errors* has been strongly associated with the Inn's 1594 Christmas revels (described in the *Gesta Grayorum,*

---

1 Henning notes the universal consensus on this dating (*Var.*, 280).
2 Since Meres mentions several works that were not yet in print, Gurr speculates that he copied their titles from playbills (*Companies*, 281).

first published in 1688), and some scholars argue that *Errors* was created for that event.[1] Standish Henning, however, has raised doubts – decisively, I think – that *Errors* could have been composed explicitly for the Gray's Inn revels. According to the *Gesta*, the Inns-men resolved to mount the revels (which had not been undertaken in three or four years) because of the great number of their members present in November and December 1594. Thus, 'about the 12th. of December, with the Consent and Assistance of the Readers and Ancients', the members decided to elect a 'Prince of Purpoole' to govern the revels, and they set in motion plans for appointing the prince's mock court, for raising funds to underwrite the proceedings and for requiring attendance.[2] As Henning points out, a decision made 'on or about December 12' to hold the revels would leave only sixteen days 'to compose, learn, and rehearse *The Comedy of Errors*' if it were a play specially written for the revels (*Var.*, 281) – and that number of days also requires the improbable assumption that someone from Gray's Inn would have commissioned a new play immediately following the 12 December decision. There is no reason to reject the *Gesta*'s account of timing, and on those grounds it is unimaginable that a new play could have been conceived, drafted and mounted in the time available. Furthermore, the plans for the 28 December Grand Night were themselves somewhat makeshift. The success of the first event on 20 December emboldened the members of Gray's Inn to enlarge their undertaking for 28 December, making even less certain the date on which the decision to hire a play was made. We must conclude that *The Comedy of Errors* was already in

---

1   See, most recently, Whitworth, who argues that the play was composed for performance at Gray's Inn and that it was too short and insubstantial for the public theatre repertoire of Shakespeare's company (2–11); see also Greg, *Problem*, 140; *Folio*, 200. For a sustained argument that *Errors* was written explicitly for the Gray's Inn performance, see Thomas, 'Date'; see also, more recently, Clare, 103–10.

2   Nelson & Elliott, 2.380; on the revels, see Nelson & Elliott, 2.380–435; also Bland.

existence when the Gray's Inn men solicited a theatre-piece and that it may well have been performed before then on the public stage. For the Gray's Inn revels, Shakespeare could have introduced into *Errors* some especially prepared material: for example, the joking between Antipholus and Dromio of Syracuse in 2.2 that plays on the legal terms 'fine' and 'recovery' (see 2.2.76–7 and n.). Likewise, Dromio of Syracuse's agitated descriptions of the judicial Officer in 4.2 and 4.3 might contain embellishments meant for the Gray's Inn audience. Yet the play's legal language is woven deeply into the dialogue, just as the framing issue of a criminal prosecution is fundamental to its structure, the arrest for debt key to its crisis and resolution and the question of justice pertinent to its start and finish: such matters are part of the play's conception and could not have been inserted belatedly for the amusement of Gray's Inn spectators. Indeed, Shakespeare would already have been fully aware of Inns students as 'regular playgoers from the start, and a conspicuous presence at the amphitheatres from early on'.[1] John Davies remarked, circa 1593, on the numerous and 'clamorous fry of the Innes of court' at the Theatre,[2] and there are various other contemporary references to the Inns members' haunting of the playhouses. The commissioning of a piece for an Inns performance does not need to be hypothesized in order to account for *Errors*'s legal language, interest in legal issues, use of legal situations and jokes upon legal personnel, although such matters might have made the play attractive for the Gray's Inn revels.[3] While some legal references might have been added for the Inns performance, *Errors* was probably written with the public theatre in mind.

Scholars agree that the earliest possible date for *Errors*'s composition, the *terminus a quo*, is 1589. That date has been

1 Gurr, *Playgoing*, 80; see 80–2.
2 Cited in Gurr, *Playgoing*, 81.
3 On *Errors*'s legal interests and their relationship to the Inns of Court, see Kreps.

inferred from a line spoken by Dromio of Syracuse as he lampoons Nell's features in geographical terms: 'Where France?', asks Antipholus of Syracuse, and Dromio responds, 'In her forehead, armed and reverted, making war against her hair' (3.2.125–7). Besides alluding to syphilis, Dromio's speech refers obliquely to the contemporaneous war in France over the prospective succession to the kingship of the Protestant Henri of Navarre, designated as heir in 1589 but, because of the hostilities, unable to take the throne until 1594.[1] In Dromio's comment, 'hair' is taken as a pun for 'heir', so that the line apparently glances at the French internal wars. Since Henri of Navarre's succession was confirmed by Henri III in 1589, Dromio's speech would probably have been composed after the events of that year. Although Navarre's coronation took place early in 1594, the French tribulations would still have been fresh enough in English minds to merit a gibe even if the scene were written after Henri's ascent to the throne.

In narrowing the five-year period, two kinds of evidence are helpful: (1) evidence outside the play, as well as allusions in the play to real-world events, people or writings, as exemplified by

1 The war was a proxy battle undertaken by the King of Spain, Philip II, to suppress Protestantism and overthrow the Queen of England, Elizabeth, who was providing financial and military support to the Protestant cause in France and the Netherlands. Following the death in 1584 of the French King Henri III's brother and heir, François, Duke of Alençon, a Catholic, the claim to succession fell legally to Henri, King of Navarre, a Huguenot. The prospect of a Protestant heir apparent touched off the 'War of the Three Henries' (1587–9), which involved Henri III and Henri of Guise in an unstable alliance against Henri of Navarre. After Henri III had Guise assassinated in 1588 and, in return, was himself mortally wounded by an assailant's knife in 1589, he gave his deathbed approval to Navarre as his heir. Nonetheless, further warfare ensued as the Catholic League, assisted by Spain, attempted to prevent the nominal king, now Henri IV, aided by England, from gaining military control of the country and taking full possession of the throne. In 1591 Elizabeth sent 4,000 soldiers to support Navarre. Eventually, in 1593, Navarre renounced Protestantism in order to secure his kingdom; his coronation took place in February 1594, in Navarre. The court of Navarre was to be the setting for one of Shakespeare's next comedies, *Love's Labour's Lost* (*c*. 1594–5).

Dromio's pun about French wars; and (2) aspects within the play that suggest temporal affinities to other of Shakespeare's works. Although all such evidence remains partial and circumstantial, cumulatively it indicates a date of composition somewhat before, but not far removed from, the first recorded production of *Errors* in 1594.

EXTERNAL EVIDENCE

In Henning's calculation, the cast of *Errors* calls for a total of twelve male actors and four boy actors,[1] a smaller cast size than typical of Shakespeare's plays before the closing of the theatres in mid-1592. That difference, according to Stanley Wells and Gary Taylor, argues that *Errors* was composed later.[2] In the same vein, the time markers in *Errors* parallel new hours of performance for the public theatre. On 8 October 1594, the Lord Chamberlain, the patron of Shakespeare's company, assured the Lord Mayor of London that his actors, who used to begin their plays 'towardes fower a clock, . . . will now begin at two, & haue don betwene fower and fiue' (quoted from Chambers, *ES*, 4.316). This promise was meant to ease complaints about plays interfering with evening prayer and, in winter-time, concluding after sunset (*Var.*, 283). If *Errors* was written in the autumn of 1594, then its announcing of 5 p.m. as the time for the execution of Egeon (when all the story-lines intersect) might allude to the promised time when a Lord Chamberlain's play in the public theatre would 'haue don', as if narrative time and real time were converging upon each other. Such a connection remains conjectural but attractive.[3]

1   See *Var.*, 509; see also Appendix 3.
2   *TxC*, 95; see also *Var.*, 283.
3   In 1980 the German scholar and editor Tetzeli von Rosador drew attention to the time references in *Errors* and the Lord Chamberlain's promise to end his plays 'betwene fower and fiue'; see *Var.*, 283.

Errors may refer to other outside events. Dromio of Syracuse's *tour de force* comic fantasia about Nell the globular kitchen wench (3.2.116–44) arguably reflects an increased public interest in cartographic globes prompted by the new English manufacture of them, begun by Emery Molyneux in 1592 (see 3.2.116n.). In the same scene, Dromio also uses the phrase 'armadas of carracks' (140) in reference to Spain, alluding presumably to the Spanish Armada's 1588 attempt to invade England (see 3.2.140n., on *armadas of carracks*), although the reference does little to resolve the date of *Errors*'s composition. In the prospective beheading in Act 5, T.W. Baldwin saw an allusion to the 1588 execution for treason of a Catholic priest behind the Holywell Priory ditches in Finsbury Field, near the Theatre and the Curtain, where Shakespeare's company performed (*Hanging*). But the conjecture has limited value, since public executions were a fact of life in Elizabethan England, and can contribute little towards fixing the play's date.

Doctor Pinch figures in a possible echo of *Arden of Feversham* (published 1592) suggested by E.K. Chambers (*WS*, 1.310–11). A felonious character in *Arden* is described as 'lean-faced' and 'hollow-eyed' (2.48, 49), terms that appear in Ephesian Antipholus' memorable description of Pinch as a 'hollow-eyed', 'lean-faced villain' (5.1.241, 238). The same time period offers other possible allusions. According to J. Dover Wilson, Dromio of Ephesus's 'Heart and good will you might, / But surely, master, not a rag of money' (4.4.86–7) reflects almost identical language found in Nashe's *Strange News* (Stationers' Register, January 1593): 'heart and good will, but neuer a ragge of money' (see 4.4.86–76n.). (The phrase 'rag of money' also occurs in Thomas Lodge's *Deaf Man's Dialogue*, 1592.) Nashe's pamphlet was an attack on the university academic Gabriel Harvey, prompted by the complicated 'Martin Marprelate' controversy and perhaps by earlier events.[1] According to J.J.M. Tobin, *Errors* echoes further terms and phrases from Nashe; the character of Doctor Pinch in particular may allude satirically to Nashe's antagonist Gabriel Harvey ('Pinch').[2] Ephesian Dromio's lines, 'Mistress, *respice finem*, "respect your end"; or rather, to prophesy like the parrot, "beware the rope's end" ' (4.4.42–4), presumably refer to the same controversy (Tobin, 'Pinch', 23). With an implied pun on the Latin accusatives *finem* (end) and *funem* (rope), Dromio is recalling Nashe's '*respice funem*' in *Strange News*, that phrase pointing to Harvey's lineage as the son of a rope-maker.[3] Doctor Pinch's complexion is also described as 'saffron' (4.4.62), a word that occurs nowhere else in Shakespeare. Harvey was from Saffron Walden, another fact to which Nashe refers in *Strange News*.[4] One might add that, in *The Terrors of the Night*,[5] Nashe mocks conjurors of the sort satirized in the figure of Doctor Pinch. These and other apparent scattered allusions or borrowings of specific terms (e.g. 'mountebank') convince Tobin that Shakespeare draws from Nashe rather than the other way around.

Tobin's conjectures about *Errors*'s allusions to Nashe and to the Harvey–Nashe quarrel are compelling, although they invite further questions. Why was Shakespeare inserting into *Errors* references to the controversy along with an apparent parody of Harvey in the figure of Doctor Pinch? And what might that material tell us about dating? For the first question, only a

---

1   The Puritan Marprelate tracts of 1588 and 1589 had assailed the episcopal governance of the Church of England. Harvey's brother Richard had participated in the defence, and Nashe (like Lyly and Greene) had championed the other side as an anti-Martin pamphleteer. Since Harvey had attacked Greene posthumously, Nashe may have wished to defend the memory of his friend and associate. See Nashe, 5.34–110.

2   In *Romeo and Juliet*, Shakespeare alludes to Nashe's later anti-Harvey pamphlet, *Have With You to Saffron Walden* (1596); see Weis, 39–41.

3   Tobin, 'Pinch', 23; see 4.4.43n.

4   On Harvey, ropes and Saffron Walden, see Nashe, 1.267, 268, 270, 274.

5   *Terrors* was probably written in 1592–3.

general answer is available. Shakespeare was an associate of Nashe and was closer to the Nashe/Lyly/Greene side than to that of the Harveys. The satirical allusion in support of his colleagues would have added topical interest to his play. For the second question, the Harvey reference suggests a composition date for *Errors* in 1593–4, after the publication of Nashe's *Strange News*. The Harvey reference also squares with the argument that *Errors* was conceived for the public theatre, which featured topical satire. Conversely, it is less obvious why Shakespeare would have introduced this specific material if the play had been commissioned for an Inns of Court revel. Other references in relation to Doctor Pinch add modest probability to a 1593–4 dating. Pinch's burning beard doused with 'puddled mire' (5.1.173) may recall the 'puddle water' in Marlowe's *Edward II* (Stationers' Register, 1593) with which the murderers wash the king's face.[1] *Edward II* may also be reflected in Antipholus of Ephesus's 'What, will you murder me?' (4.4.110),[2] although the phrase is not sufficiently unusual to warrant much of a claim.

As further support for the dating of *Errors* in 1593–4, Dromio of Syracuse's wildly agitated descriptions to Adriana and subsequently to Syracusan Antipholus of the sergeant who has arrested Ephesian Antipholus bear similarity to a description of such a figure in Greene's *A Quip for an Upstart Courtier* (1592). Although matter-of-fact references in Elizabethan writing to arresting sergeants are common, Greene employed a new and different style in offering the first sustained satirical description of a sergeant as venal and cruel, with his corruption manifested in his appearance and behaviour.[3] Nothing comparable precedes it. Greene depicts his officer as wearing

---

1 Brooks, 'Marlowe', 79; see *Edward II*, 5.3.30, 5.5.59, and *CE* 5.1.170–3 LN.

2 See *Edward II*, 5.3.29; see also Ard², xix, 4.4.107n.

3 Greene's attack is preceded by an equally harsh treatment of a lawyer; see Greene, 11.249–52. Kinney notes that Greene changed the nature of rogue pamphlets by giving them robust language, irony, satire and wit (*Rogues*, 54–5).

'a *buffe leather* ierkin' and carrying a mace for '*clapping* it on [one's] *shoulder*' so as to convey his victim 'to *Limbo*', 'to the *counter*'; as behaving as 'eager . . . as a *dog*' or 'a butcher's *cur*', 'his *hart* . . . robd of al remorse & *pity*'; and as being 'framd by the *Diuell*, of the rotten carion of a *woolfe*, and his soule of an vsurers damned ghost turned out of *hell* into his body' (italics added here and subsequently).[1] By comparison, the Officer in Dromio's description dresses 'all in *buff*', in 'calf's skin', 'a case of *leather*' (4.2.36, 4.3.18, 23); he is a '*shoulder-clapper*' doing 'exploits with his mace' (4.2.37, 4.3.27); he imprisons debtors in 'Tartar *limbo*' (4.2.32); his commandings of his arrestees to the Counter constitute '*counter*mands', and thus he 'runs *counter*' (4.2.37, 39); he is a '*wolf*', a hunting '*hound*', '*pitiless*' and with 'hard *heart*' (4.2.36, 39, 35, 34); he is likewise a '*devil*', a '*fiend*, a fairy' and an '*evil angel*' who 'carries poor souls to *hell*' (4.2.33, 35, 4.3.19, 4.2.40). Although the passages by Greene and Shakespeare sometimes deploy terms differently and although Greene stresses the officer's corruption while Dromio emphasizes demonism, they share an intensity and a resemblance in tone and diction that suggest kinship. It seems more likely that Shakespeare would have imported images from Greene's trend-setting two-page treatment of the sergeant-figure than that a few words from a speech by Dromio would have been parlayed by Greene into his own longer passage, so that influence, if operating, probably flows from Greene's *Quip* to Shakespeare's *Errors*. For a different allusion to Greene, Dromio of Ephesus's phrase 'A crow without feather' (3.1.81; see n.) might be a comic reference to 'an upstart Crow, beautified with our Feathers' from *Greene's Groatsworth of Wit* (1592).

To the inferential evidence for a 1593–4 date of composition can be added Shakespeare's use of the name Dromio, which occurs in John Lyly's *Mother Bombie* (*c.* 1590; Stationers'

---

1 *Quip*, 11.249, 252–5 (see *CE* 4.2.32–40n.); emphasis added here and in the subsequent quotations from *CE* 4.2, 4.3.

Register, 1594), where a witty and conniving servant with a prominent role bears that name. There are no apparent verbal parallels between Lyly's Dromio and Shakespeare's twin servants, but, like *Errors*, *Mother Bombie* is both modelled on Roman comedy and aimed at a popular audience. Likewise, if Shakespeare used Twine's *Pattern of Painful Adventures* as one of his sources for the Apollonius story, and if the edition he used was published in 1594,[1] then there is further reason to accept a contemporaneous date for *Errors* (see Introduction, pp. 87–9). Additionally, if Shakespeare had been familiar with Warner's English translation of Plautus' *Menaechmi* before it was entered in the Stationers' Register in 1595, then a date of composition not long before the Gray's Inn performance would again have been probable;[2] most scholars now agree, however, that despite some resemblances between *Errors* and Warner's translation, the evidence that Shakespeare was borrowing from Warner proves thin. Given the proximate timing of Warner's translation with Shakespeare's play, perhaps their interests ran concurrently.

INTERNAL EVIDENCE

Errors's affinities with other Shakespearean works also throw light on its probable time of composition. Such evidence, although conjectural, tends to support the case for a late date. With *Errors*, critics have looked to its verse and rhyme to locate it chronologically in relationship to other of Shakespeare's works. According to Sidney Thomas, in a judgement widely shared, Shakespeare's verse in *Errors* is 'of a piece with the verse of such works of 1593 and 1594 as *Venus and Adonis* and

---

1 For this argument, see Thomas, 'Date', 382.
2 Thomas argues that the Stationers' Register entry for Warner's translation reads as if copied from an already published book title; that is, earlier than 1595 ('Date', 381–2); Foakes contends that the Stationers' Register title could have been taken from the manuscript and that Warner's 1595 edition was the only one printed (xxii).

The Rape of Lucrece' ('Date', 383). Shakespeare wrote those long narrative poems during the period from mid-1592 to mid-1594 when the theatres were closed, an interval that gave him the opportunity to develop his skill at rhyme. More specifically, as Malone noted long ago, the alternating rhyme of *Venus and Adonis* and *Lucrece* resembles that of *Errors* (see 3.2.1–52 and 4.2.1–4); indeed, the first six lines of 4.2 employ the same rhyme scheme, ABABCC, used throughout *Venus and Adonis* and are not far removed from that of *Lucrece* (ABABBCC). Wells and Taylor argue that Shakespeare's experiments with rhyme in these narrative poems, and also in his contemporaneous early sonnets, greatly encouraged his use of rhyme in the comedies that followed soon after.[1]

Errors might also be considered a precursor to a set of plays known as the 'lyrical group', originally identified and so described by Walter Pater, that includes *Love's Labour's Lost*, *Richard II*, *Romeo and Juliet* and *A Midsummer Night's Dream*, all typically dated within the period 1594–5.[2] Although probably composed earlier than those plays, *Errors* shares with them a metrical regularity and a high proportion of verse lines (87%) and of rhymed lines within its verse (25%). By comparison, the percentages of verse and of rhyme-within-verse for *Love's Labour's* are 68% and 66%; *Richard II*, 100% and 19%; *Romeo and Juliet*, 87% and 18%; and *Dream*, 80% and 52%.[3] Drawing upon Wells and Taylor, Charles Whitworth argues for designating *Errors* as part of a 'rhyme group', composed of the plays of the lyrical group with the addition of *Lucrece* and *Venus and Adonis* (7–9). The term 'rhyme group' redescribes those works in a way that draws attention to their common prosodic features, and thus makes a case for their

---

1   *TxC*, 95; see also Duncan-Jones, 19.

2   See e.g. *TxC*, 117–19; also Woudhuysen, 59–61; Forker, 112; Weis, 41–3.

3   *TxC*, 96; see also p. 65, n. 3. For a recent, detailed study of the stylistic relationships among *Love's Labour's*, *Romeo and Juliet* and *Richard II*, see Shurbanov, 56–163.

composition within a few years of each other. Of course, stylistic arguments are based on the premise that Shakespeare produced certain kinds of works at certain times, and they step over the difficulties in dating many of the works that would be associated with *Errors*; nonetheless, the comparisons carry force and support other evidence for a late date. Finally, Henning summarizes a range of vocabulary tests – especially rare words and specific word-forms – that give some credence to a dating of *Errors* prior to *Love's Labour's Lost* and its related plays (*Var.*, 294–6).

The overwhelming probability is that Shakespeare wrote *The Comedy of Errors* in 1593–4. To narrow that period further, much of the evidence – including the name Dromio, the play's stylistic similarities to works of 1594–5, the matter of cast size and the possible connections to Warner and Twine – point towards the middle or latter half of 1594. Wells and Taylor date the play to 1594 (*TxC*, 95) and Henning, in the most exhaustive study, concludes, 'I believe that Sh. wrote the play after he joined the Chamberlain's men in mid-1594, but well before December', when the Gray's Inn performance occurred (*Var.*, 394). The case for such dating is convincing.

APPENDIX 2

The text and editorial procedures

THE TEXT

The Comedy of Errors *in the First Folio*

All editions of *The Comedy of Errors* derive from the First Folio of Shakespeare's dramatic works (1623). The First Folio was compiled by John Heminges and Henry Condell, fellow members and leaders of Shakespeare's former acting company, the King's Men, seven years after their colleague's death in 1616. *The Comedy of Errors* was entered in the Stationers' Register (the entry establishing claim to the work) on 8 November 1623 by Isaac Jaggard and Edward Blount (Arber, 4.69). Of the thirty-six plays in the First Folio, *Errors* was one of eighteen published for the first time. Given the play's single source, bibliographical discussions of *Errors* have focused on understanding the nature of the F text and of the manuscript on which it was based. *Errors* has attracted special and controversial interest because various scholars have judged that F's underlying copy was an early draft in Shakespeare's autograph, one that preceded a tidied-up version used for performance.

The First Folio was produced by the London printing office of William and Isaac Jaggard.[1] *The Comedy of Errors* – the only Folio play with 'Comedy' in its title – is grouped in the first set of plays, the 'Comedies', and is the fifth of fourteen in that sequence, coming after *Measure for Measure* and before *Much Ado About Nothing*. In contrast to the 1616 Folio edition of Ben Jonson's works, the volume does not present

---

1   For introductions to the Folio and its history, see Hinman, *First Folio*, ix–xxxvii; also *TxC*, 1–52. For textual analysis of F *Errors*, see *Var.*, 262–80.

Shakespeare's plays in order of composition, even within their groupings as comedies, histories or tragedies. According to the leading hypothesis, the order within genres relates, at least in part, to the nature of the copy with which the publishers were working. Thus, for example, the first four of the Folio's comedies were all printed from transcripts prepared by the professional scribe Ralph Crane, while the sixth to ninth were of plays that had already appeared in quarto editions (*TxC*, 39). The Folio's typesetters, known as compositors, apparently began with those comedies available in the most readable and consistent copy.[1]

The Comedy of Errors occupies sigs H1^r–I2^v of the First Folio, pp. 85–100 (86 is misnumbered as 88). According to the ground-breaking work of Charlton Hinman, quire H (comprising the first four acts of *Errors* and the opening of Act 5) was typeset by multiple compositors.[2] While quire H begins *The Comedy of Errors*, quire I finishes it, containing most of the last act (three-and-a-third printed pages), before the rest of that quire is given over to *Much Ado About Nothing*. As Wells and Taylor describe it, the seven comedies typeset immediately after *Errors* differ from it by being based on copies that all show some degree of annotation for the purposes of theatrical performance; following them are two final comedies again derived from scribal transcripts.[3] Although these groupings are subject to debate and lead to no clear conclusions about the nature of the printer's copy for *Errors*, they do draw attention to the claim that the play is anomalous for being the only

---

1 On Crane, see Howard-Hill, *Crane*.

2 See Hinman, *Printing*, 2.388–97. A quire in the Folio consists of three sheets making up six leaves, or twelve printed pages. A folio sheet is a large sheet of paper folded in half so that each winged half, or leaf, can accommodate two pages of text.

3 See *TxC*, 145–7. Complicating this picture, Wells and Taylor consider the underlying copy for *The Winter's Tale* (the last of the 'Comedies') to be another Crane transcript, 'possibly' of an authorial copy and 'probably' of a promptbook (*TxC*, 147).

comedy originating from a holograph manuscript. Disagreement has persisted, however, about the nature of that manuscript.

Refining Hinman's foundational work, recent scholars have concluded that three compositors – compositors C, D and B (we do not know their names) – were responsible for typesetting *The Comedy of Errors*. A chart of the compositors and the sections of *Errors* set by each appears below.[1]

Compositor	Signature[2]	TLN[3]	Act/scene/line
C	H1ʳ–H1ᵛa	1–164	1.1.1–1.2.2
	H2ʳb–H3ʳa	289–549	2.1.15–2.2.160
	H4ʳa	743–808	3.1.82–3.2.22
	H5ᵛ (*part*)	1235–54	4.3.53 ('and')–74 ('nail,')
D	H1ᵛb–H2ʳa	165–288	1.2.3–2.1.14
	H3ʳb–H3ᵛ	550–742	2.2.161–3.1.81
	H4ʳb	809–74	3.2.23–80
	H5ᵛ (*part*)	1128–234	4.2.22–4.3.53 ('dam;')
B	H4ᵛ–H5ʳ	875–1127	3.2.81–4.2.21
	H6ʳ–I2ᵛ	1255–919	4.3.74 ('a rush')–5.1.426

This chart, though useful for easily identifying the work of a compositor, can be misleading, for Folio typesetting did not start with the first act, scene and line of a play and then advance progressively through the text. Rather, the process began in

---

1   This chart is drawn from *TxC*, 152. It follows the distribution laid out by Werstine in 'Copy', 234, and agrees with that offered by *Var.*, 264. The key contributions that have refined Hinman's analysis include Howard-Hill, 'Compositors'; O'Connor; and Werstine, 'Cases'.

2   The capital letter refers to the signature (an identifying letter placed at the foot of a leaf), with the number after the letter indicating position in the sequence within the signature; the superscript *r* or *v* identifies recto or verso, the recto page facing the reader in the way that p. 1 of a book would, with the verso being its other (reverse) side; *a* and *b* indicate the first and second columns on a folio page.

3   A system for giving a through-line number (TLN) to each printed line of each play was established in Hinman's edition of the First Folio and has been universally adopted.

the middle of the six-leaf quire and moved simultaneously backwards and forwards in the play, with compositors, as they proceeded, estimating the amount of the manuscript that could be fitted into each column and page.[1] They used large sheets of paper, each leaf of which could accommodate a page of print on either side, making a total of four folio pages. Three of these sheets laid on top of one another amounted to the standard quire of twelve printed pages. Thus, in the case of quire H, the top sheet in the quire had on one side the facing pages 90 and 91, constituting a forme,[2] while the other side of the sheet contained non-adjacent pages, 89 and 92, with the pages of text becoming farther apart as the compositors worked through the quire. A new quire might have been needed part-way through the setting of a play; conversely, a play might have been fully set before a quire was used up, in which case the compositor applied the remainder to the next play. As the typesetting progressed, different compositors might have worked at the same time on different columns or on different pages of the same forme. In the case of *Errors*, compositor D began work on page 90 (sig. H3^{v}a), while the facing page, 91 (sig. H4^{r}a), was started by

---

1 For a related chart showing 'the order in which the pages were printed and the stints of the three typesetters', see Werstine, 'Copy', 234. The one below, adapted from the chart on p. 328, shows the compositors in order of act, scene and line:

Act/scene/line	TLN	Signature	Compositor
1.1.1–1.2.2	1–164	H1^r–H1^{v}a	C
1.2.3–2.1.14	165–288	H1^{v}b–H2^{r}a	D
2.1.15–2.2.160	289–549	H2^{r}b–H3^{r}a	C
2.2.161–3.1.81	550–742	H3^{r}b–H3^v	D
3.1.82–3.2.22	743–808	H4^{r}a	C
3.2.23–80	809–74	H4^{r}b	D
3.2.81–4.2.21	875–1127	H4^v–H5^r	B
4.2.22–4.3.53 ('dam;')	1128–234	H5^v (*part*)	D
4.3.53 ('and')–74 ('nail,')	1235–54	H5^v (*part*)	C
4.3.74 ('a rush')–5.1.426	1255–919	H6^r–I2^v	B

2 A forme is the type as set and locked in place for printing on one face of a folio sheet.

compositor C and completed (sig. H4^{r}b) by compositor D (Werstine, 'Copy', 234). Those pages include *Errors* 3.1 and part of 3.2. The conditions of typesetting – the multiple compositors, their sometimes backwards movement through a play – meant that compositors could not easily resort to the narrative to clarify a confusion in the manuscript.

Although the F text of *Errors* has fewer textual anomalies than many other plays, it still suffers from typical problems that arise in early printed books. Variations in spelling and typesetting habits of individual compositors can create uncertainty for a modern editor. Such problems sometimes arise in *Errors* when considering whether a passage is meant to be verse or prose. For example, when compositor D sets a line of verse that is too long for the width of the column, so that the 'flow-over' words need to be set on the line below, he typically indents the flow-over text to signal that it is a continuation of verse (as, for example, at TLN 575–6, 2.2.187), a practice helpful for the reader.[1] By contrast, compositor B does not necessarily indent verse flow-overs, so that when a character speaks a single such line, the page will offer no signal that confirms the speech as verse (as at TLN 1023–8, 4.1.40–2).[2] In those cases, an editor must decide whether the speech is verse or prose on the basis of context, scansion and style. Such choices can be especially tricky regarding the Dromios, who might speak either prose or verse, including sometimes a verse-like rhythmic prose and sometimes a prose-like 'tumbling verse' (see Introduction, pp. 66–7). Busy compositors probably did not worry greatly about distinctions such as those between prose and tumbling verse. The protocols of Arden and other modern

---

1   On flow-overs, see O'Connor, 89–91.
2   Compositor D practises another variation: at TLN 258–9 (1.2.93) he prints a verse-line flow-over ('hands:') below the end part of the line, justified right and given an initial parenthesis, even though doing so means setting it on the same line as the succeeding line of text.

editions call for making them, however, so that editors must proceed at times by conjecture. In a variation of these problems, on sig. H5ᵛb, compositor C takes over from compositor D (at TLN 1235, 4.3.53, 'and') after the first line of a speech by Syracusan Dromio – a somewhat unusual event, since compositors more commonly set at least to the foot of a column; perhaps compositor D was confronted with an emergency. The end-spacing of the first line of Dromio's speech (TLN 1234, 4.3.53, 'dam;') gives the appearance of verse, and the line scans as iambic pentameter, while the rest of the speech is set as prose: did one compositor see the speech as verse, the other not? But end-spacing practices could vary, and in this case the whole speech is probably prose.

Besides confusions caused by differences in compositorial styles, plain mistakes also happen. Compositors discover that they have too much or too little space for text; misread words and phrases in the manuscript; transpose lines or SDs out of position; accidentally repeat a word from a previous or subsequent line in another line; or even leave out a line (or parts of lines), often because of eye-skip as the compositor's head turns back and forth from manuscript to composing stick. Sometimes a compositor may be confused by handwriting. For instance, the character Luciana is misnamed '*Iuliana*' in the entrance direction to 3.2 (TLN 786, 3.2.0.1) and '*Iulia.*' in her subsequent SP (TLN 787, 3.2.1). According to Werstine, the two errors derive from compositor C's difficulty in reading the manuscript on his first typesetting of the name.[1] Sometimes a compositor will run out of room at the foot of a column and, to accommodate all the text that must be set, will string verse lines together as prose. Compositor C encountered just that problem at the foot of H2ʳb (TLN 347–50, 2.1.69–73) where five and a half lines of verse are compacted into four lines of prose. The

---

1 Werstine, 'Copy', 240. Some scholars have considered this naming error an uncorrected trace of an earlier draft of the play; see *Var.*, 123, 269, 275.

same compositor ran into a related difficulty at the foot of the next column, H2^{v}a (TLN 418, 2.2.23), where, in order to make room for a SD at the end of a line, he set 'thou' as the abbreviation 'y^u' and 'and' as an ampersand. After TLN 693 (3.1.54), at least one line of speech (perhaps more) by Luce or Dromio is lost, as is made clear by the absence of an end-word to rhyme with 'hope' in a series of couplets. In that same scene, TLN 683–701 (the lines from the second part of 3.1.49, and continuing to 58) illustrate another kind of problem, the absence of early modern typesetting protocols for indicating that lines of verse are divided among different speakers. Thus, in a series of stichomythic speeches with rhymed couplets, an end-rhyming word, 'laugh' (3.1.50) (which pairs with 'staff'), appears in the middle of a line (TLN 685) rather than at the end.

Although *Errors* has only a few textual cruxes (i.e. significantly garbled passages), one of the most notorious and intractable comes in an important speech of six lines in couplets spoken by Adriana towards the end of her first scene (TLN 385–9, 2.1.108–12), set by compositor C. Adriana has just been thinking about a necklace that her husband has promised her, and now her imagination leads to the metaphor of an enamelled jewel, which she compares implicitly to her own beauty. But after the first line F's grammar and syntax turn so convoluted that for centuries editors have been left struggling to clarify the speech's meaning (see 2.1.108–12 LN). Compositorial misreading seems to be the problem. The confusion is especially unfortunate, because, in a sustained speech at the culmination of Adriana's first, vexed scene, the planting of the jewellery metaphor prepares spectators for the later appearance of an actual piece of jewellery, the necklace, or chain, procured by Adriana's husband as a love-offering to appease his wife. Thoughts of jewels beget the later appearance of the real jewellery, but we will never be quite sure what Adriana meant to express in this proleptic passage. Compositors influenced the text more subtly, too, for they were probably responsible for much of the punctuation (some scholars argue that Shakespeare himself punctuated lightly). Likewise, the absence in the compositor's case of type-pieces (or 'sorts') for certain punctuation marks and the presence of sorts for other marks can make a difference to how a passage is understood (question marks were frequently used in the printing office in place of exclamation marks, for example).

For a glimpse of some of these textual problems, one can turn to sig. H6ᵛ (TLN 1382–1503, 4.4.95–5.1.37.1), set by compositor B (see Fig. 23). Visible here are several features, including the 'permissive' or 'indefinite' SD '*Enter three or foure . . .*' (TLN 1394) – so called because of its unfixed number of performers – and the prose-like flow-over of verse lines (TLN 1419–23). Stage directions pose interesting problems on this page. The first ('permissive') SD in column a, for example, requires several characters to enter even before Adriana calls out for their help: perhaps the direction was written in the margin of the manuscript, forcing the compositor to make a decision about where to place it among the lines. The next SD, two-thirds of the way down column a, '*Exeunt. Manet Offic. Adri. Luci.Courtizan*' (TLN 1426), offers a general '*Exeunt*' immediately corrected by the character-specified '*Manet*'[1] (for a close-up, see Fig. 24). (The end of Act 5 contains a similar SD.) This SD, like the previous one, also appears to be slightly out of place, for it makes better sense coming immediately after Adriana's preceding line (TLN 1424), in which she orders her husband to be carried off and asks her sister to stay. Perhaps the compositor was confused by the SD's ambiguous placing in the margin of the manuscript, or perhaps the order of SDs in the text somehow reflects the flow of Shakespeare's writing. In the third SD of column a, '*Enter Antipholus Siracusia with his Rapier drawne, / and Dromio Sirac.*' (TLN 1440–1), Antipholus

---

1 '*Manet*' is the third-person singular present indicative form of the Latin verb *manere*, 'to remain', used where *manent*, the third-person plural, might be expected. Similarly, the singular *exit* often takes the place of the plural *exeunt*.

They muſt be bound and laide in ſome darke roome.

Ant. Say wherefore did'ſt thou locke me forth to day,
And why doſt thou denie the bagge of gold?

Adr. I did not gentle husband locke thee forth.

Dro. And gentle M^r I receiu'd no gold :
But I coofeſſe ſir, that we were lock'd out.

Adr. Diſſembling Villain, thou ſpeak'ſt falſe in both

Ant. Diſſembling harlot, thou art falſe in all,
And art confederate with a damned packe,
To make a loathſome abiect ſcorne of me :
But with theſe nailes, Ile plucke out theſe falſe eyes,
That would behold in me this ſhamefull ſport.

*Enter three or foure, and offer to binde him:
Hee ſtriues.*

Adr. Oh binde him, binde him, let him not come
neere me.

Pinch. More company, the fiend is ſtrong within him
Luc. Aye me poore man, how pale and wan he looks.

Ant. What will you murther me, thou Iailor thou ?
I am thy priſoner, wilt thou ſuffer them to make a reſ-
cue ?

Offi. Maſters let him go : he is my priſoner, and you
ſhall not haue him.

Pinch. Go binde this man, for he is franticke too.

Adr. What wilt thou do, thou peeuiſh Officer ?
Haſt thou delight to ſee a wretched man
Do outrage and diſpleaſure to himſelfe?

Offi. He is my priſoner, if I let him go,
The debt he owes will be requir'd of me.

Adr. I will diſcharge thee ere I go from thee,
Beare me forthwith vnto his Creditor,
And knowing how the debt growes I will pay it.
Good Maſter Doctor ſee him ſafe conuey'd
Home to my houſe, oh moſt vnhappy day.

Ant. Oh moſt vnhappie ſtrumpet.

Dro. Maſter, I am heere entred in bond for you,

Ant. Out on thee Villaine, wherefore doſt thou mad
mee ?

Dro. Will you be bound for nothing, be mad good
Maſter, cry the diuell.

Luc. God helpe poore ſoules, how idlely doe they
talke.

Adr. Go beate him hence, ſiſter go you with me:
Say now, whoſe ſuite is he arreſted at ?

Exeunt. Manet Offic. Adri. Luci. Courtizan.

Off. One *Angelo* a Goldſmith, do you know him?

Adr. I know the man : what is the ſumme he owes?

Off. Two hundred Duckets.

Adr. Say, how growes it due.

Off. Due for a Chaine your husband had of him.

Adi. He did beſpeake a Chaine for me, but had it not.

Cur. When as your husband all in rage to day
Came to my houſe, and tooke away my Ring,
The Ring I ſaw vpon his finger now,
Straight after did I meete him with a Chaine.

Adr. It may be ſo, but I did neuer ſee it.
Come Iailor, bring me where the Goldſmith is,
I long to know the truth heereof at large.

*Enter Antipholus Siracusa with his Rapier drawne,
and Dromio Sirac.*

Luc. God for thy mercy, they are looſe againe.

Adr. And come with naked ſwords,
Let's call more helpe to haue them bound againe.

Runne all out.

Off. Away, they'l kill vs.

Exeunt omnes, as faſt as may be, frighted.

S. Ant. I ſee theſe Witches are affraid of ſwords.

S. Dro. She that would be your wife, now ran from
you.

Ant. Come to the Centaur, fetch our ſtuffe from
thence :
I long that we were ſafe and ſound aboord.

Dro. Faith ſtay heere this night, they will ſurely do
vs no harme : you ſaw they ſpeake vs faire, giue vs gold:
me thinkes they are ſuch a gentle Nation, that but for
the Mountaine of mad fleſh that claimes mariage of me,
I could finde in my heart to ſtay heere ſtill, and turne
Witch.

Ant. I will not ſtay to night for all the Towne,
Therefore away, to get our ſtuffe aboord. *Exeunt*

Actus Quintus. Scæna Prima.

Enter the Merchant and the Goldſmith.

Gold. I am ſorry Sir that I haue hindred you,
But I proteſt he had the Chaine of me,
Though moſt diſhoneſtly he doth denie it.

Mar. How is the man eſteem'd heere in the Citie?

Gold. Of very reuerent reputation ſir,
Of credit infinite, highly belou'd,
Second to none that liues heere in the Citie :
His word might beare my wealth at any t me.

Mar. Speake ſoftly, yonder as I thinke he walkes.

Enter Antipholus and Dromio againe.

Gold. Tis ſo : and that ſelfe chaine about his necke,
Which he forſwore moſt monſtrouſly to haue.
Good ſir draw neere to me, Ile ſpeake to him:
Signior *Antipholus,* I wonder much
That you would put me to this ſhame and trouble,
And not without ſome ſcandall to your ſelfe,
With circumſtance and oaths, ſo to denie
This Chaine, which now you weare ſo openly.
Beſide the charge, the ſhame, impriſonment,
You haue done wrong to this my honeſt friend,
Who but for ſtaying on our Controuerſie,
Had hoiſted ſaile, and put to ſea to day:
This Chaine you had of me, can you deny it?

Ant. I thinke I had, I neuer did deny it.

Mar. Yes that you did ſir, and forſwore it too.

Ant. Who heard me to denie it or forſweare it?

Mar. Theſe eares of mine thou knowſt did heare thee:
Fie on thee wretch, 'tis pitty that thou liu'ſt
To walke where any honeſt men reſort.

Ant. Thou art a Villaine to impeach and wrong,
Ile proue mine honor, and mine honeſtie
Againſt thee preſently, if thou dar'ſt ſtand:

Mar. I dare and do defie thee for a villaine.

They draw. Enter Adriana, Luciana, Courtezan, & others.

Adr. Hold, hurt him not for God ſake, he is mad,
Some get within him, take his ſword away:
Binde *Dromio* too, and beare them to my houſe.

S. Dro. Runne maſter run, for Gods ſake take a houſe,
This is ſome Prioric, in, or we are ſpoyl'd. *Exeunt to the Priorie.*

Enter

---

23   First Folio, sig. H6ᵛ (p. 96 of the 'Comedies'), comprising *CE* TLN
1382–1503, 4.4.95–5.1.37.1

Adr. Go beare him hence, fifter go you with me:
Say now, whofe fuite is he arrefted at?
             Exeunt. Manet Offic. ~Adri. Luci.Courtizan
   Off. One ~Angelo a Goldfmith, do you know him?
   Adr. I know the man : what is the fumme he owes?
   Off. Two hundred Duckets.
   Adr. Say, how growes it due.
   Off. Due for a Chaine your husband had of him.
   Adr. He did befpeake a Chaine for me,but had it not.
   Cur. When as your husband all in rage to day,
Came to my houfe, and tooke away my Ring,
The Ring I faw vpon his finger now,
Straight after did I meete him with a Chaine.'
   Adr. It may be fo, but I did neuer fee it.
Come Iailor,bring me where the Goldfmith is,
I long to know the truth heereof at large.

     Enter Antipholus Siracufia with his Rapier drawne,
             and Dromio Sirac.

   Luc. God for thy mercy, they are loofe againe.
   Adr. And come with naked fwords,
Let's call more helpe to haue them bound againe.
                         Runne all out.

24   First Folio, sig. H6ᵛ, close-up of the foot of column a

is given a drawn rapier, but Dromio nothing, even though
Adriana thereafter says that both 'come with naked swords'
(TLN 1443); it is as if the writing hand had forgotten (or
ignored) what Dromio's sword hand was doing.

But the major problem on this page occurs at the foot of
column a, which carries the SD '*Runne all out.*' on the last line,[1]

1   Such a line at the foot of a column, called the 'direction line', was typically left
    blank of text and used, in *Errors*, for a catchword and sometimes a signature
    number. Werstine notes that none of the other Folio comedies puts an SD in this
    line, and wonders whether compositor B 'was ready to take extraordinary measures
    to avoid setting a marginal stage direction at the top of a column' ('Copy', 244; see
    243–4).

and the head of column b, which, after a line from the Officer (who should have just exited), offers a second exit direction, this one in both Latin and English: '*Exeunt omnes, as fast as may be, frighted.*': two SDs in different styles and different columns, but separated by only one five-syllable line of dialogue, calling redundantly for the same exit. That the second employs Latin clarifies little, since Shakespeare wrote SDs in both Latin and English. The possibility that two SDs rather than one might genuinely be intended led the production at Stratford-upon-Avon in 2000 to launch, at the first SD, a Keystone Cops-like chase off the stage and back on to it, and then, after the Officer's 'Away, they'l kill vs.' (TLN 1446), another mass departure to fulfil the second SD (see also Cam[2a]'s '*Run all out [and re-enter with others]*'). The double chase made for theatrical fun, but the two SDs probably refer to the same exit. Since '*Runne all out.*' expresses a different sense of theatrical language than does '*Exeunt omnes*', it may be that the directions are by different hands, especially since the first is the play's only exit direction not to use '*Exeunt*' or '*Exit*' (its closest analogue is '*All gather to see them.*' at TLN 1815). That first SD succinctly summarizes the second, without worrying about the characters' emotions ('*frighted*') or their speed ('*as fast as may be*'); it is crisp and functional. Perhaps this first SD was added at a later date by someone other than Shakespeare – a theatrical bookkeeper? – with the intention of slightly separating the exits of the women and the Officer, since the latter gets one further line. If the compositor saw before him the two SDs written close to each other on the manuscript page, perhaps on two lines but as if they were collectively one unit, he was faced with the problem of a rather lengthy exit direction and an insufficient amount of space left at the foot of column a into which to squeeze it. If he did not want to put a 'marginal stage direction' at the head of a column, as Werstine speculates, then one pragmatic solution was to retain all the language of the directions but to split it up, with part of it placed at the foot of column a, even before the Officer's 'Away', and the rest coming after the Officer's line. Foakes favours such an explanation.[1] Wells and Taylor dismiss it (*TxC*, 266), although Whitworth offers a conjecture similar to that of Foakes. Still, the explanation does not quite satisfy. Compositor B, just before he set these SDs, seems not to have been bothered about insufficient space, since he left empty lines around the SD at TLN 1440–1. And if he saw the two SDs as one unit, he could simply have left the last line of column a empty (the standard procedure), begun column b with the Officer's 'Away . . .' and then beneath that speech-line set the composite exit direction. Perhaps the directions' different voices (and possibly handwriting) and perhaps their placement in the manuscript made the compositor assume that they were actually two rather than one. Alternatively, maybe the double directions offer an awkward attempt to orchestrate a complex exit, with some in Adriana's party quickly disappearing, the Officer hesitating but then delivering his own exit line, and any lingering characters, with fears heightened, completing the retreat. Evidence and conjecture cannot take us much further.

The printer's copy: authorial 'foul fapers'? A text suitable for performance?

Beyond the question of compositorial practices, a second large issue has occupied textual scholars: whether or not the F text of *The Comedy of Errors* was set from a manuscript in Shakespeare's own hand, possibly his 'foul papers' (i.e. his working draft of the play before it might have been transcribed into a 'fair copy' for subsequent use).[2] The play exhibits certain

---

1 See Foakes, xiii–xv; 86, 144n.
2 Werstine cautions that, '[c]ontrary to Greg's assumption, *foul papers* need not refer exclusively to authorial drafts, whether these are messy or not; the term simply describes papers that, for whatever, reason, are to be or have already been transcribed' ('Method', 44). On critical debates over the nature of Shakespeare's drafts, or foul papers, see Werstine, 'Narratives', and esp. Werstine, *Manuscripts*.

anomalies often attributed to an author in the flow of composition – changing SPs and character descriptors, or, in SDs, thinking out loud about characters' backgrounds or including extraneous bits of narrative. The Antipholus brothers, for example, are first named in a way that suggests that Shakespeare was writing with a copy of Plautus' *Menaechmi* fresh in his memory or even open on his desk. The resident (Ephesian) brother is referred to as '*Antipholis Sereptus*' (TLN 273); that cognomen, close to Latin *surreptus*, 'stolen', recalls *Men.*, in which one of the twins was kidnapped from a market at an early age (see List of Roles, 4n.). Likewise, the wandering (Syracusan) brother first enters the stage as '*Antipholis Erotes*' (TLN 162); here the Latinate addition is harder to parse, though one of its associations is with the Latin verb *errare*, to wander (see List of Roles, 3n.). Next time around, that name has become '*Antipholis Errotis*' (TLN 394), another near miss at a form of *errare*, before it settles down geographically as, more or less, '*Antipholus of Siracusia*' (TLN 786; for variants, see TLN 1183, 1811). Speech prefixes can change. Egeon, the Merchant of Syracuse, has '*Marchant*' for his first SP (TLN 4), but in Act 5 he will be identified first as '*Mar. Fat.*' (TLN 1671), for '*Merchant Father*' and finally just '*Fa*[*ther*].' (TLN 1762 and subsequently), as if Shakespeare were adjusting terms as, in his imagination, the character became less a merchant and more a father.[1] Monikers and SPs can also be shared. In addition to the Syracusan Merchant, F has two other characters identified as '*a Marchant*', '*a Merchant*' or '*the Merchant*' (TLN 162, 981, 1463), implying that overall distinctions were not troubling the author in the moment-by-moment act of composition. In 3.1, a maid called '*Luce*' (TLN 679) suddenly enters to Syracusan Dromio behind a door and joins him in railing against Ephesian Antipholus; scholars agree that she is the same character who is later described as the wife (or possibly fiancée) of Dromio of

1   See List of Roles, 1n.; van Elke, 'Genre', 53.

Ephesus, but who takes on a different name, 'Nell' (see 3.2.110n.). Shakespeare may have changed his idea about the name as he worked through the play, not wanting it in 3.2 to sound too close to that of Adriana's sister, Luciana, but without feeling that enough was at stake to require him to go back and rewrite dialogue in the earlier scene.

F also contains in its SDs bits and pieces of information that function less as instructions to the actors than as musings about actions and characters within the narrative: '*Enter Adriana, wife to Antipholis Sereptus,with / Luciana her Sister.*' (TLN 273–4); '*Enter . . . Angelo the / Goldsmith, and Balthaser the Merchant.*' (TLN 617–18); '*Enter . . . from the Courtizans.*' (TLN 995); '*Enter . . . from the Bay.*' (TLN 1073); '*Exeunt to the Priorie.*' (TLN 1503).[1] These directions read as if they envisioned characters within the story rather than actors in the theatre, and locations within the narrative rather than places on the stage; again, they give the impression of the author in the process of composition. Perhaps the most interesting of such directions is '*Enter . . . a Schoole- / master, call'd Pinch.*' (TLN 1321–2; see 4.4.40.2n.). The descriptive information about Pinch has no stage utility. Adriana refers to him as 'Doctor *Pinch*', 'a Coniurer' (TLN 1330, 4.4.48) and 'Good Master Doctor' (TLN 1414, 4.4.123), which might favour identifying him as a pedagogue, although he binds and carries off Ephesian Antipholus and Dromio as if, like a physician, he might effect a cure of their madness. When Shakespeare wrote Pinch's entrance direction, he may have been defining the character in his mind. With Pinch's type and manner once established conceptually, the need for vocational exactitude falls away. Likewise, the SD information about Adriana, '*wife to Antipholis Sereptus*' (TLN 273), serves less a theatrical than a narrative purpose.

Because the manuscript underlying F seems so close to the story as it is being invented and put to paper, a number of

---

1 Signs might have been hung over stage doors to identify certain houses, such as the Phoenix, the Centaur or the Porpentine, but less probably to indicate the bay.

textual scholars have argued strongly that the version must be Shakespeare's 'foul papers', his working draft of *Errors*, with some light annotations, perhaps made by a bookkeeper with eventual performance in mind – although these scholars maintain that the printer's copy could not have served for a promptbook, or playbook.[1] Such a text would afford a rare opportunity to glimpse the playwright in the act of creating his original version, before it was, perhaps, marked up by others for theatrical practice. The foul-papers scholars argue that preparation of the author's draft for the theatre would have involved regularizing *Errors*'s SPs and names, filling out SDs and clarifying indefinite ones. Because the printer's copy for *Errors* is deficient in all these regards, it presumably could not have served for a promptbook. But William B. Long has demonstrated in a series of essays that many surviving playbooks from the era show exactly the kind of variable information that scholars such as Greg believed to be confined only to foul papers.[2]

Likewise, Paul Werstine has contended that the play's authorial papers could have been used as a promptbook, that compositorial errors account for many of the editorial problems and that the F text in matters such as names and SPs is quite sufficiently clear and consistent to have been derived from a theatrical playbook. He argues, for example, that the cognomens

---

1 See McKerrow; Chambers, *WS*, 1.305–12; Greg, *Problem*, 140–1; Greg, *Folio*, 200–2; *TxC*, 266. Werstine favours the term 'playbook' over Greg's 'prompt-book' in part because the latter came into use for 'a highly regularized and thoroughly annotated theatrical manuscript quite different from those that survive from Shakespeare's time' ('Copy', 245, n. 5); see also Werstine, *Manuscripts*, esp. 107–41.

2 See Long, 'Directions'; Long, 'Dulwich'; Long, 'Playbook'. For a further argument against the presumed dichotomy between messy authorial papers and clean promptbooks, first articulated by McKerrow, see Werstine, 'McKerrow'. See also Werstine, *Manuscripts*, esp. 116–18, which demonstrates that many of the presumed confusions in F were perpetuated, even worsened, in seventeenth-century promptbooks of *Errors*.

'*Erotes*' and '*Errotis*' for Antipholus of Syracuse would have occasioned no confusion in theatrical practice and that ambiguous SPs, such as *Ant.* used for both of the Antipholus brothers, are made distinct enough when they need to be, as in the last act where the Antipholuses are onstage together and the text distinguishes them as *E. Ant.* and *S. Ant.* Werstine attributes other related inconsistencies to compositorial practice or carelessness. Further, for the duplicate SDs in 4.4 (sig. H6ᵛ) – '*Runne all out.*', '*Exeunt omnes, as fast as may be, frighted.*' – he maintains that it is difficult to sort out whether Shakespeare wrote one and a bookkeeper another, since both forms have Shakespearean analogues. Werstine concludes that the printer's copy for *Errors* could as easily have been a playbook as foul papers and, perhaps more important, that the F text simply resists the rigid distinction between these categories maintained by mid-twentieth-century scholars; the problem, he concludes, may be the assumed dichotomies themselves.[1]

Werstine's perspective has been resisted by Wells and Taylor, who point out that the F text lacks evidence of theatrical use (such as 'actors' names, duplicated directions, isolated extra-syntactical calls for essential properties, warning directions') so that '[t]he orthodox view – that the play was set from foul papers – is thus probably correct' (*TxC*, 266). The orthodox Chambers–Greg foul-papers argument, however, assumes the difficult task of maintaining a negative; that is, the claim that the manuscript underlying the F text could never have been used as a playbook. The evidence and arguments offered by Long and Werstine about the state of contemporary playbooks run against that conclusion, and Werstine's analysis of *Errors*'s textual problems provides a convincing approach. Indeed, Wells and Taylor acknowledge that the F text is to some extent a performance document: they accept the possibility of 'a few annotations related (indeterminably) to performance' and see

---

1 For his extended discussion of this matter, see Werstine, *Manuscripts*.

the act divisions 'as a genuine reflection' of the 1594 enactment at Gray's Inn (*TxC*, 266). Standish Henning, the *Variorum* editor, concludes that the F text is close to authorial papers yet acknowledges that the difference between foul papers and promptbook is difficult to sustain.[1]

Arguments about the nature of the printer's copy always make their way to those disputed SDs, mentioned previously, on sig. H6^v (TLN 1382–503, 4.4.95–5.1.37.1). How do we understand the two duplicative SDs, one at the foot of column a, the other on the second line at the head of column b, repetitious in effect but different in style (see Figs 24 and 25)?

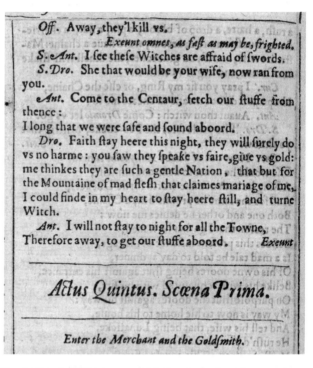

Off. Away, they'l kill vs.

Exeunt omnes, as fast as may be, frighted.

S. Ant. I fee thefe Witches are affraid of fwords.

S. Dro. She that would be your wife, now ran from you.

Ant. Come to the Centaur, fetch our ftuffe from thence :

I long that we were fafe and found aboord.

Dro. Faith ftay heere this night, they will furely do vs no harme : you faw they fpeake vs faire, giue vs gold: me thinkes they are fuch a gentle Nation, that but for the Mountaine of mad flefh that claimes mariage of me, I could finde in my heart to ftay heere ftill, and turne Witch.

Ant. I will not ftay to night for all the Towne, Therefore away, to get our ftuffe aboord. *Exeunt*

Actus Quintus. Scœna Prima.

Enter the Merchant and the Goldfmith.

25 First Folio, sig. H6^v, close-up of the head of column b

1 See *Var.*, 29–80.

The orthodox view, proposed by Greg (*Problem*, 140), contends that the first of these directions is by Shakespeare, the second a later annotation in the manuscript margin by a bookkeeper, a view that Wells and Taylor accept. According to Werstine, however, both forms of the direction could have been written by Shakespeare. '*Exeunt omnes, as fast as may be,frighted.*' resembles a SD in F *Taming of the Shrew*: '*Exit Biondello, Tranio and Pedant as fast as may be.*' (TLN 2490). That direction is thought to have been Shakespeare's, and the printer's copy for *Shrew*, as with *Errors*, is considered authorial foul papers. '*Runne all out.*', notes Werstine, bears some similarity to a SD in a fragment from the first printing of *1H6*: ' "*. . . they all runne away . . .*" ' ('Copy', 244). It also shares something in manner with a later *Errors* SD: '*All gather to see them.*' (TLN 1815; see 5.1.330 SD and n.), which Wells and Taylor consider authorial (*TxC*, 266). Werstine concludes sensibly that the 'unusual position' in the text of this split or doubled SD 'forbids an editor from using it to draw inferences about the nature of the printer's copy' ('Copy', 244; see 243–4). We are left, then, with the view that the manuscript behind the F text of *Errors* was probably authorial papers that could have served as a playbook for performance. Perhaps the most important inference that we might draw is that the text of *Errors* should not be separated from the play's theatrical life.

The printer's copy: the question of performance venue

That inference invites a related question: whether the F text seems oriented towards public performance, as at the playhouses, or private performance, as at venues such as Gray's Inn or the court. Almost thirty years separate the composition of *Errors* in about 1594 and its first appearance in print in 1623; in that interim the play was probably performed in the 1594–5 season at the Theatre, played at the Gray's Inn revels in December 1594, perhaps revived in the 1597–8 season and again in 1604–5 at the playhouses (the first season entailing performance at the Curtain and the last at the Globe), and produced at court before King James in December 1604 (see Introduction, pp. 102–12). Although the printer's copy bears signs of authorial composition, it also may have traces of performance (or revision), more likely so if it had been used as a playbook. What kind of venue, public or private, does the printer's copy reflect?

One bit of evidence is equivocal but deserves mention: the absence of music. *Errors* is unusual among the early comedies in having no music within the action, unlike, say, *The Two Gentlemen of Verona* or *The Taming of the Shrew*. Plays performed indoors needed pauses for the trimming, mending and replacing of candles, and such pauses would be used, almost as a matter of course, for entr'acte music and other business. That *Errors* retains no indications of music may reflect the fact that music was treated as something separate and detachable, a notion that squares with performance at a private venue featuring hired music from other sources. In general, however, lost theatrical music is not uncommon, as Stern points out (*Documents*, 120–73). Nonetheless, *Errors*'s anomalous absence of songs, singing or music is worth noting, if inconclusively.

F's act–scene divisions also make for tricky evidence. They may have been introduced by Shakespeare in anticipation of the Inns of Court performance (see *TxC*, 266). Alternatively, they may have been inserted as aids in outlining the complicated action as Shakespeare was drafting the play, without reference to where it would be performed. Or they may have been added somehow at a later time. If the divisions are by one hand, such as Shakespeare's, then the lack of a scene one indication in Act 2 (scene one designations being present with all the other act headings) makes for an anomaly. Likewise, the act divisions, though sensible, work against the text's implicitly continuous flow of stage action from 2.2 to 3.1 and from 4.4 to 5.1. Taylor establishes that in plays at the public playhouses from 1592 to *c.* 1607, continuous flow rather than act intervals was the performance practice (see 'Act-intervals'). As an odd case, *Errors*'s act divisions might have been meant for the performance at Gray's Inn Hall, as Taylor believes ('Act-intervals', 45), but that view cannot explain the presence of scene one designations for four of the five acts which lack any obvious performance function. Like the double SDs of 4.4, the act divisions provide little evidence for any particular theory of the text.

While the staging demands of *The Comedy of Errors* are modest and flexible enough that they could have been satisfied by almost any venue, the F text does assume certain stage resources. *Errors*'s most complicated scene for staging is 3.1. In the only close analysis of the configuration of Gray's Inn Hall for the presenting of *Errors* during the 1594 revels, Margaret Knapp and Michal Kobialka conclude that a stage for the revels must have been built between the hall's dais at one end of the long hall and the temporarily erected scaffolds at the other (and close to the dais itself). Dignitaries would have been seated on the dais, with other spectators seated opposite them, on the scaffolds. The playing space in between would have been 'about nine feet [*c.* 2.75 metres] deep and as wide as the hall, that is, thirty-four feet, eight inches [*c.* 10.5 metres]' (438), with audiences perhaps not only on two sides (the dais and the scaffold sides) but on all four. Given that the performance of *Errors* followed immediately after dancing at the end of a long night, it is doubtful that the players would have been afforded time for a disruptive erecting of booth houses on the stage, especially since such booths would block some sight-lines (see Introduction, pp. 109–10).

The Gray's Inn stage also poorly satisfies the needs of the playtext in 3.1 (see Introduction, pp. 95–101) in other ways. The central physical fact of that scene is the Phoenix's door: it is locked against Antipholus of Ephesus and his outdoor party, who pound on it for entrance; conversely, the door provides the barrier behind which the indoor party lurks and gibes. The public theatre stages, typically with balcony and central and side doors, are the locales envisioned by the text: Dromio of Syracuse could hide behind the central door (or double doors), while Adriana could emerge on the balcony, as from dining. The stage at Gray's Inn has no such advantages. Imaginative actors, of course, could have found various ways around any difficulties, but that is exactly the point: for a private venue, the text imposes a staging obstacle that must be overcome. *Errors* is adaptable enough to be played almost anywhere, but the venue imagined in 3.1 is the public theatre.

It is also sometimes argued that the F text must have been for private performance because of its shortness, which would have perfectly suited an evening at Gray's Inn or at court, packed with other entertainments. *Errors*'s shortness, however, does not constitute a liability for the public theatre. At 1,919 lines in the Folio, *Errors* has the fewest of any Shakespearean play, but there were other such plays of the era: for example, the First Quarto of *The Taming of a Shrew*, published in 1594 and apparently performed on the public stage by Pembroke's Men, was only 1,550 lines (*TxC*, 169). Indeed, in contemporary times, *Errors* has become a frequently performed Shakespearean comedy, and in modern performances cuts are often made to passages such as Adriana's 'jewel best enamelled' speech in 2.1 and the wit-contest between Antipholus and Dromio of Syracuse in 2.2. As Mariko Ichikawa has recently summarized, 'the F1 text of *The Comedy of Errors* as a whole is designed to be acted on the stage of a public playhouse' ('Staging', 81).

EDITORIAL PROCEDURES

This edition is based on the 1623 First Folio text of the play. Some fifty subsequent editions of *The Comedy of Errors* have been collated, up to very recent ones from Oxford, Cambridge and Norton. The commentary notes credit parenthetically many of the contributions of prior editions.

Following Arden guidelines, the text modernizes spelling and punctuation and word-forms (except in a few cases, such as 'fraughtage' (4.1.87), where the original was favoured for its sound over the modern 'freightage'). The text also regularizes and standardizes SPs and generally employs personal names, as is the custom with Arden editions. Thus, F's 'Merchant of Syracuse' becomes 'Egeon', the SP adopted by Rowe and by almost all subsequent editors. Emilia, however, remains the 'Abbess', as she is traditionally called, for purposes of surprise. Arden guidelines also call for textual distinctions between prose and verse, the former set immediately following a SP, the latter set on the line below. When speakers share a verse line, the second or subsequent speaker's line is indented in relation to the preceding line (as, for example, at 3.1.15). Alternating rhyme, such as at 3.2.1–52, is shown graphically by the slight indentation of alternate lines, making the rhymes visible. The First Folio did not distinguish prose and verse to this degree (although Folio verse lines generally begin with capital letters). Thus, when a line in F might be reasonably read as prose or as verse, Arden guidelines nonetheless require editors to decide on one or the other.

Concerning punctuation, the F text lavishes colons and semicolons but spares full stops, more so than in modern writing. Punctuation was changing, as rhetorical (or 'physiological') punctuation, attuned to the rhythms of words as spoken, ceded ground to grammatical (or 'syntactical') punctuation, attuned to the formal structure of a sentence.[1] Rhetorically, certain marks – comma, colon, semicolon, full stop – might represent pauses of different lengths. Grammatically,

---

1   See Parkes; also Crewe.

however, such marks signify relationships between clauses or phrases. Thus, punctuation can indicate both oral rhythm and flow of logic. Sometimes in F, the grounds on which a punctuation mark is used are unclear, and an editor must decide on a mark by interpreting the sentence. Likewise, a compositor's choice of punctuation marks can be influenced by what pieces of type are available in the type-case at any given moment: perhaps all the colons are busy but not the semicolons. Additionally, some punctuation in F may derive from compositors or from editor(s) who prepared the text underlying F, rather than from Shakespeare.

The procedure here has been generally to follow F's punctuation, although sometimes clauses have been shortened with the insertions of full stops, semicolons have been substituted for colons, and the like. I have avoided the practice of frequent editorial end-stopping, which might help the novice reader but which makes speeches sound choppy. Generally, I have preferred to allow the shifting rhythms and subtle grammatical relationships of long clauses to show through, such as in Egeon's several sustained speeches in 1.1. Retaining long sentences allows the reader and the performer to observe the nuances and potentialities of the lines as they might be spoken. Readers will also find some attention paid to punctuation in textual notes. Relevant features of Elizabethan English also receive mention, for sometimes what looks to the modern eye like sloppy grammar, such as a singular subject acting as a plural (e.g. 'man' at 2.1.7 and 20), can conform to Elizabethan usage and, even more, can reveal sudden, energizing Shakespearean shifts in thought.[1]

Following Arden practice, I have silently introduced dashes to indicate a break in a train of thought, a noticeable shift in grammatical construction, the interruption of a speech or the redirection of a speech to a different hearer. Where the

---

1 See Davis, esp. 75–7.

editorial dash deserves a comment, as when Adriana turns away from Luciana at 2.1.32 and addresses the audience, I have added a textual note on the punctuation's source and a note of explanation. Unfortunately, series protocols leave dashes unavailable for other occasions, such as when a tertiary phrase or clause is enclosed, as it were, in a secondary one, as in the difficult sentence at 1.1.5–10; in such cases, commas must suffice. Sometimes, of course, an editor must struggle to make sense out of a passage that is manifestly corrupt, such as Adriana's speech at 2.1.108–12, and must balance the desire to make as few changes as possible with the wish to make as much sense as possible through emendation. Readers will find discussions of departures from F's wording in the commentary notes and longer notes.

This edition intrudes upon F in several ways. It introduces quotation marks inside speeches to indicate when a speaker self-consciously repeats the words of another back to the speaker, such as at 1.2.87, where Syracusan Antipholus repeats Ephesian Dromio's phrase, 'mistress' marks', which asserts, surprisingly to Antipholus, that he has a wife. Such commandeering of words and phrases is so recurrent a linguistic feature of *Errors* and so much of a piece with the play's larger patterns of repetition and doubling that this edition calls attention to the practice by enclosing overtly borrowed language in quotation marks not found in F. That 'connective repetition' constitutes a time-honoured device of improvisation (see Introduction, pp. 33–4), as when a clown appropriates another speaker's phrase to launch a comic riff. Readers will also find editorially introduced SDs that mark certain actions, especially the passing of an object – a purse, a key, a chain – from one character to another (as at 1.2.7 SD) or the striking of one character by another, such as a servant by a master (as at 1.2.92 SD). Such emendations contravene the call from some editorial scholars for an 'open text' (see Kidnie). Farcical plays, however, trade in displaced objects and harmless beatings, and drawing attention to them helps readers to grasp both the business of the stage and the qualities of the play's generic world. Indeed, to emphasize the circulation of objects, such as a chain, in a play of interlinking errors, is to underscore the way that farce can make visual the symbolic action of the play. On several occasions, I have also repositioned SDs to suit the stage business and to reflect the practicalities of exiting and entering, with explanations in the commentary notes. In particular, several entrance directions have been moved to precede an onstage speaker's announcement of that entrance (see 2.1.42.1 LN). In general, my editing has assumed that the public theatre constitutes the performance venue imagined in F.

Arden editions are known for their attention to language and nuances of meaning, a tradition followed here. Furthermore, linking a particular word or phrase to its usage elsewhere by Shakespeare or another Elizabethan writer can illuminate the play's internal verbal structure and evoke the rich and rapidly developing linguistic landscape of Shakespeare's world. Likewise, following Arden practice, proverbial phrases and biblical allusions are glossed.[1] Commentary notes can lead in almost any direction, depending on the needs of the occasion; the present ones have been written with the goal of opening the text as much as possible to the reader. I have occasionally identified rhetorical devices in the commentary notes, in order to draw attention to the sophistication and even self-consciousness of *Errors*'s rhetoric.[2] This edition, in its introduction and commentary notes, also pays much more attention to versification than do most modern editions. I do so on the principle that how a line or a word is actually pronounced

---

1 Except in special cases, the commentary notes do not repeat Tilley's and Dent's cross-references to Shakespearean plays other than *Errors* that employ a given proverb. Proverbs included in both Tilley and Dent are cited from Dent.

2 My main source for terminology has been Richard Lanham's *A Handlist of Rhetorical Terms*, although I have also had recourse to Lee Soninno's *A Handbook of Sixteenth-Century Rhetoric* and other works.

(or silently heard) makes an enormous difference to how dramatic meaning and experience are created.

Finally, a note on 'first occurrences' in *Errors* of certain words as recorded in the *Oxford English Dictionary*. In this edition I have used the online *OED*, and have continuously checked and rechecked various words. Some readers might notice that fewer 'first occurrences' are recorded here than in Henning's *Variorum* edition. The reasons are twofold. (1) Henning worked from a printed copy of the second edition of the *OED*; however, as the *OED* project has continued online, entries have been steadily updated (and renumbered) and examples added, so that some 'first occurrences' are no longer so. (2) Henning generally applied his 1594 dating of *Errors* in determining a 'first occurrence', so that he claims more such instances in *Errors* than does the *OED*, which typically (and confusingly) employs either 1616 (Shakespeare's death) or 1623 (the year of the First Folio's publication) to date an *Errors* entry. There is something to be said for Henning's use of 1594, yet we cannot say exactly what words were spoken on the public stage in the autumn of 1594, whereas we can be certain what was printed in 1623 (using the *OED* 1616 date assumes that no word of a Shakespearean play had been changed between then and 1623). The present edition thus records a 'first occurrence' only when there is no citation prior to 1623.

APPENDIX 3

Casting and doubling

The chart on p. 354 lists speaking parts by scene. *The Comedy of Errors* has nineteen speaking roles; its non-speaking ones include the assistants to Doctor Pinch (see 4.4.108 SD) and the '*Headsman*' and '*other Officers*' (5.1.127.3) attending the Duke in the last act. Act 5 requires thirteen speaking characters and several additional attendants to be onstage at the same time, presumably accounting for all the available actors. If the Headsman and a minimum of two officers, all enacted by hired men, are assumed for the Duke's entourage, and if those same extras could have served earlier in the scene as '*others*' (5.1.32.2), then the minimum number of performers needed for *Errors* is sixteen. The five female speaking parts would require at least three boy actors (for Adriana, Luciana and the Courtesan). The Abbess could have been played by a fourth boy actor or perhaps by an adult. The part of Luce could be doubled either with that of the Abbess or (see *Var.*, 509) with the Courtesan. To distribute nineteen speaking roles among thirteen actors, doubling would be required. A range of combinations is possible, two attractive ones being the Jailer doubled with the Officer, and, especially, Egeon doubled with Doctor Pinch. The first possibility links Egeon's potentially fatal detention with his Ephesian son's comic arrest. The second draws Egeon's romance melancholy closer to the dark madness of the farce. The Syracusan merchant, deprived, wan and weary, bears some resemblance to the ragged, beggarly and hungry Pinch whom Ephesian Antipholus describes with revulsion as Egeon stands by (see 5.1.238–46). Ephesian Dromio likewise associates the two (at 5.1.295). The hired man John Sinkler was noted for taking the parts of thin, narrow-faced characters, so he may have played Doctor Pinch and also doubled as Egeon.

According to Donald W. Foster, however, Shakespeare (rather than Sinkler) played Egeon (see p. 103); if so, Shakespeare might have doubled as Doctor Pinch: the playwright as false conjuror has metatheatrical appeal. In either case, that possible doubling allows for a shadow of sadness to touch both the romantic and farcical domains. Some productions also double the Antipholuses and the Dromios, the staging problems of the last scene notwithstanding (see Introduction, p. 101).

DOUBLING

Richard Burbage probably took the role of Antipholus of Syracuse and Will Kemp that of Dromio of Syracuse, the largest and second largest parts respectively (on lines per part, see King, *Casting*, 168). Thomas Pope specialized in clown characters (Gurr, *Company*, 238) and may have played Dromio of Ephesus. Beyond Shakespeare, the other 1594 Chamberlain's Men shareholders and likely performers were George Bryan, John Heminges, Augustine Phillips and probably Will Sly (Gurr, *Company*, 13), whose roles are harder to specify.[1] Heminges, according to Astington, was apparently a 'chief player in most of Shakespeare's plays', so he may have taken the part of Antipholus of Ephesus (201).

---

1   In his will, Augustine Phillips left a 'bass viol' (Astington, 209), an instrument that Syracusan Dromio associates with the Officer's appearance (4.3.23). It is tempting to wonder whether Dromio might just be making an extra-dramatic allusion to the Officer-actor's musical interests.

DOUBLING CHART

Actor	1.1	1.2	2.1	2.2	3.1	3.2	4.1	4.2	4.3	4.4	5.1
1	Duke										Duke
2	Egeon										Egeon
3	Jail.										
4		Ant. Syr.		Ant. Syr.		Ant. Syr.			Ant. Syr.	Ant. Syr.	Ant. Syr.
5		1 Mer.									
6		Dro. Syr.		Dro. Syr.	Dro. Syr.	Dro. Syr.	Dro. Syr.	Dro. Syr.	Dro. Syr.	Dro. Syr.	Dro. Syr.
7		Dro. Eph.	Dro. Eph.		Dro. Eph.		Dro. Eph.			Dro. Eph.	Dro. Eph.
8			Adr.	Adr.	Adr.			Adr.		Adr.	Adr.
9			Luci.	Luci.		Luci.		Luci.		Luci.	Luci.
10					Ant. Eph.		Ant. Eph.			Ant. Eph.	Ant. Eph.
11					Ang.	Ang.	Ang.				Ang.
12					Balt.						
13					Luce						
14							2 Mer.				2 Mer.
15							Off.			Off.	
16									Court.	Court.	Court.
17										Pinch	
18											Mess.
19											Abb.

ABBREVIATIONS AND REFERENCES

Unless otherwise stated, the place of publication is London. References to Shakespeare's works other than *The Comedy of Errors* are to *The Riverside Shakespeare*, with exceptions as indicated. All biblical references are to the Bishops' Bible (1568) (STC 2099), except as otherwise noted. Abbreviations of parts of speech follow the conventions of the *OED*.

ABBREVIATIONS
ABBREVIATIONS USED IN THE NOTES, INTRODUCTION AND APPENDICES

attrib.	attributed to
ed.	edited by
edn	edition
eds	editors
EM	Early Modern
LN	Longer Notes
ME	Medieval English
n.d.	no date
n(n).	commentary note(s)
om.	omitted (in)
opp.	opposite
pt	part
repr.	reprinted (in)
rev.	revised (by)
SD	stage direction
sig., sigs	signature, signatures
SP	speech prefix
STC	Short Title Catalogue
subst.	substantively or substantially
TLN	through-line numbering in Hinman, *First Folio*
t.n(n).	textual note(s)
trans.	translated (by)
( )	surrounding a reading in the textual notes indicates original spelling; surrounding an editor's or scholar's name indicates a conjectural reading
*	precedes commentary notes when they involve readings in this edn substantively altered from F

WORKS BY AND PARTLY BY SHAKESPEARE

AC	*Antony and Cleopatra*
AW	*All's Well That Ends Well*
AYL	*As You Like It*
CE	*The Comedy of Errors*
Cor	*Coriolanus*
Cym	*Cymbeline*
E3	*King Edward III*
Ham	*Hamlet*
1H4	*King Henry IV, Part 1*
2H4	*King Henry IV, Part 2*
H5	*King Henry V*
1H6	*King Henry VI, Part 1*
2H6	*King Henry VI, Part 2*
3H6	*King Henry VI, Part 3*
H8	*King Henry VIII*
JC	*Julius Caesar*
KJ	*King John*
KL	*King Lear*
LC	*A Lover's Complaint*
LLL	*Love's Labour's Lost*
Luc	*The Rape of Lucrece*
MA	*Much Ado About Nothing*
Mac	*Macbeth*
MM	*Measure for Measure*
MND	*A Midsummer Night's Dream*
MV	*The Merchant of Venice*
MW	*The Merry Wives of Windsor*
Oth	*Othello*
Per	*Pericles*
PP	*The Passionate Pilgrim*
PT	*The Phoenix and Turtle*
R2	*King Richard II*
R3	*King Richard III*
RJ	*Romeo and Juliet*
Son	*Sonnets*
STM	*Sir Thomas More*
TC	*Troilus and Cressida*
Tem	*The Tempest*
TGV	*The Two Gentlemen of Verona*
Tim	*Timon of Athens*
Tit	*Titus Andronicus*

TN	*Twelfth Night*
TNK	*The Two Noble Kinsmen*
TS	*The Taming of the Shrew*
VA	*Venus and Adonis*
WT	*The Winter's Tale*

REFERENCES

EDITIONS OF SHAKESPEARE COLLATED

Alexander	*William Shakespeare: The Compete Works*, ed. Peter Alexander (1951)
Andrews	*The Guild Shakespeare: 'The Comedy of Errors', 'Much Ado about Nothing'*, ed. John F. Andrews (Garden City, NY, 1990)
Arber	*A Transcript of the Registers of the Company of Stationers of London, 1554–1640 AD*, ed. Edward Arber, 5 vols (London, 1875–94)
Ard[1]	*The Comedy of Errors*, ed. Henry Cuningham, The Arden Shakespeare (1907)
Ard[2]	*The Comedy of Errors*, ed. R.A. Foakes, The Arden Shakespeare, Second Series (1962)
Ayscough	*Stockdale's Edition of Shakespeare*, ed. Samuel Ayscough (1784)
Baldwin	*The Comedy of Errors*, ed. Thomas Whitfield Baldwin (Boston, Mass., 1928)
Bevington[4]	*The Complete Works of Shakespeare*, ed. David Bevington, 4th edn (New York, 1997)
Boswell–Malone	*The Plays and Poems of William Shakespeare*, ed. Edmond Malone and James Boswell, 21 vols (1821)
Cam	*The Works of William Shakespeare*, ed. William George Clark, John Glover and William Aldis Wright, 9 vols (Cambridge, 1863–6)
Cam[1]	*The Comedy of Errors*, ed. Arthur Quiller-Couch and John Dover Wilson, The New Shakespeare (Cambridge, 1922)
Cam[1a]	*The Comedy of Errors*, ed. John Dover Wilson, The New Shakespeare, 2nd edn (Cambridge, 1962; repr. 1968)
Cam[2]	*The Comedy of Errors*, ed. T.S. Dorsch, The New Cambridge Shakespeare (Cambridge, 1988)
Cam[2a]	*The Comedy of Errors*, ed. T.S. Dorsch, rev. with new intro. Ros King, The New Cambridge Shakespeare (Cambridge, 2004)

Capell	*Mr William Shakespeare: His Comedies, Histories, and Tragedies*, ed. Edward Capell, 10 vols (1767–8)
Clark & Glover	see Cam
Collier	*The Works of William Shakespeare*, ed. John Payne Collier, 8 vols (1842–4)
Collier[2]	*The Plays of Shakespeare*, ed. John Payne Collier, 8 vols (1853)
Collier[3]	*Shakespeare's Comedies, Histories, Tragedies, and Poems*, ed. John Payne Collier, 6 vols (1858)
Collier[4]	*The Plays and Poems of William Shakespeare*, ed. John Payne Collier, 6 vols (1878)
Cowden Clarke	*The Works of William Shakespeare*, ed. Charles and Mary Cowden Clarke, 4 vols (1864)
Cuningham	see Ard[1]
Delius	*Shakspere's Werke*, ed. Nicolaus Delius, 7 vols (Elberfeld, 1854–61)
Dyce	*The Works of Shakespeare*, ed. Alexander Dyce, 6 vols (1857)
Dyce[2]	*The Works of William Shakespeare*, ed. Alexander Dyce, 9 vols (1864–7)
Dyce[3]	*The Works of William Shakespeare*, ed. Alexander Dyce, 9 vols (1875–7)
F	*Mr William Shakespeares Comedies, Histories, and Tragedies*, The First Folio (1623)
Fc	First Folio, corrected state
Fu	First Folio, uncorrected state
F2	*Mr William Shakespeares Comedies, Histories, and Tragedies*, The Second Folio (1632)
F3	*Mr William Shakespear's Comedies, Histories, and Tragedies*, The Third Folio (1663)
F4	*Mr William Shakespear's Comedies, Histories, and Tragedies*, The Fourth Folio (1685)
Foakes	see Ard[2]
Folg[2]	*The Comedy of Errors*, ed. Barbara A. Mowat and Paul Werstine, The New Folger Library Shakespeare (New York, 1998)
Gentleman	*Bell's Edition of Shakespeare's Plays, As they were performed at the Theatres Royal in London*, ed. Francis Gentleman, 10 vols (York, 1774)
Halliwell	*The Works of William Shakespeare*, ed. James O. Halliwell, 16 vols (1853–65)
Hanmer	*The Works of Shakespear*, ed. Thomas Hanmer, 6 vols (Oxford, 1743)

Hanmer[2]   *The Works of Shakespear*, ed. Thomas Hanmer, 6 vols
                   (1745)
Harness   *The Dramatic Works of William Shakespeare*, ed.
                   William Harness, 8 vols (1825)
Henning   see *Var*.
Hudson   *The Works of Shakespeare*, ed. Henry N. Hudson,
                   11 vols (Boston and Cambridge, Mass., 1852)
Hudson[2]   *The Complete Works of William Shakespeare*, ed.
                   Henry N. Hudson, 20 vols (Boston, Mass., 1880–1)
Johnson   *The Plays of William Shakespeare*, ed. Samuel
                   Johnson, 8 vols (1765)
Jorgensen   *The Comedy of Errors*, ed. Paul A. Jorgensen, in
                   Alfred Harbage (ed.), *William Shakespeare: The
                   Complete Works* (Baltimore, 1969)
Keightley   *The Plays of Shakespeare*, ed. Thomas Keightley,
                   6 vols (1864)
King   see *Cam*[2a]
Kittredge   *The Complete Works of William Shakespeare*, ed.
                   George Lyman Kittredge (Boston, Mass., 1936)
Knight   *The Pictorial Edition of Shakspere*, ed. Charles
                   Knight, 55 parts (1838–43)
Knight[2]   *The Comedies, Histories, Tragedies, and Poems of
                   William Shakspere*, ed. Charles Knight, 12 vols
                   (1842–4)
Levin   *The Comedy of Errors*, ed. Harry Levin, Signet
                   Classic Shakespeare (New York, 1965)
Malone   *The Plays and Poems of William Shakespeare*, ed.
                   Edmond Malone, 10 vols (1790)
Martin   *The Comedy of Errors*, ed. Stanley Wells, intro.
                   Randall Martin (New York, 2005)
Mowat & Werstine   see *Folg*[2]
Munro   *The London Shakespeare*, ed. John Munro, 6 vols
                   (New York, 1958)
Norton   *The Norton Shakespeare*, ed. Stephen Greenblatt *et al.*,
                   (New York, 1997)
Norton[2]   *The Norton Shakespeare*, ed. Stephen Greenblatt *et al.*,
                   2nd edn (New York, 2008)
Oxf   *William Shakespeare: The Complete Works*, ed.
                   Stanley Wells and Gary Taylor (Oxford, 1986)
Oxf[1]   *The Comedy of Errors*, ed. Charles Whitworth, The
                   Oxford Shakespeare (Oxford, 2002)
Pope   *The Works of Shakespear*, ed. Alexander Pope, 6 vols
                   (1723–5)

Pope[2]	*The Works of Shakespear*, ed. Alexander Pope, 8 vols (1728)
Rann	*The Dramatic Works of Shakespeare*, ed. Joseph Rann, 6 vols (Oxford, 1786–94)
Reed	*The Plays of William Shakespeare*, ed. Isaac Reed, 21 vols (1803)
Reed[2]	*The Plays of William Shakespeare*, ed. Isaac Reed, 21 vols (1813)
Riv	*The Riverside Shakespeare*, ed. G. Blakemore Evans, with J.J.M. Tobin, 2nd edn (Boston, Mass., 1997)
Rowe	*The Works of Mr. William Shakespear*, ed. Nicholas Rowe, 6 vols (1709)
Rowe[2]	*The Works of Mr. William Shakespear*, ed. Nicholas Rowe, 6 vols (1709)
Rowe[3]	*The Works of Mr. William Shakespear*, ed. Nicholas Rowe, 8 vols (1714)
Singer	*The Dramatic Works of William Shakespeare*, ed. Samuel Weller Singer, 10 vols (Chiswick, 1826)
Singer[2]	*The Dramatic Works of William Shakespeare*, ed. Samuel Weller Singer, 10 vols (1856)
Staunton	*The Plays of Shakespeare*, ed. Howard Staunton, 3 vols (1858–60)
Steevens	*The Plays of William Shakespeare*, ed. Samuel Johnson and George Steevens, 10 vols (1773)
Steevens[2]	*The Plays of William Shakspeare*, ed. Samuel Johnson and George Steevens, 10 vols (1778)
Steevens[3]	*The Plays of William Shakspeare*, ed. Samuel Johnson and George Steevens, rev. Isaac Reed, 10 vols (1785)
Steevens[4]	*The Plays of William Shakspeare*, ed. Samuel Johnson, George Steevens, rev. Isaac Reed, 15 vols (1793)
Theobald	*The Works of Shakespeare*, ed. Lewis Theobald, 7 vols (1733)
Theobald[2]	*The Works of Shakespeare*, ed. Lewis Theobald, 8 vols (1740)
Theobald[3]	*The Works of Shakespeare*, ed. Lewis Theobald, 8 vols (1752)
Theobald[4]	*The Works of Shakespeare*, ed. Lewis Theobald, 8 vols (1757)
Var.	*'The Comedy of Errors': A New Variorum Edition of Shakespeare*, ed. Standish Henning (New York, 2011)
Verplanck	*The Illustrated Shakespeare*, ed. Gulian C. Verplanck, 3 vols (New York, 1847)

Warburton	*The Works of Shakespear*, ed. William Warburton, 8 vols (1747)
Wells	*The Comedy of Errors*, ed. Stanley Wells, New Penguin Shakespeare (Harmondsworth, 1972)
White	*The Works of William Shakespeare*, ed. Richard Grant White, 12 vols (Boston, Mass., 1857–66)
White[2]	*Mr. William Shakespeare's Comedies, Histories, Tragedies, and Poems*, ed. Richard Grant White, 3 vols (1883)
Whitworth	see Oxf[1]
Wright	*The Works of William Shakespeare*, ed. William Aldis Wright, 9 vols, The Cambridge Shakespeare (1891–5)

OTHER WORKS CITED

Abbott	E.A. Abbott, *A Shakespearian Grammar* (1886)
Aen.	Virgil, *Aeneid*, in *Virgil*, trans. H. Rushton Fairclough, 2 vols, Loeb Classical Library, rev. edn (Cambridge, Mass., 1978–86)
Allen	Shirley S. Allen, *Samuel Phelps and Sadler's Wells Theatre* (Middletown, Conn., 1971)
Almond	Philip C. Almond, *Demonic Possession and Exorcism in Early Modern England: Contemporary Texts and their Cultural Contexts* (Cambridge, 2004)
Altman	Joel B. Altman, *The Tudor Play of Mind: Rhetorical Inquiry and the Development of Elizabethan Drama* (Berkeley, Calif., 1978)
Amph.	Plautus, *Amphitruo*, in *Plautus*, vol. 1 (2011)
Archibald	Elizabeth Archibald, *Apollonius of Tyre: Medieval and Romance Themes and Variations* (Cambridge, 1991)
Arden of Feversham	in Bevington, *RD*
Aristotle	Aristotle, *The Poetics of Aristotle*, trans. and ed. Stephen Halliwell (1987)
Astington	John H. Astington, *Actors and Acting in Shakespeare's Time: The Art of Stage Playing* (Cambridge, 2010)
Axton	Marie Axton (ed.), *Three Classical Tudor Interludes* (Cambridge, 1982)
Bacon	Francis Bacon, *The Advancement of Learning*, in *Francis Bacon: A Critical Edition of the Major Works*, ed. Brian Vickers (Oxford, 1996)
Baldwin, '*Finem*'	T.W. Baldwin, '*Respice finem: respice funem*', in James G. McManaway *et al.* (eds), *Joseph Quincy*

	Adams Memorial Studies (Washington, DC, 1948), 141–55
Baldwin, *Genetics*	T.W. Baldwin, *The Compositional Genetics of 'The Comedy of Errors'* (Urbana, Ill., 1965)
Baldwin, *Hanging*	Thomas Whitfield Baldwin, *William Shakespeare Adapts a Hanging* (Princeton, NJ, 1931)
Baldwin, *Small Latine*	T.W. Baldwin, *William Shakspere's Small Latine & Lesse Greeke*, 2 vols (Urbana, Ill., 1944)
Baldwin, *Structure*	T.W. Baldwin, *Shakspere's Five-Act Structure* (Urbana, Ill., 1947)
Bate	Jonathan Bate, *Shakespeare and Ovid* (Oxford, 1993)
BCP	*The Book of Common Prayer* (1559)
Bentley	Eric Bentley, 'Farce', in *The Life of Drama* (New York, 1964; repr. 1983), 219–56
Bergson	Henri Bergson, *Laughter*, in Wylie Sypher (ed.), *Comedy: 'An Essay on Comedy', George Meredith; 'Laughter', Henri Bergson* (New York, 1956), 59–190
Berry, 'Komisarjevsky'	Ralph Berry, 'Komisarjevsky at Stratford-upon-Avon', *SS 36* (1983), 73–84
Berry, 'Prosodies'	Eleanor Berry, 'The reading and uses of Elizabethan prosodies', *Language and Style*, 14 (1981), 116–52
Betteridge & Walker	Thomas Betteridge and Greg Walker (eds), *The Oxford Handbook of Tudor Drama* (Oxford, 2012)
Bevington, *RD*	David Bevington *et al.* (eds), *English Renaissance Drama* (New York, 2002)
Billington	Michael Billington, '*Comedy of Errors* at Stratford: Williams production, 1962/1972', in Miola, *Essays*, 487–8; orig. pub. *Manchester Guardian*, 21 June 1972, 8
Bishop	T.G. Bishop, *Shakespeare and the Theatre of Wonder* (Cambridge, 1996)
Blake	N.F. Blake, *A Grammar of Shakespeare's Language* (Houndmills, Basingstoke, 2002)
Bland	*Gesta Grayorum, or the History of the High and Mighty Prince Henry, Prince of Purpoole, Anno Domini 1594* (1688), ed. Desmond Bland (Liverpool, 1968)
Boehrer	Bruce Boehrer, *Shakespeare Among the Animals: Nature and Society in the Drama of Early Modern England* (New York, 2002)
Boose	Lynda E. Boose, 'Scolding brides and bridling scolds: taming the unruly woman's member', *SQ*, 42 (1991), 179–213

Bowers	Fredson Bowers, 'Establishing Shakespeare's text: notes on short lines and the problem of verse division', *StB*, 33 (1980), 74–130
Breton	Nicholas Breton, *Fantastics: Serving for a Perpetual Prognostication* (1626)
Brooks, 'Marlowe'	Harold F. Brooks, 'Marlowe and the early Shakespeare', in Brian Morris (ed.), *Christopher Marlowe*, Mermaid Critical Commentaries (New York, 1969), 65–94
Brooks, 'Themes'	Harold F. Brooks, 'Themes and structures in *The Comedy of Errors*', in Miola, *Essays*, 71–91; orig. pub. John Russell Brown and Bernard Harris (eds), *Early Shakespeare* (1961), 54–71
Brown	Charles Armitage Brown, *Shakespeare's Autobiographical Poems* (1838)
Bruster	Douglas Bruster, *Drama and the Market in the Age of Shakespeare* (Cambridge, 1992)
Bullough	Geoffrey Bullough (ed.), *Narrative and Dramatic Sources of Shakespeare*, 8 vols (1957–75)
Burns	*Henry VI, Part 1*, ed. Edward Burns, The Arden Shakespeare, Third Series (2000)
Burrow	Colin Burrow, *Shakespeare and Classical Antiquity* (Oxford, 2013)
Burt	Richard Burt, *Shakespeare after Shakespeare: An Encyclopedia of the Bard in Mass Media and Popular Culture*, 2 vols (Westport, Conn., 2007)
Butler	Samuel Butler, *Hudibras. The First Part* (1663)
Butterworth	Philip Butterworth, *Magic on the Early English Stage* (Cambridge, 2005)
Candido	Joseph Candido, 'Dining out in Ephesus: food in *The Comedy of Errors*', *SEL*, 30 (1990), 217–41
Capell, *Notes*	Edward Capell, *Notes and Various Readings to Shakespeare, Part the First* (1774)
Caputo	Nicoletta Caputo, 'Entertainers "on the vagabond fringe": jugglers in Tudor and Stuart England', in Paolo Pugliatti and Alessandro Serpieri (eds), *English Renaissance Scenes* (Berne, 2008), 311–42
Carroll, *Metamorphosis*	William C. Carroll, *The Metamorphosis of Shakespearean Comedy* (Princeton, NJ, 1985)
Carroll, *Two Gentlemen*	*The Two Gentlemen of Verona*, ed. William C. Carroll, The Arden Shakespeare, Third Series (2004)
Cartwright, 'Language'	Kent Cartwright, 'Language, magic, the Dromios, and *The Comedy of Errors*', *SEL*, 47 (2007), 331–54

Cartwright, 'Scepticism'	Kent Cartwright, 'Scepticism and theatre in *Macbeth*', *SS 55* (2002), 219–36
Cartwright, 'Staging'	Kent Cartwright, 'Staging the "lock-out" scene in the Folio *Comedy of Errors*', *SB*, 24 (2006), 1–12
Cartwright, 'Surprising'	Kent Cartwright, 'Surprising the audience in *The Comedy of Errors*', in Evelyn Gajowski (ed.), *Re-visions of Shakespeare: Essays in Honor of Robert Ornstein* (Newark, Del., 2004), 15–30
Cercignani	Fausto Cercignani, *Shakespeare's Works and Elizabethan Pronunciation* (Oxford, 1981)
Chambers, *ES*	E.K. Chambers, *The Elizabethan Stage*, 4 vols (Oxford, 1923)
Chambers, *WS*	E.K. Chambers, *William Shakespeare: A Study of Facts and Problems*, 2 vols (Oxford, 1930)
Chaucer	*The Riverside Chaucer*, ed. Larry D. Benson, 3rd edn (Boston, Mass., 1986)
Cicero, *TD*	Cicero, *Tusculan Disputations*, trans. J.E. King, Loeb Classical Library (Cambridge, Mass., 1927)
Clare	Janet Clare, *Shakespeare's Stage Traffic: Imitation, Borrowing and Competition in Renaissance Theatre* (Cambridge, 2014)
Clay	C.G.A. Clay, *Economic Expansion and Social Change: England 1500–1700*, 2 vols (Cambridge, 1984)
Clayton	Thomas Clayton, 'The text, imagery, and sense of the Abbess's final speech in *The Comedy of Errors*', *Anglia*, 91 (1973), 479–84
Clubb, *Italian Drama*	Louise George Clubb, *Italian Drama in Shakespeare's Time* (New Haven, Conn., 1989)
Clubb, *Pollastra*	Louise George Clubb, *Pollastra and the Origins of 'Twelfth Night'* (Farnham, Surrey, 2010)
Cohen	Adam Max Cohen, *Shakespeare and Technology: Dramatizing Early Modern Technological Revolutions* (New York, 2006)
Coleridge	*Coleridge's Shakespearean Criticism*, ed. Thomas Middleton Raysor, 2 vols (Cambridge, Mass., 1930)
Collier, *Notes*	John Payne Collier, *Notes and Emendations to the Text of Shakespeare's Plays* (1853)
Cooper, *Romance*	Helen Cooper, *The English Romance in Time: Transforming Motifs from Geoffrey of Monmouth to the Death of Shakespeare* (Oxford, 2004)
Cooper, *Thesaurus*	'Dictionarivm Historicum & Poeticum', in *Thesaurus Linguae Romanae & Britannicae* (1565), facsimile reprint (Menston, Yorks., 1969)

Crewe	Jonathan Crewe, 'Punctuating Shakespeare', *SSt*, 28 (2000), 23–41
Crystal & Crystal	David Crystal and Ben Crystal, *Shakespeare's Words: A Glossary and Language Companion* (2002)
Daniel	*The Complete Works in Verse and Prose of Samuel Daniel*, ed. Alexander B. Grosart, 5 vols (1885–96)
Dash	Irene G. Dash, *Shakespeare and the American Musical* (Bloomington, Ind., 2010)
Davis	Philip Davis, *Shakespeare Thinking* (2007)
Davis & Frankforter	J. Madison Davis and A. Daniel Frankforter, *The Shakespeare Name Dictionary* (New York, 1995)
Dawson	see Dawson & Yachnin
Dawson & Yachnin	Anthony B. Dawson and Paul Yachnin, *The Culture of Playgoing in Shakespeare's England: A Collaborative Debate* (Cambridge, 2001)
Dean	Winton Dean, 'Shakespeare and opera', in Phyllis Hartnoll (ed.), *Shakespeare in Music* (1964), 89–175
Degenhardt	Jane Hwang Degenhardt, *Islamic Conversion and Christian Resistance on the Early Modern Stage* (Edinburgh, 2010)
Dekker	*The Dramatic Works of Thomas Dekker*, ed. Fredson Bowers, 4 vols (Cambridge, 1953–61)
Dent	R.W. Dent, *Shakespeare's Proverbial Language: An Index* (Berkeley, Calif., 1981)
Dessen	Alan Dessen, *Recovering Shakespeare's Theatrical Vocabulary* (Cambridge, 1995)
Dessen & Thomson	Alan C. Dessen and Leslie Thomson, *A Dictionary of Stage Directions in English Drama, 1580–1642* (Cambridge, 1999)
Digges	Leonard Digges, *Stratioticos: An Arithmetical Military Treatise* (1579)
Dolan	Frances E. Dolan, *Dangerous Familiars: Representations of Domestic Crime in England, 1550–1700* (Ithaca, NY, 1994)
Dolven	Jeff Dolven, *Scenes of Instruction in Renaissance Romance* (Chicago, Ill., 2007)
Donatus	Aelius Donatus, *De comedia*, trans. O.B. Hardison, Jr, in Preminger *et al.*, 305–9
Donne	*John Donne: A Critical Edition of the Major Works*, ed. John Carey (Oxford, 1990)
Douce	Francis Douce, *Illustrations of Shakespeare and of Ancient Manners* (1839)

Drayton	*The Works of Michael Drayton*, ed. J. William Hebel, 5 vols (Oxford, 1931; corrected edn, 1961)
Drew-Bear	Annette Drew-Bear, *Painted Faces on the Renaissance Stage: The Moral Significance of Face-Painting Conventions* (Cranbury, NJ, 1994)
Duncan-Jones	*Shakespeare's Sonnets*, ed. Katherine Duncan-Jones, The Arden Shakespeare, Third Series (2010)
Dutton	Richard Dutton, '*The Comedy of Errors* and *The Calumny of Apelles*: an exercise in source study', in Richard Dutton and Jean E. Howard (eds), *A Companion to Shakespeare's Works: The Comedies* (Oxford, 2003), 307–19
Dyce, *Remarks*	Alexander Dyce, *Remarks on Mr. J.P. Collier's and Mr. C. Knight's Editions of Shakespeare* (1844)
Edelman	Charles Edelman, *Shakespeare's Military Language* (2000)
Edwards, *DP*	Richard Edwards, *Damon and Pythias*, in Edwards, *Works*
Edwards, *Works*	Richard Edwards, *The Works of Richard Edwards*, ed. Ros King (Manchester, 2001)
Ellacombe	Henry Nicholson Ellacombe, *The Plant Lore & Garden Craft of Shakespeare*, new edn (1896)
Elliott	G.R. Elliott, 'Weirdness in *The Comedy of Errors*', in Miola, *Essays*, 57–70; orig. pub. *University of Toronto Quarterly*, 9 (1939), 95–106
ELR	*English Literary Renaissance*
Elyot	*A Critical Edition of Sir Thomas Elyot's 'The Boke named the Governour'*, ed. Donald W. Rude (New York, 1992)
Emerson	Sally Emerson, 'Trevor Nunn's musical production, 1976', in Miola, *Essays*, 497–8; orig. pub. *Plays and Players*, 24 (December 1976), 37
Erasmus, *Adages*	*The Collected Works of Erasmus: Adages II i 1 to II vi 100*, trans. and annotated by R.A.B. Mynors, vol. 33 (Toronto, 1991)
Erasmus, *Colloquies*	*The Collected Works of Erasmus: Colloquies*, trans. and annotated by Craig R. Thompson, vols 39–40 (Toronto, 1997)
Evans	G. Blakemore Evans (ed.), *Shakespearean Prompt-books of the Seventeenth Century*, 8 vols (Charlottesville, Va., 1960–96)
Evanthius	Evanthius, '*De fabula*', trans. O.B. Hardison, Jr, in Preminger *et al.*, 301–5

Everyman	*Everyman*, in *Medieval Drama*, ed. David Bevington (Boston, Mass., 1975)
Ewen	C. L'Estrange Ewen, *Witchcraft and Demonianism* (1933)
Feldman	A. Bronson Feldman, 'Shakespeare's early errors', *Journal of International Psychoanalysis*, 36 (1955), 114–33
Fennor	William Fennor, *The Compter's Commonwealth, or A Voyage Made to an Infernal Island* (1617)
Findlay	Alison Findlay, 'Ceremony and selfhood in *The Comedy of Errors* (*c.* 1592)', in Betteridge & Walker, 338–54
Finkelstein	Richard Finkelstein, '*The Comedy of Errors* and the theology of things', *SEL*, 42 (2012), 325–44
Fischer	Sandra K. Fischer, *Econolingua: A Glossary of Coins and Economic Language in Renaissance Drama* (Newark, Del., 1985)
Fitzpatrick & Millyard	Tim Fitzpatrick and Wendy Millyard, 'Hanging doors and discoveries: conflicting evidence or problematical assumptions?', *ThN*, 54 (2000), 2–23
Fletcher	Giles Fletcher, *Of the Russe Common Wealth* (1591)
Ford	John R. Ford, ' "Methinks you are my glass": looking for *The Comedy of Errors* in performance', *SB*, 24 (2006), 11–28
Forker	*King Richard II*, ed. Charles R. Forker, The Arden Shakespeare, Third Series (2002)
Foster	Donald W. Foster, '*A Funeral Elegy*: W[illiam] S[hakespeare]'s "best-speaking witnesses" ', *SSt*, 25 (1997), 115–40
Freedman, 'Farce'	Barbara Freedman, 'Errors in comedy: a psycho-analytic theory of farce', in Maurice Charney (ed.), *Shakespearean Comedy* (New York, 1980), 233–43
Freedman, *Gaze*	Barbara Freedman, *Staging the Gaze: Postmodernism, Psychoanalysis, and Shakespearean Comedy* (Ithaca, NY, 1991)
Freud	*Sigmund Freud: Studies in Parapsychology*, ed. Philip Rieff (New York, 1963)
Frith	*The Works of the English Reformers: William Tyndale and John Frith*, ed. Thomas Russell, 3 vols (1831)
Frye	Northrop Frye, 'The argument of comedy', in D.A. Robertson, Jr (ed.), *English Institute Essays 1948* (New York, 1949), 58–73
Fuchs	Barbara Fuchs, *Romance* (New York, 2004)

Fuller	Thomas Fuller, *The Worthies of England* (1662), ed. John Freeman (1952)
Gardner	Edmund Gardner, 'The Act of Uniformity: Williams production, 1962', in Miola, *Essays*, 481–3; orig. pub. *Stratford-upon-Avon Herald*, 14 September 1962
Gascoigne, *Glass*	George Gascoigne, *The Steel Glass, Together with the Complaint of Philomene* (1576)
Gascoigne, 'Notes'	George Gascoigne, 'Certayne Notes of Instruction', in Vickers, *Criticism*, 162–71
Geneva Bible	*The Geneva Bible, A Facsimile of the 1560 Edition*, intro. Lloyd E. Berry (Madison, Wis., 1969)
Ghose	Indira Ghose, *Shakespeare and Laughter: A Cultural History* (Manchester, 2008)
Gifford	George Gifford, *A Dialogue Concerning Witches and Witchcraft* (1603)
Gillies	John Gillies, *Shakespeare and the Geography of Difference* (Cambridge, 1994)
Godman	Maureen Godman, ' "Plucking a crow" in *The Comedy of Errors*', *Early Theatre*, 8 (2005), 53–68
Golding	*Ovid's 'Metamorphoses'*, trans. Arthur Golding (1567), ed. John Frederick Nims (Philadelphia, Pa., 2000)
Gosson	Stephen Gosson, *The School of Abuse* (1579)
Gould	George Gould, *Corrigenda and Explanations of the Text of Shakespere* (1884)
Gower	John Gower, *Confessio Amantis*, ed. Russell A. Peck, trans. Andrew Galloway, vol. 1, 2nd edn (Kalamazoo, Mich., 2006)
Gratwick	*Plautus: 'Menaechmi'*, ed. A.S. Gratwick (Cambridge, 1993)
Greene	*The Life and Complete Works in Prose and Verse of Robert Greene*, ed. Alexander B. Grosart, 15 vols (1881–6)
Greg, *Bibliography*	W.W. Greg, *A Bibliography of the English Printed Drama to the Restoration*, 4 vols (1939–59)
Greg, *Folio*	W.W. Greg, *The Shakespeare First Folio: Its Bibliographical and Textual History* (Oxford, 1955)
Greg, *Problem*	W.W. Greg, *The Editorial Problem in Shakespeare: A Survey of the Foundations of the Text*, 3rd edn (Oxford, 1954)
Grennan	Eamon Grennan, 'Arm and sleeve: nature and custom in *The Comedy of Errors*', *Philological Quarterly*, 59 (1980), 150–64

Grey	Zachary Grey, *Critical, Historical, and Explanatory Notes on Shakespeare*, 2 vols (1754)
Griffiths	Eric Griffiths, 'Ludwig Wittgenstein and the comedy of errors', in Michael Cordner *et al.* (eds), *English Comedy* (Cambridge, 1994), 288–316
Gurr, *Companies*	Andrew Gurr, *The Shakespearian Playing Companies* (Oxford, 1996)
Gurr, *Company*	Andrew Gurr, *The Shakespeare Company, 1594–1642* (Cambridge, 2004)
Gurr, 'Gulf'	Andew Gurr, 'Doors at the Globe: the gulf between page and stage', *ThN*, 55 (2001), 59–71
Gurr, *Playgoing*	Andrew Gurr, *Playgoing in Shakespeare's London*, 3rd edn (Cambridge, 2004)
Gurr, 'Stage doors'	Andrew Gurr, 'Stage doors at the Globe', *ThN*, 52 (1999), 8–18
Gurr & Egan	Andrew Gurr and Gabriel Egan, 'Prompting, backstage activity, and the openings onto the Shakespearean stage', *ThN*, 56 (2002), 138–42
Gurr & Ichikawa	Andrew Gurr and Mariko Ichikawa, *Staging in Shakespeare's Theatres* (Oxford, 2000)
Hadfield	Andrew Hadfield, 'Shakespeare, John Derricke and Ireland: *The Comedy of Errors*, III.ii.105–6', *N&Q*, 242 (1997), 53–4
Hamilton	Donna B. Hamilton, *Shakespeare and the Politics of Protestant England* (Lexington, Ky, 1992)
Harris	Jonathan Gil Harris, *Sick Economies: Drama, Mercantilism, and Disease in Shakespeare's England* (Philadelphia, Pa., 2004)
Harrison	William Harrison, *'The Description of England': The Classic Contemporary Account of Tudor Social Life*, ed. Georges Edelen (Washington, DC, 1968)
Harsnett	Samuel Harsnett, *A Declaration of Egregious Popish Impostures* (1603)
Hart	Elizabeth Hart, '"Great is Diana" of Shakespeare's Ephesus', *SEL*, 43 (2003), 347–74
Hartley	Andrew James Hartley, 'Character, agency, and the familiar actor', in Paul Yachnin and Jessica Slights (eds), *Shakespeare and Character: Theory, History, Performance, and Theatrical Persons* (Houndmills, Basingstoke, 2009), 158–76
Hazlitt	William Hazlitt, *The Characters of Shakespear's Plays* (1817)
Heath	Benjamin Heath, *A Revisal of Shakespear's Text* (1765)

Heller	Agnes Heller, *Immortal Comedy* (Lanham, Md, 2005)
Hennings	Thomas P. Hennings, 'The Anglican doctrine of affectionate marriage in *The Comedy of Errors*', *Modern Language Quarterly*, 47 (1986), 91–107
Henze	Richard Henze, '*The Comedy of Errors*: a freely binding chain', *SQ*, 22 (1971), 35–41
Herodotus	*Herodotus*, trans. A.D. Godley, 4 vols (1921–61)
Herrick, *Italian Comedy*	Marvin T. Herrick, *Italian Comedy in the Renaissance* (Urbana, Ill., 1960)
Herrick, *Theory*	Marvin T. Herrick, *Comic Theory in the Sixteenth Century* (Urbana, Ill., 1964)
Heywood, *Stuckeley*	Thomas Heywood, *Captain Thomas Stuckeley* (c. 1594), in Charles Edelman (ed.), *The Stukeley Plays* (Manchester, 2005)
Heywood, *Wife*	*How a Man May Choose a Good Wife from a Bad* (1602)
Hills	Erato Hills, 'Shakespeariana', *N&Q*, ser. 4, vol. 11, pt 1 (1873), 152
Hinman, *First Folio*	Charlton Hinman (ed.), *The First Folio of Shakespeare: The Norton Facsimile* (New York, 1968; 2nd edn, 1996)
Hinman, *Printing*	Charlton Hinman, *The Printing and Proof-Reading of the First Folio of Shakespeare*, 2 vols (Oxford, 1963)
Hodgdon	*The Taming of the Shrew*, ed. Barbara Hodgdon, The Arden Shakespeare, Third Series (2010)
Hogan	Charles Beecher Hogan, *Shakespeare in the Theatre, 1701–1800*, 2 vols (1952–7)
Hollander	John Hollander, 'Romantic verse form and the metrical contract', in Harold Bloom (ed.), *Romanticism and Consciousness* (New York, 1970), 181–200
Homer, *Il.*	*The Iliad*, trans. A.T. Murray, rev. William F. Wyatt, 2 vols, Loeb Classical Library, 2nd edn (Cambridge, Mass., 1999)
Homer, *Od.*	*The Odyssey*, trans. A.T. Murray, rev. George E. Dimock, 2 vols, Loeb Classical Library, 2nd edn (Cambridge, Mass., 1995)
Homilies	*Certain Sermons or Homilies Appointed to be Read in Churches in the Time of Queen Elizabeth of Famous Memory*, ed. John Griffiths (1864)
Honigmann	E.A.J. Honigmann, 'Re-enter the stage direction: Shakespeare and some contemporaries', *SS 29* (1976), 117–25

Hope	Jonathan Hope, *Shakespeare's Grammar* (2003)
Hotson	Leslie Hotson, *The First Night of 'Twelfth Night'* (1954)
Howard-Hill, 'Compositors'	T.H. Howard-Hill, 'The compositors of Shakespeare's Folio comedies', *StB*, 26 (1973), 61–106
Howard-Hill, *Crane*	T.H. Howard-Hill, *Ralph Crane and Some Shakespeare First Folio Comedies* (Charlottesville, Va., 1972)
Hull	*The Comedy of Errors; with Alterations from Shakspeare as Performed at the Theatre-Royal, Covent Garden*, adapted by Thomas Hull (1793)
Hunt	Maurice Hunt, 'Slavery, English servitude, and *The Comedy of Errors*', *ELR*, 27 (1997), 31–56
Hutton	Luke Hutton, *The Black Dog of Newgate* (1596)
Ichikawa, 'Acting'	Mariko Ichikawa, '"*Maluolio within*": acting on the threshold between onstage and offstage spaces', *MRDE*, 18 (2005), 123–45
Ichikawa, *Entrances*	Mariko Ichikawa, *Shakespearean Entrances* (Houndmills, Basingstoke, 2002)
Ichikawa, 'Staging'	Mariko Ichikawa, 'The staging of *The Comedy of Errors*, Act 3, Scene 1', *Journal of the Graduate School of International Studies* (Tohoku University, Japan), 15 (2007), 81–97
Isherwood	Charles Isherwood, 'Shakespeare at large in Runyonland', *New York Times*, 18 June 2013 (http://theater.nytimes.com/2013/06/19/theater/reviews/a-comedy-of-errors-unfolds-in-the-40s-with-fedoras.html?emc=eta1&_r=0&pagewanted=1) (accessed 20 June 2013)
Jack	Sybil M. Jack, *Trade and Industry in Tudor and Stuart England* (1977)
James VI/I	*Basilikon Doron* (Edinburgh, 1599)
Jervis	Swynfen Jervis, *Proposed Emendations of the Text of Shakespeare's Plays* (1861)
Johnson, *Dictionary*	Samuel Johnson, *A Dictionary of the English Language*, 2 vols (1755; facsimile edn, New York, 1967)
Johnson, 'Preface'	Samuel Johnson, 'Preface to "The Plays of William Shakespeare"' (1765), in D. Nichol Smith (ed.), *Eighteenth Century Essays on Shakespeare* (Oxford, 1963), 104–51
Jonson	*Ben Jonson*, ed. C.H. Herford and Percy and Evelyn Simpson, 11 vols (Oxford, 1925–52)
Judges	A.V. Judges (ed.), *The Elizabethan Underworld* (New York, 1930)

Kahn   Coppélia Kahn, *Man's Estate: Masculine Identity in Shakespeare* (Berkeley, Calif., 1981)

Kehler   Dorothea Kehler, '*The Comedy of Errors* as a problem comedy', *Rocky Mountain Review of Language and Literature*, 41 (1987), 229–40

Kellner   Leon Kellner, *Restoring Shakespeare: A Critical Analysis of Misreadings in Shakespeare's Work* (1925)

Kennedy   Dennis Kennedy, *Looking at Shakespeare: A Visual History of Twentieth-Century Performances* (Cambridge, 1993)

Kidnie   Margaret Jane Kidnie, 'Text, performance, and the editors: staging Shakespeare's drama', *SQ*, 51 (2000), 456–73

King, *Casting*   T.J. King, *Casting Shakespeare's Plays* (Cambridge, 1992)

Kinney, 'Kinds'   Arthur F. Kinney, 'Shakespeare's *The Comedy of Errors* and the nature of kinds', *SEL*, 85 (1988), 29–52

Kinney, *Rogues*   Arthur Kinney (ed.), *Rogues, Vagabonds, & Sturdy Beggars* (Barre, Mass., 1973)

Kish   see Solinus

Knapp & Kobialka   Margaret Knapp and Michal Kobialka, 'Shakespeare and the Prince of Purpoole: the 1594 production of *The Comedy of Errors* at Gray's Inn Hall', in Miola, *Essays*, 431–44; orig. pub. *Theatre History Studies*, 4 (1984), 71–81

Knight, *Buffs*   H.R. Knight, *Historical Record of the Buffs*, 2 vols (1905)

Knutson   Roslyn Lander Knutson, *The Repertory of Shakespeare's Company, 1594–1613* (Fayetteville, Ark., 1991)

Kökeritz   Helge Kökeritz, *Shakespeare's Pronunciation* (New Haven, Conn., 1953)

Kreps   Barbara Kreps, 'Playing the law for lawyers: witnessing, evidence and the law of contracts in *The Comedy of Errors*', *SS 63* (2010), 262–71

Kyd, *ST*   Thomas Kyd, *The Spanish Tragedy*, in Bevington, *RD*

Landau   Aaron Landau, ' "Past thought of human reason": confounding reason in *The Comedy of Errors*', *English Studies*, 85 (2004), 189–205

Lanham   Richard A. Lanham, *A Handlist of Rhetorical Terms* (Berkeley, Calif., 1991)

Lanier, 'Character'	Douglas Lanier, ' "Stigmatical in making": the material character of *The Comedy of Errors*', in Miola, *Essays*, 299–334; orig. pub. *ELR*, 23 (1993), 81–112
Lanier, *Popular*	Douglas Lanier, *Shakespeare and Modern Popular Culture* (Oxford, 2002)
Latham	Minor White Latham, *The Elizabethan Fairies* (New York, 1930)
Lawrence	Jason Lawrence, *'Who the Devil Taught Thee So Much Italian?': Italian Language Learning and Literary Imitation in Early Modern England* (Manchester, 2005)
Lawson	Jane A. Lawson (ed.), *The Elizabethan New Year's Gift Exchanges, 1559–1603* (2013)
Leinwand	Theodore B. Leinwand, *Theatre, Finance and Society in Early Modern England* (Cambridge, 1999)
Levin, 'Rope'	Richard Levin, 'Grumio's "rope-tricks" and the Nurse's "ropery" ', *SQ*, 22 (1971), 82–6
Levinson	Jill L. Levinson (ed.), *Romeo and Juliet* (Oxford, 2000)
Levith	Murray J. Levith, *What's in Shakespeare's Names* (Hamden, Conn., 1978)
Lewis	C.S. Lewis, *The Discarded Image* (Cambridge, 1964)
Lin	Erika T. Lin, *Shakespeare and the Materiality of Performance* (New York, 2012)
Long, 'Directions'	William B. Long, 'Stage directions: a misinterpreted factor in determining textual provenance', *Text*, 2 (1985), 121–37
Long, 'Dulwich'	William B. Long, 'Dulwich MS. XX, *The Telltale*: clues to provenance', *MRDE*, 17 (2005), 180–204
Long, 'Playbook'	William B. Long, '*John a Kent and John a Cumber*: an Elizabethan playbook with implications', in W.R. Elton and William B. Long (eds), *Shakespeare and Dramatic Tradition* (Newark, Del., 1989), 125–43
Lothian & Craik	*Twelfth Night*, ed. J.M. Lothian and T.W. Craik, The Arden Shakespeare, Second Series (1975)
Low	Jennifer A. Low, 'Door number three: time, space, and the audience in *The Menaechmi* and *The Comedy of Errors*', in Low & Myhill, 71–91
Low & Myhill	Jennifer A. Low and Nova Myhill (eds), *Imagining the Audience in Early Modern Drama, 1558–1642* (New York, 2011)
Luxon	Thomas H. Luxon, 'Humanist marriage and *The Comedy of Errors*', *Renaissance and Reformation / Renaissance et Réforme*, 25 (2001), 45–65

Lyly, *Campaspe*	John Lyly, *Campaspe*, ed. G.K. Hunter, in *Campaspe; Sappho and Phao*, ed. G.K. Hunter and David Bevington (Manchester, 1991)
Lyly, *Endymion*	John Lyly, *Endymion*, ed. David Bevington (Manchester, 1996)
Lyly, *Euphues*	John Lyly, *Euphues: The Anatomy of Wit and Euphues and His England*, ed. Leah Scragg (Manchester, 2003)
Lyly, *MB*	John Lyly, *Mother Bombie*, ed. Leah Scragg (Manchester, 2010)
Lyly, *Midas*	John Lyly, *Midas*, ed. George K. Hunter, in *Galatea and Midas*, ed. George K. Hunter and David Bevington (Manchester, 2000)
MacCary	W. Thomas MacCary, '*The Comedy of Errors*: a different kind of comedy', *New Literary History*, 9 (1978), 525–36
Macey	Samuel L. Macey, *Patriarchs of Time: Dualisms in Saturn-Cronos, Father Time, the Watchmaker God, and Father Christmas* (Athens, Ga., 1987)
McJannet	Linda McJannet, 'Genre and geography: the eastern Mediterranean in *Pericles* and *The Comedy of Errors*', in John Gillies and Virginia Mason Vaughan (eds), *Playing the Globe: Genre and Geography in English Renaissance Drama* (Madison, NJ, 1998), 86–106
McKerrow	R.B. McKerrow, 'A suggestion regarding Shakespeare's manuscripts', *Review of English Studies*, 2 (1935), 459–65
Maguire	Laurie Maguire, 'The girls from Ephesus', in Miola, *Essays*, 355–91
Maisano	Scott Maisano, 'Rise of the Poet of the Apes', *SSt*, 14 (2013), 64–76
Malleus Maleficarum	Heinrich Kramer and James Sprenger, *The Malleus Maleficarum*, trans. Montague Summers (1928; repr. New York, 1971)
Manningham	*The Diary of John Manningham of the Middle Temple, 1602–1603*, ed. Robert Parker Sorlien (Hanover, NH, 1976)
Marino	James J. Marino, 'The anachronistic *Shrews*', *SQ*, 60 (2009), 25–46
Marlowe	*The Complete Works of Christopher Marlowe*, ed. Fredson Bowers, 2 vols (Cambridge, 1973)
Marrapodi	Michele Marrapodi (ed.), *Shakespeare, Italy, and Intertextuality* (Manchester, 2004)

Martin, 'Artemis'	Randall Martin, 'Rediscovering Artemis in *The Comedy of Errors*', in Tom Clayton *et al.* (eds), *Shakespeare and the Mediterranean* (Newark, Del., 2004), 363–79
Mason	John Monck Mason, *Comments on the Last Edition of Shakespeare's Plays* (Dublin, 1785)
Matz	Robert Matz (ed.), *Two Early Modern Marriage Sermons: Henry Smith's 'A Preparative to Marriage' (1591) and William Whately's 'A Bride-Bush' (1623)* (Farnham, Surrey, 2016)
Maus	Katharine Eisaman Maus, *Inwardness and Theater in the English Renaissance* (Chicago, Ill., 1995)
Men.	Plautus, *Menaechmi*, in *Plautus*, vol. 2 (2011)
Mentz	Steve Mentz, *At the Bottom of Shakespeare's Ocean* (2009)
Meres	Francis Meres, *Palladis Tamia: Wit's Treasury, Being the Second Part of Wit's Commonwealth* (1598)
Middleton	*Thomas Middleton: The Collected Works*, ed. Gary Taylor and John Lavagnino (Oxford, 2007)
Milton	John Milton, *Complete Poems and Major Prose*, ed. Merritt Y. Hughes (New York, 1957)
Milward	Peter Milward, '*The Comedy of Errors* in Japan', in Miola, *Essays*, 489–96
Miola, *Comedy*	Robert S. Miola, *Shakespeare and Classical Comedy* (Oxford, 1994)
Miola, *Essays*	Robert S. Miola (ed.), *'The Comedy of Errors': Critical Essays* (New York, 1997)
Miola, 'Intertextuality'	Robert S. Miola, 'Seven types of intertextuality', in Marrapodi, 13–25
Miola, 'Play'	Robert S. Miola, 'The play and the critics', in Miola, *Essays*, 3–52
MRDE	*Medieval and Renaissance Drama in England*
Mullaney	Steven Mullaney, *The Place of the Stage: License, Play, and Power in Renaissance England* (Chicago, Ill., 1988)
N&Q	*Notes and Queries*
Nashe	Thomas Nashe, *The Works of Thomas Nashe*, ed. Ronald B. McKerrow, rev. F.P. Wilson, 5 vols (Oxford, 1958)
Nelson & Elliott	Alan H. Nelson and John R. Elliott, Jr, *Inns of Court*, Records of Early English Drama, 3 vols (Cambridge, 2011)
Noble	Richmond Noble, *Shakespeare's Biblical Knowledge and the Use of the Book of Common Prayer* (1935)

OCD	*The Oxford Classical Dictionary*, ed. Simon Hornblower *et al.*, 4th edn (Oxford, 2012), online by subscription (accessed 12 August 2014)
O'Connor	John O'Connor, 'Compositors D and F of the Shakespeare First Folio', *StB*, 28 (1975), 81–117
Odell, *Annals*	George C.D. Odell, *Annals of the New York Stage*, 15 vols (New York, 1927–49)
Odell, *Shakespeare*	George C.D. Odell, *Shakespeare from Betterton to Irving*, 2 vols (New York, 1920)
ODNB	*Oxford Dictionary of National Biography*, ed. Lawrence Goldman (Oxford, 2004–14), online by subscription (accessed 12 August 2014)
O'Donnell	Brennan O'Donnell, 'The errors of the verse: metrical reading and performance in *The Comedy of Errors*', in Miola, *Essays*, 393–422
OED	*The Oxford English Dictionary Online*, by subscription (accessed 15 February 2014)
OLD	*The Oxford Latin Dictionary*, ed. P.G.W. Glare (Oxford, 1996)
Ollard	S.L. Ollard, *A Dictionary of English Church History* (1919)
Onions	C.T. Onions, *A Shakespeare Glossary*, rev. Robert D. Eagleson (Oxford, 1986)
Ovid, *Fasti*	Ovid, *Fasti*, trans. Sir James G. Frazer, rev. G.P. Goold, Loeb Classical Library, 2nd edn (Cambridge, Mass., 1988)
Ovid, *Met.*	Ovid, *Metamorphoses,* ed. Frank Justus Miller, rev. G.P. Goold, 2 vols, Loeb Classical Library, 3rd edn (Cambridge, Mass., 1977)
Page & Round	William Page and J. Horace Round (eds), *The Victoria History of the County of Essex*, 3 vols (1907)
Panofsky	Erwin Panofsky, *Studies in Iconology: Humanistic Themes in the Art of the Renaissance* (New York, 1939)
Paradin	Claude Paradin, *Heroical Devices* (1591)
Parker, 'Bible'	Patricia Parker, 'The Bible and the marketplace: *The Comedy of Errors*', in *Shakespeare from the Margins* (Chicago, Ill., 1996), 56–82
Parker, *Romance*	Patricia Parker, *Inescapable Romance: Studies in the Poetics of a Mode* (Princeton, NJ, 1979)
Parkes	M.B. Parkes, *Pause and Effect: An Introduction to the History of Punctuation in the West* (Aldershot, 1992)

Parks
George B. Parks, 'Shakespeare's map for *The Comedy of Errors*', *Journal of English and Germanic Philology*, 39 (1940), 93–7

Peck
Linda Levy Peck, 'Creating a silk industry in seventeenth-century England', *SSt*, 28 (2000), 225–8

Perry
Curtis Perry, 'Commerce, community, and nostalgia in *The Comedy of Errors*', in Linda Woodbridge (ed.), *Money and the Age of Shakespeare: Essays in New Economic Criticism* (New York, 2003), 39–51

Petrarch
The Poetry of Petrarch, trans. David Young (New York, 2004)

Phillips
Susan E. Phillips, *Transforming Talk: The Problem with Gossip in Late Medieval England* (University Park, Pa., 2007)

Piesse
Amanda Piesse, 'Space for the self: place, persona and self-projection in *The Comedy of Errors* and *Pericles*', in Gordon McMullan (ed.), *Renaissance Configurations: Voices/Bodies/Spaces, 1580–1690* (Houndmills, Basingstoke, 1998), 151–70

Plato
The Collected Dialogues of Plato, ed. Edith Hamilton and Huntington Cairns (Princeton, NJ, 1961)

Plautus
Plautus, ed. and trans. Wolfgang de Melo, 5 vols, Loeb Classical Library (Cambridge, Mass., 2011–13)

Plautus, Segal
Plautus: Four Comedies, trans. Erich Segal (Oxford, 1996)

Preminger *et al.*
Alex Preminger *et al.* (eds), *Classical and Medieval Literary Criticism* (New York, 1974)

Pressler
Charlotte Pressler, 'Intertextual transformations: the *Novella* as mediator between Italian and English Renaissance drama', in Marrapodi, 107–17

Puttenham
George Puttenham, *The Art of English Poesy: A Critical Edition*, ed. Frank Whigham and Wayne A. Rebhorn (Ithaca, NY, 2007)

Quince
Rohan Quince, 'Crinkles in the carnival: ideology in South African productions of *The Comedy of Errors* to 1985', in Miola, *Essays*, 547–61

Raman
Shankar Raman, 'Marking time: memory and market in *The Comedy of Errors*', *SQ*, 56 (2005), 176–205

RD
Renaissance Drama

Reed, *Bedlam*
Robert Rentoul Reed, Jr, *Bedlam on the Jacobean Stage* (Cambridge, Mass., 1952)

Rhatigan
Emma K. Rhatigan, 'Audience, actors, and "taking part" in the revels', in Low & Myhill, 151–69

Richens	R.H. Richens, *Elm* (Cambridge, 1983)
Rid	Samuel Rid, *The Art of Juggling or Legerdemain* (1612)
Riehle	Wolfgang Riehle, *Shakespeare, Plautus and the Humanist Tradition* (Cambridge, 1990)
Rigolot	François Rigolot, 'The Renaissance fascination with error: mannerism and early modern poetry', *Renaissance Quarterly*, 57 (2004), 1219–34
Ring	Lars Ring, 'Leif Söderström's Stockholm production, 1983', trans. Gunnar Sorelius, in Miola, *Essays*, 521–4
Ritson	Joseph Ritson, *Remarks, Critical and Illustrative, on the Text and Notes of the Last Edition of Shakespeare* (1778)
Roberts, 'Circe'	Gareth Roberts, 'The descendants of Circe: witches and Renaissance fictions', in Jonathan Barry *et al.* (eds), *Witchcraft in Early Modern Europe* (Cambridge, 1996), 183–206
Roberts, 'Owl'	Gareth Roberts, '*The Comedy of Errors* II.ii.190: "owl" or "elves"?', *N&Q*, 232 (1987), 202–4
Rosen	Barbara Rosen (ed.), *Witchcraft in England, 1558–1618* (New York, 1969)
Rouse	W.H.D. Rouse (ed.), *The Menaechmi: The Original of Shakespeare's 'Comedy of Errors': The Latin Text together with the Elizabethan Translation* (1912)
RSC	Royal Shakespeare Company
Rutter	Carol Chillington Rutter, 'Shakespeare performances in England (and Wales) 2011', *SS 65* (2013), 445–83
Salgādo	Gāmini Salgādo, ' "Time's deformed hand": sequence, consequence, and inconsequence in *The Comedy of Errors*', *SS 25* (1972), 81–91
Salingar	Leo Salingar, *Shakespeare and the Traditions of Comedy* (Cambridge, 1974)
SB	*Shakespeare Bulletin*
Scot	Reginald Scot, *The Discovery of Witchcraft* (1584; repr. New York, 1930)
Scouten	Arthur B. Scouten (ed.), *The London Stage, 1660–1800*, 5 parts (Carbondale, Ill., 1961)
Scragg	see Lyly, *MB*
Segal	Erich Segal, *Roman Laughter: The Comedy of Plautus* (Cambridge, Mass., 1968)
SEL	*Studies in English Literature*

Selleck	Nancy Selleck, *The Interpersonal Idiom in Shakespeare, Donne, and Early Modern Culture* (Houndmills, Basingstoke, 2008)
Seltzer	Leon E. Seltzer (ed.), *The Columbia Lipincott Gazetteer of the World* (New York, 1952)
Seymour	E.H. Seymour, *Remarks, Critical, Conjectural, and Explanatory, upon the Plays of Shakespeare*, 2 vols (1805)
Shaheen	Naseeb Shaheen, *Biblical References in Shakespeare's Plays* (Newark, Del., 1999)
Shakespeare's England	Walter Raleigh *et al.*, *Shakespeare's England: An Account of the Life and Manners of his Age*, 2 vols (Oxford, 1916)
Shattuck	Richard H. Shattuck, *The Shakespeare Promptbooks: A Descriptive Catalogue* (Urbana, Ill., 1965)
Shaw	George Bernard Shaw, *Our Theatres in the Nineties*, 3 vols (1932)
Shelburne	Steven R. Shelburne, 'The nature of "error" in *The Comedy of Errors*', *Explorations in Renaissance Culture*, 18 (1992), 137–51
Shurbanov	Alexander Shurbanov, *Shakespeare's Lyricized Drama* (Newark, Del., 2010)
Sidney, *A&S*	Sir Philip Sidney, *Astrophil and Stella*, in W.A. Ringler (ed.), *The Poems of Sir Philip Sidney* (Oxford, 1962)
Sidney, *Apology*	Sir Philip Sidney, *An Apology for Poetry: or, the Defence of Poesy*, ed. R.W. Maslen (Manchester, 2002)
Sidney, *Arcadia*	Sir Philip Sidney, *The Countess of Pembroke's Arcadia*, ed. Maurice Evans (1977)
Sidney, *Old Arcadia*	Sir Philip Sidney, *The Countess of Pembroke's Arcadia (The Old Arcadia)*, ed. Katherine Duncan-Jones (Oxford, 1985)
Sillars	Stuart Sillars, 'Image, genre, interpretation: the visual identities of *The Comedy of Errors*', *Interfaces: Image, Texte, Langage*, 25 (2007), 11–34
Sisson	C.J. Sisson, *New Readings in Shakespeare*, 2 vols (Cambridge, 1956)
Slater	Niall W. Slater, *Plautus in Performance: The Theatre of the Mind*, 2nd edn (Amsterdam, 2000)
Slights	Camille Wells Slights, 'Time's debt to season: *The Comedy of Errors*, IV.ii.58', *English Language Notes*, 24 (1986), 22–4

Smallwood	Robert Smallwood, 'Shakespeare performances in England, 1996', *SS 50* (1997), 201–24
Smith, *Acoustic*	Bruce R. Smith, *The Acoustic World of Early Modern England: Attending to the O-Factor* (Chicago, Ill., 1999)
Smith, *Ancient*	Bruce R. Smith, *Ancient Scripts and Modern Experience on the English Stage, 1500–1700* (Princeton, NJ, 1988)
Smith, *Marriage*	Henry Smith, *A Preparative to Marriage* (1591)
Solinus	*The Excellent and Pleasant Work of Julius Solinus Polyhistor*, trans. Arthur Golding (1587)
Soninno	Lee A. Soninno, *A Handbook of Sixteenth-Century Rhetoric* (1968)
Speaight, *Poel*	Robert Speaight, *William Poel and the Elizabethan Revival* (1954)
Speaight, 'Williams'	Robert Speaight, 'Shakespeare in Britain: Williams production, 1962', in Miola, *Essays*, 485–6; orig. pub. *SQ*, 14 (1963), 427–8
Spenser, *FQ*	Edmund Spenser, *The Faerie Queene*, ed. A.C. Hamilton, rev. 2nd edn, textual eds Hiroshi Yamashita and Toshiyuki Suzuki (Harlow, 2007)
Spevack	Marvin Spevack, *A Complete and Systematic Concordance to the Works of Shakespeare*, 9 vols (Hildesheim, 1968–80)
SQ	*Shakespeare Quarterly*
SS	*Shakespeare Survey*
SSt	*Shakespeare Studies*
StB	*Studies in Bibliography*
Steevens, *Dramatic Works*	George Steevens, ed., *The Dramatic Works of Shakespeare*, vol. 2 (1802) (with illustrations from Boydell Gallery)
Steggle	Matthew Steggle, 'Arrest for debt in *The Comedy of Errors*', paper presented at the annual meeting of the Shakespeare Association of America, Bermuda, March 2005
Stern, 'Arras'	Tiffany Stern, 'Behind the arras: the prompter's place in the Shakespearean theatre', *ThN*, 55 (2001), 110–18
Stern, *Documents*	Tiffany Stern, *Documents of Performance in Early Modern England* (Cambridge, 2009)
Stern, *Rehearsal*	Tiffany Stern, *Rehearsal from Shakespeare to Sheridan* (Oxford, 2000)
Strier	Richard Strier, 'Sanctifying the bourgeoisie: the cultural work of *The Comedy of Errors*', in Kenneth

	J.E. Graham and Philip D. Collington (eds), *Shakespeare and Religious Change* (Houndmills, Basingstoke, 2009), 17–36
Sugden	Edward H. Sugden, *A Topographical Dictionary to the Works of Shakespeare and His Fellow Dramatists* (Manchester, 1925)
Sullivan	Garrett A. Sullivan, Jr, 'Shakespeare's comic geographies', in Dutton & Howard, 182–99
Tannenbaum	Samuel A. Tannenbaum, 'Notes on *The Comedy of Errors*', *Shakespeare Jahrbuch*, 68 (Leipzig, 1932), 103–24
Tarlinskaja	Marina Tarlinskaja, *Shakespeare and the Versification of English Drama, 1561–1642* (Farnham, Surrey, 2014)
Taylor, 'Act-intervals'	Gary Taylor, 'The structure of performance: act-intervals in the London theatres, 1576–1642', in Gary Taylor and John Jowett, *Shakespeare Reshaped, 1606–1623* (Oxford, 1993), 3–50
Taylor, 'Crux'	Gary Taylor, 'Textual and sexual criticism: a crux in *The Comedy of Errors*', *RD*, 19 (1988), 195–225
ThN	*Theatre Notebook*
Thomas, 'Date'	Sidney Thomas, 'The date of *The Comedy of Errors*', *SQ*, 7 (1956), 377–84
Thomas, *Religion*	Keith Thomas, *Religion and the Decline of Magic* (1971)
Tilley	Morris Palmer Tilley, *A Dictionary of the Proverbs in England in the Sixteenth and Seventeenth Centuries* (Ann Arbor, Mich., 1950)
Tobin, 'Pinch'	J.J.M. Tobin, 'Dr Pinch and Gabriel Harvey', *N&Q*, 248 (2003), 23–5
Tobin, 'Touch'	J.J.M. Tobin, 'A touch of Greene, much Nashe, and all Shakespeare', in Thomas A. Pendleton (ed.), *Henry VI: Critical Essays* (New York, 2001), 39–56
Traill	Ariana Traill, '*Casina* and *The Comedy of Errors*', *International Journal of the Classical Tradition*, 18 (2011), 497–522
Trewin, 'Britain'	J.C. Trewin, 'Shakespeare in Britain', *SQ*, 29 (1978), 212–22
Trewin, *Shakespeare*	J.C. Trewin, *Shakespeare on the English Stage, 1900–1964* (1964)
Turner	Robert Y. Turner, *Shakespeare's Apprenticeship* (Chicago, Ill., 1974)

Twine	Lawrence Twine, *The Pattern of Painful Adventures* (1594)
TxC	Stanley Wells and Gary Taylor, *William Shakespeare: A Textual Companion* (Oxford, 1987)
van Elk, 'Genre'	Martine van Elk, '"This sympathized one day's error": genre, representation, and subjectivity in *The Comedy of Errors*', *SQ*, 60 (2009), 47–72
van Elk, 'Misidentification'	Martine van Elk, 'Urban misidentification in *The Comedy of Errors* and the cony-catching pamphlets', *SEL*, 43 (2003), 323–46
Var. KJ	*The New Variorum King John*, ed. H.H. Furness (Philadelphia, Pa., 1919)
Vaughan	William Vaughan, *The Golden-Grove* (1600)
Vickers, *Artistry*	Brian Vickers, *The Artistry of Shakespeare's Prose* (1968)
Vickers, *Criticism*	Brian Vickers (ed.), *English Renaissance Literary Criticism* (Oxford, 1999)
Vitkus	Daniel Vitkus, *Turning Turk: English Theater and the Multicultural Mediterranean, 1570–1630* (New York, 2003)
Voragine	Jacobus de Voragine, *The Golden Legend*, trans. William Granger Ryan, 2 vols (Princeton, NJ, 1993)
Walch	Günter Walch, '*Die Irrungen*: The Comedy of Errors in Germany', in Miola, *Essays*, 449–71
Walker, *Critical*	William Sidney Walker, *A Critical Examination of the Text of Shakespeare*, 3 vols (1860)
Walker, *Versification*	William Sidney Walker, *Shakespeare's Versification* (1854)
Walkington	Thomas Walkington, *The Optick Glasse of Humors* (1607)
Warner	Plautus, *'Menaechmi': A Pleasant and Fine-Conceited Comedy Taken out of the Most Excellent Witty Poet Plautus . . . Written in English by W.W.* [William Warner], (1595), in Bullough, 1.12–39
Warren	Roger Warren, 'Theory and practice: Stratford, 1976', in Miola, *Essays*, 499–500; orig. pub. *SS 30* (1978), 176–7
Wayne	Valerie Wayne, 'Introduction' to Edmund Tilney, *The Flower of Friendship*, ed. Valerie Wayne (Ithaca, NY, 1992), 1–93
Weis	*Romeo and Juliet*, ed. René Weis, The Arden Shakespeare, Third Series (2012)

Weiss	Larry Weiss, 'A solution to the stubborn crux in *The Comedy of Errors*', *Shakespeare*, published online 27 October 2014 (http://dx.doi.org/10.1080/17450918.2014.963658) (accessed 26 November 2014)
Wells, *Burlesques*	Stanley Wells (ed.), *Nineteenth-Century Shakespeare Burlesques* (1977)
Werstine, 'Cases'	Paul Werstine, 'Cases and compositors in the Shakespeare First Folio comedies', *StB*, 35 (1982), 206–34
Werstine, 'Copy'	Paul Werstine, ' "Foul papers" and "prompt-books": printer's copy for Shakespeare's *Comedy of Errors*', *StB*, 41 (1988), 232–46
Werstine, 'Line division'	Paul Werstine, 'Line division in Shakespeare's dramatic verse: an editorial problem', *Analytical and Enumerative Bibliography*, 8 (1984), 73–126
Werstine, 'McKerrow'	Paul Werstine, 'McKerrow's "Suggestion" and twentieth-century Shakespeare textual criticism', in Stephen Orgel and Sean Keilen (eds), *Shakespeare: The Critical Complex* (New York, 1999), 153–73; orig. pub. *RD*, 19 (1988), 149–73
Werstine, *Manuscripts*	Paul Werstine, *Early Modern Playhouse Manuscripts and the Editing of Shakespeare* (Cambridge, 2013)
Werstine, 'Method'	Paul Werstine, 'The continuing importance of New Bibliographic Method', *SS 62* (2009), 30–45
Werstine, 'Narratives'	Paul Werstine, 'Narratives about printed Shakespeare texts: "foul papers" and "bad quartos" ', *SQ*, 41 (1990), 65–86
Weyer	Johann Weyer, *On Witchcraft: An Abridged Translation of 'De praestigiis daemonum'*, ed. Benjamin G. Kohn and H.C. Erik Midelfort (Asheville, NC, 1998)
White	Paul Whitfield White, *Theatre and Reformation* (Cambridge, 1993)
Whitney	Geffrey Whitney, *A Choice of Emblems, and Other Devices* (Leiden, 1586)
Williams, 'Correcting'	George Walton Williams, 'Correcting double vision in *The Comedy of Errors*', in Christopher Cobb and M. Thomas Hester (eds), *Renaissance Papers 2006* (Rochester, NY, 2007), 91–6
Williams, *Dictionary*	Gordon Williams, *A Dictionary of Sexual Imagery in Shakespearean and Stuart Literature*, 3 vols (1994)
Williams, *Glossary*	Gordon Williams, *Shakespeare's Sexual Language: A Glossary* (2006)

Wilson   F.P. Wilson (ed.), *The Oxford Dictionary of English Proverbs*, 3rd edn (Oxford, 1970)

Witmore   Michael Witmore, *Culture of Accidents: Unexpected Knowledges in Early Modern England* (Stanford, Calif., 2001)

Woodcock   Matthew Woodcock, *Fairy in the Faerie Queene: Renaissance Elf-Fashioning and Elizabethan Myth-Making* (Aldershot, 2004)

Wotton   *The Life and Letters of Sir Henry Wotton*, ed. Logan Pearsall Smith, 2 vols (Oxford, 1907)

Woudhuysen   *Love's Labour's Lost*, ed. H.R. Woudhuysen, The Arden Shakespeare, Third Series (Walton-on-Thames, 1998)

Wright, *Metrical*   George T. Wright, *Shakespeare's Metrical Art* (Berkeley, Calif., 1988)

Wyatt   *Sir Thomas Wyatt: The Collected Poems*, ed. R.A. Rebholz (New Haven, Conn., 1978)

Yachnin   in Dawson & Yachnin

Yamada   Akihiro Yamada (ed.), *The First Folio of Shakespeare: A Transcript of Contemporary Marginalia in a Copy of the Kodama Memorial Library of Meisei University* (Tokyo, 1998)

INDEX

This index covers the Introduction, the commentary notes (including the longer notes) and Appendices 1, 2 and 3. The abbreviation 'n' is used only for footnotes in the Introduction and the Appendices; it is not used for commentary notes. Entries in italics indicate figures.